Edgar Saltus, Alfred Rambaud

Russia by Alfred Rambaud

Vol. 1

Edgar Saltus, Alfred Rambaud

Russia by Alfred Rambaud
Vol. 1

ISBN/EAN: 9783337297299

Printed in Europe, USA, Canada, Australia, Japan

Cover: Foto ©ninafisch / pixelio.de

More available books at **www.hansebooks.com**

RUSSIA

BY

ALFRED RAMBAUD

TRANSLATED BY LEONORA B. LANG

IN TWO VOLUMES

WITH A SUPPLEMENTARY CHAPTER OF RECENT EVENTS
By EDGAR SALTUS

ILLUSTRATED

VOL. I

NEW YORK
PETER FENELON COLLIER
MDCCCXCVIII

PREFACE.

THIS Translation of M. Alfred Rambaud's "Historie de la Russie" (Paris, 1878) contains a number of emendations by the Author. M. Rambaud has also written many additional pages: on Russian ethnography; on the Esthonian Epic; on the early relations of England and Russia; and on the Emperor Paul's project of attacking England in India. The Translator has to express a grateful sense of M. Rambaud's constant and courteous aid. In whatever is hasty or inaccurate in these volumes, he has no share. The Translator has compiled Genealogical Tables, of which M. Rambaud has approved. The French book has no index, and an attempt has been made to supply this deficiency. The Translator regrets that, by a too close following of the French spelling of the ancient tribal names, new varieties have been introduced, where variety was already too plentiful and confusing. There seem, for example, to be about thirteen ways of spelling "Patzinak." A list of some of these names as here printed, and of the forms used by Dr. Latham ("Russian and Turk." London, 1878), is subjoined:

	DR. LATHAM.
Tchouvach	Tshuvash.
Tcheremiss	Tsherimis.
Mordvians	Mordvins (otherwise Mordwa).
Tchoud	Tshud.
Dregovitch	Dragovitsae, Dregoviczi.
Polovtsi	Poloveszi.
Iatvegues	Yatshvings.
Patzinaks	Petshinegs.
Zaporogues	Zaporogs.

CONTENTS, VOL. I.

THE BEGINNINGS OF RUSSIA.

CHAPTER I.
GEOGRAPHY OF RUSSIA.

Eastern and Western Europe compared : seas, mountains, climate — The four zones — Russian rivers and history — Geographical unity of Russia, - - - - - - - 13–23

CHAPTER II.
ETHNOGRAPHY OF RUSSIA.

Greek colonies and the Scythia of Herodotus — The Russian Slavs of Nestor — Lithuanian, Finnish, and Turkish hordes in the 9th century — Division of the Russians proper into three branches — How Russia was colonized, - - - - - 24–37

CHAPTER III.
PRIMITIVE RUSSIA : THE SLAVS.

Religion of the Slavs — Funeral rites — Domestic and political customs : the family, the *mir* or commune, the *volost* or canton, the tribe — Cities — Industry — Agriculture, - - - 38–44

CHAPTER IV.
THE VARANGIANS : FORMATION OF RUSSIA ; THE FIRST EXPEDITIONS AGAINST CONSTANTINOPLE, 862-972.

The Northmen of Russia — Origin and customs of the Varangians — The first Russian princes : Rurik, Oleg, Igor — Expeditions against Constantinople — Olga — Christianity in Russia — Sviatoslaf — The Danube disputed between the Russians and Greeks, 45–57

PRINCELY RUSSIA.

CHAPTER V.
THE CLOVIS AND CHARLEMAGNE OF THE RUSSIANS : SAINT VLADIMIR AND IAROSLAF THE GREAT, 972–1054.

Vladimir (972–1015) — Conversion of the Russians — Iaroslaf the Great (1016–1054) — Union of Russia — Splendor of Kief — Varangian-Russian society at the time of Iaroslaf — Progress of Christianity — Social, political, literary, and artistic results, - 58–71

CONTENTS.

CHAPTER VI.
RUSSIA DIVIDED INTO PRINCIPALITIES — SUPREMACY AND FALL OF KIEF, 1054-1169.

Distribution of Russia into principalities — Unity in division — The successors of Iaroslaf the Great — Wars about the right of headship of the royal family, and the throne of Kief — Vladimir Monomachus — Wars between the heirs of Vladimir Monomachus — Fall of Kief, - - - - - - 72–83

CHAPTER VII.
RUSSIA AFTER THE FALL OF KIEF — POWER OF SOUZDAL AND GALLICIA, 1169-1224.

Andrew Bogolioubski of Souzdal (1157-1174), and the first attempt at autocracy — George II. (1212-1238) — Wars with Novgorod — Battle of Lipetsk (1216) — Foundation of Nijni-Novgorod (1220) — Roman (1188-1205) and his son Daniel (1205-1264, in Gallicia, 84–94

CHAPTER VIII.
THE RUSSIAN REPUBLICS: NOVGOROD, PSKOF, AND VIATKA, UP TO 1224.

Novgorod the Great — Her struggles with the princes — Novgorodian institutions — Commerce — National Church — Literature — Pskof and Viatka, - - - - - - - 95–106

THE INVASIONS FROM THE 12TH TO THE 14TH CENTURY.

CHAPTER IX.
THE LIVONIAN KNIGHTS: CONQUEST OF THE BALTIC PROVINCES BY THE GERMANS.

Conversion of Livonia — Rise of the Livonian knights: union with the Teutonic knights, - - - - - 106–111

CHAPTER X.
THE TATAR MONGOLS: ENSLAVEMENT OF RUSSIA.

Origin and manners of the Mongols — Battles of the Kalka, of Riazan, of Kolomna, and of the Sit — Conquest of Russia — Alexander Nevski — The Mongol yoke — Influence of the Tatars on the Russian development, - - - - - 112–129

CHAPTER XI.
THE LITHUANIANS: CONQUEST OF WESTERN RUSSIA (1240–1430).

The Lithuanians — Conquests of Mindvog (1240-1263), of Gedimin (1315-1340), and of Olgerd (1345-1377) — Jagellon — Union of Lithuania with Poland (1386) — The Grand Prince Vitovt (1392-1430) — Battles of the Vorskla (1399) and of Tannenberg (1410), 130–137

CONTENTS.   ix.

MUSCOVITE RUSSIA.
CHAPTER XII.
THE GRAND PRINCES OF MOSCOW: ORGANIZATION OF EASTERN RUSSIA (1303–1462).

Origin of Moscow — Daniel — George Danielovitch (1303–1325) and Ivan Kalita (1328–1341) — Contest with the house of Tver — Simeon the Proud and Ivan the Débonnaire (1341—1359) — Dmitri Donskoï (1363–1389) — Battle of Koulikovo — Vassili Dmitriévitch and Vassili the Blind (1389–1462), - - - - 138–160

CHAPTER XIII.
IVAN THE GREAT, THE UNITER OF THE RUSSIAN LAND (1462–1505).

Submission of Novgorod — Annexation of Tver, Rostof, and Iaroslavl — Wars with the Great Horde and Kazan — End of the Tatar yoke — Wars with Lithuania — Western Russia as far as the Soja reconquered — Marriage with Sophia Palæologus — Greeks and Italians at the Court of Moscow, - - - - 161–174

CHAPTER XIV.
VASSILI IVANOVITCH (1505–1533).

Annexation of Pskof, Riazan, and Novgorod-Severski — Wars with Lithuania — Acquisition of Smolensk — Wars with the Tatars — Diplomatic relations with Europe, • - - 175–181

CHAPTER XV.
IVAN THE TERRIBLE (1533–1584).

Minority of Ivan IV. — He takes the title of Tzar (1547) — Conquest of Kazan (1552) and of Astrakhan (1554) — Contests with the Livonian Order, Poland, the Tatars, Sweden, and the Russian aristocracy — The English in Russia — Conquest of Siberia,   182-208

CHAPTER XVI.
MUSCOVITE RUSSIA AND THE RENAISSANCE.

The Muscovite government — The *kin* and the *men* of the Tzar — The *prikazes* — Rural classes — Citizens — Commerce — Domestic slavery — Seclusion of women — The Renaissance : Literature, popular songs, and cathedrals — Moscow in the 16th century,
209–230

CHAPTER XVII.
THE SUCCESSORS OF IVAN THE TERRIBLE : FEODOR IVANOVITCH AND BORIS GODOUNOF (1584–1605).

Feodor Ivanovitch (1584–1598) — The peasant attached to the glebe — The patriarchate — Boris Godounof (1598–1605) — Appearance of the false Dmitri,   -   -   -   -   -   231–241

CONTENTS.

CHAPTER XVIII.
THE TIME OF THE TROUBLES (1605-1613).
Murder of the false Dmitri — Vassili Chouïski — The brigand of Touchino — Vladislas of Poland — The Poles at the Kremlin — National rising — Minine and Pojarski — Election of Michael Romanof, - - - - - - - 242-253

CHAPTER XIX.
THE ROMANOFS: MICHAEL FEODOROVITCH AND THE PATRIARCH PHILARETE (1613-1645).
Restorative measures — End of the Polish war — Relations with Europe — The States-general, - - - - 254-262

CHAPTER XX.
WESTERN RUSSIA IN THE 17TH CENTURY.
The political union of Lublin (1509), and the religious *Union* (1595) — Complaints of White Russia — Risings in Little Russia, 263-271

CHAPTER XXI.
ALEXIS MIKHAILOVITCH (1645-1676) AND HIS SON FEODOR.
Early years of Alexis — Seditions — Khmelnitski — Conquest of Smolensk and the Eastern Ukraine — Stenko Razine — Ecclesiastical reforms of Nicon — The precursors of Peter the Great — Reign of Feodor Alexiévitch (1676-1582), - - - 272-290

CHAPTER XXII.
PETER THE GREAT: EARLY YEARS (1682-1709).
Regency of Sophia (1682-1689) — Peter I. — Expeditions against Azof (1695-1696) — First journey to the West (1697) — Revolt and destruction of the *streltsi* — Contest with the Cossacks: revolt of the Don (1706); Mazeppa (1709), • • • 291-309

LIST OF ILLUSTRATIONS

RUSSIA
VOL. I

Frontispiece—Peter the Great
The City of Novgorod
The New Palace
View of the City of Tobolsk

HISTORY OF RUSSIA.

HISTORY OF RUSSIA.

CHAPTER I.

GEOGRAPHY OF RUSSIA.

Eastern and Western Europe compared: seas, mountains, climate—The four zones—Russian rivers and history—Geographical unity of Russia.

EASTERN AND WESTERN EUROPE COMPARED: SEAS, MOUNTAINS, CLIMATE.

EUROPE may be roughly divided into two unequal parts. If we give 4,000,000 square miles to the whole of Europe, only 1,800,000 belong to the western, 2,200,000 to the eastern part. The former division is shared between all the monarchies and republics of Europe, Russia excepted; the latter is united under the Russian sceptre. Nature, not less than policy or religion, has established a strong opposition between the two regions, between Eastern and Western Europe.

The shores of the latter are everywhere broken up by inland seas, pierced by deep gulfs, jagged with peninsulas, isthmuses, capes, and promontories; islands and crowded archipelagos are thickly sprinkled along the coasts. Great Britain and the Greek peninsula particularly, which have a coast-line out of all proportion to their area, contrast with the impenetrable compact mass of Eastern Europe. This strongly-marked outline of the western lands is the characteristic feature of European geography, while the immense spaces of which Russia is composed seem the continuation of the plains and plateaux of Northern and Central Asia. No doubt Russia is washed by many seas: in the north by the Icy Ocean, which bites deep into the country through the great fissure of the White Sea; in the south by the Caspian, the

Sea of Azof, and the Black Sea; in the north-west by the Baltic and the gulfs of Bothnia, Finland, and Livonia; but, with all these seas, it has only a comparatively meagre share of seaboard. While the rest of Europe has about 15,525 miles of coast, Russia, with a much more considerable surface, possesses only 5514 miles of coast; and of this nearly half (2680 miles) belongs to the Icy Ocean and the White Sea. Now, these two seas are only navigable during a few months of the year, from June to September, at furthest. The Baltic, in its two most northern gulfs, freezes easily; armies have been able to cross on the ice, with all their artillery supplies; navigation is stopped from the month of November to the end of April. The Caspian often freezes, especially in its northern half, which includes Astrakhan, its most flourishing port. The Sea of Azof, here and there, is little better than a marsh. It may be said that, with the exception of the Euxine, the Russian seas have an anti-European character; they cannot be of the same use as our western seas. From this point of view Russia is worse endowed by nature than any other European country; compared with the privileged lands of the West, she might be styled *continental* Europe, in opposition to *maritime* Europe.

Western Europe, so jagged in its contour, is no less broken in its surface. Without speaking of the vast central mass of the Alps, there is not one European land which does not possess, either in its length or breadth, a great mountain system forming the scaffolding or the backbone of the country. England has her chain of the Peak and her Highlands; France has her Cevennes and her central support in Auvergne; Spain her Pyrenees and the Sierras; Italy her Apennines; Germany her ranges in Suabia, Franconia, and the Hartz; Sweden her Scandinavian Alps; the Greco-Slav peninsula has the Balkan and Pindus. What mountains Russia possesses on the other hand, are banished, as it were, to the extremities of her territory. She is bounded on the north-west by the granitic system of Finland, on the south-east by the branches of the Carpathians, to the south by the rocky plateaux of the Crimea with the Yalïa and Tchardyr-Dagh (5183 feet), by the Caucasus, extending over 687 miles, where Elburz (18,000 feet) surpasses by more than 2000 feet the highest mountain in Europe, Mont Blanc. To the east is the Oural range, the longest chain of mountains (1531 miles) in Europe or Asia, running parallel to the meridians of longitude, with peaks 6233 feet high. In the Tatar language, the word *Oural* signifies *girdle*, but it is not only the Ourals which may be called the mountain girdle; all the mountains of Russia deserve this name. They bound her, they confine her, but have only a slight influence on the configuration of her interior and the distribution of her waters. From the Carpathians and the Caucasus only secondary rivers flow, while the four great Russian streams take their rise in hills not 300 feet high.* We must observe also that none of these great mountains form a separate system; they are nearly all fragments of systems belonging to other countries. The empire of the Tzars is thus a huge plain, which is continued on the west by the level lands of Poland and Prussia, and on the east by the limitless steppes of Siberia and Turkestan, and is in striking contrast with the rugged and multiform soil of the west. From this point of view, Russia may be defined as the Europe of plains, in opposition to the Europe of mountains.

Uniformity of surface is never quite complete, and Russia does present inequalities of soil, though these are far less notable than the depressions and elevations of the West. In the faintly-marked soil of Russia, we must notice, in the centre of the country, a kind of square table-land, called the central plateau, or the plateau of Alaoune, from the name of its northern part. The north-eastern angle is formed by the heights of the Valdaï plateau, where the hills are 300 feet high; the western side of the central plateau by the small hills of the Dnieper, which extend as far as the *Cataracts;* the southern side by the heights which reach from Koursk to Saratof; the eastern side by the sandy stretches which extend along the right bank of the Volga and the Kama; the northern side by the undulations of the land which separate the basin of the Volga from the rivers that drain into the Icy Ocean. The central plateau is besides divided into two unequal parts by the deep valleys of the Upper Volga, of the Oka, and their tributaries.

Considerable depressions correspond to this swelling in the centre of the Russian plateau:—1. Between the plateau of the Valdaï and the north-east slope of the Carpathians lies a deep valley, in which during the quaternary age the Baltic and Euxine mingled their waves. It is traversed on the north by the southern Düna or Dwina, and the Niemen; on the south by the Dnieper, and its affluents; it reaches its lowest level in the wide marshes of Pinsk. 2. Between the low rocks on the right bank of the Volga and the spurs of the Oural (*obchtchiisirt*), the soil gradually sinks throughout the whole length of the Volga, and reaches the level of the sea at the Caspian, which is 80 feet lower than the Black Sea : here are the steppes of Kirghiz, the lowest part of European Russia, formerly the bed of a great inland mere which was gradually dried up, and of which the Caspian, the Lake of Aral, and other sheets of water are only the remains.

* 1100 feet above the level of the sea.

If the Caspian could only regain the level of the Black Sea, a large part of this sterile plain, now covered with saline efflorescence, would be inundated anew. 3. The third great depression of the Russian soil is the slope of the north, covered with lakes and marshes, where the frozen *toundra* are lost amongst the icefields of the Polar Ocean and the White Sea. 4. The region of the lakes Saïma, Onega, Ladoga, which is continued by the sandy tracts of the Baltic, and which forms a series of deep cavities, where the waters of the Baltic and the White Sea must once have found a meeting-point.

From the fact that Russia, taken as a whole, is only a vast plain, it follows that her surface is swept by Polar winds, which no mountain barrier keeps out, for the Oural chain runs in a direction parallel to their course. From the fact, again, that Russia is only washed by seas, small in proportion to the extent of the land, it results that the temperature is modified neither by sea-breezes, which in the West warm in winter and refresh in summer, nor by the aërial and marine current of the Gulf Stream, which finally expires on the coasts and on the mountains of Scandinavia, without being able to influence the shores of the Baltic. In parallel latitudes this Scandinavian mountain-chain makes a notable difference between the Norwegian and the Swedish-Russian climate.

Russia then, like the interior of Asia, Africa, or Australia, has to undergo the effects of a purely continental climate. The first of these effects is a violent contrast between the seasons. The Russian plain is subject in turn to the influences of Polar regions and to those of Central and Southern Asia, of the deserts of ice and the deserts of burning sand. " Under the latitude of Paris and of Venice," says M. Anatole Leroy-Beaulieu, " the countries situated to the north of the Black Sea and the Caspian have the temperature of Stockholm in January, and the temperature of Madeira in July. At Astrakhan, in the latitude of Geneva, it is by no means rare for the temperature to vary from 70 to 75 degrees * in a period of six months. On the coasts of the Caspian, in the latitude of Avignon, the cold descends to 30° below freezing; in summer, on the contrary, the heat rises to upwards of 40°. In the steppes of the Kirghiz, in the latitude of the centre of France, the mercury is sometimes frozen for whole days ; while in the summer the same thermometer, if not carefully watched, bursts in the sun. Near the shores of the Sea of Aral these extremes of temperature reach their maximum ; there are intervals of 80°, perhaps of 90° centigrade, between the greatest cold and the greatest heat." Even at Moscow, they have had cold of 33° and heat of 28 °; at St.

* Centigrade.

Petersburg, the temperature may shift between the extremes of from 30° to 35° of cold to 31° of heat.

The second consequence of the continental climate of Russia is that the winds do not reach the country till they have lost on the way part of their humidity. Russia suffers generally from dryness. At Kazan the rainfall is only half that of Paris; it is for this reason that Russia contains so many barren and unwooded plains, while this absence of forests all through the south is, in its turn, an obstacle to the formation of hills and springs and to the development of a healthy moisture.

St. Petersburg, situated on the 60th parallel of northern latitude, is the most northern capital of the whole world. The longest day in this city lasts 18 hours 45 minutes; the sun rises on that day at 20 minutes to three, and sets at 25 minutes past 9, but the twilight is prolonged to the moment of dawn. For two months there is no night. The shortest day is 5 hours 47 minutes; the sun rises at 5 minutes past 9, and sets at 8 minutes to 3. The Aurora Borealis is frequent in the north of Russia, while the mirage is often seen in the steppes of the south.

Russia being a country of plains, the geological beds of which the soil is formed are nearly always horizontal; no raising of the soil has broken them, rent the beds of stone, and driven the fragments through the layers of mould or sand. It follows that, except in the neighborhood of mountains, stone is very scarce in Russia. This fact has had much influence on the economic and artistic development of the country. The people were obliged to build with other materials than in the West. The public buildings were everywhere of oak and pine, or of brick; the old churches, the palaces of the Tzars, the ramparts of the towns, were of wood; of wood are the present houses of the citizens, and the *isbas* of the peasants. Russian villages, and most of the towns, are a collection of combustible materials: hence the fires which break out periodically, and justify the saying that Russia, as a rule, was burned every seven years. Buildings of such materials cannot assume the colossal proportions of the castles of the Isle de France, or of the Rhenish cathedrals; the old churches of Russia are small. It is only since the conquest of the Baltic and the Black Sea that the empire has had cities of stone. Peter the Great gave Russia her first stone capital. From the geological point of view, then, Russia may be defined, according to the expression of M. Solovief, as the *Europe of wood,* in opposition to the *Europe of stone.*

RUSSIAN RIVERS AND HISTORY.

In a country so extensive and so destitute of **seaboard as** Russia, rivers have an immense importance, and with rivers Eastern Europe is well endowed. It is her watercourses which prevent Russia from being a continent closed and sealed, like Africa or Australia. In place of arms of the sea, she has great rivers which penetrate to her centre, and have sometimes almost the proportions of seas. In the level plains they have not the impetuous current of the Rhone, they flow peacefully through great beds cut in the sand or clay. The rivers were for a long while the only means of communication. When the Russian princes wished to make a progress through their dominions, or begin a campaign, they had either to take advantage of winter, which from the Dnieper to the Oural gave them a flat surface for their sledges, or await the thaw and follow the course of the rivers. Boats in summer, sledges in winter, were the only means of conveyance ; in spring, the thaw and floods, which transformed the plain into a marsh, brought the *raspoutitsa* (the season of bad roads). Commerce followed the same routes as war or government. The rivers which, in Russia especially, are "the roads that run," explain the rapidity with which we see the characters of Russian history traverse immense spaces, and go as easily from Novgorod to Kief, from Moscow to Kazan, as a French king from his good city of Paris to Rheims or Orleans. The rivers are the allies of the Russians against what they call "their great enemy"—space. Russian conquest or colonization has everywhere followed the course of the waters ; it was on the banks of the Oka, the Kama, the Don, and the Volga, that the Russian element of the population chiefly gathered, the aboriginal races everywhere retreating into the thickness of the primitive forests.

The plateau of Valdaï is the dominant point in the river-system of Russia. It is near this plateau, in the lake Volgo, that the Volga, which ultimately falls into the Caspian, takes its rise. In this neighborhood also are the sources of the Dnieper (flowing to the Black Sea), the Niemen, the Dwina, which falls into the Baltic, the Velikaïa, a tributary of the Peïpus, the rivers forming lake Ilmen, and those which feed the lakes Ladoga and Onega, whence rises the Neva. The hydrographic centre of Russia being at the north-west angle of the central plateau, it follows that the slopes are turned to the south and to the east ; a disposition which has had its influence on the development of the national history. This history, indeed, begins in the north-west, near the Valdaï plateau ; on the Peïpus and the Ilmen the old commercial cities of Pskof and Novgorod are established.

What is their opening to the sea? Not the Narova, which falls out of lake Peïpus, and of which the course is broken by cataracts, but the network of rivers and lakes which terminates in the Neva, the Thames of Russia, a river of little length but immense breadth, on which St. Petersburg, the Novgorod of the 18th century, was afterwards to be built. In primitive times Novgorod was safer in the centre of this network of rivers and lakes than she would have been on the Neva. By the Volkhof her vessels sailed from the Ilmen to the Ladoga, and by the Neva from the Ladoga to the Gulf of Finland, and the great Baltic Sea. Other small rivers put her in communication with the lake Onega and the White Lake (Biéloe-Ozéro); by the Soukhona and the northern Dwina she had relations with the White Sea, where later the port of Arkhangel arose. By the tributaries of the Dwina the Novgorod explorers penetrated deep into the northern forests, peopled by aboriginal races, on whom they imposed tribute. The watersheds between the slope to the White Sea, the basin of the Novgorod lakes, and the basin of the Volga, are scarcely marked at all. The rivers seem to hesitate at their rise between two opposite courses: some of them never make up their minds, like the sluggish Cheksna which connects the White Sea and the Volga. This interlacement of the water-system, which makes the northern Dwina, the Neva, the Niemen, and the southern Dwina mere prolongations of the Volga and the Dnieper, and puts the four Russian seas in unbroken communication, is in itself a sufficient explanation of the extent of the conquests and great commercial position of Novgorod the Great.

On the Dnieper, Russia, to rival the Russia of Novgorod, founded at a very early date the *Rouss* of Kief. She too followed the line marked out for her by the course of the Dnieper, which necessarily led her to the Black Sea and the Byzantine world.

It was by the Dnieper that the fleets of war descended against Constantinople; it was by this river too that Greek civilization and Christianity reached Kief. The Dnieper, which had made the greatness of Kief, hastened its decay. As a medium of communication it was imperfect. The celebrated cataracts below Kief formed an insurmountable barrier to navigation, and consequently the city could not remain the political and commercial capital of Russia.

The Don, notwithstanding its length of 621 miles, has had little influence on the evolution of Russian history. During the whole period of the growth of the nation it remained in the power of the Asiatic hordes. In later years it fell, with Azov, into the possession of the Turks. The sandy shallows near its mouth would in any case have proved fatal to its commercial importance. The Dwina and the Niemen also remained till the 18th century in the hands of the native Finns and Lithuanians, or of the German conquerors.

The river, *par excellence*, of Russia is the Volga — the " mother Volga," as the popular singers call it. If the Neva, with the great lakes which feed it, may be compared to the St. Lawrence, the Volga may be compared to the Mississippi. With a length of 2336 miles, it has a course 250 leagues longer than that of the Danube. Many of its tributaries may be reckoned among the great rivers of the world. The Oka, with its 633 miles of length, surpasses the Meuse and the Oder; the Kama, 1266 miles long, outvies all other European rivers except the Danube; for the Elbe is only 643 miles, the Loire 681, and the Rhine 812 in length. The junction of the Volga and Oka at Nijni-Novgorod is like the meeting of two arms of the sea; it is an imposing spectacle to contemplate from the hill on which the upper town is built, while the lower town or the fair, with its 100,000 fluctuating inhabitants, spreads its buildings on the banks of both rivers. The Volga, which near Iaroslavl is 2106 feet broad, has a breadth of 4593 above Kazan; towards Samara sometimes it decreases to 2446 feet; sometimes it spreads, with its tributary streams and lateral branches, over a breadth of 17 miles. At the Caspian it divides into seventy-five branches, forming numerous islands, and its delta spreads over 93 miles. This immense river, the waters of which abound with fish as large as sea-fish,—sturgeon, salmon, lampreys,— and where the sterlet sometimes weighs 1073 pounds, would be the wonder of Europe, if it was not frost-bound during many months in the year. But at the thaw the ports, the dockyards, the wharves, are full of life. Two hundred thousand workmen flock from all parts of Russia to its banks. Fifteen thousand ships and 500 steamboats plough its waters. Kostroma, Nijni-Novgorod, Kazan, Simbirsk, Samara, Saratof, Astrakhan, are filled with noise and movement. The whole life of Russia seems concentrated on the Volga.

The basin of the Volga and its tributaries embraces an extent of surface nearly treble that of France. The basin of the Oka alone has three times the extent of the basin of the Loire. In her vast domain the Volga included nearly the whole of the Russia of the 16th century, and has exercised an irresistible influence over the destiny of the land. From the day that the Grand Princes established their capital on the Moskowa, a tributary of the Oka and sub-tributary of the Volga, Russia turned to the east, and began her struggle with the Turks and Tatars. The Dnieper made Russia Byzantine, the Volga made her Asiatic: it was for the Neva to make her European. The whole history of this country is the history of its three great rivers, and is divided into three periods: that of the Dnieper with Kief, that of the Volga with Moscow, that of the Neva with Novgorod in the 8th century, and St. Petersburg in the 18th. The greatness of this creation of Peter I. consisted in his transporting his capital to the Baltic, without abandoning the Caspian and the Volga, and in seeking for the great Eastern river a new outlet which should open a communication with Western seas. Thanks to the canals of the Tikvinka and of the Ladoga, which furnished that outlet, the Neva has become, as it were, the northern mouth, the European estuary of the Volga.

THE FOUR ZONES—THE GEOGRAPHICAL UNITY OF RUSSIA.

From the point of view of production, Russia may be divided into four unequal bands, which run from the south-west to the north-east, namely: the zone of forests, that of the *Tchernoziom* or Black Land, that of the arable steppes or prairies, and that of the barren steppes.

1. The most northerly and largest zone is the *poliessa* or Russian forest, which borders on one side on the frozen marshes and the *toundra* of the icy shore, and on the other on the wide clearings formed by the agricultural enterprise of Novgorod, Moscow, and Iaroslavl. In the north the forest begins with the larch; in the centre resinous trees, with their dark foliage, alternate with the small leaves and white bark of the birch; further south come the lime, the elm, and the sycamore, and the oak appears at the southern limit.

2. The Black Land extends from the banks of the Pruth to the Caucasus, over the widest extent of Russia; it even passes the Oural and the Caucasus, and is prolonged into Asia. It derives its name from a deep bed of black mould of inexhaustible fertility, which produces without manure the richest harvests, and may be compared to a gigantic Beauce, 375,000 miles square, a corn-field as large as the whole of France. From this alone twenty-five millions are fed, and the population increases daily. From time immemorial this soil has been the granary of Eastern Europe. It was here Herodotus placed his agricultural Scythians, and hence Athens drew her grain.

3. The zone of arable steppes lies parallel to the Black Land; to the south it descends nearly to the sea: the country is fertile, though it cannot do without manure. It formed before tillage a bare grass-grown plain, completely devoid of wood, and with its 375,000 miles square recalls the American prairie. The

vegetation of the steppe, where men and flocks can hide themselves as in a forest, is often five, six, and even eight feet high. This monotonous steppe, unbroken except by the barrows that cover the bones of early races,—this steppe, which is an ocean of verdure in spring, but russet and burnt up in the autumn, is very dear to her children. It was for long the Russia of heroes, the property of nomad horsemen, the country of the Cossack. The Black Land and the prairie, which is nearly as fertile, have a superficies of 750,000 miles square, or 300,000,000 of acres of excellent earth, a surface equal to that of France and Austrian Hungary united.

4. The fourth zone, that of the barren steppes, steppes which are sandy at the mouth of the Dnieper, clay to the north of the Crimea, saline to the north of the Caspian, only contains 1,500,000 inhabitants in its whole extent of 250,000 miles. "Unsuited to agriculture, and in a great degree to civilized life," says M. Leroy-Beaulieu, " these vast spaces, like the neighboring plains of Asia, seem only fit for the raising of cattle and the nomad existence. Of all Russia in Europe, these are the only parts which even at the present day are inhabited by the Kirghiz and the Kalmucks, nomad tribes of Asia, and up to a few years ago by the Tatars of the Crimea and the Nogais. Here the Asiatics appear as much at home as in their native country."

The productive parts of Russia are these: the *prairie*, the *Black Land*, and in the zone of forests the agriculture and industrial region of Novgorod, Moscow, Nijni-Novgorod, and Kazan. Were the sea-level to rise and drown the northern part of the *poliessa* and the barren steppes of the south, nothing would be taken from the real force and riches of Russia.

These alternations of low plains and plateaux, this diversity in the direction of the great rivers, this division into forests and barren and arable steppes, does not hinder Eastern Europe from presenting a remarkable unity. None of the parts of Russia could remain isolated from the others; the plains admit of no barrier, no frontier; those which the rivers might impose would be effaced in winter under the chariot-wheels of armies, when the land is ice-bound from the White Sea to the Euxine, and the climate is almost as severe at Kief as at Arkhangel. All these regions, which resume their different characters in spring, are kept together by economical interests and needs. The forest zone needs the corn of the Dnieper, the cattle of the Volga; the steppes of the south need the wood of the north. The commerce with Europe, which was conducted by means of the northern Dwina, the Neva and the southern Dwina, was completed by that with the south and the east, carried on by the Dnieper and the Volga.

Only the region of Moscow, where fields and woods alternate, was long sufficient for its own wants; but since Moscow has turned to industrial arts, she needs help from others. In early times she united the products of the north and the south; she thus formed the connecting link between them, and ended by becoming their ruler. Even Novgorod was forced to acknowledge her dependence on the princes established on the Oka, who had only to forbid the transportation of corn from the Upper Volga to the region of the lakes to reduce the Great Republic to obedience.

The wide plains of Russia are as evidently destined to be united as Switzerland to be divided. Between the Carpathians and the Ourals, between the Caucasus and the system of Finland, nature has marked out a vast empire of which the mountain girdle forms the framework. How this framework has been filled in is the lesson that history has to teach us.

CHAPTER II.

ETHNOGRAPHY OF RUSSIA.

Greek Colonies and the Scythia of Herodotus—The Russian Slavs of Nester—Lithuanian, Finnish, and Turkish hordes in the ninth century—Division of the Russians proper into three branches—How Russia was colonized.

GREEK COLONIES AND THE SCYTHIA OF HERODOTUS.

THE early Greeks had established factories and founded flourishing colonies on the northern shores of the Black Sea. The Milesians and Megarians built Tomi or Kustenje, near the Danube, Istros at its mouth, Tyras at that of the Dniester, Odessos at that of the Bug, Olbia at that of the Dnieper, Chersonesos or Cherson on the roadstead of Sebastopol, Palakion which afterwards became Balaclava, Theodosia which became Kaffa, Panticapea (Kertch), and Phanagoria on the two shores of the Strait of Ienikale, Tanaïs at the mouth of the Don, Apatouros in the Kuban, Phasis, Dioscurias, Pityus at the foot of the Caucasus, on the coast of ancient Colchis. Panticapea, Phanagoria and Theodosia formed, in the 4th century B.C., a confederation with a hereditary chief called the Archon of the Bosphorus at its head, whose authority was also acknowledged by some of the barbarous tribes.

Russian archæologists, and quite recently, M. Ouvarof, have brought to light many monuments of Greek civilization, funeral pillars, inscriptions, bas-reliefs, statues of gods and heroes. We know that the colonists carefully preserved the Greek civilization, cultivated the arts of their mother cities, repeated the poems of Homer as they marched to battle, loved eloquent speeches as late as the time of Dion Chrysostom, and offered a special cult to the memory of Achilles. Beyond the line of Greek colonies dwelt a whole world of tribes, whom the Greeks designated by the common name of Scythians, with whom they entered into wars and alliances, and who served them as middlemen in their trade with the countries of the north. Herodotus has handed on to us nearly all that was known of these barbarians in the 5th century B.C.

The Scythians worshipped a sword fixed in the earth as an

image of the god of war, and bedewed it with sacrifices of human gore. They drank the blood of the first enemy killed in battle, scalped their prisoners, and used their skulls as drinking-cups, They gave their kings terrible burial-rites, and celebrated the anniversaries of their death by strangling their horses and slaves, and leaving the impaled corpses to surround the royal *kourgan* with a circle of horsemen. They honored the memory of the wise Anacharsis, who travelled among the Greeks. Their nomad hordes defied the power of Darius Hystaspes.

Among the Scythians properly so called, Herodotus distinguished the *agricultural* Scythians established on the Dnieper, probably in the *tchernoziom* of the Ukraine ; the *nomad* Scythians, who extended fourteen days' journey to the east ; the *royal* Scythians encamped round the Sea of Azof, who regarded the other Scythians as their slaves.

The barbarism of the inland tribes became rapidly modified under the influence of the powerful cities of Olbia and Chersonesos, and the Greco-Scythian state of the Bosphorus. In the tombs of the Scythian kings of what is now the government of Ekaterinoslaf, as well as in those of the Greco-Scythian princes of the Bosphorus, works of art have been found which show the genius of the Greeks accommodating itself to the taste of the barbarians, precious vases chiselled for them by Athenian artists, and all the jewels which at present enrich the museums of Kertch, Odessa, and St. Petersburg.

The Hermitage Museum at St. Petersburg, in particular, possesses two vases of an incomparable artistic and archæologic value. They are the silver vase of Nicopol (government of Ekaterinoslaf) and the golden vase of Kertch, and date from the 4th century B.C., or about the period when Herodotus wrote his history, of which they are the lively commentary. The Scythians of the silver vase, with their long hair, their long beards, large features, tunics and trousers, reproduce very fairly the physiognomy, stature and costume of the present inhabitants of the same countries ; we see them breaking-in and bridling their horses in exactly the same way as they do it to-day in those plains. The Scythians of the golden vase, notwithstanding their pointed caps, their garments embroidered and ornamented after the Asiatic taste, and their strangely-shaped bows, are of a very marked Aryan type. The former might very well have been the agricultural Scythians of Herodotus, perhaps the ancestors of the agricultural Slavs of the Dnieper ; the latter, the royal Scythians who led a nomad and warlike life. The philological studies of M. Bergmann and M. Mullendorf tend to identify the Scythian idiom with the Indo-European family of languages. " They were then," says M. Georges Perrot, " in spite of many apparent differences of language, customs and civilization, nearly related to the Greeks, and this kinship perhaps contributed, without the knowledge of either Greeks or barbarians, to facilitate the relations between Hellenes and Scythians."

Herodotus takes care to make an emphatic distinction between the Scythians properly so called, and certain other peoples about whom he has strange stories to tell. These peoples are the Melanchlainai, who wear black raiment; the Neuri, who, once a year, become were-wolves; the Agathyrsi, who array themselves in golden ornaments, and have their women in common; the Sauromati, sprung from the loves of the Scythians with the Amazons; the Budini and Geloni, slightly tinged with Greek culture; the Thysagetæ, the Massageæ the Iyrx, who lived on the produce of the chase; the Argippei, who were bald and snub-nosed from their birth; the Issedones, who used to devour their dead parents with great pomp and ceremony; the one-eyed Arimaspians; the Gryphons, guardians of fabled gold; the Hyperboreans, who dwell in a land where, summer and winter, the snow-flakes fall, like a shower of white feathers.

It seems probable that among all these peoples there may be some who have since emigrated westwards, and who may belong to the German and Gothic races. Others, again, may have continued to maintain themselves, under different names, in Eastern Europe, such as the Slavs, the Finns, and even a certain number of Turkish tribes. M. Rittich believes he can identify the *Melanchlainai* of Herodotus with the Esthonians, who still prefer dark raiment; the *Androphagi* with the Samoyedes, whose name is derived from the Finnish word *suomeadnæ*; the *Issedones* with the Vogouls, who may very well have dwelt on the Isseta, a sub-tributary of the Obi; the *Arimaspians* with Votiaks, whom the Turks now call Ari; the *Argippei*, Aorses, and Zyrians of Strabo with the Erzes or Zyrians; the *Massagetes* with the Bachkirs. M. Vivien de Saint-Martin recognizes the *Agathyrsi* in the Agatzirs of Priscus (A.D. 449), and Acatzirs of Jornandes, who are the Khazars. The Finns, then, have formed the most widely-spread race of Scythia.

THE RUSSIAN SLAVS OF NESTOR THE CHRONICLER—LITHUANIAN, FINNISH, AND TURKISH CLANS IN THE NINTH CENTURY.

The great barbaric invasions in the 4th century of our era formed a period of change and terrible catastrophe in Eastern Europe. The Goths, under Hermanaric, founded a vast empire in Eastern Scythia. The Huns, under Attila, overthrew this Gothic dominion, and a cloud of Finnish peoples, Avars and

Bulgarians, followed later by Magyars and Khazars, hurried swiftly on the traces of the Huns. In the midst of this strife and medley of peoples, the Slavs came to the front with their own marked character, and appeared in history under their proper name. They were described by the Greek chroniclers and by the Emperors Maurice and Constantine Porphyrogenitus. They clashed against the Roman Empire of the East ; they began the secular duel between the Greek and Slavonic races, a duel which is still being waged for the prize of mastery in the peninsula of the Balkans. Certain tribes formed a separate group among the others, and received the name of the Russian Slavs. Nestor, the first Russian historian, a monk of Kief, of the 12th century, has described their geographical distribution as it existed two hundred years before his time. The *Slavs*, properly so called, inhabited the basin of the Ilmen, and the west bank of Lake Peïpus ; their towns, Novgorod, Pskof, Izborsk, appear in the very beginning of the history of Russia. The Krivitches, again, were settled on the sources of the Dwina and the Dnieper, round their city of Smolensk. The Polotchans had Polotsk, on the Upper Dwina. The Dregovitches dwelt on the west of the Dwina, and of the Upper Dnieper, and held Tourof. The Radimitches abode on the Soja, a tributary of the Dnieper, and possessed the old cities of Ouvritch and Korosthenes ; the Viatitches on the Higher Oka ; the Drevlians, so called from the thick forests which covered their territory, in the basin of the Pripet. Between the Desna and the Dnieper the Severians were established ; their towns were Loubetch, Tchernigof, and Pereiaslavl. The Polians faced the Severians on the right bank of the Dnieper ; Kief was their centre. The White Croats abode between the Dniester and the Carpathians ; the Tivertses and the Loutitches on the Lower Dniester and the Pruth ; the Doulebes and the Boujans on the Bug, a tributary of the Vistula.

Nestor's list of the Russian Slavs shows that, in the 9th century of our era, when their history begins, they occupied but a small part of the Russia of to-day. They were almost completely penned in the districts of the Dwina and the Upper Dnieper, of the Ilmen and the Dniester. In all the immense basin of the Caspian, their share was only the land they occupied around the sources of the Volga and the Oka.

On the west and north, the Russian Slavs bordered on other Slavonic tribes, which, about this period, acquired distinct national names. Some groups, scattered about the Upper Elbe and the two banks of the Vistula, after the invasion of the Tcheques and the Liakhs or Lechites (from the 4th to the 7th century), formed themselves into the States of Bohemia and Poland.

Other tribes on the March, or Morava, made, in the kingdom of Moravia, their first attempt to secure political existence (9th century). Certain others scattered on the Lower Danube formed the kingdom of Bulgaria, after the invasion of the Bulgarians under Asparuch (680). In a more distant land on the Adriatic, the Servian and Croatian tribes were preparing to organize themselves into the kingdoms of Croatia, Dalmatia, and Servia. On the Baltic were the Slavs of Pomerania, of Brandenburg (Havelians), and Sprevanians of the banks of the Elbe (Obotrites, Wiltzes, Lutitzes, and Sorabians or Sorbes), all one day to be absorbed by the German Conquest.

At this period there was little difference between Russian and Polish Slavs. M. Koulich thinks that conquests achieved by two different races of men; that the adoption of two irreconcilable creeds (those of Rome and of Byzantium); that the influence of two rival civilizations, the Greek and the Latin, with their separate literatures and alphabets;—that all these influences created two antagonistic peoples in the midst of a race of one blood, and stamped on the inert and unconscious material of the Slavonic kindred the impress of two hostile nationalities. The Slav, moulded by the Lechites, converted to the Church of Rome, and subject to the influences of the west, became the Pole. The Slav, moulded by the Varangians, converted to the Greek church, and subject to Byzantine influences, became the Russian. In the beginning, on the Vistula as on the Dnieper, all were Slavs alike; all practised the same heathen ritual; all were governed by the same traditions, and spoke almost the same language. Indeed, the affinities of the Russian and Polish idioms, between which the dialects of White Russia, of Red Russia, and of Little Russia serve as links, sufficiently demonstrate an original brotherhood, which the strifes of churches and of thrones have destroyed.

The Russian Slavs, before taking possession of all the domain assigned to them by history. had to struggle in the north and east against the nations belonging to three principal races, the Letto-Lithuanians, the Finns and the Turks, in whom Finnish and Tatar elements were more or less mingled. The Finns and the Turks belong to that branch of the human family which has been named, from its twofold cradle of the Oural and the Altai, Ouralo-Altaic. The first of these races belongs to the Aryan family, but is nevertheless distinct from the Germanic or Slav races, and its dialects have more resemblance to Sanscrit than any other European tongue. The Jmouds and the Lithuanians, properly so called, dwell on the Niemen, the Iatviagues on the Narev. On the western shore of the Gulf of Riga and on the Baltic, the *Korses*, who give their name to

Courland, are to be found, while the *Semigalli* inhabit the left bank of the Dwina; and the Letgols, from whom are descended by a mingling with the Finnish race of Livonians, the Letts or Latiches of Southern Livonia. The Livonians on the Gulfs of Livonia and Finland, and the Tchoud-Estonians, who gave their name to Peïpus, the *Lake of the Tchouds*, belong to the Finnish race. They are the ancestors of the present inhabitants of Northern Livonia and Esthonia. The three so-called German provinces of the Baltic are then Lettish in the south, Finnish in the north. The Narovians were established on the Narova, which is a territory of the Peïpus; the Votes or Vodes, between the Volkhof and the sea, in a country called by the Novgorodians, *Vodskaïa Piatina;* the Ingrians or Ijors, on the Ijora or Ingra, a tributary on the left bank of the Neva. The Tchoud-Estonians at the present day number 719,000, the Livonians 2540, the Vodes 5000, and the Ingrians 18,000.

Finland or Suomen-maa (land of the Suomi) is still inhabited by the Suomi, who were divided into three tribes, the Iames or Tavasts on the south-east, round Inamburg and Tavastehus; the Kvins or Kaïans, on the Gulf of Bothnia; the Carelians, who were more numerous than the two other nations put together, occupied the rest of Finland. These three peoples at present amount to a total of 1,450,000. The north of Finland was and is inhabited by the Laps or Laplanders, who form a special division of the Finnish race, and reckon in Russia about 4000 souls. The shores of the Icy Ocean, from the Mezen to the Yenissei, have been always occupied by the Samoyedes, a very wide-spread but far from numerous people, who amount in Europe to about 5000 souls. In the time of Nestor the Vesses dwelt on the Cheksna and the White Lake; the Mouromians (whose name is repeated in that of Mourom) on the Oka and its affluents, the Moskowa and the Kliazma; the Merians on the Upper Volga around the Lake Klechtchine and Lake Nero or Rostof. These three tribes have completely disappeared, having been absorbed or transformed by the Russian colonization, but leave behind them innumerable *kourgans* or *tumuli*. Between 1851 and 1854, M. Ouvarof and M. Savelief excavated 7729 in the Merian country alone. Besides these monuments and the remains which they contain, the only traces left of these tribes are to be found in names of places, and in certain peculiarities of the local dialects. It was around their territory that the Muscovite State and the Russian empire were formed. The Tchoud-Zavolotchians were encamped on the Lower Dwina; the Erzes, or Zyrians, inhabited the basin of the Petchora; the Permians, the source of the Dwina and the Kama; the Votiaks or Ari lived on the Viatka, where the town of Viatka still preserves their name. These races form what is called the Permian branch of the Finnish nation; their country was named by the Scandinavians, Biarmia or Biarmaland, and "Great Permia" by the Muscovites. Biarmaland was discovered in the 9th century by the Norwegian navigator Other, who not long afterwards entered the Service of Alfred the Great, king of England, and has left in Anglo-Saxon an account of his travels. This narrative proves that the Permians were then a civilized people, who traded with India and Persia. The temple of their god Ioumala was so richly ornamented with precious stones, that its brilliance illuminated all the surrounding country. The Erzes number at the present day only 80,000, the Permians 70,000, the Votiaks 234,000.

The Ougrian branch is composed first of the Ostiaks, amounting to 20,000 and of the Voguls (7000). On the east they inhabit the Ourals, and only border on Europe. Formerly they lived more to the south. The Magyars, who made Europe tremble in the 10th century, and founded the kingdom of Hungary, belonged to this race.

Between the Kama and the Oural were already to be found the Bach-Kourtes (shaven-heads) or Bachkirs of the 16th to the 17th centuries, originally a Finnish people, no doubt of the Ugrian branch, but profoundly Tatarized, with whom were mingled the Metcheraks, a tribe named by Nestor. There are at present 500,000 Bachkirs, and 100,000 Metcheraks. On the Middle Volga dwelt the Tcheremisses, the Tchouvaches, and the Mordvians; the Tcheremisses are found again to-day in the government of Kazan, Nijni-Novgorod, and Viatka; the Tchouvaches in Kazan, Nijni-Novgorod, and Simbirsk; the Mordvians in Kazan, Tambof, Pensa, Simbirsk, Samara, and Saratof, but these are now only small islets amid the Russian colonization, whereas in the time of Nestor they formed a compact mass. The Tcheremisses now only number 165,000, the Tchouvaches 430,000, and the Mordvians 500,000; all the rest have become Russians except a few who have become Tatar.

All seems strange among these ancient peoples. The type of countenance is blurred and, as it were, unfinished; the costume seems to have been adopted from some antediluvian fashion; the manners and superstitions preserve the trace of early religions beyond the date of any known paganisms; the language is sometimes so very primitive that the Tchouvaches for example do not possess more than a thousand original words.

The Tcheremiss women wear on their breasts two plates forming a cuirass, and ornamented with pieces of silver, transmitted from generation to generation. A numismatist would make wonderful discoveries in these walking museums of medals.

They drape their legs in a piece of tightly "tied back" black cloth, and think that modesty consists in never showing the legs, just as the Tatar women make a point of never unveiling the face.

The Tchouvach women cover their heads with a little peaked cap like a Saracen helmet, carry on their backs a covering of leather and metal, like the trapping of a war-horse, and wear on fête-days a stiff and rectangular mantle like a chasuble. Among this singular people, "black" and "beautiful" are synonymous, and when they wish to revenge themselves they hang themselves at their enemy's door.

In spite of three centuries of Christian missions, these tribes dwelling in the heart of Russia and on the great artery of the Volga are not even yet complete converts to Christianity.

There are still some pagan districts. It may even be said that a considerable portion of the Tcheremisses, Tchouvaches, Mordvians, and Votiaks remain attached to the worship of the ancient deities, which they sometimes mingle with the orthodox practices and the worship of St. Nicholas. Their religion consisted essentially in dualism: the good principle is called by the Tchouvaches, Thora; Iouma (the "Ioumal" of the Finns) by the Tcheremisses; Inma by the Votiaks, etc. The bad principle was named Chaïtan or Satan. Between the two is a divinity whom men had in former times cruelly offended, who is called Keremet. From the good god proceeded an infinity of gods and goddesses; from Keremet a numerous progeny of male and female Keremets, genii more mischievous and malevolent, to whom the aborigines offer pieces of money, and sacrifice horses, oxen, sheep, swans, and cocks and hens, in sanctuaries also named Keremet, built in the depths of the forests and far from Russian spies.

Human sacrifices have been talked of. The worship of the dead inspired ideas which guide the savage everywhere. Men have preserved the custom of wife-capture, or buying brides from the fathers by paying the *kalym*; they practise agricultural communism. In a word, the life of these races of the Volga in the 19th century is the living commentary of the accounts of Nestor of the Russian Slavs of the 9th century.

It is probable that Slavs and Russians then lived in an absolutely identical state of civilization, and had almost the same religious ideas and the same customs.

There remain two Finnish peoples still to be spoken of, who, mentioned by Nestor, have at present disappeared, but who were far more remarkable than any of the preceding. These are the Khazars, who, although mingled with Turkish elements, were essentially Finnish. Remarkable for their aptitude for civilization, they had formed in the 9th century a vast empire, which embraced the regions of the Lower Dnieper, the Don, and the Lower Volga, round the Sea of Azof and the Caspian; they had built Itil on the Volga, and Sarkel or the White City on the Don; they had sometimes governors at Bosporos and Cherson in the Taurid peninsula; in the Kuban they possessed the Tamatarchia of the Greeks. They had commercial and friendly relations with Byzantium, the caliphate of Bagdad, and even the caliphate of Cordova, the only civilized states of the then known world. The Khazars had flourishing schools, and tolerated all religions besides the national paganism. Mussulman missionaries appeared in the 7th, Jewish missionaries in the 8th century, and Saint Cyril arrived about 860 at the court of their Chagan. A Jewish Chagan of the name of Joseph interchanged some curious letters with the Rabbi Hasdai of Cordova, announcing to him that the people of God, the Israel Khazar, ruled over nine nations of the nineteen of the Caucasus, and thirteen of the Black Sea, and that he did not allow the Russians to descend the Volga to ravage the territory of the Caliph of Bagdad. The Israelitish Khazars became afterwards mingled with the Kharaite Jews, and the Moslem Khazars with the Tatars of the Crimea. Among the vassal nations of the Khazars enumerated by the Chagan Joseph, were the Bourtass and the Bulgars of the Volga the latter, kinsmen of the Bulgars who were subjected by the Danubian Slavs, and apparently nearly related to the Tchouvaches, were a mixture of Finnish, Turkish, and even Slav elements, according to an Arabian account. Sedentary, industrious, and destined to inherit the commercial splendor of the Khazars, they blended with the native superstitions the Islamism which was preached to them in 922 by missionaries from Bagdad, and possessed in the 10th century a flourishing state. Their capital was Bolgary or the "Great City," on the junction of the Volga and the Kama. They also owned the cities of Bouliar or Biliarsk, Souvar, Krementchoug, &c. Their descendants were fused with the Tatar conquerors of the 13th century.

The Finnish races, even more than the Slavs, are the real aborigines of Russia. In the 5th century B.C. Herodotus writes of them as already long possessed of the soil. Everywhere in these wide regions the traces of their occupation are visible. At different periods they extended from the Livonian Gulf to the Ourals, and from the Icy Ocean to the Black Sea. They withdrew at various times, especially from the 5th to the 9th centuries, to allow the passage of the great migrations and of the great invasions; but in the 10th century they occupied, with the

Khazars, the shores of the Sea of Azof and of the Caspian, while the Finns of Esthonia held the Lithuanians in check.

The Turkish races, on the contrary, made their appearance much later in Russia. In the 9th century the Lower Volga and the Lower Oural began to fall a prey to the Patzinaks, incorrigible brigands who marched over the bodies of the Khazars to establish themselves on the Lower Dnieper. After them appeared the Polovtsi or Koumans, the Ouzes or Torques. The invasion of the Tatars was more Turkish than Mongolian. The nomads vanished or, according to Nestor, were absorbed by new arrivals, namely the Nogaïs, formed in the 13th century of the remnants of the Polovtsi, and of the Turko-Kanglis, at present numbering 50,000; the Kirghis, who entered Europe about 1721, and to-day amount to about 82,000 souls; the Kalmucks, who are Mongols not Turks, belong to the Œleutes or Western Mongols, invaders of Russia in 1636, number 87,0co in the provinces of Astrakhan, Stavropol, and the Don, and in spite of the efforts of Christians and Mussulmans have remained Lamaists. As to the Tatars, properly so called, or sedentary Turks (more or less a mixture of Finnish and Mongol elements), who inhabit the governments of the Volga, Kazan, and Astrakhan, as well as those of Stavropol and the Crimea, they number altogether about 1,420,000 heads.

DIVISION OF THE RUSSIANS OF TO-DAY INTO THREE BRANCHES—
HOW RUSSIA WAS COLONIZED.

In the time of Nestor (end of the 11th century), the Russian Slavs confined between the Lithuanians on the west, the Finns on the north, and the Turks on the east, hardly occupied one-fifth part of Russia in Europe. To-day we see the Russian race extend from Finland to the Oural, from the Icy Ocean to the Caucasus and Crimea, amounting to 56,000,000 men, besides 3,000,000 colonists in the Asiatic provinces. The Letto-Lithuanians on the contrary are reduced to 2,420,000 souls; the Finns, including the inhabitants of Finland, to less than 4,000,000; and the Turko-Tatars to less than 2,000,000. The Russians form six-sevenths of the population of Russia. The proportions are more than reversed. What a change has been wrought in ten centuries! The present Russians may be divided into three branches, deriving their names from certain historical circumstances. 1. The name of *White Russia* is given to the provinces conquered from the 13th to the 14th century by the Grand Dukes of Lithuania. These were the ancient territories of the Krivitches, Polotchans, Dregovitches,

Drevlians, Doulebes, now forming the governments of Vitepsk, Mohilef, and Minsk. The governments of Kovno, Grodno and Wilna, at present unequally Russicized, were originally Lithuanian. The Lithuanian territories of Grodno, Novogrodek and Belostok were sometimes called *Black Russia*. 2. *Little Russia* includes the country of the ancient Severians and Polians increased by colonies; that is, the governments of Kief, Tchernigof, Pultowa, Kharkof, Volhynia, and Podolia. It even extends beyond the frontiers of the empire into *Red Russia* or Old Gallicia (Galitch, Iaroslavl, Terebovl, Zvenigorod, Lemberg, or Lvof), belonging to Austria, and peopled by 3,000,000 of Ruthenians or Russians. 3. *Great Russia* grouped around the ancient Muscovy, and occupying the place held in the 9th century by many Turkish or Finnish tribes. To Great Russia belong *Northern Russia* (Arkhangel), *Eastern Russia* (the Volga, Kazan, Astrakhan), and *New Russia or South Russia* (Cherson, Ekaterinoslaf, Kharkof, Odessa, the Crimea). Great Russia as a whole, apart from Novgorod and Pskof, was won from foreign races by Russian colonization. It was a colony of Kievian Russia, and, though for a time subjugated by the Tatars, was able to shake off their yoke, while Kief still remained a Lithuanian province. It continued to extend its conquests in the East; then turning to the West in the 17th and 18th centuries, was able to recover White Russia and Little Russia.

In the empire the White Russians number 3,000,000, the Little Russians 12,000,000, and the Great Russians 41,000,000. There are dialectical differences between the idioms of these three families, which historical and literary influences easily explain. Some writers have been anxious to establish the existence of a profound difference between Great Russia and her two neighbors. They have reserved the name of Russians and the character of Slavs for the White Russians and the Little Russians, and have pretended to see in the "Muscovites" nothing but descendants of Finns, Turks and Tatars, in a word Turanians, Russian only in language. The Muscovite Empire, founded in the midst of Vesses, of Mouromians, and of Merians, extended at the expense of the Tchouvaches, the Mordvians, Tatars and Kirghiz, with its two capitals Moscow and St. Petersburg in the Tchoudic region, is not, if these writers are to be trusted, even a European state. A more careful study shows us that Muscovy was formed in the first place by the migrations of Russian colonists, in the second place by the assimilation of certain foreign races. 1. When the steppes of the south became the prey of Asiatic nomads, the Russian population flowed back in a vast wave, from the banks of the Dnieper to the Upper and Middle Volga. We see the princes of Souzdal calling to their aid the inhabitants of the banks of the Dnieper, while in the forests of the north new cities are constantly founded by the people of Novgorod. The Russia of Kief once destroyed, a new Russia begins to form itself, almost out of the same elements, at the opposite extremity of the Oriental plain. The names given to the new towns of Souzdal and Muscovy must be noticed. There is a Vladimir on the Kliazma as there is a Vladimir in Volhynia, a Zvenigorod on the Moskowa as on the Dniester, a Galitch in Souzdal as in Gallicia, a Iaroslavl on the Volga as on the San. Souzdal and Riazan, like Kief, have their Pereiaslavl; that of the former bears the title of Zaliesski, or "beyond the forests." In a different land and under another sky the emigrants clearly tried to restore the name, if they could not find the image of their native country. Is it not thus that the English in America founded New York, and the French New Orleans? Moreover, when we have seen a population of 3,000,000 Russians gather in the Caucasus and in Siberia—when we see that the steppes of the south which were deserts in the time of Catherine II. reckon to-day their 5,000,000 to 6,000,000 inhabitants,—it is easy to understand how, at a more distant epoch, the basin of the Volga was colonized. As for saying that the inhabitants of New Russia are nothing but Finns and Russified Turks, one might as well pretend that the 30,000,000 or 40,000,000 of North America are Red-skins who have learnt English and embraced Protestantism.

We must recognize that the Russian, almost as much as the Anglo-Saxon, has the instinct which drives men to emigrate and found colonies. The Russians do in the far East of Europe what the Anglo-Saxons do in the far West of America. They belong to one of the great races of pioneers and backwoodsmen. All the history of the Russian people, from the foundation of Moscow, is that of their advance into the forest, into the Black Land, into the prairie. The Russian has his trappers and settlers in the Cossacks of the Dnieper, Don, and Tereck; in the tireless fur-hunters of Siberia; in the gold-diggers of the Oural and the Altai; in the adventurous monks who ever lead the way, founding in regions always more distant, a monastery which is to be the centre of a town; lastly, in the Raskolnicks, or Dissenters, Russian Puritans or Mormons, who are persecuted by laws human and divine, and seek from forest to forest the Jerusalem of their dreams. The level plains of Russia naturally tempted men to migration. The mountain keeps her own, the mountain calls her wanderers to return; while the steppe, stretching away to the dimmest horizon, invites you to advance, to ride at adventure, to "go where the eyes glance."

The flat and monotonous soil has no hold on its inhabitants; they will find as bare a landscape anywhere As for their hovel, how can they care for their hovel? it is burned down often. The Western expression, the "ancestral roof," has no meaning for the Russian peasant. The native of Great Russia, accustomed to live on little, and endure the extremes of heat and cold, was born to brave the dangers and privations of the emigrant's life. With his crucifix, his axe in his belt, and his boots slung behind his back, he will go to the end of the Eastern world. However weak may be the infusion of the Russian element in an Asiatic population, it cannot transmute itself nor disappear—it must become the dominant power.

History has helped to make this movement irresistible. When the Russian took refuge in Souzdal, he was compelled to clear and cultivate the very worst land of his future domain, for the *Tchernoziom* was then overrun by nomads. How could he escape the temptation to go and look in the south for more fertile soil which without labor or manure would yield four times as great a harvest? Villages and whole cantons in Muscovy have been known to empty themselves in a moment, the peasants marching in a body, as in the old times of the invasions, towards the "Black Soil," the "Warm Soil" of the south. Government and the landholders were obliged to use the most terrible means to stop these migrations of the husbandmen. Without these repressive measures the steppes would have been colonized two centuries earlier than they actually were. The report that the Tzar authorized the emigration—a forged ukase, a rumor—anything was enough to uproot whole peoples from the soil. The peasant's passion for wandering explains the development of Cossack life in the plains of the south; it explains the legislation which from the beginning of the 16th century chained the serf to the glebe and bound him to the soil. In the 13th century, on the other hand, the peasant was free. His prince encouraged him to emigrate, and hence came the colonization of Eastern Russia.

2. The Russian race, it is true, has the faculty of absorbing certain aboriginal stocks. The Little Russians assimilated the remnants of Turkish tribes, the Great Russians swallowed up the Finnish nations of the East. There must, however, be no religious barrier between the conquerors and the conquered, for the Tchoud, while still heathen, is easily assimilated; but once converted to Islamism, he is a refractory element that can scarcely be brought to order. A baptized Tchouvach inevitably becomes a Russian, a circumcised Tchouvach inevitably becomes a Tatar. We have seen the Vesses, the Mouromians, the Merians disappear without leaving a trace; the Tchouvaches, the Mordvians, the Tcheremisses become more Russian every day. The successive stages, and the steps which lead to the

accomplishment of this change, were lately observed by Mr. Wallace, an English traveller :—

" During my wanderings in these northern provinces I have found villages in every stage of Russification. In one everything seemed thoroughly Finnish: the inhabitants had a reddish-olive skin, very high cheek-bones, obliquely-set eyes, and a peculiar costume; none of the women and very few of the men could understand Russian, and any Russian who visited the place was regarded as a foreigner. In a second there were already some Russian inhabitants; the others had lost something of their pure Finnish type, many of the men had discarded the old costume and spoke Russian fluently, and a Russian visitor was no longer shunned. In a third, the Finnish type was still further weakened; all the men spoke Russian, and nearly all the women understood it; the old male costume had entirely disappeared, and the old female costume was rapidly following it, and the intermarriage with the Russian population was no longer rare. In a fourth, intermarriage had almost completely done its work, and the old Finnish element could be detected merely in certain peculiarities of physiognomy and accent" (vol. i. p. 231).

The density and resisting power of these ancient peoples, scattered over such immense spaces of the continent, must have been comparatively slight, while the Russian emigrants came on in vast waves, or stole in like the constant dropping of water. The aboriginals must often have recoiled and concentrated their forces, thus leaving room and verge for the pure Slavonic element. The more or less considerable mixture of races, on the other hand, cannot but have influenced the physical type, character, and powers of the Great Russian in a peculiar way. The bright Slavonic nature, when blended with tribes of a duller cast, gained in strength and weight what it lost in vivacity. Hence, of all the Slavonic peoples, the Great Russian alone has been able to create and to maintain, in face of every obstacle, a vast and durable empire.

CHAPTER III.

PRIMITIVE RUSSIA: THE SLAVS.

Religion of the Slavs—Funeral rites—Domestic and political customs, the family, the *mir* or commune, the *volost* or canton, the tribe—Cities—Industry—Agriculture.

RELIGION OF THE SLAVS—FUNERAL RITES.

THE religion of the Russian Slavs, like that of all Aryan races, was founded on nature and its phenomena. It was a pantheism which, as its original meaning was lost, necessarily became a polytheism. Just as the Homeric deities were preceded by the gods of Hesiod, Ouranos and Demeter, or Heaven and Earth, so the most ancient gods of the Russian Slavs seem to have been Svarog, the heaven, and "our mother, the dank earth." Then new conceptions appeared in the first rank in the historic period. 1. Ancient poets and chroniclers (see the Song of Igor, and Nestor) have preserved to us the names of *Dagh-Bog*, god of the sun, father of nature; *Voloss*, a solar deity, and, like the Greek Apollo, inspirer of poets and protector of flocks; *Perun*, god of thunder, another personification of the Sun at war with the Cloud; *Stribog*, the Russian Æolus, father of winds, protector of warriors; *Khors*, a solar god; *Semargl* and *Mokoch*, whose attributes are unknown. 2. In some of the early hymns they sing of *Koupalo* or *Iarilo*, god of the summer sun, and *Did-Lado*, goddess of fecundity. 3. In the epic songs are celebrated *Sviatogor*, the giant-hero, whose weight the earth can scarcely bear; *Mikoula Selianinovitch*, the good laborer, a kind of Slav Triptolemus, the divine personification of the race's passionate love of agriculture, striking with the iron share of his plough the stones of the furrow, with a noise that is heard three days' journey off; *Volga Vseslavitch*, a Proteus who can take all manner of shapes; *Polkan*, a centaur; *Dounai, Don Ivanovitch, Dnieper Korolevitch*, who are rivers; then a series of heroes, conquerors of dragons like *Ilia of Mourom*, who seem to be solar gods degraded to the rank of paladins. 4. In the stories which beguile the village evening assemblies, appear *Morena*, goddess of death; *Kochtchei* and *Moroz*, personifications of the bitter winter weather; *Baba-Yaga*, an ogress who lives on the edge of the forest, in a hut built on the foot of a fowl, and swayed by the winds; and the *King of the Sea*, who entices sailors to his watery palaces. 5. Popular superstition continues to people nature with good and bad spirits: the *Russalki*, water sprites; *Vodianoi*, river genii; the *Liechii* and the *Liesnik*, forest demons; the *Domovoi* (*dom*, house), the brownie of the domestic hearth; and the *Vampires*, ghosts who steal by night from their tombs, and suck the blood of the living during their sleep.

Since Mythology reproduces under so many forms the struggle of the heroes of the light with the monsters of darkness, it is possible that she may have admitted a bad principle at variance with a good principle, an ill-doing god, of whom Morena, Kochtchei, Baba-Yaga, the dragon, the mountain-serpent, are only types. We cannot find any positive confirmation of this hypothesis, as far as the Russian Slavs are concerned, but Helmold asserts that the Baltic Slavs recognize *Bielibog*, the White God, and *Tchernobog*, the Black God.

The Russians do not seem to have had either temples or priests in the proper sense of the word. They erected rude idols on the hills, and venerated the oak consecrated to Perun; the leaders of the people offered the sacrifices. They also had sorcerers, or magicians, analogous to the Tatar Shamans, whose counsels appear to have had great weight.

It has been the study of the Russian Church to combat paganism by purifying the superstitions she cannot uproot. She has turned to account any similarity in names or symbols. She has been able to honor Saint Dmitri and Saint George, the slayers of dragons; Saint John, who thunders in the spring; Saint Elias, who recalls Ilia of Mourom; Saint Blaise or Vlaise, who has succeeded to Voloss as guardian of the flocks; Saint Nicholas, or Mikoula, patron of laborers, like Mikoula Selianinovitch; Saint Cosmas, or Kouzma, protector of blacksmiths, who has taken the place of *kouznets*, the mysterious blacksmith forger of the destinies of man in the mountains of the north. In some popular songs the Virgin Mary replaces Did-Lado, and then Saint John succeeds to Perun or Iarilo. Who can fail to recognize the myth of the spring and the fruitful rains accompanied by thunder, in this White Russian song that is repeated at the festival of St. John? "John and Mary—bathed on the hill—while John bathed—the earth shook—while Mary bathed—the earth germinated." The Church has taken care to consecrate to the Saints of her calendar or to purify by holy rites the sacred trees and mysterious wells to which crowds of pilgrims continued to flock.

Russian Slavs certainly had visions of another life, but, like all primitive peoples, they looked forward to a life which was gross and material. In the 7th century among the Wends, German Slavs, women refused to survive their husbands, and burned themselves on their funeral pile. This ancient Aryan custom must have been in vigor among the Russian Slavs at an equally early epoch. The Arabic writer, Ibn-Foszlan, gives an account of the Russian funeral rites which he himself witnessed in the 9th century. For ten days the friends of the deceased bewailed him, and intoxicated themselves over his corpse. Then the men-servants were asked, which of them would be buried with his master? One of them replied in the affirmative, and was ininstantly strangled. The same question was also put to the women-servants, one of whom likewise devoted herself. She was then washed, adorned, and treated like a princess, and did nothing but drink and sing. On the appointed day the dead man was laid in a boat, with part of his arms and his garments. The man-servant was slain with the favorite horse and other domestic animals and was laid in the boat, to which the young girl was then led. She took off her jewels, and with a glass of kvass in her hand sang a song that she would only too willingly have prolonged. "All at once," says the eye-witness, "the old woman who accompanied her, and whom they called the angel of death, ordered her to drink quickly, and to enter into the cabin of the boat, where lay the dead body of her master. At these words she changed color, and as she made some difficulties about entering, the old woman seized her by the hair, dragged her in, and entered with her. The men immediately began to beat their shields with clubs to prevent the other girls from hearing the cries of their companion, which might prevent them from one day dying for their masters." While the funeral pile blazed, one of the Russians said to our narrator, "You Arabs are fools: you hide in the earth the man you have loved best, and there he becomes the prey of worms. We, on the contrary, burn him up in the twinkling of an eye, that he may the quicker enter paradise." Nestor found the rite among the Russian Slavs. The excavations made in a great number of *kourgans* (barrows) confirm his testimony. The discoveries recently made in the tombs of Novgorod by M. Ivanouski, prove that the Slavs of Ilmen had preserved or adopted the custom of burying their dead. In these tombs are found a great quantity of arms, instruments, jewels, animals, bones, and grains of wheat; from which we may conclude that the Russian Slavs expected the future life to be an exact continuation of the present one, and that they surrounded the dead with all the objects that here contributed to his happiness. The examination of the human bones preserved in the *kourgans* also confirms the historical accounts, and proves that **servants and female slaves were sacrificed over the corpse.**

DOMESTIC AND POLITICAL CUSTOMS : THE FAMILY ; THE MIR OR COMMUNE ; THE VOLOST OR CANTON ; THE TRIBE.

The Slav family was founded on the patriarchal principle. The father was the absolute head, and after his death the power passed to the eldest of the members composing it : first, to the brothers of the deceased, if he had any under his care, then successively to his sons, beginning with the eldest. The chief had the same rights over the women who entered his family by marriage, as over its natural members.

Their domestic manners seemed to have been very barbarous. The monk Nestor may be suspected of exaggeration wherever he describes the condition of pagan Russia, which baptism was to regenerate. There is no exception to this exaggerated censure but in the case of the Polians. " The Drevlians," he tells us, " lived after the manner of wild beasts. They cut each other's throats, ate impure food, declined all marriage-ties ; they ravished and stole young girls who came for water to the fountains. . . . . The Radimitches, the Viatitches, the Severians lived like wild animals in the forests, were fed on all sorts of horrors, and spoke of all kinds of shameful things in the presence of their sisters-in-law and relatives. . . . They captured women, who were willing parties to the transaction, often two or three at a time."

The charges which Nestor chiefly urges against the Slavs, are the capture of women and polygamy. This latter charge is completely established ; as to the capture, it might be symbolical. In the text quoted above we see the women " came " to the fountain, and that they were parties to the transaction. This capture, if we take it for a simple ceremony, may imply, in very early times the existence of abduction by violence. To-day, the marriage-customs of Russia still preserve traces of these ancient usages. There is still a pretended capture of the woman ; a custom to be found in the Germany of the 8th century, where the very name of marriage has a pointed signification—*Brautlauft*, the flight of the bride. The songs at Russian weddings also imply the existence of a time when the maiden was bought. One of these songs accuses the kindred of avarice : " Thy brother—the accursed Tatar—has sold his sister for a piece of silver."

Some historians have thought, with Karamsin, that the Slavs held women in less consideration than the Germans did, and in fact " treated them as slaves." We may doubt if there was so great a difference between the two nations. The chronicles speak of Lybed, sister of Kii, the fabulous founder of Kief, dividing her paternal inheritance with her brothers, and of

Princess Olga becoming heir and avenger of her husband and guardian of his son. The epic songs show us many bold heroines side by side with the heroes of the Kievian cycle, and mothers of heroes surrounded with wonderful luxury and extraordinary honors. The excavations of the *kourgans* show us skeletons of women richly ornamented with jewels.

The commune, or *mir*, was only the expansion of the family; it was subject to the authority of the elders of each household, who assembled in a council or *vetché*. The village lands were held in common by all the members of the association; the individual only possessed his harvest, and the *dvor* or enclosure immediately surrounding his house. This primitive condition of property, existing in Russia up to the present day, was once common to all European peoples.

The communes nearest together formed a group called *volost* or *pagost* (canton, parish). The volost was governed by a council formed of the elders of the communes: one of these elders, either by hereditary right, age, or election, was recognized as more powerful than the rest, and became chief of the canton. His authority seems much to have resembled that of Ulysses over the numerous kings of little Ithaca. In times of danger, the *volosts* of the same tribe could elect a temporary head, but decline to submit to a general and permanent ruler. The Emperor Maurice had already observed that passion for liberty among the Slavs, which made them detest all sovereignty. The Russian Slavs easily rose from the idea of a commune to that of a canton, with a chief chosen from the elders of the family; in an emergency they might permit a temporary confederation of all the cantons of one tribe (dlemia), but we never find that there was a prince of the Severians, Polians, or Radimitches. Only princes of the *volost* could exist among them, like the prince of Korosthenes in the legend of Olga. The idea of the unity of a tribe, and *à fortiori* the unity of the Russian nation, was absolutely foreign to the race. The ideas of government and of the State had to come to them from without.

TOWNS—TRADE—AGRICULTURE.

Nestor declares that the Russian Slavs, for the most part, "lived in forests like the wild beast." Karamsin and Schloezer have concluded from this that they had no towns. Now there exist a number of monuments in Russia which have for long puzzled archæologists. There are the *gorodichtchés* (from *gorod*, town), enclosures formed by the earth being thrown up, and these we find invariably on the steep bank of a watercourse, or on a small hill. M. Samokvassof, who has explored this very country of the Severians, described by Nestor as living wholly in forests, has been able to prove that these *gorodichtchés* are the *oppida*, the primitive towns of Russia. In the government of Tchernigof alone, M. Samokvassof has reckoned 160; in that of Koursk, 50. We may calculate from this that numbers exist in Russia, and that every *volost* had at least one. About these earth-enclosures, which were capped by wooden palisades or hedges of osier, and were the common means of defence for each group of families, we usually find grouped, as in a cemetery, the *kourgans* or *tumuli* of the dead.

The excavations made, either in the *kourgans* or in the soil of the *gorodichtchés*, have shown us the Slavs were more civilized than Nestor supposed. Vessels of pottery, tolerably well designed, iron and bronze, gold and silver objects, glass, false pearls, rattles, prove that they had a certain amount of trade, and a fairly extensive commerce, particularly with Asia. Oriental coins have been dug up, dating from 699, or near two hundred years before the arrival of the Varangians. There are a great number of these coins in the country. Near Novgorod a vase was discovered, containing about 7000 roubles' worth of this early money. The fame of the swords made by the Russian Slavs extended to Arabia. Nestor relates that the Khazars imposed a tribute of swords on the Polians. When the latter brought the arms to the Khazars, they were afraid, and said to their princes, " Our swords have only one edge—these have two. We tremble lest one day this people should levy a tribute on us and other tribes."

Agriculture was the favorite occupation of the Slavs. Nearly all their deities are of an agricultural character. The favorite heroes of their epic cycle, Mikoula and Ilia, were the sons of laborers. They had the more liking for field life, as the serfage of the glebe was still unknown amongst them. It has been said that the Germans borrowed the plough from the Slavs, and that the German name of *pflug* is derived from the Slav *ploug*. With the wax and honey of their hives, the corn of the *Tchernoziom*, and the furs of the north, the Russians carried on a great trade. Their need of strangers, together with a sociable instinct, natural to primitive races, made them very hospitable: it was even permitted to steal for the benefit of the unexpected guest. A peaceful race, devoted to liberty, music, and dancing. appears in the idyllic picture painted for us of the early Slavs. The Emperor Maurice, on the contrary, who had had dealings with all kinds of adventurous tribes, assures us that they were warlike, cruel in battle, full of savage wiles, able to conceal themselves in places where it seemed impossible their bodies could be hidden, or to lie in ambush in streams for hours together, the water over their heads, breathing by means of a reed. Their armor was defective, they had no breast-plates, they fought on foot, were naked to the waist, and had for weapons, pikes, large shields, wooden bows, poisoned arrows, and lassoes to catch their victims. This sketch specially applies to the invaders of the Roman provinces of the Danube. It is probable that these agricultural races had in general a military organization inferior to that of their Turkish and Scandinavian neighbors who lived by plunder. The imperfection of their political condition, their minute division into clans and *volosts*, the incessant warfare of canton with canton, delivered them up, defenceless, to their invaders. Whilst the Slavs of the south paid tribute to the Khazars, the Slavs of Ilmen, exhausted by their divisions, decided on calling in the Varangians. "'Let us seek,' they said, 'a prince who will govern us and reason with us justly.' Then," continues Nestor, "the Tchouds,* the Slavs (Novgorod), the Krivitches, and other confederate races, said to the princes of Varangia, 'Our land is great and fruitful, but it lacks order and justice; come and take possession, and govern us.'"

* The Tchouds here mentioned are rather Slavs who had colonized the Tchoud country about Pskof and Izborsk.

CHAPTER IV.

THE VARANGIANS: FORMATION OF RUSSIA; THE FIRST EXPEDITIONS AGAINST CONSTANTINOPLE, 862-972.

The Northmen of Russia—Origin and customs of the Varangians—The first Russian princes: Rurik, Oleg, Igor—Expeditions against Constantinople —Olga—Christianity in Russia—Sviatoslaf—The Danube disputed between the Russians and Greeks.

NORTHMEN IN RUSSIA—ORIGIN AND CUSTOMS OF THE VARANGIANS.

WHO were these Varangians? To what race did they belong? No questions in the early history of Russia are more eagerly debated. After more than a century of controversy, the various views have been reduced to three :—

1. The Varangians were of Scandinavian origin, and it was they who imposed the name of Russia on the Slav countries. A most weighty argument in support of this theory is the large number of Scandinavian names in the list of Varangian princes reigning in Russia. The Emperor Constantine Porphyrogenitus, speaking of Russia, makes a distinction between the Slavs and the Russians proper. Describing the cataracts of the Dnieper, he gives to each the *Russian* and the *Slav* name. Now these *Russian* names may nearly all be understood by reference to Scandinavian roots. Liutprand, speaking of the Russians, expresses himself in these terms :—" *Græci vocant Russos . . . nos vero Normannos.*" The *Annals of Saint Bertinus* say, that the Emperor Theophilus recommended some Russian envoys to Louis le Débonnaire, but he, taking them for Norman spies, threw them into prison. Finally, the first Russian Code of Laws, compiled by Iaroslaf, presents a striking analogy with the Scandinavian laws. The Partisans of this opinion place the mother country of the Russians in Sweden, where they point particularly to a spot called *Roslog*, and associations of oarsmen called *Roslagen*. At the present day the Finns call the Swedes *Rootzi*.

2. The Varangians were Slavs, and came either from the Slav shores of the Baltic, or from some Scandinavian region where the Slavs had founded a colony. The word *Russia* is not of Swedish origin; it is applied very early to the country of the Dnieper. To come from *Rouss* or to go to *Rouss* are ex-

pressions to be met with in the ancient documents, and *Rouss* there signifies the country of Kief. Arabic writers give the name of Russians to a nation they consider very numerous, and they mean in this case, not Scandinavians, but indigenous Slavs.

3. The Varangians were not a nation, but a band of warriors formed of exiled adventurers, some Slavs, other Scandinavians. The partisans of this opinion show us the Slav and Scandinavian races from very early times, in frequent commercial and political relations. The leaders of the band were generally Scandinavian, but part of the soldiers were Slav. This hypothesis, which diminishes the Norman element in the Varangians, serves to explain how the establishment of these adventurers in the country but little affected the Slavs of the Ilmen and the Dnieper. It explains, too, the rapid absorption of the new comers in the conquered race, an absorption so complete that the grandson of Rurik, Sviatoslaf, already bears a Slav name, while his great-grandson, Vladimir, remains in the memory of the people as the type of Slav prince. Whether the Varangians were pure Scandinavians, or whether they were mingled with Slav adventurers, it seems certain that the former element predominated, and that we may identify these men from the North with the sea-kings so celebrated in the West during the decay of the Carolings. M. Samokvassof has lately opened, near Tchernigof, the *black tomb* containing the bones and arms of an unknown prince who lived in the 10th century, and was probably a Varangian. His coat-of-mail and pointed helmet completely resemble the arms of the Norman warriors. The Russian princes that we find in the early miniatures, are clothed and armed like the Norman chiefs in the Bayeux Tapestry of Queen Matilda. It is therefore not surprising that, in our own age, art has made almost identical representations of Rurik on the monument lately erected at Novgorod, and of William the Conqueror on the monument at Falaise. The Varangians, like the Normans, astonished the nations of the South by their reckless courage and gigantic stature. "They were as tall as palm-trees," said the Arabs. Bold sailors, admirable foot-soldiers, the Varangians differed widely from the mounted and nomad races of Southern Russia, Hungarians, Khazars, Patzinaks, whose tactics were always Parthian. The Russians, according to Leo the Deacon, who was an eye-witness of the fact, fought in a compact mass, and seemed like a wall of iron, bristling with lances, glittering with shields, whence rang a ceaseless clamor like the waves of the sea—the famous *barditus* or *barritus* of the Germans of Tacitus. A huge shield **covered** them to their feet, and, when they fought in retreat,

they turned this enormous buckler on their backs, and became invulnerable. The fury of battle at last made them beside themselves, like the Bersarks. Never, says the same author, were they seen to surrender. When victory was lost, they stabbed themselves, for they held that those who died by the hand of an enemy were condemned to serve him in another life. The Greeks had for long highly esteemed these heroes worthy of the Edda. Under the name of *Ros* or Varangians, they formed the body-guard of the Emperor, and figured in all the Byzantine armies. In the expedition of 902 against Crete, 700 Russians took part; 415 in that of Lombardy in 925; 584 in that of Greece in 949.

The Russian Varangians readily took the pay of foreign nations of Novgorod as well as Byzantium. This is one more feature of resemblance with the Normans of France, whom the Greek emperors also employed in their wars with the Saracens of Italy. Sometimes, instead of fighting for others, they made war for themselves. This was the case with the Danes in England, the Normans in Neustria, the descendants of Tancred in Naples and Sicily, the companions of Rurik in Russia. As they were usually a very small number, they blended rapidly with the conquered nations. Thus the descendants of Rollo quickly became Frenchmen, and those of Robert Guiscard, Sicilians. In the Varangian bands, Slavs as well as Scandinavians were mixed; but we likewise know that in the bands of Northmen that ravaged the country of France, there was a large number of Gallo-Romans, renegades from Christianity, who thirsted more for pillage and murder than did the Vikings themselves. This mingling of the adventurers and the indigenous race explains the rapidity with which both the Normans of Russia and the Normans of France lost their language, customs and religion. The Varangians only retained one thing, their military superiority, the habit of obeying the chosen or hereditary chief. Into the Slav anarchy they brought this element of warlike and disciplined force, without which a State cannot exist. They imposed on the natives the amount of constraint necessary to drag them from their isolation and division into *gorodichtchés* and *volosts*. The Slavs of the Danube also owe their constitution to a band of Finno-Bulgarian adventurers under Aspar Asparuch; the Polish Slavs to the invasion of the Liakhs or Lechites; the Tcheques to the Frank Samo, who enabled them to shake off the yoke of the Avars.

The spontaneous appeal of the Slavs to the Varangian princes may seem to us strange. We might believe that the annalist, like the old French historians, has tried to disguise the fact of a conquest, by representing that the Slavs submitted voluntarily to the Varangians of Rurik, as the Gauls are supposed to have done to the Franks of Clovis. In reality there was no conquest, a statement which is proved by the fact that the muncipal organization remained intact, that the *vetché* continued to deliberate by the side of the prince, the local army to fight in conjunction with the band of adventurers. The laws of Iaroslaf established the same wer-gild for the murder of either Slav or Varangian, while the Merovingian laws recognize a great difference between a Gallo-Roman and a Frank. The defence of the country, the administration of justice, and the collection of the tribute were the special cares of the prince, the last being considered his legitimate reward. He played in the Slav towns a *rôle* similar to that of the Italian *podestàs* in the 15th century, who were called in to administer justice impartially, or that of the leaders of *condottieri*, to whom the cities entrusted their defence.

As early as 859 the Varangians exacted tribute from the Slavs of Ilmen and the Krivitches, as well as the Tchouds, Vesses, and Merians. The natives had once expelled the Varangians, but as divisions once more became rife among them, they decided that they needed a strong government, and recalled the Varangians in 862. Whether the name of *Russia* or of *Rouss* was originally derived from a province of Sweden, or from the banks of the Dnieper, the fact remains that with the arrival of the Varangians in Slavonia, the true history of Russia commences It was the 1000th anniversary of this event that was commemorated at Novgorod in 1862. With the Varangians the Russian name became famous in Eastern Europe. It was the epoch of brilliant and adventurous expeditions; it was the heroic age of Russia.

The Varangians of Novgorod and Kief are not unworthy mates of the Normans of the West—the bold conquerors who sought their fortunes from the coasts of England, Sicily, and Syria. They are to be found nearly at the same time under the walls of Constantinople and at the foot of the Caucasus, where they captured the town of Berdaa from the Arabs (944). Nestor, the monk of the Petcherski convent at Kief, whose history extends to 1116, adds to his conscientious accounts many legendary traits, which seem an echo of Scandinavian *sagas* and early Russian *bylinas*. His Annals, which Greek and French authorities enable us to check, and which are tolerably exact in all essentials, seem at times, like the first books of Livy, to be epic poetry converted into prose.

THE EARLY RUSSIAN PRINCES: RURIK, OLEG, IGOR—EXPEDITIONS AGAINST CONSTANTINOPLE.

At the call of the Slavs, Rurik, Sineous and Trouvor, three Varangian brothers, whose Scandinavian names signify the *Peaceful*, the *Victorious*, and the *Faithful*, gathered together "their brothers and their families," that is, their warriors or *droujines* (resembling the *truste* of the Frank kings), crossed the Baltic and took up their positions on the borders of the territory they were summoned to defend. Rurik, the eldest, established himself on the lake Ladoga, near to which, on the southern side, he founded the city of Ladoga; Sineous on the White Lake (Biéloe-Ozéro), in the Vess country; Trouvor at Izborsk, to hold the Livonians in check. When the two latter died, Rurik established himself at Novgorod, where he built, not a town as Nestor would have us believe, but a castle. It is thus we must explain the pretended foundation by his orders of Polotsk and of Rostof, which had existed long before the arrival of the Varangians. What he probably did was to transform ancient *gorodichtchés* with ramparts of mud into fortresses. Two other Varangians, Askold and Dir, who were not of the family of Rurik, went down to Kief, and reigned over the Polians. It was they who began the expeditions against *Tzargrad* (Byzantium), the *queen of cities*. With 200 vessels, says Nestor, they entered the *Sound*, in old Slav *Soud* (the Bosphorus or the Golden Horn), and besieged Constantinople. But the patriarch Photius, according to the Byzantine accounts, took the wonder-working robe of Our Lady of Blachernes, and plunged it in the waves. A fierce tempest instantly arose, and the whole Russian fleet was destroyed.

Rurik's successor was not his son Igor, then a minor, but the *eldest* member of the family, his fourth brother, the enterprising Oleg. At the head of an army composed of Varangians, Slavs and Finns, he marched to the south, received the submission of Smolensk and Loubetch, and arrived under the walls of Kief. By means of treachery he took Askold and Dir prisoners, and put them to death, observing: "You are neither princes yourselves, nor of the blood of princes; this is the son of Rurik," pointing to Igor. The tomb of Askold is still shown near Kief. Oleg was charmed with his new conquest, and took up his abode there, saying, "Let Kief be the mother of Russian cities." The Varangian chief held communication both with the Baltic and the Black Sea by means of Novgorod, Smolensk, and Kief. He subdued the Novgorodians, the Krivitches, the Merians, the Drevlians, the Severians, the Polians, the Radimitches, and thus united nearly all the Russian tribes under his sceptre. It was about this time that the Hungarians crossed the Dnieper near Kief, and invaded Pannonia. The Magyar chronicles speak of their having defeated Oleg; Nestor is silent on the subject.

In 907 Oleg collected a large army from among the tributary races, equipped 2000 boats, and prepared to invade Tzargrad by land and sea. Russian legends have embellished this expedition with many wonderful details. Oleg built wheels to his vessels, and spread their sails; blown by the wind they reached the gates of the city. Leo VI. the Philosopher, horror-stricken, agreed to pay tribute, but the Greeks tried to get rid of the Russians by offering them poisoned food. Oleg divined their perfidy. He imposed a heavy contribution, a commerical treaty advantageous to the Russians, and suspended his shield on the Golden Door.

To his subjects Oleg was more than a hero. Terror-stricken by his wisdom, this "foolish and idolatrous people" looked on him as a sorcerer. In the Scandinavian *sagas* we find many instances of chiefs, such as Odin, Gylf and Raude, being at the same time great warriors and great magicians. It is strange that neither Greek, Frank, nor Venetian historians allude to this campaign. Nestor cites the names of the Russian envoys who negotiated the peace, and gives the text of the treaty.

A magician had predicted to Oleg that his favorite horse would cause his death. It was kept apart from him, and when, five years after, the animal died, he insisted on being taken to see its body, as a triumph over the ignorance and imposture of the sorcerers. But from the skull of the horse issued a serpent which inflicted a mortal sting on the foot of the hero.

Igor led a third expedition against Tzargrad. The Dnieper conducted, as it were of her own will, the Russian flotilla to the seas of Greece. Igor had 10,000 vessels according to the Greek historians, 1000 according to the more probable calculation of Liutprand. This would allow 400,000 men in the first case, and only 40,000 in the second. Instead of attacking the town, he cruelly ravaged the Greek provinces. The Byzantine admirals and generals united, and destroyed the Russian army in a series of engagements by the aid of Greek fire. Nestor has not copied the numerous details the Byzantine historians give of this battle, but we have the evidence of Liutprand, bishop of Cremona, derived from his father-in-law, the ambassador of the king of Italy at Constantinople, who saw with his own eyes the defeat of Igor, and was present at the sacrifice of prisoners, beheaded by order of the Emperor Romanus Lecapenus. In 944 Igor secured the help of the formidable Patzinaks, and organized an expedition to avenge his defeat. The Greek Emperor, now seriously alarmed, offered to pay tribute, and signed a new commercial treaty, of which the text is given by Nestor. Byzantine and Western writers do not mention this second expedition of Igor. On his return from Russia, he was assassinated by the Drevlians, from whom he had tried to exact tribute. Leo the Deacon, a Greek writer, says he was torn in pieces by means of two young trees, bent forcibly to the earth, and then allowed to take their natural direction (945).

OLGA—CHRISTIANITY IN RUSSIA.

Olga, widow of Igor, assumed the regency in the name of her son Sviatoslaf, then a minor. Her first care was to revenge herself on the Drevlians. In Nestor's account it is impossible to distinguish between the history and the epic. The Russian chronicler relates in detail how the Drevlians sent two deputations to Olga to appease her, and to offer her the hand of their prince, and how she disposed of them by treachery, burying some alive, and causing others to be stifled in a bathing-house. Next, says Nestor, she besieged their city Korosthenes, and she offered them peace on payment of a tribute of three pigeons and three sparrows for each house. Lighted tow was tied to the tails of the birds, and they were set free. They flew straight home to the wooden town, where the barns and thatched roofs instantly took fire. Lastly the legend relates that Olga massacred part of the Korosthenians, and the rest became slaves.

This vindictive Scandinavian woman, in spite of all, was destined to be the first apostle of Russia. Nestor relates that she went to Tzargrad to the Emperor Constantine Porphyrogenitus, astonished him by the strength and adroitness of her character, and was baptized under the name of Helen, the Greek Tzar being her godfather. Only two facts in Nestor's account are historical, namely, the reception of Olga at the imperial palace of Constantinople, related in detail in the 'Book of Ceremonies,' and perhaps her baptism. If the Greek historians do not mention it in the contemporary chronicles, it is because they did not perceive the important consequences of this event. If writers allude to it in the chronicles of the 11th and 12th centuries, it is because the consequences of the event had by that time been completely developed. *

Even in Russia Olga's conversion passed almost unnoticed. Christianity had made but little progress in that country. No doubt since Cyril and Methodius had invented the Slavonic alphabet, and translated the Holy Books for th Bulgari. e,

* A. Rambaud, ' L'Empire grec au dixième siècle, p. 383.

Christianity, which had already triumphed over some Slav peoples, was being handed on from one to the other. Some missions were already established in Russia. The Byzantines say, that alarmed by the miraculous defeat of Askold and Dir, and seized with a respectful awe of the Christian talismans of the Patriarch Photius, the Russians "sent envoys to Constantinople to ask for baptism." The Emperor Basil the Macedonian then gave them an archbishop, who performed a miracle before them. He threw a copy of the Gospels into a brazier, and drew it out unharmed. According to this account, Askold was the first Russian prince who became a Christian. Hence the worship rendered to his tomb and memory. In the list of Byzantine Eparchies under Leo VI., the Bishopric of Russia figures, of which no doubt Kief was the metropolis. These missions, however, do not seem to have been very successful; at the time of the treaty concluded between Oleg and Leo VI., the Russians still swore by their swords, by Voloss and Perun. In the treaty concluded by Igor, when the Russians swore at Kief before the Emperor's envoy, to confirm it, some ascended the hill of Perun and performed the vows in the ancient way; others went to the chapel of Saint Elias, and laid their hand on the Gospel. There existed then, in the "mother of Russian cities," a Christian community, though a very weak one, if it is true that Olga refused to be baptized in Kief "for fear of the pagans." The mass of warriors kept Christianity at a distance. In their expeditions against the Byzantine provinces, we find them attacking monasteries and churches by preference, giving them up to the flames, and finding a peculiar pleasure in torturing priests and monks by driving nails into their heads. It was thus that the Normans of France, the fanatics of Odinism, treated the ecclesiastics with refinements of cruelty, boasting that they "sang them the Mass of lances." "When one of the soldiers of the Grand Prince wished to become a convert," says Nestor, "he was not prevented, but only laughed at." The efforts of Olga for the conversion of her son Sviatoslaf, who had assumed the reins of government on reaching his majority, were fruitless. He did not like exposing himself to the ridicule of his soldiers by embracing a new faith. "My men will mock me," he replied to the prayers of his mother. "And often," Nestor affirms sadly, "he became furious with her." Olga vainly assured him that if he would be baptized, all his subjects would soon follow his example. The public mind was not yet in a condition for the example of the prince to be all-powerful. The Christian Olga, canonized by the Church, "the first Russian who *wanted* to the heavenly kingdom," remained an exception, little noticed or thought of in the midst of the pagan aristocracy

SVIATOSLAF—THE DANUBE DISPUTED BETWEEN GREEKS AND RUSSIANS.

The reign of Sviatoslaf, 664-972, though short, was signalized by two memorable events: the defeat of the Khazars, and the great war against the Byzantine Empire for the possession of Bulgaria. About the former event the annalist gives few details; but Sviatoslaf must have gained a complete victory, if it be true that he took the White City, capital of the Khazar Empire on the Don, and that he exacted tribute from the Iasses or Ossets of the Caucasus, and the Kassogans or Tcherkesses. The Russians had no reason to rejoice in their success, for the decline of the Khazars, who were a civilized people, favored the progress of the Patzinaks, the most ferocious of all barbarians. The Arabs spoke of them as wild beasts and Matthew of Edessa calls them "a greedy people, devouring the bodies of men, corrupt and impure, bloody and cruel beasts." During one of the frequent absences of Sviatoslaf, the Patzinaks suddenly appeared under the walls of Kief, where the mother and children of the Grand Prince had taken refuge, and reduced it to the last extremity. The bold manœuvre of a voïevode saved the Kievians, who were starving. On his return to his capital, Sviatoslaf was horrified at the risks it had encountered. It was at the hands of these same Patzinaks that he was one day to perish.

On the subject of the Bulgarian war the narrative of Nestor is confused and incomplete. He is silent about the Russian defeats, and legend mixes largely with historical facts. Nestor relates that the Greeks wished to ascertain what sort of man Sviatoslaf was. They sent him gifts of gold and fine tissues, but the Grand Prince looked on them with disdain, and said to his soldiers, "Take them away." Then they sent him a sword and other weapons, and the hero seized them and kissed them enthusiastically. The Greeks were afraid, and said, "This must be a fierce man, since he despises wealth and accepts a sword for tribute." Happily the very minute account of Leo the Deacon appears both exact and impartial, and we are enabled to follow this campaign, where a chief of infant Russia crosses that Danube which the Russian armies are not again to see till the reign of Catherine II. and Nicholas. The Greek Emperor Nicephorus Phocas, in order to avenge himself on Peter the Tzar of Bulgaria, had recourse to the dangerous expedient so frequent in Byzantine policy. He called in the barbarians. A certain Kalokyr was sent as envoy to Sviatoslaf with a sufficient sum of money to allow him to take the field. It was thus that these two Slav races—

who owned their constitutions, one to the Varangian *droujina* of Rurik, the other to the Turanian *droujina* of Asparuch—were urged to conflict by Greek diplomacy. Sviatoslaf descended on Bulgaria with a thoroughly-equipped fleet, reassured the Byzantines by bringing 60,000 men to their assistance, took Pereiaslaf, the Bulgarian capital, and all their fortresses.

The Tzar Peter yielded to his evil destiny at the moment the Patzinaks were besieging Kief. This lesson was, however, lost on Sviatoslaf. He was overjoyed at his conquest, and wished to transport his capital to Pereiaslaf on the Danube, a city distinct from Pereiaslaf or Prislaf, the modern Eski-Stamboul, which was the capital of the Bulgarians in the 10th century. "This place," he said to his mother, "is the central point of my possessions, and abounds in wealth. From Greece come precious stuffs, wine, gold, and all kinds of fruit; from the country of the Tcheques and Hungarians, horses and silver; from Russia, furs, money, wax, and slaves." This resolution of Sviatoslaf was fraught with immense danger to the Greek Empire. If Byzantium feared the neighborhood of an enfeebled Bulgaria, how was she to resist a power that extended from the Baltic to the Balkans, and which could add to the Bulgarian legions, disciplined after the Roman fashion by the Tzar Simeon, the Varangians of Scandinavia, the Russian Slavs, the Finnish hordes of the Vesses, Tchouds, and Merians, and even the light cavalry of the Patzinaks?

The formation of a great Slav Empire so close to Constantinople would have been rendered more formidable by the ethnographical constitution of the peninsula. Ancient Thrace and ancient Macedon were peopled by Slav tribes, some of whom were offshoots from the Russian tribes; for example, Dregovitches and Smolenes were to be found there as much as at Minsk and Smolensk. Thessaly, Attica, and the Peloponnesus were invaded by these emigrants, who became the subjects of the Greek Empire. The famous mountain Taygetus, in Laconia, was inhabited by two Slav tribes, still unsubdued—the Milingians and the Ezerites. We must not forget that Bulgaria extended as far as the Ochrid, and that the ancient provinces under the names of Croatia, Servia, and Dalmatia, had become almost entirely Slav. This great race extended then almost unbroken from the Peloponnesus, already called by the Slav name of Morea, to Novgorod. Thus, if the town of Pereiaslaf on the Danube had really become the centre of the Russian dominions, according to the wish of Sviatoslaf, the Greek race and the Roman domination in the Balkan peninsula would speedily have come to an end. The Greek emperors had been able to resist Askold, Oleg, and Igor. The Russians of their day had lived far from the Empire, and were obliged to go by water, which limited greatly the number of their armies. With their canoes hollowed out of the trunks of trees, such as are now to be seen in the Russian villages, they had to descend the Dnieper, disembark at each of the seven cataracts, carry canoes (monoxyles) till they could re-embark further on, and all the while gave battle to the Patzinaks, who were in ambush behind the rocks. After they had escaped these perils, they had to brave with their frail barks the tempests of the Black Sea, the powerful Roman galleys manned by the best sailors of the East, and the mysterious Greek fire which filled them with terror. Few reached the walls of Constantinople, and their defeat was certain. Now, on the contrary, masters of the Danube, masters of the land-route, they could precipitate on Constantinople all the hordes of Scythia.

Fortunately for the Greek Empire, it then chanced to be renewing its youth. A series of great captains succeeded each other on this tottering throne. In John Zimisces the Russian prince was to find an adversary worthy of him. Sviatoslaf, recalled to Bulgaria, had been obliged to reconquer it. It was at this moment that Zimisces summoned him to execute the conditions of the treaty concluded with his predecessor; that is, to evacuate the country. Sviatoslaf, who had just taken Philippopolis and exterminated the inhabitants, replied haughtily that he hoped soon to be at Constantinople. Zimisces then began his preparations. In the beginning of March 972, he despatched a fleet to the north of the Danube, and himself marched to Adrianople. He surprised the Russians, who had not expected him so soon, in the defiles of the Balkans: appeared suddenly under the walls of Pereiaslaf, defeated a body of many thousand Russians, and obliged them to retire within the walls; then he gave the order for the assault, and took the town by escalade. Eight thousand Russians shut up in the royal castle made a frantic resistance, refused to capitulate, and perished in the flames.

When the news of this disaster reached Sviatoslaf, he advanced with the greater part of his army to meet the Emperor, and came up with him near Dorostol (Silistria). The Greek historians make the Russian army to have consisted of at least 60,000 men; Nestor only reckons 10,000. Here a bloody battle took place, and twelve times victory appeared to shift from one side to the other. The solidity of the Russian infantry defied the charges of the cavalry—"the Ironside" ($\kappa\alpha\tau\acute{\alpha}\phi\rho\alpha\kappa\tau\omicron\iota$). At last they gave way under a desperate charge, and fell back on Dorostol. There they were besieged by the Emperor, and displayed a wild courage in their sallies. Even their women, like the ancient Amazons, or the heroines of the Scandinavian *sagas* or Russian songs, took part in the *mêlée*. The Russians slew themselves rather than ask for mercy. The night following on an action, they were seen to leave the town by moonlight to burn their dead. On their ashes they sacrificed prisoners of war, and drowned in the Danube cocks and little children. Provisions failed, and Sviatoslaf stole out one stormy night with canoes manned by 2000 warriors, rowed round the Greek fleet, collected millet and corn in the neighboring villages, and, falling suddenly on the Greeks, re-entered the town victoriously. Zimisces then took measures to prevent any boat from getting out. This epic siege was signalized by some strange combats. One of the bravest of the Russian chiefs was slain by Apemas, a baptized Arab, son of an Emir of Crete, and himself one of the guards of Zimisces.

Sviatoslaf resolved to make one last effort, and issued from the town with all his forces. Before the battle Zimisces proposed to Sviatoslaf to terminate the war by a duel between themselves. It was the barbarian who refused: "I know better than my enemy what I have to do," said Sviatoslaf. "If he is weary of life, there are a thousand means by which he can end his days." This battle was as obstinate and bloody as the former. Sviatoslaf came near being slain by Apemas. At last the Russians gave way, leaving on the battlefield, says Leo the Deacon, 15,500 dead and 20,000 shields. The survivors retired into the town. They were forced to treat. Zimisces allowed them to retire from Bulgaria, and they swore by Perun and Voloss never again to invade the empire, but to help to defend it against all enemies. If they broke their vows, might they "become as yellow as gold, and perish by their own arms." Nestor gives us the text of this convention, which was really a capitulation, and confirms the account of the Greek historians rather than his own. These relate that Zimisces sent deputies to the Patzinaks to beg them to grant a free passage to the remnant of the Russian army. It is certain that the barbarians awaited the Russians at the Cataracts, or *porogs* of the Dnieper. They killed Sviatoslaf, cut off his head, and his skull was used by their Prince Kouria as a drinking-cup. Sviatoslaf was, in spite of his Slav name, the very type of a Varangian prince of the intrepid, wily, and ambitious Northmen. Nestor boasts his good faith. When he wished to make war on a people, he sent to warn them. "I march against you," he said.

After the surrender of Dorostol, he had an interview with his enemy Zimisces. Leo the Deacon profits by the occasion to give us his portrait. The Emperor being on horseback by the shore, Sviatoslaf approached him by boat, handling the oar like his companions. He was of middle height, but very robust; he had a wide chest, a thick neck, blue eyes, thick eyebrows, a flat nose, long mustaches, a thin beard, and a tuft of hair on his shaven head as a mark of his nobility. He wore a gold ring in one of his ears, ornamented with rubies and two pearls. Let us notice this portrait; we shall have to search far into Russian annals to find another. Between the description given by Leo the Deacon and those of the Russian annalists, there is the same difference **as between the** *eikon* **of a saint and an authentic likeness.**

CHAPTER V.

THE CLOVIS AND CHARLEMAGNE OF THE RUSSIANS: SAINT VLADIMIR AND IAROSLAF THE GREAT 972-1054.

Vladimir (972-1015)—Conversion of the Russians—Iaroslaf the Great (1016-1054—Union of Russia—Splendor of Kief—Varangian-Russian society at the time of Iaroslaf—Progress of Christianity—Social, political, literary, and artistic results.

VLADIMIR (972-1015)—CONVERSION OF THE RUSSIANS.

THE Slav tribes owe their organization to a twofold conquest—a military conquest which came from the North, and an ecclesiastical conquest which came from the South. The Varangians sent them chiefs of war, who welded their scattered tribes into a nation; the Byzantines sent missionaries, who united the Slavs among themselves and to their civilized neighbors by the bonds of a common religion.

The man destined to conclude the work of propagandism begun by Olga did not at first seem fitted for this great task. Vladimir, like Clovis, was at first nothing but a barbarian—wily, voluptuous, and bloody. Only while Clovis after his baptism is not perceptibly better than he was before, and becomes the assassin of his royal Frankish relations, the Russian annalist seems to wish to establish a contrast between the life led by Vladimir prior to his conversion and the life he led after it. Sviatoslaf left three sons: Iaropolk at Kief, Oleg ruler of the Drevlians, Vladimir at Novgorod. In the civil wars which followed, and which recall the bloody Merovingian anarchy, Iaropolk slew Oleg, and in his turn died by the hand of Vladimir. He fell in love with Rogneda, Iaropolk's betrothed, and demanded her in marriage from the Varangian Rogvolod, who ruled over Polotsk. The princess answered, that she would never marry the son of a slave, in allusion to Vladimir's mother having been a servant, though he himself had always been treated by his father as his brother's equal. Maddened by this insult, Vladimir sacked Polotsk, killed Rogvolod and his two sons, and forced Rogneda to marry him. After the murder of Iaropolk, Vladimir also took the wife whom Iaropolk had left *enceinte*, a beautiful Greek nun, captured in an expedition against Byzantium. These two women he had deprived, one of her husband, the other of her father and brothers. He had, besides, a Bohemian and a Bulgarian wife, and another, all of whom bore him sons. Finally this bastard, this " son of a slave," was so abandoned in his profligacy, that he kept 300 concubines at Vychegorod, 3000 at Biélgorod, near Kief, and 200 at Berestof. Lusting no less after war and plunder, he reconquered Red Russia from the Poles, quelled a revolt of the Viatitches and Radimitches, and exacted tribute from the Lithuanian Iatvaguians, and Livonian tribes of Letts or Finns.

The soul of the sensual and passionate barbarian was troubled, notwithstanding, by religious aspirations. At first he turned to the Slav gods, and his reign was inaugurated by a new growth of paganism. On the high sandy cliffs of Kief, which tower above the Dnieper, he erected idols; among them one of Perun, with a head of silver and a beard of gold. Two Varangians, father and son, both Christians, were stabbed at the feet of Perun. But the day of the ancient gods was passed; Vladimir was undergoing the religious crisis in which all Russia labored. He felt other faiths were necessary to him; so, according to the testimony of Nestor, he took it into his head, like the Japanese of to-day, to institute a search after the best religion. His ambassadors forthwith visited Mussulmans, Jews, and Catholics: the first represented by the Bulgarians of the Volga, the second probably by the Khazars or the Jewish Kharaites, the third by the Poles and Germans. Vladimir declined Islamism, which prescribed circumcision and forbade "the wine, which was dear to the Russians;" Judaism, whose disciples wandered through the earth; and Catholicism, whose ceremonies appeared wanting in magnificence. The deputies that he sent to Constantinople, on the contrary, returned awestricken. The splendors of Saint Sophia, the brilliancy of the sacerdotal vestments, the magnificence of the ceremonies, heightened by the presence of the Emperor and his Court, the patriarch and the numerous clergy, the incense, the religious songs, had powerfully appealed to the imagination of the barbarians. One final argument triumphed over the scruples of Vladimir. "If the Greek religion had not been the best, your grandmother Olga, the wisest of mortals, would not have adopted it," said the boyards. The proud Vladimir did not intend to beg for baptism at the hands of the Greeks—he would conquer it by his own arms, and ravish it like a prey. He descended into the Taurid and besieged Cherson, the last city of this region that remained subject to the Emperors. A certain Anastasius, possibly from religious motives, betrayed his country. Rendered prouder than ever by this important conquest,

Vladimir sent an embassy to the Greek Emperors Basil and Constantine, demanding their sister Anne in marriage, and threatening, in case of refusal, to march on Constantinople; It was not the first time the barbarians had made this proposal to the Greek Cæsars, and Constantine Porphyrogenitus himself teaches his successors how to get rid of these inconvenient demands. But on this occasion the Emperors, who were occupied with revolts in the interior, thought themselves driven to consent, on condition that Vladimir was baptized. It was in Cherson that the Russian prince received baptism, and celebrated his marriage with the heiress of the Emperors of Rome. The priests he brought to Kief were his captives; the sacred ornaments, the holy relics with which he enriched and sanctified his capital, were his booty. When he returned to Kief it was as an Apostle (*Isapostolos*), but as an armed Apostle that he catechized his people. The idols were pulled down amid the tears and fright of the people. Perun was flogged and thrown into the Dnieper. They still show on the side of the Kievan cliffs the rock called "The Devil's Leap;" and further away, the the place where Perun was thrown up by the waters on the shore. The people instantly rushed to worship him, but the soldiers of Vladimir cast him back into the river. Then, by Vladimir's order, all the Kievans, men and women, masters and slaves, old people and little children, plunged naked into the consecrated waters of the old pagan stream, while the Greek priests standing on the bank with Vladimir read the baptismal service. After a sturdy resistance, the Novgorodians were in like manner forced to hurl Perun into the Volkhoff, and enter it themselves.

We have already seen that the Russians had not lost all recollections of their ancient gods, and that nature was still the home of a whole world of deities. A long time had to pass before Christianity could penetrate into their hearts and customs. M. Bouslaef assures us that, even in the 12th century, Christian rites were only practised by the higher classes. The peasants kept their old pagan ceremonies, and continued to contract their marriages "around the bush of broom." They preserved even longer their faith in magicians and sorcerers, who were often of more authority than the priests. Vladimir, at any rate, wished to prepare the transformation. It does not appear that he persecuted the idolaters, but he occupied himself in adorning the churches of his capital, which he had shorn of its idols. On the spot where Perun stood he built the church of Saint Basil, the Greek name which he had taken at his baptism. On the place where the two Varangian martyrs had been slain by his orders he raised the church of the *Déciatine* or the

Dine, embellished and ornamented with Greek inscriptions by artists who came from the South. He founded schools, where boys studied the holy books translated into Slavonic, but he was obliged to compel the attendance of the children, whose parents, convinced that writing was a dangerous kind of magic, shed tears of despair. Nestor cannot sufficiently praise the reformation of Vladimir after his baptism. He was faithful to his Greek wife, he no longer loved war, he distributed his revenues to the churches and to the poor, and, in spite of the increase of crime, hesitated to inflict capital puhishment. "I fear to sin," he replied to his councillors. It was the bishops who had to recall to him the fact that "criminals must be chastised, though with discretion," and that the country must not be left a prey to the Patzinaks. Vladimir, who reminded us formerly of a Northman of the type of Robert the Devil, suddenly becomes the "good King Robert" of Russia.

His wars with the Patzinaks are recorded by Nestor with all kinds of episodes borrowed from the epic poetry. There is the Russian champion who tears in pieces the furious bull, or stifles a Patzinak giant in his arms; there are the inhabitants of Bielgorod, who, having been reduced to famine by the barbarians, let down into wells two large caldrons, one full of hydromel and the other of meal, to make the Patzinaks believe these were natural productions of the soil. We see in the popular songs of what a marvellous cycle of legends Vladimir has become the centre; but in these *bylinas* he is neither Vladimir, the Baptist, nor the Saint Vladimir of the orthodox Church, but a solar hero, successor of the divinities whom he destroyed. To the people, still pagans at heart, Vladimir is always the "Beautiful Sun" of Kief.

IAROSLAF THE GREAT (1016–1054)—UNION OF RUSSIA—SPLENDOR OF KIEF.

Vladimir died in 1015, leaving a large number of heirs by his numerous wives. The partition that he made between them of his states tells us what was the extent of Russia at that epoch. To Iaroslaf he gave Novgorod; to Isiaslaf, son of Rogneda, and grandson of the Varangian Rogvolod, Polotsk; to Boris, Rostof; to Gleb, Mourom (these two principalities were in the Finn country); to Sviatoslaf, the Drevlians; to Vsevolod, Vladimir in Volhynia; to Mstislaf, Tmoutorakan, the Tamatarchia of the Greeks; finally, to his nephew Sviatopolk, the son of his brother and victim Iaropolk, the principality of Tourof, in the country of Minsk, founded by a Varangian named Tour, who did not belong to the "blood of princes" any more than Askold and Dir. The history of Vladimir's successors recalls that of the heirs of Clovis. The murder of the sons of Clodomir is paralleled by the assassination of Boris and Gleb, sons of *Isapostolos*, by the order of Sviatopolk, who usurped the throne of Kief. His two victims were canonized, and henceforth became inseparable, and are, as it were, the Dioscuri of orthodoxy. The prince of the Drevlians perished by the same hand. Iaroslaf resolved to avenge his brothers and to save himself. At this moment, however, he had alienated his Novgorodian subjects, having enticed the principal citizens into his castle, and then treacherously slain them. When he learnt the crimes of Sviatopolk, he trembled for his own life, and threw himself on the generosity of those he had so cruelly outraged. He wept for his sins before them, and besought their help. "Prince," replied the Novgorodians, with one voice, "you have destroyed our brethren, but we are ready to fight for you." After a bloody war, in which Boleslas the Brave, king of Poland took part, the usurper fled, and died miserably in exile. Iaroslaf had still to defend himself against the Prince of Polotsk and Mstislaf of Tmoutorakan. The latter had acquired great fame from his wars with the Khazars, whom, with the aid of the Greek Emperor, Basil II., he finally annihilated, and with the Tcherkess, whose chief, a giant named Rhededia, he slew in single combat. At last, Iaroslaf remained the sole master of Russia, and reigned gloriously at Kief. He recalls Charles the Great by some successful wars, but particularly by his code of laws, his taste for building, and his love of letters in a barbarous age. He owes part of his reputation to the anarchy which followed his death, and which caused his reign to be regretted as the climax of Kievian greatness.

In Poland Iaroslaf revenged on the son of Boleslas the Brave the invasions of his father, and took from him the towns of Red Russia. He fought a bloody battle with the Patzinaks under the walls of Kief, and in their flight part of the vanquished barbarians were drowned in crossing the rivers. It was as fatal a blow to the Patzinaks as that struck by Sviatoslaf at the Khazars: they never recovered it. But in the same manner as the defeat of the Khazars opened the way to the Patzinaks, the ruin of the Patzinaks opened the way to the Polovtsi. The steppes of the Don were incessantly filled by new hordes from Asia. Iaroslaf also fought against the Finnish and Lithuanian tribes. In the country of the Tchouds he founded Iourief (Saint George) on the Embach, near the Peïpus (the Germans called it Dorpat): in the country of the Merians, he founded Iaroslavl on the Upper Volga. Finally, his reign was marked by a new war with Greece, brought on by mercantile disputes. His son Vladimir, leader of the expedition, rejected proudly the propositions of the Emperor Constantine Monomachus. A naval battle was fought in the Bosphorus; Greek fire and the tempests of the Black Sea dispersed the Russian armament. Part of the army, a body of 8000 men, which was retreating into Russia by land, was attacked and exterminated by a Greek force : 800 prisoners were sent to Constantinople, where their eyes were put out. Notwithstanding the bonds of religion which had been riveted between the Byzantines and their neophytes on the Dnieper, the Russians were always dreaded by Constantinople. An inscription hidden in the boot of one of the equestrian statues of Byzantium announced that the day would come when the capital of the empire would fall a prey to the men of the North. The decay of Kievian Russia after the death of Iaroslaf, adjourned or nullified the fulfilment of this prophecy.

The legislation of the Russian Charlemagne is comprised in the Code entitled *Rousskaïa Pravda* the *Russian right* or *verity*. This Code strangely recalls that of Scandinavia. It consecrates private revenge, and the pursuit of an assassin by all the relatives of the dead ; it fixes the *wergeld* for different crimes, as well as the fine paid into the royal treasury ; it allows the judicial duel ; the ordeal by red-hot iron and boiling water ; the oath corroborated by those of the *compurgatores ;* it also established by the side of the judges nominated by the Prince, a jury of twelve citizens. In the " Rousskaïa Pravda," there is not, properly speaking, any criminal law. Capital punishment, death by refinements of cruelty, corporal chastisement, torture to wring out confessions, even a public prison, were all unknown. These are Scandinavian and German principles in all their purity. At this period Russia had almost the same laws as the West.

Iaroslaf occupied a glorious place among the princes of his time. His sister Mary was married to Casimir, king of Poland ; his daughters also became the wives of kings : Elizabeth, of Harold the Brave, king of Norway ; Anne, of Henry I., king of France ; Anastasia, of Andrew I., king of Hungary. Of his sons, Vladimir, the eldest, is said to have married Githa, daughter of Harold, king of England ; Isiaslaf, a daughter of Micislas II., king of Poland ; Vseslaf, a Greek princess, daughter of Constantine Monomachus ; Viatcheslaf and Igor, two German princesses. Iaroslaf gave an asylum to the proscribed princes, Saint Olaf, king of Norway, and his two sons ; a prince of Sweden ; Edwin and Edward, sons of Edmund Ironside, king of England, expelled from their country by Knut the Great. The Varangian dynasty was thus mingled with the families of the

Christian princes, and we may say of the Russia of the 11th century, what we can no longer say of the Russia of the 16th century, that she was a European State.

To Kief was destined the lot of Anchen, the capital of Charles the Great, which, glorious in his life, after his death fell into decay. Under Iaroslaf, kief reached the highest pinnacle of splendor. He wished to make his capital the rival of Constantinople; like Byzantium, she had her cathedral and her Golden Gate. The Grand Prince also founded the monastery of Saint Irene, of which only a few ruins now remain, and those of Saint George and the Catacombs, the latter made illustrious by the virtues of its first superiors, Saint Theodosius and Saint Antony. He repaired the church of the Dîme, and surrounded the city with ramparts. The population began to increase, and the lower town to grow at the feet of the upper. Kief, situated on the Dnieper, the great road to Byzantium, seemed to be part of Greece. Adam of Bremen calls her *æmula sceptri Constantinopolitani et clarissimum decus Græciæ*, She was the rendezvous of the merchants from Holland, Hungary, Germany, and Scandinavia, who lived in separate quarters of the town. She had eight markets, and the Dnieper was constantly covered with merchant-ships. Iaroslaf had not enough Greek artists to decorate all the churches, nor enough priests to serve them, for Kief was at that time " the city of 400 churches," so much admired by the writers of the West. What she was then we may partly realize by seeing what she is still at certain seasons of the year. The Monastery of the Catacombs, with the incorruptible bodies of its ascetics and thaumaturges, some of whom bricked themselves up while living, in the cell which was to be their sepulchre, draws annually, and especially at the Assumption, 50,000 pilgrims. Saint Sophia was the pride of Kief; the mosaics of the time of Iaroslaf still exist, and the traveller may admire on the " indestructible wall " the colossal image of the Mother of God, the Last Supper, with a double apparition of Christ, presenting to six of His disciples His body, and to six others His blood, the images of Saints and Doctors, the Angel of the Annunciation of the Virgin. The frescoes which have been preserved or carefully restored are still numerous, and everywhere cover the pillars, the walls, and the vaults floored with gold. The inscriptions are not in Slavonic, but in Greek. Iaroslaf did not forget Novgorod, his first residence, and there he built another Saint Sophia, one of the most precious monuments of the Russian past. Like Charles the Great, he set up schools. Vladimir had founded one at Kief; Iaroslaf instituted that of Novgorod for 300 boys. He sent for Greek singers from Byzantium, who taught the Russian clergy. Coins were struck for him by Greek artists, with his Slavonic name in Slav on one side, and his Christian name, Ioury (George), on the other. Like all other barbarian neophytes, Iaroslaf pushed devotion into superstition. He caused the bones of his uncles, who had died unconverted, to be disinterred and baptized. He died in 1054, and his stone sarcophagus is one of the most precious ornaments of Saint Sophia.

VARANGIAN-RUSSIAN SOCIETY AT THE TIME OF IAROSLAF.

Varangian-Russian society presents more than one analogy with the society which was developed in Gaul after the Frank conquest. The government of the Varangian princes somewhat resembled that of the Merovingian kings.

The germ of the future State lay in the *droujina*, the band of warriors surrounding the prince, as in Gaul it lay in the *truste*. The *droujinniki*, like the *antrustions*, were the faithful followers, the men of the prince. They formed his guard, and were his natural council in all affairs, public or private. He could constitute them a court of justice, nominate them individually *voïevodes* or governors of fortresses, or *possadniks* or lieutenants in the large towns. In the same way as the body surrounding the Merovingian kings was not composed so entirely of Franks, but that shortly Gallo-Romans crept into the *antrustions*, so the *droujina* of the Russian princes admitted many different elements, not only Varangian but Slav. Mstislaf, prince of Tmoutorakan, had enrolled Iasses and Kassogans; a Lithuanian Iatiague is mentioned as being in the *droujina* of Igor, a Hungarian in that of Boris. The military class did not form at that time a caste apart in Russia any more than in Gaul; Saint Vladimir took into his service the son of a leather-worker who had vanquished the Patzinak giant; his maternal uncle Dobryna was not even a free man.

The prince in the middle of his *droujina* seems to be only the first among his equals; all that he had seems to belong to his men. We see them eat at the same table, and listen together to the songs of the blind poets who accompanied themselves on the *gouzzla*. It was as it were a family of soldiers, from which one day the Russian administration was to come. The prince had great respect for the demands of his men. Those of Vladimir complained one day that they had to eat from wooden bowls. He gave them silver ones, and added, " I could not buy myself a *droujina* with gold and silver; but with a *droujina* I can acquire gold and silver, as did my father and my grandfather." The prince did nothing without consulting his *droujinniki.* It was this that prevented Sviatoslaf from listening to the exhortations of Olga; he said that " his *droujina* would mock him" if he became a Christian.

The administration of the Varangian princes was very elementary. Let us see what the Arab writer Ibn-Dost says of the way they distributed justice: " When a Russian has a grievance with another, he summons him before the tribunal of the prince, where both present themselves. When the prince has given sentence, his orders are executed; if both parties are displeased by the judgment, the affair must be decided by arms. He whose sword cuts sharpest gains his cause. At the moment of the combat the relations of the two adversaries appear armed, and surround the space shut off. The combatants then come to blows, and the victor may impose any conditions he pleases."

After justice, the most important of the princely functions was the collection of the tributes. The amount was fixed by the prince himself. Oleg imposed on the Drevlians a tax of a marten's skin for every house. The raising of taxes was always very arbitrary. Nestor's account of the death of Igor is a lively picture of the political customs of the time; we might imagine ourselves reading a page of Gregory of Tours about the sons of Clovis, for example the expedition of Thierry in Arvernia. " In the year 945 the *droujina* of Igor said to him, 'The men of Sveneld are richly provided with weapons and garments, while we go naked; lead us, prince, to collect the tribute, so that thou and we may become rich.' Igor consented, and conducted them to the Drevlians to raise the tribute. He increased the first imposts, and did them violence, he and his men; after having taken all he wanted, he returned to his city. While on the road he bethought himself and said to his *droujina.* ' Go on with the tribute; I will go back to try and get some more out of them.' Leaving the greater part of his men to go on their way, he returned with only a few, to the end that he might increase his riches. The Drevlians, when they learnt that Igor was returning, held council with Mal their prince. 'When the wolf enters the sheepfold he slays the whole flock, if the shepherd does not slay him. Thus it is with us and Igor; if we do not destroy him, we are lost.' Then they sent deputies and said to him, ' Why dost thou come anew unto us? Hast thou not collected all the tribute?' But Igor would not hear them, so the Drevlians came out of the town of Korosthenes, and slew Igor and his men, for they were but a few."

For the government and defence of the country the prince established the chief of his *droujinniki* in different towns, supported by adequate forces. Thus Rurik distributed the towns of his appanage; he gave to one of his *men* Polotsk, to another

Rostof, to a third Bielozersk. A principality was in some sort divided into fiefs, but the fiefs were only temporary, and always revokable. For the defence of the frontiers new towns were built, where native soldiers kept watch.

Social conditions from the 9th to the 12th century were as unequal as in the West. The *droujina* of the prince, which speedily absorbed all the Slav and Finn chiefs, constituted an aristocracy. Still we must distinguish in it those who were only simple guards or *gridi* (*girdin* among the Scandinavians), the *mouges* or men (*vir* in Latin, *baron* in French), and the *boyards* who were the most illustrious of all. The freemen of the Russian soil were "the people" or *lioudi*. The *gosti* or merchants were not at this period a class apart; it was in fact the warriors or the princes who pursued commerce with arms in their hands. Oleg was disguised as a merchant when he surprised Kief and slew Askold and Dir; the Byzantines mistrusted these terrible guests, and assigned them a separate quarter, closely watched, of Constantinople.

The rural population, on whom the weight of the growing State was beginning to rest, was already less free than in primitive times. The peasant was called *smerde* (perhaps derived from *smerdiet*, to stink), or *mougik*, insulting diminutive of *mouge*, man. Later he became the *Christian* par excellence, *krestianine*.

Below the peasant, whose situation recalls that of the Roman *colonus*, were the slaves properly so called, *rabi* or *kholopy*. The slave might have been taken in war, bought in a market, born in the house of his master, or have lost his liberty by the mere fact of fulfilling certain offices, such as that of house-steward. War was, however, the principal source of slavery. Ibn-Dost relates that the Russians, when they marched against another people, did not depart without having destroyed everything; they carried off the women, and reduced the men to slavery. They maintained a great slave-trade with foreign nations. "From Russia," said Sviatoslaf, the conqueror of Bulgaria, "will be brought skins, wax, honey, and *slaves*."

PROGRESS OF CHRISTIANITY—SOCIAL, POLITICAL, LITERARY, AND ARTISTIC RESULTS.

Russia had become Christian : it is the chief event in her primitive history. An important fact is that her Christianity was received not from Rome, like that of the Poles and other Western Slavs, but from Constantinople. Although the separation between the Churches of the East and West was not yet fully consummated, it was evident that Russia would be engaged in what the Latins called "the schism." It is usually considered in the West that this fact exercised an evil influence on Russia. Now let us see the opinion of a Russian historian, M. Bestoujef-Rioumine, on the subject. "What is no less important is that Christianity came to us from Byzantium, where the Church put forth no pretensions of governing the State, a circumstance which preserved us from struggles between the secular, a national, and the spiritual, a foreign power. Excluded from the religious unity of the Romano-Germanic world, we have perhaps gained more than we have lost. The Roman Church made her appearance with German missionaries in Slavonic lands ; and if she did not everywhere bring with her material servitude, she at least introduced an intellectual slavery by forcing men to support foreign interests, by bringing among them foreign elements, and by establishing in all parts a sharp division between the higher classes who wrote and spoke in Latin, and the lower classes who spoke the national tongue and were without literature."

No doubt an ecclesiastical language which, thanks to Cyril and Methodius, mingled with the national language, and became intelligible to all classes of society ; a purely national Church, which was subject to no foreign sway ; the absolute independence of the civil power and of national development, were the inestimable advantages that Byzantine Christianity brought into Russia. But if the Russian State was free from all obligations to Rome, she had nothing to hope for from her. She could not reckon in her days of peril on the help that Spain received when she grappled with the Moors; Germany in her crusades against the Slavs and Finns ; Hungary in her national war with the Turks. Separated from the West by difference of faith, Russia in the time of the Mongols, like Greece at the epoch of the Ottoman invasion, saw no Europe arming in her defence.

Her princes were neither laid under the pontifical interdicts, like Robert of France, nor reduced to implore pardon at the feet of a Gregory VII., like Henry IV. of Germany; humiliations always followed by a swift revenge, as on the day when Barbarossa expelled Alexander III. from Italy, and Philip the Handsome caused Boniface to be arrested in Anagni. Humiliations still more cruel awaited the Russians at the court of the Mongols. Another misfortune attending the entrance of the Russians into the Greek Church is, that they found themselves separated by religion from the races to whom they were bound by a common origin, and who spoke almost their own tongue. It was the difference of religion which inflamed their long rivalry with the Poles, and which at present deprives them of much influence over part of the Slavs. This same difference of religion delayed for them the benefits of civilization resulting from the Renaissance of the West, but it spared them the terrible crisis of the wars of the Reformation.

Oriental Christianity, with the Byzantine civilization that was inseparable from it, produced in time a considerable transformation in Russia. The first effect of Christianity was to reform society, and draw closer family ties. It condemned polygamy, and forbade equal divisions between the children of a slave and those of the lawful wife. Society resisted this new principle for some time. Saint Vladimir, even after his conversion, divided his possessions equally among the children the Church regarded as natural and those she considered legitimate. In the long run Christianity prevailed, and by the abolition of polygamy the Russian family ceased to be Asiatic, and became European.

Christianity prescribed new virtues, and gave the ancient barbaric virtues of hospitality and benevolence a more elevated character.

Vladimir Monomachus charged his children to receive strangers hospitably, because, says he, they have it in their power to give you a good or evil reputation. The hospitality of primitive peoples may often be explained by their need of merchants and foreigners. Pagan Slavs were only obliged to help those of the same association; warriors, the members of the same *droujina;* peasants, those of the same *commune;* merchants or artisans, those of the same *artel*. Christianity enjoined benevolence to all the world, without hope of reward in this life. It rendered honorable, weakness, poverty, manual labor. If it prescribed excessive humility, it was useful at least as a reaction against the brutality of overweening pride. Between these two societies, aristocratic and religious, which rest on opposite and equally exaggerated principles, there would one day be room for lay and civil society.

The influence of Christian principles was rather slow among these excitable and ardent natures, but at last we see in Russia, as in the West, princes abjure their pride and seek the peace of the cloister, like the good King Robert, or Saint Henry. In the end it became an established custom with the Russian sovereigns that, on the approach of death, they should be tonsured, change their worldly for a monkish name, and so die in the garb of one of the religious orders.

From a political point of view, the influence of Byzantine Christianity was bound in the long run to cause a complete revolution. For what was a Russian prince, after all, but the head of a band, surrounded by the men of his *droujina,* and in a sense a foreigner to the land he governed and on which he levied tribute ? Properly speaking, a Russian prince had no subjects.

The natives might always expel him—his *droujinniki* were always free to forsake him.

The princes of Kief were no more sovereigns in the modern or Roman sense of the term, than Merwig or Clodowig the long-haired. But the priests who came from Constantinople brought with them an ideal of government; in a little while it was that of the Russians who entered the ranks of the clergy. This Greek ideal was the Emperor, the *Tzar* of Constantinople, heir of Augustus and Constantine the Great, Vicar of God upon earth, the typical monarch on whom the eyes of the barbarians of Gaul as well as those of Scythia were fixed. He was a sovereign in the fullest sense of the word, as, by a legal fiction, the people by the *Lex Regia* was supposed to have yielded its power to the *imperator*. He had subjects, and subjects only. Alone he made the law; he *was* the law. He had neither *droujinniki* nor *antrustions* that he placed in such and such a town, but an host of movable functionaries, the inviolate Roman hierarchy, by means of whom his all-powerful will penetrated to the remotest parts of his dominions. He was not the leader of a band of exacting soldiers, free to quit his service for that of another, but master of a standing army, to guard both frontiers and capital. He did not consider his states as a patrimony to be divided between his children, but transmitted to his successor the Roman Empire in its integrity. He inherited his power, not only from his people, but from God. His imperial ornaments had, like his person, a sacred character: and whenever the barbarian kings demanded one of them at Constantinople, whether it was a crown enriched with precious stones, the purple mantle, the sceptre or the *brodequins* (leggings), they were answered, that when God gave the Empire to Constantinople, He sent these vestments by a holy angel; that they were not the work of man, and that they were laid on the altar, and only worn, even by the Emperor, on solemn occasions. Leo the Khazar was said to have been smitten with a fatal ulcer for having put on the crown without permission of the patriarch.

An empire one and indivisible, resting on a standing army, a hierarchy of functionaries, a national clergy, and a body of jurisconsults,—such was the Roman Empire, and such it revived in the monarchies of the 17th century. This was the conception of the State, unknown to both Slavs and Varangians, that the Greek priests brought to Russia. For a long while the reality answered little to the ideal; the princes continued in their wills to divide their soldiers and their lands among their children; but the idea did not perish, and if it was never realized in Kievian Russia, it found a more propitious soil in Muscovite Russia. Legislation likewise felt the influence of Christianity. Theft, murder, and assassination were not looked upon by the Church as private offences for which the aggrieved persons could take reprisals or accept a *wergeld*. They were crimes to be punished by human justice in the name of God.

For private revenge Byzantine influence substituted a public penalty; for the fine it substituted corporal punishment, repugnant to the free barbarian, and to the instinctive sentiment of human dignity. Imprisonment, convict labor, flogging, torture, mutilation, death itself, inflicted by more or less cruel means; such was the penal code of the Byzantines.

The Greek bishops of the time of St. Vladimir had wished that brigands should be put to death, but the custom was, and long remained, against it. Vladimir, after having employed this supreme means of repression, returned to the system of the *wergeld*, which besides helped to fill the treasury. The Byzantine mode of procedure likewise rejected the judicial duel, the judgment of God and the *compurgatores* long defended by habit. But, as in Gaul Roman law existed for Church officers and part of the natives, side by side with the Frank or Burgundian law, so in Russia the Byzantine codes of Justinian and Basil the Macedonian, were established at the side of the Scandinavian code of Iaroslaf.

During many centuries the two systems of legislation existed together, each being slightly influenced by the other, to the time when they were mingled in a new code, the Oulojenie of Ivan the Great, and the Soudebnik of Ivan the Terrible.

The Byzantine literature which found its way into Russia consisted not only of the sacred books, but also of the Fathers of the Church, among whom we may reckon some writers of the first order, like Saint Basil and Saint John Chrysostom; lives of the saints, the inexhaustible source of new poetry; chronicles destined to serve as models to the Russian annalists; philosophical and scientific books; even romances such as 'Barlaam and Josaphat,' 'Salomon and Kitovras,' &c. Though this literature was partly the fruit of Byzantine decay, we may perceive how it implanted fresh ideas in the mind of a young nation, and would largely influence the moral life of the individual, and public and family life. We shall see up to what point Russian society of the Middle Ages was modelled on the examples afforded by this literature. Finally, it must not be forgotten that Christianity brought music in its train to a people whose music was highly primitive, and architecture to a people who had absolutely none. It was she who, to use a Western expression, *illuminated* the Russian cities with magnificent churches, and her golden cupolas towered above the ramparts of mud that begirt the cities.

CHAPTER VI.

RUSSIA DIVIDED INTO PRINCIPALITIES. SUPREMACY AND FALL OF KIEF, 1054-1169.

Distribution of Russia into principalities—Unity in division—The successors of Iaroslaf the Great—Wars about the right of headship of the royal family, and the throne of Kief—Vladimir Monomachus—Wars between the heirs of Vladimir Monomachus—Fall of Kief.

DISTRIBUTION OF RUSSIA INTO PRINCIPALITIES—UNITY IN DIVISION.

THE period that extends from 1054, the year of Iaroslaf's death, to 1224, the year of the first appearance of the Tatars, or to take the French chronology, from the reign of Henry I. to the death of Philip Augustus, is one of the most confused and troubled in Russian history. As the barbarian custom of division continued to prevail over the Byzantine ideas of political unity, the national territory was ceaselessly partitioned.

The princely anarchy of Eastern Europe has its parallel in the feudal anarchy of the West. M. Pogodine reckons during this period, sixty-four principalities which had an existence more or less prolonged, 293 princes who disputed the throne of Kief and other domains, and eighty-three civil wars, in some of which the whole country was engaged. There were besides foreign wars to augment this immense heap of historical facts. Against the Polovtsi alone the chroniclers mention eighteen campaigns, while these barbarians made no less than forty-six invasions of Russia. It is impossible to follow the national chroniclers in the minute details of their annals; we will only treat of the principalities which lasted some time, and the facts which were the most important.

The ancient names of the Slav tribes have everywhere disappeared, or only remain in the names of some of the towns, for example that of the Polotchanes in Polotsk, and that of the Severians in Novgorod Severski. The elements of which Russia was now composed were no longer tribes, but principalities. We hear no more of the Krivitches or the Drevlians, but of the principalities of Smolensk and Volhynia. These little States were perpetually dismembered at each new partition between the sons of a prince, and then were reconstituted to be divided anew into appanages.

Notwithstanding all these vicissitudes, some of them maintained a steady existence, corresponding to certain topographical or ethnographical conditions. Without speaking of the distant principality of Tmoutorakan, situated at the foot of the Caucasus in the centre of Turkish and Circassian tribes, and reckoning eight successive princes, the following are the great divisions of Russia from the 11th to the 13th century:—

1. The principality of Smolensk occupied the important territory which is, as it were, the central point in the mountain system of Russia. It comprehends the ancient forest of Okof, where three of the largest Russian rivers, the Volga, the Dnieper, and the Dwina, take their rise. Hence the political importance of Smolensk, attested by all the wars to gain possession of her; hence, also, her commercial prosperity. We must observe that all her towns were built on one or the other of these three great rivers; all the commerce, therefore, of ancient Russia passed through her hands. Besides Smolensk, we must mention Mojaïsk, Viasma, and Toropetz, which was the capital of a secondary principality, the property of two celebrated princes, Mstislaf the Brave (*Khrabryi*) and Mstislaf the Bold (*Oudaloï*).

2. The principality of Kief was *Rouss*, Russia in the strict sense of the word. Her situation on the Dnieper, the neighborhood of the Greek Empire, the fertility of the *Black Land*, for long secured to this State the supremacy over the other Russian principalities. On the south she bordered directly on the nomads of the steppe, against whom her princes were forced to raise a barrier of frontier towns. They often took these barbarians into their pay, granted them lands, and constituted them into military colonies. The principality of *Peréiaslavl* was a dependence of Kief; Vychegorod, Bielgorod, Tripoli, Torchesk, were at times erected into principalities for princes of the same family.

3. On the tributaries of the right bank of the Dnieper, notably the Soja, the Desna and the *Seïme*, extended the two principalities of *Tchernigof*, with Starodoub and Loubetch; and of *Novgorod-Severski*, with Poutivl, Koursk, and Briansk. The principality of Tchernigof, which reached towards the Upper Oka, had therefore one foot in the basin of the Volga; her princes, the Olgovitches, were the most formidable rivals of Kief. The princes of Severski were always occupied with their ceaseless wars against the Polovtsi, their neighbors on the south. It was

a prince of Severski whose exploits against these barbarians formed the subject of a sort of *chanson de geste*, the *Song of Igor*, or the *Account of the Expedition of Igor* (*Slovo o polkou Igorévič.*)

4. Another principality, whose very existence consisted in endless war against the nomads, was the double principality of *Riazan* and *Mourom*. Her principal towns were Riazan, Mourom, Peréiaslavl-Riazanski, situated on the Oka, Kolomna at the junction of the Moskowa with the Oka, and the Pronsk on the Prona. The Upper Don formed its western boundary. This principality was placed in the very heart of the Mouromians and Mechtcheraks, Finnish tribes. The reputation of her inhabitants, who were reckoned warlike in character, and rough and brutal in manners, was no doubt partly the result of the mixture of the Russian race with the ancient inhabitants of the country, and of their perpetual and bloody struggle with the nomad tribes.

5. The double principalities of *Souzdal*, with their towns of Souzdal, Rostof, Iourief-Polski on the Kolocha, Vladimir on the Kliazma, Iaroslavl, and Peréiaslavl-Zaliesski, were situated on the Volga and the Oka amongst the thickest of northern forests, and in the middle of the Finnish tribes of Mouromians, Merians, Vesses, and Tcheremisses. Although placed at the furthest extremity of the Russian world, Souzdal exercised an important influence over it. We shall find her princes now establishing a certain political authority over Novgorod and the Russia of the Lakes, the result of a double economic dependence; now intervening victoriously in the quarrels of the Russia of the Dnieper. The Souzdalians were rough and warlike, like the Riazanese. Already we can distinguish among these two peoples the characteristics of a new nationality. That which divides them from the Kievians and the men of Novgorod-Severski, occupied like themselves in the great war with the barbarians, is the fact that the Russians of the Dnieper sometimes mingled their blood with that of their enemies, and became fused with the nomad, essentially mobile Turkish races, whilst the Russians of the Oka and the Volga united with the Finnish tribes, agricultural and essentially sedentary. This distinction between the two foreign elements that entered the Slav blood, had doubtless contributed to the difference in the characters of the two branches of the Russian race. From the 11th to the 13th century, in passing from the basin of the Dnieper to the basin of the Volga, we can already watch the formation of Great and Little Russia.

6. The principalities of Kief, Tchernigof, Novgorod-Severski, Riazan, Mourom, and Souzdal, situated on the side of the

steppe with its devastating hordes, formed the frontier States, the *Marches* of Russia. The same *rôle*, on the north-west opposite the Lithuanians, Letts, and Tchouds, fell to the principality of *Polotsk*, which occupied the basin of the Dwina; and to the republican principalities of *Novgorod* and *Pskof* on the lakes Ilmen and Peïpus. To the principality of Polotsk, that of *Minsk* was attached, which lay in the basin of the Dnieper. The possession of Minsk, thanks to its situation, was often disputed by the Grand Princes of Kief. To Novgorod belonged the towns of Torjok, Volok-Lamski, Izborsk, and Veliki-Louki, which were at times capitals of particular States.

South-east Russia comprehended—1. *Volhynia* in the fan-shaped distribution of rivers formed by the Pripet and its tributaries, with Vladimir-in-Volhynia, Loutsk, Tourof, Brest, and even Lublin, which is certainly Polish. 2. *Gallicia* proper, or Red Russia, in the basin of the San, the Dniester, and the Pripet, whose ancient inhabitants the White Croats seemed to have sprung from the stock of the Danubian Slavs. Her chief towns were Galitch, founded by Vladimirko about 1144, Peremysl, Terebovl, and Zvenigorod. The neighborhood of Hungary and Poland gave a special character to these principalities, as well as a more advanced civilization. The epic songs speak of Gallicia, the native land of the hero Diouk Stepanovitch, as a fabulously-rich country. The *Tale of the Expedition of Igor* gives us a high idea of the power of these princes. " Iaroslaf Osmomysl of Gallicia!" cried the poet to one of them, " thou art seated very high on thy throne of wrought gold; with thy regiments of iron thou sustainest the Carpathians; thou closest the gates of the Danube; thou barrest the way to the king of Hungary; thou openest at thy will the gates of Kief, and with thine arrows thou strikest from afar!"

The disposition of these fifteen or sixteen principalities confirms all that we have said about the essential unity of the configuration of the Russian soil. Not one of the river-basins forms an isolated and closed region. There is no line of heights to establish barriers between them or political frontiers. The greater number of the Russian principalities belong to the basin of the Dneiper, but extend everywhere beyond its limits. The principality of Kief, with Peréiaslavl, is nearly the only one completely confined within it; but Volhynia puts the basin of the Dnieper in communication with those of the Bug and the Vistula, Polotsk with the basins of the Dnieper and the Dwina, Novgorod-Severski with the basin of the Don, Tchernigof and Smolensk with the basin of the Volga. Water-courses every-where established communications between the principalities.

Already Russia, though broken up into appanages, had the germs of a great united empire. The slight cohesion of nearly all the States, and their frequent dismemberments, prevented them from ever becoming the homes of real nationalities. The principalities of Smolensk, Tchernigof, and Riazan have never possessed as definite an historic existence as the duchy of Bretagne or the county of Toulouse in France, or the duchies of Saxony, Suabia, and Bavaria in Germany.

The interests of the princes, their desire to create appanages for each of their children, caused a fresh division of the Russian territory at the death of every sovereign. There was, however, a certain cohesion in the midst of all these vicissitudes. There was a unity of race and language, the more sensible, notwithstanding all dialectic differences, because the Russian people was surrounded everywhere, except at the south-west, by entirely strange races, Lithuanians, Tchouds, Finns, Turks, Magyars. There was a unity of religion; the Russians differed from nearly all their neighbors, for in contrast with the Western Slavs, Poles, Tcheques, and Moravians, they represented a particular form of Christianity, not owning any tie to Rome, and rejecting Latin as the language of the Church. There was the unity of historical development, as up to that time the Russo-Slavs had all followed the same road, had accepted Greek civilization, submitted to the Varangians, pursued certain great enterprises in common—such as the expeditions against Byzantium and the war with the nomads. Finally, there was political unity, since after all in Gallicia as in Novgorod, on the Dnieper as in the forests of Souzdal, it was the same family that filled all the thrones. All these princes descended from Rurik, Saint Vladimir, and Iaroslaf the Great. The fact that the wars that laid waste the country were civil wars, was a new proof of this unity. The different parts of Russia could not consider themselves strangers one to the other, when they saw the princes of Tchernigof and Souzdal taking up arms to prove which of them was the *eldest*, and which consequently had most right to the title of Grand Prince and the throne of Kief. There were descendants of Rurik who governed successively the remotest States of Russia, and who, after having reigned at Tmoutorakan on the Straits of Ienikale, at Novgorod the Great, at Toropetz in the country of Smolensk, ended by establishing their right to reign at Kief. In spite of the division into appanages, Kief continued to be the centre of Russia. It was there that Oleg and Igor had reigned, that Vladimir had baptized his people, and Iaroslaf had established the metropolis of the faith, of arts, and of national civilization. It is not surprising that she should have been more fiercely disputed than all the other Russian cities. Russia had many *princes;* but she had only one *Grand Prince* (*Veliki-kniaz*)—the one who reigned at Kief. He had a recognized supremacy over the others which he owed not only to the importance of his capital, but to his position as *eldest* of the royal family. Kief, the mother of Russian cities, was always to belong to the *eldest* of the descendants of Rurik; this was the consequence of the patriarchal system of the Slavs, as was the custom of division. When the Grand Prince of Kief died, his son was not his rightful heir; but his uncle or brother, or which ever of the princes was the *eldest.* Then the whole of Russia, from the Baltic to the Black Sea, held itself in readiness to support the claims of this or that candidate. It was the same with the other principalities, where the possessors of different appanages aspired to reign in the metropolis of the region. The civil wars, then, themselves strengthened the sentiments of Russian unity. What were they, after all, but family quarrels?

THE SUCCESSORS OF IAROSLAF THE GREAT — WARS FOR THE RIGHTS OF ELDERSHIP AND THE THRONE OF KIEF—VLADIMIR MONOMACHUS.

The persistent conflict between the Byzantine law, by which the son inherited the possessions of the father, and the old national law of the Slavs which caused them to pass to the eldest of all the family, was an inexhaustible source of civil wars. Even had the law been perfectly clear, the princes were not always disposed to recognize it. Thus, although the eldest of Iaroslaf's sons had in his favor the formal will of his father, giving him the throne of Kief, and though Iaroslaf on his deathbed had desired his other sons to respect their elder brother as they had done their parent, and look on him as their father, Isiaslaf at once found his brother Sviatoslaf ready to take up arms and overturn his throne (1073). He was obliged to seek refuge at the Court of Henry IV. of Germany, who sent an embassy to Kief, commanding Sviatoslaf to restore the throne of Isiaslaf. Sviatoslaf received the German envoys with such courtesy, made them such a display of his treasures and riches, that, dazzled by the gold, they adopted a pacific policy. Henry IV. himself, disarmed by the liberalities of the Russian prince, spoke no more of chastising the usurper. Isiaslaf did not return to Kief till after the death of his rival (1076).

When his own death took place (1078), his son Sviatopolk did not succeed him immediately. It was necessary that all the heirs of Iaroslof should be exhausted. Vsevolod, a brother of Isiaslaf, whose daughter married the Emperor Henry IV., or Henry V.—it is not quite certain which—reigned for fifteen years (1078-1093). In accordance with the same principle, it was not the son of Vsevolod, Vladimir Monomachus, who succeeded his father; but after the crown had been worn by a new generation of princes, it returned to the blood of Isiaslaf. Vladimir Monomachus made no opposition to the claims of Sviatopolk Isiaslavitch. "His father was older than mine," he said, "and reigned first in Kief," so he quitted the principality which he had governed with his father, and valiantly defended against the barbarians. But everyone was not so respectful to the national law as Vladimir Monomachus.

Two terrible civil wars desolated Russia in the reign of the Grand Prince Sviatopolk (1093-1113): one about the principality of Tchernigof, the other about Volhynia and Red Russia. Sviatoslaf had enjoyed Tchernigof as his share, to which Tmoutoraken in the Taurid, Mourom and Riazan in the Finn country, were annexed. Isiaslaf and Vsevolod, Grand Princes of Kief, had despoiled the sons of Sviatoslaf, their brother, depriving them of the rich territory of Tchernigof, and only leaving them Tmoutorakan and the Finnish country. Even Vladimir Monomachus, whom we have seen so disinterested, had accepted a share of the spoil. The injured princes were not people to bear this meekly, especially the eldest, Oleg Sviatoslavitch, one of the most energetic men of the 11th century. He called the terrible Polovtsi to his aid, and subjected Russia to frightful ravages. Vladimir Monomachus was moved by these misfortunes; he wrote a touching letter to Oleg, expressing his sorrow for having accepted Tchernigof. At his instigation a Congress of Princes met at Loubetch, on the Dnieper (1097). Seated on the same carpet, they resolved to put an end to the civil wars that handed the country as a prey to the barbarians. Oleg recovered Tchernigof, and promised to unite with the Grand Prince of Kief and Vladimir Monomachus against the Polovtsi. The treaty was ratified by the oath of each prince, who kissed the cross and swore, "That henceforth the Russian land shall be considered as the country of us all; and whoso shall dare to arm himself against his brother becomes our common enemy."

In Volhynia, the prince, David, was at war with his nephews, Vassilko and Volodar. The Congress of Loubetch had divided the disputed territories between them, but scarcely was the treaty ratified when David went to the Grand Prince Sviatopolk and persuaded him that Vassilko had a design on his life. With the light faith habitual to the men of that date, the Grand Prince joined David in framing a plot to attract Vassilko to Kief on the occasion of a religious fête. When he arrived he was loaded with chains, and the Grand Prince convoked the boyards and citizens of Kief, to denounce to them the pretended projects of Vassilko. "Prince," replied the boyards, much embarrassed, "thy tranquillity is dear to us. Vassilko merits death, if it is true that he is thine enemy; but if he is calumniated by David, God will avenge on David the blood of the innocent." Thereon the Grand Prince delivered Vassilko to his enemy David, who put out his eyes. The other descendants of Iaroslaf I. were indignant at this crime. Vladimir Monomachus united with Oleg of Tchernigof, his ancient enemy, and marched against Sviatopolk. The people and clergy of Kief succeeded in preventing a civil war between the Grand Prince and the confederates of Loubetch. Sviatopolk was forced to disavow David, and swear to join the avengers of Vassilko. David defended himself with vigor, and summoned to his help, first the Poles, and then the Hungarians. At last a new congress was assembled at Vititchevo (1100), on the left bank of the Dnieper, a town of which a deserted *gorodichtché* is all that now remains. As a punishment for his crime, David was deprived of his principality of Vladimir in Volhynia, and had to content himself with four small towns. After the new settlement of this affair, Monomachus led the other princes against the Polovtsi, and inflicted on them a bloody defeat; seventeen of their khans remained on the field of battle. One khan who was made prisoner offered a ransom to Monomachus; but the prince showed how deeply he felt the injuries of the Christians—he refused the gold, and cut the brigand chief in pieces.

When Sviatopolk died, the Kievians unanimously declared they would have no Grand Prince but Vladimir Monomachus. Vladimir declined the honor, alleging the claims of Oleg and his brothers to the throne of Kief. During these negotiations, a sedition broke out in the city, and the Jews, whom Sviatopolk had made the instruments of his fiscal exactions, were pillaged. Monomachus was forced to yield to the prayers of the citizens. During his reign (1113–1125) he obtained great successes against the Polovtsi, the Patzinaks, the Torques, the Tcherkesses, and other nomads, He gave an asylum to the remains of the Khazars, who built on the Oster, not far from Tchernigof, the town of Belovega. The ruins of this city that remain to-day prove that this Finnish people, eminently perfectible, and already civilized by the Greeks, were further advanced in the arts of construction and fortification than even the Russians themselves.

According to one tradition, Monomachus also made war on the Emperor Alexis Comnenus, a Russian army invaded Thrace, and the Bishop of Ephesus is said to have brought gifts to Kief, among others a cup of cornelian that had belonged to Augustus, besides a crown and a throne, still preserved in the Museum at Moscow under the name of the crown and throne of Monomachus. It is at present ascertained that they never belonged to Vladimir, but it was the policy of his descendants, the Tzars of Moscow, to propagate this legend. It was of consequence to them to prove that these ensigns of their power were traceable to their Kievian ancestor, and that the Russian Monomachus, grandson of the Greek Monomachus, had been solemnly crowned by the Bishop of Ephesus as sovereign of Russia.

The Grand Prince made his authority felt in other parts of Russia. A Prince of Minsk who had the temerity to kindle a civil war, was promptly dethroned, and died in captivity at Kief. The Novgorodians saw many of their boyards kept as hostages, or exiled. The Prince of Vladimir in Volhynia was deposed, and his states given to a son of the Grand Prince.

Monomachus has left us a curious paper of instructions that he compiled for his sons, and in which he gives them much good advice, enforced by examples drawn from his own life. "It is neither fasting, nor solitude, nor the monastic life, that will procure you the life eternal—it is well-doing. Do not forget the poor, but nourish them. Do not bury your riches in the bosom of the earth, for that is contrary to the precepts of Christianity.* Be a father to orphans, judge the cause of widows yourself.... Put to death no one, *be he innocent or guilty*, for nothing is more sacred than the soul of a Christian. . . . . Love your wives, but beware lest they get the power over you. When you have learnt anything useful, try to preserve it in your memory and strive ceaselessly to get knowledge. Without ever leaving his palace, my father spoke five languages, *a thing that foreigners admire in us*. . . I have made altogether twenty-three campaigns without counting those of minor importance. I have concluded nineteen treaties of peace with the Polovtsi, taken at least 100 of their princes prisoners, and afterwards restored them to liberty; besides more than 200 whom I threw into the rivers. No one has travelled more rapidly than I. If I left Tchernigof very early in the morning, I arrived at Kief before vespers. Some

---

* To bury riches in the earth is the custom with which the Emperor Maurice reproaches the Slavs of his time, and which is to this day characteristic of the Russian peasants. Often the head of the family dies, without having revealed the hiding-place to his children. Treasure trove is frequent in Russia.

times in the middle of the thickest forests, I caught wild horses
myself, and bound them together with my own hands. How
many times I have been thrown from the saddle by buffaloes,
struck by the horns of the deer, trampled under foot by the
elands ! A furious boar once tore my sword from my belt ; my
saddle was rent by a bear, which threw my horse down under
me ! How many falls I had from my horse in my youth, when,
heedless of danger, I broke my head, I wounded my arms and
legs ! But the Lord watched over me ! "

Vladimir completed the establishment of the Slav race in
Souzdal, and founded a city on the Kliazma that bore his name,
and that was destined to play a great part. Such, in the beginning of the 12th century, when Louis VI. was fighting with his
barons of the Isle de France, was the ideal of a Grand Prince
of Russia.

WARS BETWEEN THE HEIRS OF VLADIMIR MONOMACHUS—FALL OF
KIEF.

Of the sons of Vladimir Monomachus, George Dolgorouki
became the father of the Princes of Souzdal and Moscow, and
Mstislaf the father of the Princes of Galitch and Kief. These
two branches were often at enmity, and it was their rivalry that
struck the final blow at the prosperity of Kief. When Isiaslaf,
son of Mstislaf (1146–1154), was called to the throne by the
inhabitants of the capital, his uncle, George Dolgorouki, put
forward his rights as the *eldest* of the family. Kief, which had
been already many times taken and re-taken in the strife between
the *Olgovitches* (descendants of Oleg of Tchernigof) and the
Monomachivitches (descendants of Vladimir Monomachus), was
fated to be disputed anew between the uncle and the nephew.
It was almost a war between the Old and New Russia, the
Russia of the Dnieper and that of the Volga. The Princes of
Souzdal, who dwelt afar in the forests in the north-west, establishing their rule over the remnants of the Finnish races, were to
become greater and greater strangers to Kievian Russia. If
they still coveted the "mother of Russian cities," because the
title of Grand Prince was attached to it, they at least began to
obey and to venerate it less than the other princes.

George Dolgorouki found an ally against Isiaslaf in one of
the Olgovitches, Sviatoslaf, who thirsted to avenge his brother
Igor, dethroned and kept prisoner in Kief by the Grand Prince.
The Kievians hesitated to support the sovereign they had chosen ;
they hated the Olgovitches, but in their attachment to the blood

of Monomachus, they respected his son and his grandson equally. "We are ready," they said to Isiaslaf, "we and our children, to make war on the sons of Oleg. But George is your uncle, and can we dare to raise our hands against the son of Monomachus?" After the war had lasted some time, a decisive dattle was fought. At the battle of Peréiaslavl, Isiaslaf was completely defeated, and took refuge, with two attendants, in Kief. The inhabitants, who had lost many citizens in this war, declared they were unable to stand a siege. The Grand Prince then abandoned his capital to George Dolgorouki and retired to Vladimir in Volhynia, whence he demanded help from his brother-in-law, the King of Hungary, and the kings of Poland and Bohemia. With these reinforcements he surprised Kief, and nearly made his uncle prisoner. Understanding that the national law was against him, he opposed *eldest with eldest* and declared himself the partisan of another son of Monomachus, the old Viatcheslaf, Prince of Tourof. He was proclaimed Grand Prince of Kief (1150–1154), adopted his nephew Isiaslaf as his heir, and gave splendid fêtes to the Russians and Hungarians. George returned to the charge, and was beaten under the walls of Kief. Each of these princes had taken barbarians into his pay: George, the Polovtsi; Isiaslaf the *Black Caps*, that is the Torques, the Patzinaks, and the Berendians.

The obstinate Prince of Souzdal did not allow himself to be discouraged by this check. The old Viatcheslaf, who only desired peace and quiet, in vain addressed him letters, setting forth his rights as *elder*. "I had already a beard when you entered the world," he said. George proved himself intractable, and went into Gallicia to effect a junction with his ally, Vladimirko, Prince of Galitch. This Vladimirko had violated the oath he had taken and confirmed by kissing the cross. When they reproached him, he said, with a sneer, "It was such a little cross." To prevent this dangerous co-operation, Isiaslaf, without waiting the expected arrival of the Hungarians, began the pursuit of George, and came up with him on the borders of the Rout, a small tributary of the Dnieper. A bloody battle was fought, where he himself was wounded and thrown from his horse, but the Souzdalians and their allies the Polovtsi were completely defeated (1151). Isiaslaf survived this victory only three years. After his death and that of Viatcheslaf, Kief passed from hand to hand. George ended by reaching the supreme object of his desires. He made his entry into the capital in 1155, and had the consolation of dying Grand Prince of Kief at the moment that a league was being formed for his expulsion (1157). "I thank Thee, great **God**," cried one of the confederates on learning the news, "for having spared us, by the sudden death of our enemy, the obligation of shedding his blood!"

The confederates entered the town; one of them assumed the title of Grand Prince, the others divided his territories. Henceforth there existed no Grand Principality, properly speaking, and with the growing power of Souzdal, Kief ceased to be the capital of Russia. A final disaster was still reserved for her.

In 1169, Andrew Bogolioubski, son of George Dolgorouki and Prince of Souzdal, being disaffected to Mstislaf, Prince of Kief, formed against him a coalition of eleven princes. He confided to his son Mstislaf and his voïevode Boris an immense army of Rostovians, Vladimiris, and Souzdalians to march against Kief. This time the Russia of the forests triumphed over Russia of the steppes, and after a three days' siege Kief was taken by assault. "This mother of Russian cities," says Karamsin, "had been many times besieged and oppressed. She had often opened her Golden Gate to her enemies, but none had ever yet entered by force. To their eternal shame, the victors forgot that they too were Russians! During three days not only the houses, but the monasteries, churches, and even the temples of Saint Sophia and the Dime, were given over to pillage. The precious images, the sacerdotal ornaments, the books, and the bells, all were taken away."

From this time the lot of the capital of Saint Vladimir, pillaged and dishonored by his descendants, ceases to have a general interest for Russia. Like other parts of Slavonia, she has her princes, but the heads of the reigning families of Smolensk, Tchernigof, and Galitch assume the title, formerly unique, of Grand Prince. The centre of Russia is changed. It is now in the basin of the Volga, at Souzdal. Many causes conspired to render the disaster of 1169 irremediable. The chronic civil wars of this part of Russia, and the multitudes and growing power of nomad hordes, rendered the banks of the Dnieper uninhabitable. In 1203 Kief was again sacked by the Polovtsi, whom the Olgovitches of Tchernigof had taken into their pay. On this soil, incessantly the prey of war and invasion, it was impossible to found a lasting order of things; it was impossible that a regular system of government should be established—that civilization should develop and maintain itself. Less richly endowed by nature, and less civilized, the Russia of the forests was at least more tranquil. It was there that a grand principality was formed, called to fulfil high destinies, but which unhappily was to be separated for three hundred years, by the southern steppes and the nomads who dwelt there, from the Black Sea; that is, from Byzantine and Occidental civilization.

CHAPTER VII.

RUSSIA AFTER THE FALL OF KIEF. POWER OF SOUZDAL AND GALLICIA, 1169–1224.

Andrew Bogolioubski of Souzdal (1157–1174), and the first attempt at autocracy—George II. (1212–1238)—Wars with Novgorod—Battle of Lipetsk (1216)—Foundation of Nijni-Novgorod (1220)—Roman (1188–1205) and his son Daniel (1205–1264) in Gallicia.

ANDREW BOGOLIOUBSKI OF SOUZDAL (1157–1174) AND THE FIRST ATTEMPT AT AUTOCRACY.

AFTER the fall of the grand principality of Kief, Russia ceased to have a centre round which her whole mass could gravitate. Her life seemed to be withdrawn to her extremities; and during the fifty four years which preceded the arrival of the Mongols, all the interest of Russian history is concentrated on the principality of Souzdal, on that of Galitch, and on the two republics of Novgorod and Pskof.

George Dolgorouki was the founder of Souzdal, but we have seen him expend all his energy in securing possession of the throne of Kief. His son Andrew Bogolioubski was, on the contrary, a true prince of Souzdal. From him are descended the Tzars of Moscow; with him there appears in Russian history quite a new type of prince. It is no longer the chivalrous lighthearted careless *kniaz*, in turn a prey to all kinds of opposing passions, the joyous *kniaz* of the happy land of Kief—but an ambitious, restless, politic, and imperious sovereign, going straight to his goal without scruple and without pity. Andrew had taken an aversion to the turbulent cities of the Dnieper, where the assemblies of citizens sometimes held the power of the prince in check. In Souzdal, at least, he found himself in the centre of colonists planted by the prince, who never dreamed of contesting his authority: he reigned over towns which for the most part owed their existence to his ancestors or himself. During the lifetime of his father George, he had quitted the Dnieper and his palace at Vychegorod, had established himself on the Kliazma, bringing with him a Greek image of the mother of God, had enlarged and fortified Vladimir, and founded a quarter that he called Bogolioubovo.

When after the death of George the grand principality became vacant, he allowed the princes of the south to dispute it among themselves. He only wished to mix with their quarrels as far as would suffice for the recognition of his authority, not at Kief, but at Novgorod the Great, then bound by the closest ties to Souzdal. He established one of his nephews as his lieutenant at Novgorod. A glorious campaign against the Bulgarians increased his reputation in Russia. He deserved more than anyone to be Grand Prince of Kief, but we have seen that he preferred to pillage it—that he preferred a sacrilegious spoil to the throne of Monomachus.

After having destroyed the splendor and power of Kief, and guided by the sure instinct that afterwards led Ivan the Great and Ivan the Terrible against Novgorod, he longed to subdue the great republic to a narrower dependence. "The fall of Kief," says Karamsin, "seemed to presage the loss of Novgorod liberty; it was the same army, and it was the same prince (Mstislaf Andreievitch) who commanded it. But the Kievians, accustomed to change their masters—to sacrifice the vanquished to the victors—only fought for the honor of their princes, while the Novgorodians were to shed their blood for the defence of the laws and institutions established by their ancestors." Mstislaf, who had forced the princes of Smolensk, Riazan, Mourom, and Polotsk to join him, put the territories of the republic to fire and sword, but only succeeded in exasperating the courageous citizens. When fighting began under the walls of the town, the Novgorodians, to inflame themselves for the combat, reminded each other of the pillage and the sacrilege with which their adversaries had polluted the holy city of Kief. All swore to die for St. Sophia of Novgorod; their archbishop, Ivan, took the image of the Mother of God and paraded it with great pomp round the walls. It is said that an arrow shot by a Souzdalian soldier having struck the image of the Virgin, her face turned towards the city, and inundated the vestments of the archbishop with miraculous tears. Instantly a panic seized the besiegers. The victory of the Novgorodians was complete; they slew a multitude of their enemies, and made so many prisoners, that according to the contemptuous expression of their chronicler, "You could get six Souzdalians for a grivna (1170)." Their dependence on Souzdal for corn soon forced them to make peace. They abandoned none of the ancient rights of the republic, but of "their own free will," according to the consecrated expression, they accepted as sovereign the prince nominated for them by Andrew of Souzdal.

Andrew about this time lost his only son, his heir, Mstislaf.

The knowledge that in future he would be working for his collateral relatives no whit diminished his ambition or his arrogance. The princes of Smolensk, David, Rurik, and Mstislaf the Brave, could not endure his despotic ways, and, in spite of his threats, took Kief. The Olgovitches of Tchernigof, delighted to see discord kindled between the descendants of Monomachus, incited Andrew to revenge this injury. So he sent a herald to the princes of Smolensk, to say to them, " You are rebels; the principality of Kief is mine. I order Rurik to return to his patrimony of Smolensk, and David to retire to Berlad; I can no longer bear his presence in Russia, nor the presence of Mstislaf, the most guilty of you all."

Mstislaf the Brave, say the chroniclers, "feared none but God." When he received Andrew's message, he shaved the beard and hair of the messenger, and answered him: "Go, and repeat these words unto your prince—' Up to this time we have respected you like a father, but since you do not blush to treat us as your vassals and common people, since you have forgotten that you speak to princes, we mock at your menaces. Execute them—we appeal to the judgment of God.'" The judgment of God was an encounter under the walls of Vychegorod, besieged by more than twenty princes, allies or vassals of Andrew of Souzdal. Mstislaf succeeded in dividing the assailants, and completed their defeat by a victorious sortie, 1173.

When Andrew came to establish himself in the land of Souzdal, the inhabitants themselves elected him their prince, to the exclusion of other members of the family. But this enemy of municipal liberty had no intention of fixing his residence either at Rostof or Souzdal, the two most ancient cities of the principality, which had their assembly of citizens, their *vetché*. From the beginning he conceived the project of raising above them a new town, Vladimir on the Kliazma, considered by Rostof and Souzdal merely a subject borough. To give a plausible pretext to this resolution he had his tent pitched on the road to Souzdal ten versts from Vladimir, and installed himself there with his miraculous image of the Virgin which came from Constantinople, and was, we are assured, the work of St. Luke. The next day he announced that the Mother of God had appeared to him in a dream, and had commanded him to place her image, not at Rostof, but at Vladimir. He was likewise to build a church and a monastery to the Virgin on the spot where she made herself manifest; this was the origin of the village of Bogolioubovo. Andrew preferred Vladimir to the old cities, but it was in his house at Bogolioubovo that he best liked to live. He tried to make of Vladimir a new Kief, as Kief herself was a new Byzantium. There were at Vladimir a Golden Gate, a Church of the Dime consecrated to the Virgin, and numerous monasteries built by the artists summoned by Andrew from the West.

Andrew sought the friendship of the priests, whom he felt to be one of the great forces of the future. He posed as a pious prince, rose often by night to burn tapers in the churches, and publicly distributed alms in abundance. After a victory over the Bulgarians of the Volga, he obtained leave from the Patriarch of Constantinople to establish a commemorative feast. It happened that on the same day that Andrew triumphed over the Bulgarians, thanks to the image of the Virgin, the Emperor Manuel had won a victory over the Saracens by means of the true cross and the image of Christ represented on his standard. One anniversary served for both victories of orthodoxy, and Vladimir was in harmony with Byzantium. Andrew was anxious to make Vladimir a metropolitan city. At the same time that he robbed Kief of the grand principality, he would have deprived her of the religious supremacy of Russia, and given his new city the spiritual as well as the temporal power. This time the patriarch refused, but the attempt was one day to be renewed by the princes of Moscow.

What more particularly proves this prince—who had risen from the conception of appanages to that of the indivisible modern state—to have been superior to his century, to have had sure instincts as to the future, is that he declined to share his dominions with his brothers and nephews. In spite of the testamentary directions of George, he expelled his three brothers from Souzdal, and they retired with their mother, a Greek princess, to the court of the Emperor Manuel. It appears that this measure was advised by the men of Souzdal. The subjects then had the same instinct of unity as the prince. If he broke with the patriarchal custom of appanages, and wished to reign alone in Vladimir, he broke equally with the Varangian tradition of the *droujina*; he treated his men, his boyards, not as companions, but as subjects. Those who refused to bow to his will had to leave the country. We may say that Andrew Bogolioubski created autocracy 300 years before its time. He indicated in the 12th century all that the Grand Princes of Moscow had to do in the 15th and 16th centuries, to attain absolute power. His mistrust of municipal liberty, his despotic treatment of the boyards, his efforts to suppress the appanages, his proud attitude towards the other Russian princes, his alliance with the clergy, and his project of transporting to the basin of the Oka the religious metropolis of all the Russias, are the indications of a political programme that ten generations of princes did **not** suffice to carry out. The moment was not yet come; Andrew had not enough power, nor Souzdal resources enough to subjugate the rest of Russia. Andrew succeeded against Kief, but he endured a double check from Novgorod the Great, and from Mstislaf the Brave, and the princes of the south. His despotism made him terrible enemies. His boyards, whom he tried to reduce to obedience, assassinated him in his favorite residence of Bogolioubovo (1174).

GEORGE II. (1212-1238) — WARS WITH NOVGOROD — BATTLE OF LIPETSK (1216) — NIJNI-NOVGOROD FOUNDED (1220).

The death of this remarkable man was followed by great troubles. The common people attacked the houses of rich men and magistrates, gave them up to pillage, and committed so many murders that to establish quiet the clergy were forced to have a procession of images. The unpunished murders show how premature was the autocratic attempt of Andrew. His succession was disputed between his nephews and his two brothers Michael and Vsevolod, who had returned from Greece. The nephews were supported by the old cities of Rostof and Souzdal, which were animated by a violent hatred of the *parvenue* city of Vladimir, that had torn from them the title of capital, and had taken up the cause of Michael and Vsevolod. "The Vladimirians," said the Rostovians, "are our slaves, our masons; let us burn their town, and set up there a governor of our own." The Vladimirians had the advantage in the first war, and caused Michael, the elder of Andrew's brothers, to be recognized Grand Prince of Souzdal. At his death the Rostovians refused to recognize the other brother Vsevolod, surnamed the *Big-Nest*, on account of his numerous posterity. They resisted all proposals of compromise, declaring that "their arms alone should do them right on the vile populace of Vladimir." It was, on the contrary, the vile populace of Vladimir who put the boyards of Rostof in chains. The two ancient cities were forced to submit; Vladimir remained the capital of Souzdal. Vsevolod (1176–1212) managed to secure himself on the throne by defeating the princes of Riazan and Tchernigof. He extended his influence to the distant Galitch, and contracted matrimonial alliances with the princes of Kief and Smolensk. He reduced the Novgorodians to beg for one of his sons as their prince. "Lord and Grand Prince," said the envoys of the republic to him, "our country is your patrimony; we entreat you to send us the grandson of

George Dolgorouki, the great-grandson of Monomachus, to govern us." The princes of Riazan having incurred his displeasure, he united their states to his principality. Riazan rebelled, and was reduced to ashes, and the inhabitants transported to the solitudes of Souzdal. This prince, who has likewise been called "The Great," exhibited in his designs the prudence, the spirit of intrigue, constancy, and firmness which characterized the princes of the Russia of the forests. At his death (1212) the troubles began again. Dissatisfied with his eldest son Constantine, prince of Novgorod, Vsevolod had given the grand principality of Novgorod to his second son, George II. Constantine had to content himself with Rostof; a third brother, Iaroslaf, prince of Peréiaslavl-Zaliesski, had been sent to Novgorod.

Iaroslaf quarrelled with his turbulent subjects, left their town and installed himself at Torjok, a city in the territory of Novgorod, where he betook himself to hindering the passage of the merchants and boyards. Their communications with the Volga were intercepted; he preuented the arrival of corn, and reduced the town to starvation. The Novgorodians were obliged to eat the bark of pines, moss, and lime-leaves. The streets were filled with the bodies of the wretched inhabitants, which the dogs devoured. Iaroslaf was implacable. He persisted in remaining at Torjok, refused to retnrn to Novgorod, and arrested all envoys sent to him. He treated Novgorod as his father had treated Rostof and Souzdal. But help arrived to the despairing citizens in the person of a prince of Smolensk, Mstislaf the Bold, son of Mstislaf the Brave. "Torjok shall not hold herself higher than Novgorod," he cried; "I will deliver your lands and your citizens, or leave my bones among you." Thus Mstislaf became prince of Novgorod; and as he saw that the Grand Prince of Vladimir supported his brothers, he sought an ally in Constantine of Rostof, who was discontented with his inheritance. The Novgorodian quarrel speedily expanded into a general war, and Mstisaf contrived to make Souzdal the scene of strife. Before a battle he tried to effect a reconciliation between the two princes of Vladimir and Rostof. But George answered, "If my father was not able to reconcile me with Constantine, has Mstislaf the right to judge between us? Let Constantine be victorious and all will be his." This strife between the three sons of Big-Nest had all the fierceness of fraternal warefare. Before the battle George and Iaroslaf issued orders that quarter was to be given to no one, to kill even those who had "embroideries of gold on their shoulders;" that is, the princes of the blood. Already they had decided on the partition of Russia. But the troops of Novgorod, Pskof, and Smolensk attacked them with such fury that those of Souzdal and Mourom gave way, and it was the soldiers of Mstislaf who in their turn gave no quarter. Nine thousand men were killed and only sixty prisoners taken. George threw off his royal clothes, wore out the strength of three horses, and with the fourth just managed to reach Vladimir. (Battle of Lipetsk, near Peréiaslavl-Zaliesski, 1216.) Constantine then became Grand Prince of Vladimir, and ceded Souzdal to his brother George. Iaroslaf was obliged to renounce Novgorod, and release the captive citizens.

At the death of Constantine (1217) George regained the throne of Vladimir. Under him the expeditions against the Bulgarians of the Volga and the Mordvians were continued. These expeditions were organized both by land and water; the infantry descended the Oka and the Volga in boats, the cavalry marched along the banks. They attacked and burnt the wooden forts of the Bulgars, and destroyed the population.

During a campaign, conducted by George in person along the whole length of the Volga, he noticed a small hill on its right bank, near its junction with the Oka. Here, in the midst of the Mordvian tribes, he founded Nijni-Novgorod (1220). A Mordvian tradition gives its own account of this important event. "The prince of the Russians sailed down the Volga; on the mountain he perceived the Mordva in a long white coat, adoring her god; and he said to his warrors, 'What is that white birch that bends and sways up there, above its nurse the earth, and inclines towards the east?' He sent his men to look nearer, and they came back and said, 'It is not a birch that bends and sways, it is the Mordva adoring her god. In their vessels they have a delicious beer, pancakes hang on sticks, and their priests cook their meat in caldrons.' The elders of the Mordva, hearing of the Russian prince, sent young men with gifts of meat and beer. But on the road the young men ate the meat and drank the beer, and only brought the Russian prince earth and water. The prince was rejoiced at this present, which he considered as a mark of submission of the Mordva. He continued to descend the Volga: where he threw a handful of this earth on the bank, a town sprang up: where he threw a pinch of this earth, a village was born. It was thus that the Mordvian land became subject to the Russians."

ROMAN (1188-1205) AND HIS SON DANIEL (1205-1264) IN GALITCH.

Galitch offers a remarkable contrast to Souzdal ; peopled by Khorvates or White Croats, she had preserved a purely Slavonic character in spite of her conquest by Varangian princes. " The prince," says M. Kostomarof, " was a prince of the old Slavonic type. He was elected by a popular assembly, and kept his crown by its consent."

The assembly itself was governed by the richest men of the country, the boyards. Under the influence of Polish and Hungarian ideas the boyards had raised themselves above the mass of the people, and formed a strong aristocracy which really ruled the country. When Iaroslaf Osmomysl (glorified in the Song of Igor) neglected his lawful wife Olga for his mistress Anastasia, the nobles rose, burnt Anastasia alive, and obliged the prince to send away his natural son, and to recognize his legitimate son Vladimir as his heir.

When Vladimir became prince, he lost no time in incurring their hatred. He was accused of abandoning himself to vice and drunkenness, of despising the councils of wise men, of dishonoring the wives and daughters of the nobles, and of having married as his second wife the widow of a priest. It did not need all this to exhaust the patience of the Gallicians. They summoned Vladimir to give up the woman that they might punish her. Vladimir took fright, and fled to Hungary with his family and his treasures. This was all the boyards desired, and they offered the throne to Roman, prince of Volhynia (1188). But Bela, king of Hungary, brought back the fugitive prince with an army, and entered Galitch. There he suddenly changed his mind, and coveted this beautiful country, rich in salt and minerals, for himself. He threw his *protégé* Vladimir into prison, and proclaimed his own son Andrew. The Hungarian yoke seemed naturally more heavy to the Gallicians than the authority of their easy-going princes. They expelled the strangers, and recalled Vladimir, who had found means to escape, and had taken refuge with Frederick Barbarossa. When Vladimir died, Roman of Volhynia resolved at all hazards to enter Galitch. His rival had previously appealed to the Hungarians, so he applied to the Poles, and, with an auxiliary army given him by Casimir the Just, he reconquered Galitch. The turbulent boyards had at last found their master.

This time Roman held the crown, not by election, but by conquest. He resolved to subdue the proud aristocracy. The Polish Bishop Kadloubek, a contemporary writer, who sympathsized with the oligarchs, draws a frightful picture of the vengeance exercised by Roman on his enemies. They were quartered, buried alive, riddled with arrows, delivered over to horrible tortures. He had promised pardon to those who had fled; but when they returned, he accused them of conspiracy, condemned them to death, and confiscated their goods. "To eat a drop of honey in peace," he said cynically, "you must first kill the bees." The Russian chroniclers, on the contrary, praise him highly. He was another Monomachus, an invincible and redoubtable hero, who "walked in the ways of God, exterminated the heathen, flung himself like a lion upon the infidels, was savage as a wildcat, deadly as a crocodile, swooped on his prey like an eagle." More than once he vanquished the Lithuanian tribes and the Polovtsi; in the civil wars of Russia he was likewise victorious, and gave to one of his relations the throne of Kief. He attracted the attention of the great Pope, Innocent III., who sent missionaries to convert him to the Catholic faith, promising to make him a great king by the sword of Saint Peter. Drawing his own sword, Roman proudly answered the envoys of Innocent: "Has the Pope one like mine? While I wear it at my side, I have no need of another's blade." In 1205, when he was engaged in a war with Poland, he imprudently ventured too far from his army on the banks of the Vistula, and perished in an unequal combat. His exploits were long remembered in Russia, and the 'Chronicle of Volhynia' gives him the surname of "the Great," and "the Autocrat of all the Russias." A historian of Lithuania relates that, after his victories over the barbarous inhabitants of that country, he harnessed the prisoners to the plough. Hence the popular saying, "Thou art terrible, Roman; the Lithuanians are thy laboring oxen." Roman of Volhynia is a worthy contemporary of the autocrat of the north-west, Andrew of Souzdal.

Roman left two sons, minors. Daniel the elder was proclaimed prince of Galitch (1205–1264), but in such a turbulent country, rent as it was by factions, it was impossible for a child to reign under the guardianship of his mother. Red Russia fell a prey to a series of civil wars, complicated by the intervention of Poles and Hungarians. The ferocity shown by the Gallicians in their intestine struggles has gained for them the name of *atheist* in the Kievian Chronicles. The princes of the blood of Saint Vladimir were tortured and hung by the boyards. Daniel was first replaced on the throne, then expelled, then again recalled. His infancy was the toy of intriguing factions. Mstislaf the Bold also came hither in search of adventures. He chased the Hungarians from Galitch, took the title of Prince, and married his daughter to Daniel. Both were immediately obliged to turn their arms against the Poles. Daniel, whose character had been formed in such a rough school, displayed remarkable energy and courage in these campaigns. The aid of the Polovtsi had to be sought against these enemies from the west, the Hungarians and the Poles—now rivals, now allies. At the death of Mstislaf the Bold (1228), Daniel, who five years previously had taken part in the battle of Kalka against the Tatars, became prince of Galitch. Towards the boyards, whose turbulence had ruined the country, he acted with the salutary policy of Roman, though without employing the same severity.

The great Mongol invasion once more expelled him from Galitch, which it covered with ruins. Daniel, who had fled to Hungary, did his best to help his unhappy country. To fill up the void made by the Mongols in the population, he invited Germans, Armenians, and Jews, whom he loaded with privileges. The economic consequence of this measure was a rapid development of commerce and industry ; the ethnographic consequence was the introduction into Gallicia of a Jewish element, very tenacious and very persistent, but alien to the dominant nationality, and forming a separate people in the midst of the Russians. Daniel was one of the last princes to make his submission to the horde. "You have done well to come at last," said the khan of the Mongols. Bati treated him with distinction, allowed him to escape the ordinary humiliations, and, seeing that the fermented milk of the Tatars was not to his taste, gave him a cup of wine. Daniel, however, bore with impatience the yoke of these barbarians.

Feeling himself insolated in the general abasement of the orthodox world, the prince of Galitch turned towards Rome, and promised to do his best for the union of the two Churches and to add his contingent to the crusade preached in Europe against the Mongols. Innocent IV, called him his dear son, accorded him the title of king, and sent him a crown and sceptre. Daniel was solemnly crowned at Droguitchine by the abbot of Messina, Legate of the Pope (1254). Both the crusade against the Asiatics and the reconciliation between the two Churches came to nothing. Daniel braved the reproaches and threats of Alexander IV., but kept the title of king. He took part in the European wars with great success. "The Hungarians," says a chronicler, "admired the order that reigned among his troops, their Tatar weapons, the magnificence of the prince, his Greek habit embroidered with gold, his sabre and his arrows, his saddles enriched with jewels and precious metals richly chased." Encouraged by the Hungarians and the Poles, he tried to shake off the yoke of the Mongols, and expelled them from a few places; but he was soon obliged to bow to superior force, and dismantle his fortresses. No prince better deserved to free Southern Russia, but his activity and talents struggled in vain against the fate of his country. He terminated in 1264 one of the most memorable and most checkered careers in the history of Russia. The civil wars of his youth, the Tatar invasion in his ripe age, the negotiations and wars with Western Europe, left him no repose. After him, Russian Galitch passed to different princes of his family. In the 14th century, she was absorbed into the kingdom of Poland. She was lost to Russia.

CHAPTER VIII.

THE RUSSIAN REPUBLICS: NOVGOROD, PSKOF, AND VIATKA, UP TO
1224.

Novgorod the Great—Her struggles with the princes—Novgorodian institutions—Commerce—National Church—Literature—Pskof and Vitaka.

NOVGOROD THE GREAT—STRUGGLES WITH THE PRINCES.

NOVGOROD has been, from the most remote antiquity, the political centre of the Russia of the North-west. The origin of the Slavs of the Ilmen, who laid her foundations, is still uncertain. Some learned Russians, such as M. Kostomarof, suppose them to belong to the Slavs of the South, others to the Slavs of the Baltic; others, again, like M. Bielaef and M. Ilovaïski, make them a branch of the Krivitch or Smolensk Slavs. We find the Novgorodians, at the opening of Russian history, at the head of the confederation of tribes which first expelled and then recalled the Varangians to reign over Russia.

Novgorod, from very ancient times, was divided into two parts, separated by the course of the Volkhof, which rises in lake Ilmen and falls into the Ladoga. On the right bank was the *side of Saint Sophia,* where Iaroslaf the Great built his celebrated cathedral; where the Novgorod kremlin was situated, enclosing both the palaces of the Archbishop and the prince; and where the famous Russian monument was consecrated in 1862. On the left bank, the *side of commerce,* with its *Court of Iaroslaf;* the bridge which joins the two halves of the city is celebrated in the annals of Novgorod. The side of Saint Sophia includes the Nerevian quarter as well as those of "beyond the city," and of the potters (*Nerevski, Zagorodni, Gontcharni*). The side of commerce comprised the quarters of the *carpenters* and *Slavs.* Ancient documents also speak of a *Prussian* (Lithuanian) quarter. Some of these names seem to indicate that many races have concurred, as in ancient Rome, to form the city of Novgorod. Gilbert of Lannoy, who visited the republic about 1413, has left us this description of it: "Novgorod is a prodigiously large town situated in a beautiful plain, in the midst of vast forests. The soil is low, subject to inundations, marshy in places. The town is surrounded by imperfect ramparts, formed of gabions; the towers are of stone." Portions of these ramparts still exist, and allow us to form an idea of the immense extent of the ancient city. The kremlin forms its acropolis. The cathedral has preserved its frescoes of the 12th century, the pillars painted with images of saints on a golden ground, the imposing figure of Christ on the cupola, the banner of the Virgin, which was to revive the courage of the besieged on the ramparts: the tombs of Saint Vladimir Iaroslavitch, of the Archbishop Nikita, by whose prayers a fire was extinguished, of Mstislaf the Brave, the devoted defender of Novgorod, and of many other saints and illustrious people. Without counting the tributary cities of Novgorod, such as Pskof, Ladoga, Izborsk, Veliki Louki, Staraia Roussa (Old Russia), Torjok, Biejitchi, her primitive territory (the " ager Romanus " of the republic) was divided into five *fifths* (*piatines*), the *Vodskaïa*, the *Chelonskaïa*, the *Obonejs* kaïa the *Biejetskaïa*, and the *Dereveksaïa*, which included the land to the south of the lakes Ladoga and Onega. Her conquests formed five bailiwicks or *volosts* occupying the whole of Northern Russia, and extending as far as Siberia. These bailiwicks were the *Zavolotchié* between the Onega and the Mezen; the *Tré*, or Russian Lapland; *Permia*, on the Upper Kama; *Petchora*, on the river of the same name; and *Iougria*, on the other side of the Oural mountains. To these we must add Ingria, Carelia, and part of Livonia and Esthonia.

Novgorod, which had summoned the Varangian princes, was too powerful, with her 100,000 inhabitants and 300,000 subjects, to allow herself to be tyrannized over. An ancient tradition speaks vaguely of a revolt against Rurik the Old under the hero Vadim. Sviatoslaf, the conqueror of the Bulgaria of the Danube, undertook to govern her by mere agents, but Novgorod insisted on having one of his sons for her prince. "If you do not come to reign over us," said the citizens, "we shall know how to find ourselves other princes." Iaroslaf the Great, as a reward for their devotion, accorded them immense privileges, of which no record can be found, but which are constantly invoked by the Novgorodians, as were the true or false charters of Charles the Great by the German cities. These republicans could not exist without a prince, but they rarely kept one long. The assembly of the citizens, the *vetché*, convoked by the bell in the Court of Iaroslaf, was the real sovereign. The republic called herself " *My Lord Novgorod the Great* " (Gospodine Velikii Novgorod). "Who can equal God and the great Novgorod?" was a popular saying. From the distance of the city from the Russia of the Dnieper, and her position towards the Baltic and Western Europe, she took little part in the civil wars of which Kief was the object and the centre. She profited by this in a certain sense; for in the midst of the strifes of princes and of frequent changes in the grand principality, no sovereign was strong enough to give her a master. She could choose between princes of the rival families. She could impose conditions on him whom she chose to reign over her. If discontented with his management, she expelled the prince and his band of *antrustions*. According to the accustomed formula, "she made a reverence, and showed him the way" to leave Novgorod. Sometimes, to hinder his evil designs, she kept him prisoner in the archbishop's palace, and it was left to his successor to set him at liberty. Often a revolution was accompanied by a general pillage of the partisans of the fallen prince, even by *noyades* in the Volkhof. A grand Prince of Kief, Sviatopolk, wished to force his son on them. "Send him here," said the Novgorodians, "if he has a spare head." The princes themselves contributed to the frequent changes of reign. They only felt themselves half-rulers in Novgorod, so they accepted any other appanage with joy. Thus, in 1132, Vsevolod Gabriel abandoned Novgorod to reign at Peréiaslavl. When his hopes of Kief were crushed, and he wished to return to Novgorod, the citizens rejected him. "You have forgotten your oath to die with us, you have sought another principality; go where you will." Presently they thought better of it, and took him back. Four years afterwards he was again obliged to fly. In a great *vetché*, to which the citizens of Pskof and Ladoga were summoned, they solemnly condemned the exile, after reading the heads of very characteristic accusations: "He took no care of the poorer people; he desired to establish himself at Peréiaslavl: at the battle of Mount Idanof, against the men of Souzdal, he and his *droujina* were the first to leave the battle-field; he was fickle in the quarrels of the princes, sometimes uniting with the Prince of Tchernigof, sometimes with the opposite party."

The power of a prince of Novgorod rested not only on his *droujina*, which always followed his fortunes, and on his family relations with this or that powerful principality, but also on a party formed for him in the heart of the republic. It was when the opposing party grew too strong that he was dethroned, and popular vengeance exercised on his adherents. Novgorod being above all a great commercial city, her divisions were frequently caused by diverging economic interests. Among the citizens, some were occupied in trade with the Volga and the East, others with the Dnieper and Greece. The former naturally sought the alliance of the princes of Souzdal, masters of the great Oriental artery; the latter that of the princes of Kief or Tchernigof, masters of the road to the south. Each of the two parties tried to establish a prince of the family whose protection they sought. If he fell, yet succeeded in escaping from the town, he tried to regain his throne by the arms of his family, or to instal himself and his *droujina* either at Pskof, like Vsevolod-Gabriel, who became prince of that town, or at Torjok, like Iaroslaf of Souzdal, and thence blockaded and starved the great city. The prince of Souzdal was soon the most formidable neighbor of Novgorod. We have seen that Andrew Bogolioubski sent an army against it, then that his nephew Iaroslaf besieged his ancient subjects till Mstislaf the Bold freed them by the battle of Lipetsk (1216). He was the son of Mstislaf the Brave, who had defended them against Vsevolod Big-Nest, and against Souzdal and the Tchouds. The remains of "the Brave" rest at Saint Sophia, in a bronze sarcophagus. His son, "the Bold," was of far too restless a nature to leave his bones also at Novgorod. He reduced the principality to order, and then assembled the citizens in the Court of Iaroslaf, and said to them, "I salute Saint Sophia, the tomb of my father, and you. Novgorodians, I am going to reconquer Galitch from the strangers, but I shall never forget you. I hope I may lie by the tomb of my father, in Saint Sophia." The Novgorodians in vain entreated him to stay (1218). We have seen him use his last armies in the troubles of the South-east, and die Prince of Galitch.

After his departure, the republic summoned his nephew, Sviatoslaf, to the throne; but he could not come to terms with magistrates and a populace equally turbulent. The *possadnik*, Tverdislaf, caused one of the boyards of Novgorod to be arrested. This was the signal for a general rising; some took the part of the boyard, others that of the possadnik. During eight days the bell of the kremlin sounded. Finally both factions buckled on their cuirasses and drew their swords. Tverdislaf raised his eyes to Saint Sophia, and cried, "I shall fall first in the battle, or God will justify me by giving the victory to my brothers." Ten men only perished in this skirmish, and then peace was reestablished. The prince, who accused Tverdislaf of being the cause of the trouble, demanded that he should be deposed. The *vetché* inquired what crime he had committed. "None," replied the prince, "but it is my will." "I am satisfied," exclaimed the possadnik, "as they do not accuse me of any fault; as to you, my brothers, you can dispose alike of possadniks and

NOVGOROD

Russia, Vol. 2 p. 6.

princes." The assembly then gave their decision. " Prince, as you do not accuse the possadnik of any fault, remember that you have sworn to depose no magistrate without trial. He will remain our possadnik—we will not deliver him to you." On this Sviatoslaf quitted Novgorod (1219). He was replaced by Vsevolod, one of his brothers, who was expelled two years later (1221).

The Souzdalian party having made some progress, they recalled the same Iaroslaf who was beaten at Lipetsk, but the princes of Souzdal were too absolute in their ideas to be able to agree with the Novgorodians. Iaroslaf was again put to flight, and replaced by Vsevolod of Smolensk, who was expelled in his turn. The Grand Prince of Souzdal now interposed, levied a contribution on Novgorod, and a prince of Tchernigof was imposed on them, who hastened in 1225 to return to the south of Russia. In seven years the Novgorodians had five times changed their rulers. Iaroslaf himself came back for a third and even a fourth time. A famine so much reduced the Novgorodians that 42,000 corpses were buried in two cemeteries alone. These proud citizens implored strangers to take them as slaves for the price of a morsel of bread. The same year a fire destroyed the whole of one quarter of Novgorod. These calamities subdued their turbulence. Iaroslaf succeeded in governing them despotically till he was called to fill the throne of the Grand Prince (1236). He left them, as their prince, his son Alexander Nevski.

NOVGORODIAN INSTITUTIONS—COMMERCE—THE NATIONAL
CHURCH—LITERATURE.

From the fact that no dynasty of princes could establish itself at Novgorod, that no princely band could take a place among the native aristocracy, it follows that the republic kept her ancient liberties and customs intact under the short reigns of her rulers. In all Russian cities, it is true, the *country* existed side by side with the prince and *boyards*, the assembly of citizens side by side with the prince's men, and the native *militia* side by side with the foreign *droujina*; but at Novgorod, the *country*, the *vetché*, and the municipal *militia* had retained more vigor than elsewhere. The town was more powerful than the prince, who reigned by virtue of a constitution, traces of which may be observed, no doubt, in other regions of Russia, but which is found in its original form at Novgorod alone. Each **new monarch was compelled to take an oath, by which he bound** himself to observe the laws and privileges of Iaroslaf the Great. This constitution, like the *pacta conventa* of Poland, signified distrust, and was intended to limit the power of the prince and his men. The revenues to which he had a right, and which formed his civil list, were carefully limited, as also were his judicial and political functions. He levied tribute on certain *volosts*, and was entitled to the *vira* (German *Wergeld*) as well as to certain fines. In some bailiwicks he had his own lieutenant, and Novgorod had hers. He could not execute justice without help of the possadnik, nor upset any judgment; nor, above all, take the suit beyond Novgorod. This was what the Novgorodians feared most, and with reason. The day when the people of Novgorod bethought themselves of appealing to the tribunal of the Grand Prince of Moscow, was fatal to the independence of the republic. In the conflicts between the men of the prince and those of the city, a mixed court delivered judgment. The prince, no more than his men, could acquire villages in the territory of Novgorod, nor create colonies. He was forbidden to hunt in the woods of Staraïa Roussa except in the autumn, and had to reap his harvests at a specified season. Though they thus mistrusted their prince, the Novgorodians had need of him to moderate the ancient Slav anarchy. As in the days of Rurik, "family armed itself against family, and there was no justice." In Novgorod the *vetché* had more extensive powers, and acted more regularly than in the other Russian cities. It was the *vetché* which nominated and expelled princes, imprisoned them in the archiepiscopal palace, and formally accused them; elected and deposed the archbishops, decided peace and war, judged the State criminals. According to the old Slav custom (preserved in Poland till the fall of the republic), the decisions were always made, not by a majority, but by unanimity of voices. It was a kind of *liberum veto*. The majority had the resource of drowning the minority in the Volkhof. The prince as well as the possadnik, the boyards as well as the people, had the right of convoking the *vetché*. It met sometimes in the Court of Iaroslaf, sometimes in Saint Sophia's. As Poland had her confederations, her "diets under the shield," Novgorod occasionally saw on the banks of the Volkhof two rival and hostile *vetchés*, which often came to blows on the bridge. Before being submitted to the general assembly, the questions were sometimes deliberated in a smaller council, composed of notable citizens, of acting or past magistrates.

The chief Novgorodian magistrates were: 1. The *possadnik* called by contemporary German writers the *burgomaster*, who was changed nearly as often as the prince. The possadnik was chosen from some of the influential families, one of which alone gave a dozen possadniks to Novgorod. The first magistrate was charged to defend civic privileges, and shared with the prince the judicial power and the right of distributing the taxes. He governed the city, commanded her army, directed her diplomacy, sealed the acts with her seal. 2. The *tysatski* (from *tysatch*, thousand) bears in German documents the title of *dux* or *herzog*; he was therefore a military chief, a chiliarch who had the centurions of the town militia under his orders. He had a special tribunal, and seems to have been specially entrusted with the defence of the rights of the people, thus recalling the Roman tribunes. 3. Besides the *centurions* there was a *starost*, a sort of district mayor, for each quarter of the town.

The chief document of the Novgorodian law is the *Letter of Justice* (*Soudnaïa Gramota*), of which the definite publication may be placed at 1471. It contains the same principles as the *Rousskaïa Pravda* of Iaroslaf the Great. As in all the early Germanic and Scandinavian laws, we find the right of private revenge, the fixed price of blood, the "boot" or fine for injury inflicted, the oath admitted as evidence, the judgment of God, the judicial duel, which was still resorted to by Novgorod even after her decadence, in the 16th century. We also find records of corporal punishments. The thief was to be branded; on the second relapse into crime, he was to be hung. Territorial property acquires a greater importance, and, a sure evidence of Muscovite influence, a second court of appeal is admitted—the appeal to the tribunal of the Grand Prince.

From a social point of view, the constitution of Novgorod presents other analogies with the constitution of Poland. Great inequality then existed between the different classes of society. An aristocracy of boyards had ultimately formed itself, whose intestine quarrels agitated the town. Below the boyards came the *dieti boyarskië*, a kind of inferior nobility; then the different classes of citizens, the merchantmen, the *black people*, and the *smerdes* or peasants. The merchants formed an association of their own, a sort of *guild*, round the Church of Saint John. Military societies also existed, bands of independent adventurers or *droujinas* of some boyard who, impelled by hunger or a restless spirit, sought adventures afar on the great rivers of Northern Russia, pillaging alike friends and enemies, or establishing military colonies in the midst of Tchoud or Finnish tribes.

The soil of Novgorod was sandy, marshy, and unproductive: hence the famines and pestilences that so often depopulated the country. Novgorod was forced to extend itself in order to live; she became therefore a commercial and colonizing city. In the

10th century, Constantine relates how the Slavs left *Nemogard* (Novgorod), descended the Dnieper by *Milinisca* (Smolensk), *Telioutza* (Loubetch), Tchernigof, Vychegord, Kief and Vititchevo; crossed the cataracts of the Dnieper, passed the naval stations of Saint Gregory and Saint Etherius, at the mouth of the river, and spread themselves over all the shores of the Greek empire. The Oriental coins and jewels found in the *kourgans* of the Ilmen show that the Novgorodians had an early and extensive commerce with the East. We see them exchange iron and weapons for the precious metals found by the Iougrians in the mines of the Ourals. They traded with the Baltic Slavs; and when the latter lost their independence, and a flourishing centre, Wisby, was formed in the Isle of Gothland, Novgorod turned to this side also. In the 12th century there was a Gothic trading *dépôt* and a Varangian Church at Novgorod, and a Novgorodian Church in Gothland. When the Germans began to dispute the commerce of the Baltic with the Scandinavians, Novgorod became the seat of a German *dépôt*, which ended by absorbing the Gothic one. When the Hanseatic League became the mistress of the North, we find the Germans established not only at Novgorod, but at Pskof and Ladoga, at all the mouths of the network of Novgorodian lakes. There they obtained considerable privileges, even the right to acquire pastureland. They were masters, and at home in their fortified *dépôts*, in their stockade of thick planks, where no Russian had the right to penetrate without their leave. This German trading company was governed by the most narrow and exclusive ideas. No Russian was allowed to belong to the company, nor to carry the wares of a German, an Englishman, a Walloon or a Fleming. The company only authorized a wholesale commerce, and, to maintain her goods at a high price, she forbade imports beyond a certain amount. "In a word," says a German writer, "during three centuries the Hanseatic League concentrated in her own hands all the external commerce of Northern Russia. If we inquire what profit or loss she has brought this country, we must recognize that, thanks to her, Novgorod and Pskof were deprived of a free commerce with the West. Russia, in order to satisfy the first wants of civilization, fell into a complete independence. She was abandoned to the good pleasure and pitiless egotism of the German merchants." (Riesenkampf, 'Der deutsche Hof.')

The ecclesiastical constitution of Russia presents a special character. In the rest of Russia the clergy was Russian-orthodox. At Novgorod it was Novgorodian before everything. It was only in the 12th century that the Slavs of Ilmen, who had been the last to be converted, could have an archbishop that was neither Greek nor Kievian, but of their own race. From that time the archbishop was elected by the citizens, by the *vetché*. Without waiting for the metropolitan to be invested at Kief, he was at once installed in his episcopal palace. He was one of the great personages, the first dignitary of the republic. In public acts his name was placed before the others. "With the blessing of Archbishop Moses," says one letter-patent; "possadnik Daniel and tysatski Abraham salute you." He had a superiority over the prince on the ground of being a native of the country, whilst the descendant of Rurik was a foreigner. In return, the revenues of the archbishop, the treasures of Saint Sophia, were at the service of the republic. In the 14th century we find an archbishop building at his own expense a kremlin of stone. In the 15th century, the riches of the cathedral were employed to ransom the Russian prisoners captured by the Lithuanians. The Church of Novgorod was essentially a national Church; the ecclesiastics took part in the temporal affairs, the laics in the spiritual. In the 14th century the *vetché* put to death the heretical *strigolniks*, proscribed ancient superstitions, and burnt the sorcerers. As Novgorod nominated her archbishop, she could also depose him. The orthodox religion extended with the Novgorod colonization among the Finnish tribes. In face of the Finns, the interests of the Church and the Republic were identical. It was religion that contributed to the splendor of the city, and that specially profited by her wealth. Novgorod was full of churches and monasteries, founded by the piety of private individuals. Novgorod, which had shaken off the political supremacy of Kief, wished also to free herself from its religious domination, and no longer to be obliged to seek on the Dnieper the investiture of her archbishop, but to make him an independent metropolitan. She failed. When Moscow became of importance, she threatened not only the political, but the religious supremacy of Novgorod. Religion was, in the hands of the Muscovite princes, an instrument of government. The Novgorodian prelate always made common cause with his fellow-citizens, and endured with them their master's bursts of anger.

The literature of Novgorod was as national as the Church herself. The pious chronicles of the Novgorodian convents shared all the quarrels and all the passions of their fellow-citizens. "Even their style," said M. Bestoujef, "reflects vividly the active, business-like character of the Novgorodians. It is short, and sparing of words; but their narratives embrace more completely than those of other Russian countries all the phases of actual life. They are the historians not merely of the princes and boyards, but of the whole city. The lives of the saints are the lives of Novgorodian saints ; the miracles they relate are to the glory of the city. They tell you, for example, that Christ appeared to the artist charged with the paintings under the dome of Saint Sophia, and said to him : 'Do not represent me with my hand extended for blessing, but with my hand closed because in it I hold Novgorod; and when it is opened it will be the end of the city.' " The tale of the panic excited among the soldiers of Andrew Bogolioubski by the image of the Virgin wounded by a Souzdalian arrow, was spread abroad. Novgorod has her own cycle of epic songs, of *bylinas*. Her heroes are not those of the Kievian epopee. There is Vassili Bouslaévitch, the bold boyard, who with his faithful droujina stood up to his knees in blood on the bridge of the Volkhof, holding in check all the mougiks of Novgorod, whom he had defied to combat. Vassili Bouslaévitch is the true type of these proud adventurers, who knew neither friend nor enemy—a true Novgorodian oligarch, a hero of civil war. Still more popular was Sadko, the rich merchant, a kind of Novgorodian Sindbad or Ulysses, a worthy representative of a people of merchants and adventurers, who sought his fortunes on the waves. A tempest rose, and men drew lots to decide who should be sacrificed to the wrath of the gods. Sadko threw a little wooden ring into the water, the others flung in iron rings : O prodigy ! the others swam, his sank. He obeyed his destiny, and threw himself into the waves, but he was received in the palace of the king of the sea, who tested him in various ways, and wished him to marry his daughter. Then suddenly Sadko found himself on the shore with great treasures, but what were these compared to the treasures of the city ? "They see that I am a rich merchant of Novgorod, but Novgorod is still more rich than I."*

PSKOF AND VIATKA.

Of all the towns subject to Novgorod, Pskof was the most important. On the point formed by the junction of the Pskova and the Velikaïa rises her kremlin, with its crumbling ramparts, its ruined gates and towers. These once famous walls are to-day a mass of ruins, and the street-boys amuse themselves by throwing stones in the Pskova to frighten the laundresses. Pskof is only a poor little place with 10,000 souls. There only

---

* A. Rambaud, ' La Russie épique,' p. 130.

remains of her past splendor the cathedral of the Trinity at one end of the kremlin. There rest in metal coffins the bones of the best-loved princes, Vsevolod-Gabriel and Dovmont, a converted Lithuanian who came in the 13th century to defend the republic against his own compatriots. This old town has preserved many churches and monasteries. The distant view of Pskof is beautiful, and on fête-days the dead city seems to awake at the chimes of her innumerable bells, which sound as loudly as in the days of her glorious past.

Nestor makes Pskof the native land of Saint Olga. The sum of his history is nothing more than these two facts: first, the struggle against the Tchouds, and, later, against the Germans of Livonia; second, the efforts of Novgorod to secure her freedom. The independence of the city was ultimately secured by her wealth and her commerce. The first prince who ruled her as a separate state, Vsevolod-Gabriel, was expelled by his subjects, and therefore was welcomed with the greater eagerness by the Pskovians. When the Souzdalian party ruled at Novgorod, it was generally the contrary party that triumphed in Pskof. About 1214 the little republic contracted an offensive and defensive alliance with the Germans; she undertook to help them against the Lithuanians, and they were to support her against Novgorod. This was playing rather a dangerous game. In 1240, one Tverdillo delivered up Pskof to the Livonian knights; she did not free herself till 1242. From this moment Pskof ceased to mix in the civil wars of Novgorod. She had enough to do with her own affairs and her struggle against the Germans, Swedes, and Lithuanians. She also called herself "My Lord Pskof the Great;" but it was only in 1348 that the Novgorodians, needing her help against Magnus, king of Sweden, formally recognized her independence, by the treaty of Bolstof, and concluded with her a bond of fraternal friendship. Novgorod became the elder sister, and Pskof the younger. The organization of Pskof is almost that of her ancient metropolis. We again find the prince, the *vetché*, the division into quarters, up to the number of six, each one having its *starost*.

In the 12th century a new Novgorodian colony was formed between the Kama and the Viatka, which remained a republic till the end of the 15th century. "This distant country," says M. Bestoujef-Rioumine, "is still quite Novgorodian. When the traveller has passed the Viatka, he meets with a peculiar mode of constructing the huts. There are no longer whole lines of *isbas* joined one to the other, as on this side of the river, but there is a high house, where the court, rooms, and offices are surrounded by a rampart of pales, and united under the same roof; in a word, it was a Novgorodian house. You hear the Novgorodian patois, you see the Novgorodian cap. It is the Novgorod colonization still living." In 1174 some adventurers from the Great Republic came from the Kama to the Viatka, and advanced from east to west, and founded a colony on this river, which is to-day the village of Nikoulitsyne. Another band defeated the Tcheremisses, and on their territory raised Kochkarof, at present called Kotelnitch. Then the two bands reunited, and penetrated into the Votiak country. On the right bank of the Viatka, on the summit of a high mountain, they perceived a city surrounded by a rampart and a ditch, which contained one of the sanctuaries of the people. As pious as the companions of Cortez and Pizarro, the Russian adventurers prepared themselves for the assault by a fast of several days, then invoked Saints Boris and Gleb, and captured the town. Next, at the mouth of the Khlynovitsa, in the Viatka, not very far off, they built the city of Khlynof, which became, under the name of Viatka, the capital of all their colonies. She had no walls, but the houses, built close together, formed an unbroken rampart against the enemy, a wall and defence. At the news of this success, other colonists flocked from Novgorod and the forests of the north, and founded other centres of population. These bold pioneers had more than once to re-unite, sometimes against the aboriginal Finns or the Tatar invaders, sometimes against the pretensions of Novgorod, or the Grand Prince of Moscow. We find among them, as in the metropolis, boyards, merchants, and citizens. They had voïevodes or *atamans* for their military chiefs. Their spirit of religious independence equalled their political independence. Jonas, metropolitan of Moscow, writes angrily about the indocility of their clergy, and avenges himself by blaming their morals. "Your spiritual sons," he wrote to the priests of Viatka, "live contrary to the law. They have five, six, or even seven wives. And you dare to bless these marriages!"

CHAPTER IX.

THE LIVONIAN KNIGHTS: CONQUEST OF THE BALTIC PROVINCES
BY THE GERMANS.

Conversion of Livonia—Rise of the Livonian knights: union with the
Teutonic knights.

THREE new races of men, three invasions (from the 12th to the 13th century), were to modify the historical development of the different parts of Slavonia ; the Russia of the north-west was to make acquaintance with the Germans, Russia of the east and south with the Tatar-Mongols, Russia of the west with the Lithuanians.

Part of the Tchoud or Lett tribes of the Baltic were considered by the Russia' princes and republics of the north-west as their subjects or tributaries. If the Danish Cnut the Great had conquered Esthonia, Iaroslaf the Great had founded Iourief (Dorpat) on the Embach which falls into the Peïpus, and then separated the Danish and Russian dominions. It separates to-day the country of the Finns into two peoples speaking different dialects, the dialect of Revel and that of Dorpat. A Mstislaf, son of Vladimir Monomachus, had conquered the city of Odenpaeh (Finnish *bear's head*) from the Tchouds. In the Lett country the princes of Polotsk had captured the native fortresses of Gersike and Kokenhausen on the Dwina, and extended their influence along this river to Thoreïda and Ascheraden.

With the German merchants Latin missionaries soon began to make their appearance on the Baltic. The monk Meinhard, sent by the Archbishop of Bremen, converted the Livonians, and was created bishop of Livonia. That which the Germans really brought, under the cloak of Christianity, to the Lett and descendants of the Tchoud hero Kalevy, and to many other Slav, Lithuanian, or Finnish tribes, now extinct, was the ruin of their national independence and servitude. The German merchant and the German missionary appeared almost at the same time on the Dwina. The apostle Meinhard built a church at Uexküll, and a fortress round the church (1187). From this fatal day these brave tribes lost their lands and their liberty. The Livonians soon saw to what this mission tended. They rose against the missionaries, and in 1198 the second bishop of Livonia perished in battle. The natives returned to their gods, and plunged in the Dwina to wash off the baptism they had received, and to send it back to Germany. Then Innocent III. preached a crusade against them, and Albert of Buxhœwden (1198–1229), their third bishop and the true founder of the German rule in Livonia, entered the Dwina with a fleet of twenty-three ships, and built the town of Riga, which he made his capital (1200). The following year he installed the Order of the Brothers of the Army of Christ, or the Sword-bearers, to whom the Pope gave the statutes of the Templars. They wore a white mantle, with a red cross on the shoulders. The greater number were natives of Westphalia and Saxony. Vinno de Rohrbach was their first grand master. The Livonians, after having implored the help of the princes of Polotsk, marched on Riga, and suffered an entire defeat (1206). The prince of Polotsk in his turn besieged the city during the absence of the bishop, but it was saved by the arrival of a German flotilla.

Three causes were particularly favorable to the success of the knights of the sword, namely: the weakness of the princes of Polotsk, the intestine quarrels of Novgorod, which prevented her from watching over Russian interests, and the divisions among the natives who had not yet been able to raise their minds from the conception of the tribe to that of the nation. The knights were likewise far superior in their arms and tactics. The German fortresses were solidly built in cemented stone, while those of the natives were ramparts of earth, wood, or loose stones. In vain they tried to drag down with ropes the palisades of the German ramparts. The Sword-bearers afterwards undertook a series of campaigns against the Livonians and the Semigalli of the Dwina, and against the Tchouds of the north and the Letts of the south-east. If a tribe declined baptism and obedience, it was delivered a prey to fire and sword; when it submitted, hostages were taken, and castles built on its territory, these being often merely German reconstructions of the ancient native fortresses.

It was in this manner that Riga, Kirchholm, Uexküll, Lennewarden, Ascheraden, and Kreuzburg were built on the Dwina; Neuhausen, near the Peïpus, Wolmar, Wenden, Segevold, and Kremon on the Aa; Fellin and Weissenstein among the Northern Tchouds. The strangers managed to take Kokenhausen and Gersike from the princes of Polotsk, Odenpaeh and

Dorpat from the Novgorodians; Pskof was threatened. In the north Kolyvan was bought from the king of Denmark, after the fiercest disputes. Under its rock lies Kolyvan, a Titan hero of Finnish mythology. The town is now called Revel.

The conquered country was divided into fiefs, some of which belonged to the Order by whom they were distributed among the knights, the rest were at the disposal of the archbishop, who enfeoffed his own men. The new towns received the constitution of the merchant cities of Lubeck, Bremen, or Hamburg. Riga was the most powerful of them. The archbishop of Riga, the chapter, the town and the grand master of the Order, often quarrelled over their respective rights. Their divisions were one day to bring about the decline of the institution.

About 1225 another military fraternity was established among the Prussian Lithuanians, the *Teutonic Order*, which, on the remains of the subject pagan tribes, raised Thorn, Marienberg, Elbing and Kœnigsberg. The Teutons of Prussia and the knights of Livonia were certain to be friendly; the black cross fraternized with the red, and, in 1237, the two orders united into one association. The Teutonic *landmeister*, Hermann de Balk, became *landmeister* of Livonia. The grand master of the Teutonic Order took precedence of all the landmeisters. Strengthened by this alliance, the "brothers of the army of Christ" were able to impose the most cruel servitude on the aboriginal Letts, Livonians, and Finns. These brave barbarians soon became peasants attached to the glebe. The German nobility restored them their liberty at the beginning of this century, but it did not restore them their lands.

The conquering and conquered races are always separate. To the Tchoud, the word *Saxa* (Saxon, German) always signifies the *master*. A song of the Tchoud country of Pskof, called *The days of Slavery*, deplores the time when "the banners of the strangers waved, when the intruders made us slaves, enchained us as the serfs of tyrants, forced us to be their servants. Brother, what can I sing? Sadly sounds the song of tears. The lot of the slave is too hard." Another song of Wiesland (Esthonia) is entitled *The Days of the Past*. "The past, that was the time of massacre, a long time of suffering . . . Destroying fiends were unchained against us. The priests strangled us with their rosaries, the greedy knights plundered us, troops of brigands ravaged us, armed murderers cut us in pieces. The *father of the cross* stole our riches, stole the treasure from the hiding-place, attacked the tree, the sacred tree, polluted the waters and the fountain of salvation. The axe smote on the oak of Tara, the woful hatchet on the tree of Kero." (Richter, 'Geschichte der deutschen Ostseeprovinzen.')

In the *Kalevy-poeg*, or "the son of Kalev," the national poem of the Tchoud-Esthonians, the hero, who is the personification of the race, displays in his various adventures a wonderful Titanic force. He swam the Gulf of Finland, he rooted up oak-trees to make his clubs; with his horse and his colossal harrow he ploughed up the land of Esthonia; he exterminated the bears and the beasts of prey; he conquered the magician of Finland, and the genii of the caves; he descended into hell and fought with Sarvig the horned; he sailed away to explore the utmost limits of the world, and when the hot breath of the spirits of the north burnt up his wooden vessel, he disembarked in a vessel of silver with fittings of metal. He braved whirlwinds at sea; discovered the isle of flame (which is perhaps Iceland, where the three volcanoes vomit forth fire), of smoke, and boiling water; he encountered a gigantic woman who plucked up several sailors with the grass for the kine, as if the men had been insects; he rallied the courage of his pilot, horror-stricken by the flames with which the spirits of the north filled heaven, and said to him, "Let them send their darts of fire, they will only lighten us on our way, since the daylight would not accompany us, and the sun has long since gone to rest." He fought with men whose bodies were like dogs (possibly the Esquimaux of Greenland), and only retraced his steps because a magician assured him "that the wall of the world's end was still far off." It is at the close of the poem, when he is told that the men of iron (*raudamched* in Tchoud) have landed, that his unconquerable heart is troubled. The iron cannot penetrate their armor, nor the axe break it. In vain he seeks counsel at the tomb of his father; the tomb is silent, "the leaves murmur plaintively, the winds sigh drearily, the dew itself is troubled, the eye of the clouds is wet;" all Esthonian nature shares in the sinister forebodings of the national hero. He raised, however, the battle-cry, and his warriors assembled on the Embach. Bloody is the battle! The Esthonians gain the victory, but what a victory! The bravest of them are dead, the two brothers of Kalevy-poeg perish, his charger is struck down by the axe of a stranger. The end of Esthonia, the age of slavery has arrived; it is time that Kalevy-poeg, the representative of the heroic age, should disappear; he who had vanquished the demon Sarvig, the sorcerers of Finland, and the spirits of the pole, could not subdue these men whom an unknown, irresistible force sustained, superior to that of the gods. Behold him, the captive of Mana, god of death, his wrist held fast in a rock, which is the gate of hell.

Long his sons trusted that Mana would give him back his liberty, and that once again the iron men would feel the weight of his arm; but, like King Arthur, he has never appeared, bringing to his people the liberty that the Germans have taken from them.

CHAPTER X.

THE TATAR MONGOLS. ENSLAVEMENT OF RUSSIA.

Origin and manners of the Mongols—Battles of the Kalka, of Riazan, of Kolomna, and of the Sit—Conquest of Russia—Alexander Nevski—The Mongol yoke—Influence of the Tatars on the Russian development.

ORIGIN AND MANNERS OF THE MONGOLS.

UP to this time the destinies of Russia had presented some analogy with those of the West. Slavonia, like Gaul, had received Roman civilization and Christianity from the South. The Northmen had brought her an organization which recalls that of the Germans; and under Iaroslaf, like the West under Charles the Great, she had enjoyed a certain semblance of unity, while she was afterwards dismembered and divided like France in feudal times. But in the 13th century, Russia suffered an unheard-of misfortune—she was invaded and subjugated by Asiatic hordes. This fatal event contributed quite as much as the disadvantage of the soil and the climate to retard her development by many centuries. "Nature," as M. Soloviaf says, "has been a step-mother to Russia;" fate was another step-mother.

"In those times," say the Russian chroniclers, "there came upon us for our sins, unknown nations. No one could tell their origin, whence they came, what religion they professed. God alone know who they were, God and perhaps wise men learned in books." When we think of the horror of the whole of Europe at the arrival of the Mongols, and the anguish of a Frederick, of a Saint Louis, an Innocent IV., we may imagine the terror of the Russians. They bore the first shock of those mysterious foemen, who were, so the people whispered, Gog and Magog, who "were to come at the end of the world, when Antichrist is to destroy everything." (Joinville.)

The *Ta-ta* or *Tatars* seem to have been a tribe of the great Mongol race, living at the foot of the Altai, who in spite of their long-continued discords frequently found means to lay waste China by their invasions. The portrait drawn of them recalls in many ways those already traced by Chinese, Latin, and Greek authors, of the Huns, the Avars, and other nomad peoples of former invasions. "The *Ta-tzis* or the *Das*," says a Chinese writer of the 13th century, "occupy themselves exclusively with their flocks; they go wandering ceaselessly from pasture to pasture, from river to river. They are ignorant of the nature of a town or a wall. They are unacquainted with writing and books; their treaties are concluded orally. From infancy they are accustomed to ride, to aim their arrows at rats and birds, and thus acquire the courage essential to their life of wars and rapine. They have neither religious ceremonies nor judicial institutions. From the prince to the lowest among the people all are nourished by the flesh of the animals whose skin they use for clothing. The strongest among them have the largest and fattest morsels at feasts; the old men are put off with the fragments that are left. They respect nothing but strength and bravery; age and weakness are condemned. When the father dies, the son marries his youngest wives." A Mussulman writer adds, that they adore the sun, and practice polygamy and the community of wives. This pastoral people did not take an interest in any phenomenon of nature except the growth of grass. The names they gave to their months were suggested by the different aspects of the prairie. Born horsemen, they had no infantry in war. They were ignorant of the art of sieges. "But," says a Chinese author, "when they wish to take a town, they fall on the suburban villages. Each leader seizes ten men, and every prisoner is forced to carry a certain quantity of wood, stones, and other materials. They use these for filling up fosses, or digging trenches. In the capture of a town, the loss of 10,000 men was thought nothing. No place could resist them. After a siege, all the population was massacred, without distinction of old or young, rich or poor, beautiful or ugly, those who resisted or those who yielded; no distinguished person escaped death, if a defence was attempted."

It was these rough tribes that Temoutchine or Genghis-Khan (1154–1227) succeeded in uniting into one nation after forty years of obscure struggles. Then in a general congress of their princes he proclaimed himself emperor, and declared that, as there was only one sun in heaven, there ought only to be one emperor on the earth. At the head of their forces he conquered Mantchouria, the kingdom of Tangout, Northern China, Turkestan, and Great Bokhara, which never recovered this disaster, and the plains of Western Asia as far as the Crimea. When he died, he left to be divided between his **four sons** the largest empire that ever existed.

It was during his conquest of Bokhara that his lieutenants Tchepe and Souboudaï-bagadour subdued in their passage a multitude of Turkish peoples, passed the Caspian by its southern shore, invaded Georgia and the Caucasus, and in the southern steppes of Russia came in contact with the Polovtsi.

BATTLES OF THE KALKA, OF RIAZAN, OF KOLOMNA, AND OF THE SIT—CONQUEST OF RUSSIA.

The hereditary enemies of the Russians proper, the Polovsti, asked the Christian princes for help against these Mongols and Turks, who were their brothers by a common origin. "They have taken our country," said they to the descendants of Saint Vladimir; "to-morrow they will take yours." Mstislaf the Bold, then prince of Galitch, persuaded all the dynasties of Southern Russia to take up arms against the Tatars: his nephew Danial, prince of Volhynia, Mstislaf Romanovitch, Grand Prince of Kief, Oleg of Koursk, Mstislaf of Tchernigof, Vladimir of Smolensk, Vsevolod for a short time prince of Novgorod, responded to his appeal. To cement his alliance with the Russians, Basti, khan of the Polovsti, embraced orthodoxy. The Russian army had already arrived on the Lower Dnieper, when the Tatar ambassadors made their appearance. "We have come by God's command against our slaves and grooms, the accursed Polovtsi. Be at peace with us; we have no quarrel with you." The Russians, with the promptitude and thoughtlessness that characterized the men of that time, put the ambassadors to death. They then went further into the steppe, and encountered the Asiatic hordes on the Kalka, a small river running into the Sea of Azof. The Russian chivalry on this memorable day showed the same disordered, and the same ill-advised eagerness as the French chivalry at the opening of the English wars. Mstislaf the Bold, Daniel of Galitch, and Oleg of Koursk were the first to rush into the midst of the infidels, without waiting for the princes of Kief, and even without giving them warning, in. order to gain for themselves the honors of victory. In the middle of the combat, the Polovsti were seized with a panic and fell back on the Russian ranks, thus throwing them into disorder. The rout became general, and the leaders spurred on their steeds in hopes of reaching the Dnieper.

Six princes and seventy of the chief boyards or voïevodes remained on the field of battle. It was the Creçy and Poictiers of the Russian chivalry. Hardly a tenth of the army escaped; the Kievians alone left 10,000 dead. The Grand Prince of Kief, however, Mstislaf Romanovitch, still occupied a fortified camp on the banks of the Kalka. Abandoned by the rest of the army, he tried to defend himself. The Tatars offered to make terms ; he might retire on payment of a ransom for himself and his *droujina*. He capitulated, and the conditions were broken. His guard was massacred, and he and his two sons-in-law were stifled under planks. The Tatars held their festival over the inanimate bodies (1224).

After this thunderbolt, which struck terror into the whole of Russia, the Tatars paused and returned to the East. Nothing more was heard of them. Thirteen years passed, during which the princes reverted to their perpetual discords. Those in the north-east had given no help to the Russians of the Dnieper; perhaps the Grand Prince, George II. of Souzdal, may have rejoiced over the humiliation of the Kievians and Gallicians. The Mongols were forgotten ; the chronicles, however, are filled with fatal presages : in the midst of scarcity, famine and pestilence, of incendiaries in the towns and calamities of all sorts, they remark on the comet of 1224, the earthquake and eclipse of the sun of 1230.

The Tatars were busy finishing the conquest of China, but presently one of the sons of Genghis, Ougoudei or Oktaï, sent his nephew Bati to the West. As the reflux of the Polovtsi had announced the invasion of 1224, that of the Saxin nomads, related to the Khirghiz who took refuge on the lands of the Bulgarians of the Volga, warned men of a new irruption of the Tatars, and indicated its direction. It was no longer South Russia, but Souzdalian Russia that was threatened. In 1237 Bati conquered the Great City, capital of the half-civilized Bulgars, who were, like the Polovtsi, ancient enemies of Russia, and who were to be included in her ruin. Bolgary was given up to the flames, and her inhabitants were put to the sword. The Tatars next plunged into the deep forests of the Volga, and sent a sorcerer and two officers as envoys to the princes of Riazan. The three princes of Riazan, those of Pronsk, Kolomna, Moscow and Mourom, advanced to meet them. "If you want peace," said the Tatars, "give us the tenth of your goods." "When we are dead," replied the Russian princes, "you can have the whole." Though abandoned by the princes of Tchernigof and the Grand Prince George II., of whom they had implored help, the dynasty of Riazan accepted the unequal struggle. They were completely crushed ; nearly all their princes remained on the field of battle. Legend has embellished their fall. It is told how Feodor preferred to die rather than see his young wife, Euphrasia, the spoil of Bati ; and how, on learning his fate, she threw herself and her son from the window of the *terem*. Oleg the Handsome, found still alive on the battle-field, repelled the caresses, the attention, and religion of the Khan, and was cut in pieces. Riazan was immediately taken by assault, sacked, and burned. All the towns of the principality suffered the same fate.

It was now the turn of the Grand Prince, for the Russia of the North-east had not even the honor of falling in a great battle like the Russia of the South-west, united for once against the common enemy. The Souzdalian army, commanded by a son of George II., was beaten on the day of Kolomna, on the Oka. The Tatars burned Moscow, then besieged Vladimir on the Kliazma, which George II. had abandoned to seek for help in the North. His two sons were charged with the defence of the capital. Princes and boyards, feeling there was no alternative but death or servitude, prepared to die. The princesses and all the nobles prayed Bishop Metrophanes to give them the tonsure; and when the Tatars rushed into the town by all its gates, the vanquished retired into the cathedral, where they perished, men and women, in a general conflagration. Souzdal, Rostof, Iaroslavl, fourteen towns, a multitude of villages in the Grand Principality, were all given over to the flames (1238). The Tatars then went to seek the Grand Prince, who was encamped on the Sit, almost on the frontier of the possessions of Novgorod. George II. could neither avenge his people nor his family. After the battle, the bishop of Rostof found his headless corpse (1238). His nephew, Vassilko, who was taken prisoner, was stabbed for refusing to serve Bati. The immense Tatar army, after having sacked Tver, took Torjok; there "the Russian heads fell beneath the sword of the Tatars as grass beneath the scythe." The territory of Novgorod was invaded; the great republic trembled, but, the deep forests and the swollen rivers delayed Bati. The invading flood reached the Cross of Ignatius, about fifty miles from Novgorod, then returned to the South-east. On the way the small town of Kozelsk (near Kalouga) checked the Tatars for so long, and inflicted on them so much loss, that it was called by them the *wicked town*. Its population was exterminated, and the prince Vassili, still a child, was "drowned in blood."

The two following years (1239-1240) were spent by the Tatars in ravaging Southern Russia. They burnt Pereiaslaf, and Tchernigof, defended with desperation by its princes. Next Mangou, grandson of Genghis Khan, marched against the famous town of Kief, whose name resounded through the East, and in the books of the Arab writers. From the left bank of the Dnieper, the barbarian admired the great city on the heights of the right bank, towering over the wide river with her white walls and towers adorned by Byzantine artists, and innumerable churches with cupolas of gold and silver. Mangou proposed a capitulation to the Kievians; the fate of Riazan, of Tchernigof, of Vladimir, the capitals of powerful states, announced to them the lot that awaited them in case of refusal, yet the Kievians dared to massacre the envoys of the Khan. Michael, their Grand Prince, fled; his rival, Daniel of Galitch, did not care to remain. On hearing the report of Mangou, Bati came to assault Kief with the bulk of his army. The grinding of the wooden chariots, the bellowings of the buffaloes, the cries of the camels, the neighing of the horses, the howlings of the Tatars, rendered it impossible, says the annalist, to hear your own voice in the town. The Tatars as sailed the Polish Gate, and knocked down the walls with a battering-ram. "The Kievians, supported by the brave Dmitri, a Gallician boyard, defended the fallen ramparts till the end of the day, then retreated to the Church of the Dime, which they surrounded by a palisade. The last defenders of Kief found themselves grouped around the tomb of Iaroslaf. Next day they perished. The Khan gave the boyard his life, but, the 'Mother of Russian cities' was sacked. This third pillage was the most terrible. Even the tombs were not respected. All that remains of the Church of the Dime is only a few fragments of mosaic in the Museum at Kief. Saint Sophia, and the Monastery of the Catacombs, were delivered up to be plundered" (1240).

Volhynia and Gallicia still remained, but their princes could not defend them, and Russia found herself, with the exception of Novgorod and the north-west country, under the Tatar yoke. The princes had fled or were dead; hundreds of thousands of Russians were dragged into captivity. Men saw the wives of boyards, "who had never known work, who a short time ago had been clothed in rich garments, adorned with jewels and collars of gold, surrounded with slaves. now reduced to be themselves the slaves of barbarians and their wives, turning the wheel of the mill, and preparing their coarse food."

If we look for the causes which rendered the defeat of the brave Russian nation so complete, we may, with Karamsin, indicate the following :—1. Though the Tatars were not more advanced, from a military point of view, than the Russians, who had made war in Greece and in the West against the most warlike and civilized people of Europe, yet they had an enormous superiority of numbers. Bati probably had with him 500,000 warriors. 2. This immense army moved like one man; it could successively annihilate the *droujinas* of the princes, or the militia of the towns, which only presented themselves successively to its blows. The Tatars had found Russia divided against herself.

3. Even though Russia had wished to form a confederation, the sudden irruptions of an army entirely composed of horsemen did not leave her time. 4. In the tribes ruled by Bati, every man was a soldier; in Russia the nobles and citizens alone bore arms: the peasants, who formed the bulk of the population, allowed themselves to be stabbed or bound without resistance. 5. It was not by a weak nation that Russia was conquered. The Tatar-Mongols, under Genghis Khan, had filled the East with the glory of their name, and subdued nearly all Asia. They arrived, proud of their exploits, animated by the recollection of a hundred victories, and reinforced by numerous peoples whom they had vanquished, and hurried with them to the West.

When the princes of Galitch, of Volhynia, and of Kief arrived as fugitives in Poland and Hungary, Europe was terror-stricken. The Pope, whose support had been claimed by the Prince of Galitch, summoned Christendom to arms. Louis IX. prepared for a crusade. Frederic II., as Emperor, wrote to the sovereigns of the West: "This is the moment to open the eyes of body and soul, now that the brave princes on whom we reckoned are dead or in slavery." The Tatars invaded Hungary, gave battle to the Poles in Liegnitz in Silesia, had their progress a long while arrested by the courageous defence of Olmütz in Moravia, by the Tcheque voïevode Iaroslaf, and stopped finally, learning that a large army, commanded by the King of Bohemia and the dukes of Austria and Carinthia, was approaching. The news of the death of Oktaï, second Emperor of all the Tatars, in China, recalled Bati from the West, and during the long march from Germany his army necessarily diminished in number. The Tatars were no longer in the vast plains of Asia and Eastern Europe, but in a broken hilly country, bristling with fortresses, defended by a population more dense and a chivalry more numerous than those in Russia. To sum up, all the fury of the Mongol tempest spent itself on the Slavonic race. It was the Russians who fought at the Kalka, at Kolomna, at the Sit; the Poles and Silesians at Liegnitz; the Bohemians and Moravians at Olmütz. The Germans suffered nothing from the invasion of the Mongols but the fear of it. It exhausted itself principally on those plains of Russia which seem a continuation of the steppes of Asia. Only in Russian history did the invasion produce great results. About the same time Bati built on one of the arms of the Lower Volga a city called Saraï (the Castle), which became the capital of a powerful Tatar Empire, the *Golden Horde*, extending from the Oural and Caspian to the mouth of the Danube. The Golden Horde was formed not only of Tatar-Mongols or Nogaïs, who even now survive in the

Northern Crimea, but particularly of the remains of ancient nomads, such as the Patzinaks and Polovtsi, whose descendants seem to be the present Kalmucks and Bachkirs; of Turkish tribes tending to become sedentary, like the Tatars of Astrakhan in the present day; and of the Finnish populations already established in the country, and which mixed with the invaders. Oktaï, Kouïouk, and Mangou, the first three successors of Genghis Khan, elected by all the Mongol princes, took the title of Great Khans, and the Golden Horde recognized their authority; but under his fourth successor, Khouboulaï, who usurped the throne and established himself in China, this bond of vassalage was broken. The Golden Horde became an independent State (1260). United and powerful under the terrible Bati, who died in 1255, it fell to pieces under his successors; but in the 14th century the Khan Uzbeck reunited it anew, and gave the horde a second period of prosperity. The Tatars, who were pagans when they entered Russia, embraced about 1272 the faith of Islam, and became its most formidable apostles.

ALEXANDER NEVSKI (1252-1263).

Iaroslaf, after his defeat at Lipetsk, entered Souzdal on the tragic death of his brother, the Grand Prince George II. Iaroslaf (1238-1246) found his inheritance in the most deplorable condition. The towns and villages were burnt, the country and roads covered with unburied corpses; the survivors hid themselves in the woods. He recalled the fugitives and began to rebuild. Bati, who had completed the devastation of South Russia, summoned Iaroslaf to do him homage at Saraï, on the Volga. Iaroslaf was received there with distinction. Bati confirmed his title of Grand Prince, but invited him to go in person to the Great Khan, supreme chief of the Mongol nation, who lived on the banks of the river Sakhalian or Amour. To do this was to cross the whole of Russia and Asia. Iaroslaf bent his knees to the new master of the world, Oktaï, succeeded in refuting the accusations brought against him by a Russian boyard, and obtained a new confirmation of his title. On his return he died in the desert of exhaustion, and his faithful servants brought his body back to Vladimir. His son Andrew succeeded him in Souzdal (1246-1252). His other son, Alexander, reigned at Novgorod the Great.

Alexander was as brave as he was intelligent. He was the hero of the North, and yet he forced himself to accept the necessary humiliations of his terrible situation. In his youth we see him fighting with all the enemies of Novgorod, Livonian knights and Tchouds, Swedes and Finns. The Novgorodians found themselves at issue with the Scandinavians on the subject of their possessions on the Neva and the Gulf of Finland. As they had helped the natives to resist the Latin faith, King John obtained the promise of Gregory IX. that a crusade, with plenary indulgences, should be preached against the Great Republic and her *protégés*, the pagans of the Baltic. His son-in-law, Birger, with an army of Scandinavians, Finns, and Western Crusaders, took the command of the forces, and sent word to the Prince of Novgorod, " Defend yourself if you can : know that I am already in your provinces." The Russians on their side, feeling they were fighting for othodoxy, opposed the Latin crusade with a Greek one. Alexander humbled himself in Saint Sophia, received the benediction of the Archbishop Spiridion, and addressed an energetic harangue to his warriors. He had no time to await reinforcements from Souzdal. He attacked the Swedish camp, which was situated on the Ijora, one of the southern affluents of the Neva, which has given its name to Ingria. Alexander won a brilliant victory, which gained him his surname of Nevski, and the honor of becoming under Peter the Great, the second conqueror of the Swedes, one of the patrons of St. Petersburg. By the orders of his great successor his bones repose in the Monastery of Alexander Nevski. The battle of the Neva was preserved in a dramatic legend. An Ingrian chief told Alexander how, in the eve of the combat, he had seen a mysterious bark, manned by two warriors with shining brows, glide through the night. They were Boris and Gleb, who came to the rescue of their young kinsman. Other accounts have preserved to us the individual exploits of the Russian heroes— Gabriel, Skylaf of Novgorod, James of Polotsk, Sabas, who threw down the tent of Birger, and Alexander Nevski himself, who with a stroke of the lance " imprinted his seal on his face" (1240). Notwithstanding the triumph of such a service, Alexander and the Novgorodians could not agree; a short time after, he retired to Peréiaslavl-Zaliesski. The proud republicans soon had reason to regret the exile of this second Camillus. The Order of the Sword-bearers, the indefatigable enemy of orthodoxy, took Pskof, their ally ; the Germans imposed tribute on the Vojans, vassals of Novgorod, constructed the fortress of Koporié on her territory of the Neva, took the Russian town of Tessof in Esthonia, and pillaged the merchants of Novgorod within seventeen miles of their ramparts. During this time the Tchouds and the Lithuanians captured the peasants, and the cattle of the citizens. At last Alexander allowed himself to be touched by the prayers of the archbishop and the people, assembled an army, expelled the Germans from Koporié, and next from Pskof, hung as traitors the captive Vojans and Tchouds, and put to death six knights who fell into his hands. This war between the two races and two religions was cruel and pitiless. The rights of nations were hardly recognized. More than once Germans and Russians slew the ambassadors of the other side. Alexander Nevski finally gave battle to the Livonian knights on the ice of Lake Peïpus, killed 400 of them, took 50 prisoners, and exterminated a multitude of Tchouds. Such was the *Battle of the Ice* (1242). He returned in triumph to Novgorod, dragging with him his prisoners in armor of iron. The Grand Master expected to see Alexander at the gates of Riga, and implored help of Denmark. The Prince of Novgorod, satisfied with having delivered Pskof, concluded peace, recovered certain districts, and consented to the exchange of prisoners. At this time Innocent IV., deceived by false information, addressed a bull to Alexander, as a devoted son of the Church, assuring him that his father Iaroslaf, while dying among the Horde, had desired to submit himself to the throne of St. Peter. Two cardinals brought him this letter from the Pope (1251).

It is this hero of the Neva and Lake Peïpus, this vanquisher of the Scandinavians and Livonian knights, that we are presently to see grovelling at the feet of a barbarian. Alexander Nevski had understood that, in presence of this immense and brutal force of the Mongols, all resistance was madness, all pride ruin. To brave them was to complete the overthrow of Russia. His conduct may not have been chivalrous, but it was wise and humane. Alexander disdained to play the hero at the expense of his people, like his brother Andrew of Souzdal, who was immediately obliged to fly, abandoning his country to the vengeance of the Tatars. The Prince of Novgorod was the only prince in Russia who had kept his independence, but he knew Bati's hands could extend as far as the Ilmen. " God has subjected many peoples to me," wrote the barbarian to him : " will you alone refuse to recognize my power ? If you wish to keep your land, come to me ; you will see the splendor and the glory of my sway." Then Alexander went to Saraï with his brother Andrew, who disputed the Grand Principality of Vladimir with his uncle Sviatoslaf. Bati declared that fame had not exaggerated the merit of Alexander, that he far excelled the common run of Russian princes. He enjoined the two brothers to show themselves, like their father Iaroslaf, at the Great Horde ; they returned from it in 1257. Kouïouk had confirmed the one in the possession of

Vladimir, and the other in that of Novgorod, adding to it all South Russia and Kief.

The year 1260 put the patience of Alexander and his politic obedience to the Tatars to the proof. Oulavtchi, to whom the Khan Berkaï had confided the affairs of Russia, demanded that Novgorod should submit to the census and pay tribute. It was the hero of the Neva that was charged with the humiliating and dangerous mission of persuading Novgorod. When the possadnik uttered in the *vetché* the doctrine that it was necessary to submit to the strongest, the people raised a terrible cry and murdered the possadnik. Vassili himself, the son of Alexander, declared against a father " who brought servitude to free men ; " and retired to the Pskovians. It needed a soul of iron temper to resist the universal disapprobation, and counsel the Novgorodians to the commission of the cowardly though necessary act. Alexander arrested his son, and punished the boyards who had led him into the revolt with death or mutilation. The *vetché* had decided to refuse the tribute, and send back the Mongol ambassadors with presents. However, on the rumor of the approach of the Tatars, they repented, and Alexander could announce to the enemy that Novgorod submitted to the census. But when they saw the officers of the Khan at work, the population revolted again, and the prince was obliged to keep guard on the officers night and day. In vain the boyards advised the citizens to give in: assembled around St. Sophia, the people declared they would die for liberty and honor. Alexander then threatened to quit the city with his men, and abandon it to the vengeance of the Khan. This menace conquered the pride of the Novgorodians. The Mongols and their agents might go, register in hand, from house to house in the humiliated and silent city to make the list of the inhabitants. " The boyards," says Karamsin, " might yet be vain of their rank and their riches, but the simple citizens had lost with their national honor their most precious possession " (1260).

In Souzdal also Alexander found himself in the presence of insolent victors and exasperated subjects. In 1262 the inhabitants of Vladimir, of Souzdal, of Rostof, rose against the collectors of the Tatar impost. The people of Iaroslavl slew a renegade named Zozimus, a former monk, who had become a Moslem fanatic. Terrible reprisals were sure to follow. Alexander set out with presents for the Horde at the risk of leaving his head there. He had likewise to excuse himself for having refused a body of auxiliary Russians to the Mongols, wishing at least to spare the blood and religious scruples of his subjects. It is a remarkable fact, that, over the most profound humiliations of the Russian nationality, the contemporary history always throws a ray of glory. At the moment that Alexander went to prostrate himself at Saraï, the Souzdalian army, united to that of Novgorod, and commanded by his son Dmitri, defeated the Livonian knights, and took Dorpat by assault. The Khan Berkaï gave Alexander a kind greeting, accepted his explanations, dispensed with the promised contingent, but kept him for a year near his court. The health of Alexander broke down; he died on his return before reaching Vladimir. When the news arrived at his capital, the Metropolitan Cyril, who was finishing the liturgy, turned towards the faithful, and said, "Learn, my dear children, that the Sun of Russia is set, is dead." "We are lost," cried the people, breaking forth into sobs. Alexander by this policy of resignation, which his chivalrous heroism does not permit us to despise, had secured some repose for exhausted Russia. By his victories over his enemies of the West he had given her some glory, and hindered her from despairing under the most crushing tyranny, material and moral, which a European people had ever suffered.

THE MONGOL YOKE—INFLUENCE OF THE TATARS ON THE RUSSIAN DEVELOPMENT.

The Mongol khans, after having devastated and abased Russia, did not introduce any direct political change. They left to each country her laws, her courts of justice, her natural chiefs. The house of Andrew Bogolioubski continued to reign in Souzdal, that of Daniel Romanovitch in Galitch and Volhynia, the Olgovitches in Tchernigof, and the descendants of Rogvolod the Varangian at Polotsk. Novgorod might continue to expel and recall her princes, and the dynasties of the South to dispute the throne of Kief. The Russian States found themselves under the Mongol yoke, in much the same situation as that of the Christians of the Greco-Slav peninsula three centuries later, under the Ottomans. The Russians remained in possession of all their lands, which their nomad conquerors, encamped on the steppes of the East and South, disdained. They were, like their Danubian kinsmen, a sort of rayahs, over whom the authority of the khans was exerted with more or less rigor, but whom their conquerors never tried in any way to *Tatarize*. Let us see exactly in what consisted the obligations of the vanquished, and their relations with their conquerors, during the period of the Mongol yoke or *Tatarchtchina*.

1. The Russian princes were forced to visit the Horde, either as evidence of their submission, or to give the Khan opportunity of judging their disputes. We have seen how they had to go not only to the Khan of the Golden Horde, but often also to the Grand Khan at the extremity of Asia, on the borders of the Sakhalian or Amour. They met there the chiefs of the Mongol, Tatar, Thibetian and Bokharian hordes, and sometimes the ambassador of the Caliph of Bagdad, of the Pope, or of the King of France. The Grand Khans tried to play off against each other these ambassadors, who were astonished to meet at his court. Mangou Khan desired Saint Louis to recognize him as the master of the world, "for," said he, "when the universe has saluted me as sovereign, a happy tranquillity will reign on the earth." In the case of refusal, "neither deep seas nor inaccessible mountains" would place the King of France beyond the power of his wrath. To the princes of Asia and Russia he displayed the presents of the King of France, affecting to consider them as tributes and signs of submission. "We will send to seek him to confound you," he said to them, and Joinville assures us that this threat, and "the fear of the King of France," decided many to throw themselves on his mercy. This journey to the Grand Horde was terrible. The road went through deserts, or countries once rich, but changed by the Tatars into vast wastes. Few who went returned. Planus Carpinus, envoy of Innocent IV., saw in the steppes of the Kirghiz the dry bones of the boyards of the unhappy Iaroslaf, who had died of thirst in the sand. Planus Carpinus thus describes the Court of Bati on the Volga:—" It is crowded and brilliant. His army consists of 600,000 men, 150,000 of whom are Tatars, and 450,000 strangers, Christians as well as infidels. On Good Friday we were conducted to his tent, between two fires, because the Tatars pretend that a fire purifies everything, and robs even poison of its danger. We had to make many prostrations, and enter the tent without touching the threshold. Bati was on his throne with one of his wives; his brothers, his children, and the Tatar lords were seated on benches; the rest of the assembly were on the ground, the men on the right, the women on the left. . . . . The Khan and the lords of the Court emptied from time to time cups of gold and silver, while the musicians made the air ring with their melodies. Bati has a bright complexion; he is affable with his men, but inspires general terror." The Court of the Grand Khan was still more magnificent. Planus Carpinus found there a Russian named Koum, who was the favorite and special goldsmith of Gaïouk or Kouïouk, and Rubruquis discovered a Parisian goldsmith, named Guillaume. Much money was

needed for success, either at the Court of the Grand Khan or of
Bati. Presents had to be distributed to the Tatar princes, to
the favorites; above all to the wives and the mother of the
Khan. At this terrible tribunal the Russian princes had to
struggle with intrigues and corruption; the heads of the pleaders
were often the stakes of these dreadful trials. The most dangerous enemies they encountered at the Tatar Court were not
the barbarians, but the Russians, their rivals. The history of
the Russian princes at the Horde is very tragic. Thus Michael
of Tchernigof perished at the Horde of Saraï in 1246, and Michael of Tver in 1319, the one assassinated by the renegade
Doman, the other by the renegade Romanetz, at the instigation
and under the eyes of the Grand Prince of Moscow.

2. The conquered people were obliged to pay a capitation
tax, which weighed as heavily on the poor as on the rich. The
tribute was paid either in money or in furs; those who were
unable to furnish it became slaves. The Khans had for some
time farmed out this revenue to some Khiva merchants, who
collected it with the utmost rigor, and whom they protected by
appointing superior agents called *baskaks*, with strong guards to
support them. The excesses of these tax-gatherers excited
many revolts: in 1262, that of Souzdal; in 1284, that of Koursk;
in 1318, that of Kolomna; in 1327, that of Tver, where the inhabitants slew the *baskak* Chevkal, and brought down on themselves frightful reprisals. Later, the princes of Moscow themselves farmed not only the tax from their own subjects, but also
from neighboring countries. They became the farmers-general
of the invaders. This was the origin of their riches and their
power.

3. Besides the tribute, the Russians had to furnish to their
master the blood-tax, a military contingent. Already at the
time of the Huns and Avars, we have seen Slavs and Goths
accompany the Asiatic hordes, form their vanguards, and be as
it were the hounds of Baïan. In the 13th century, the Russian
princes furnished to the Tatars select troops, especially a solid
infantry, and marched in their armies at the head of their *droujinas*. It was thus that in 1276 Boris of Rostof, Gleb of Biéloiersk, Feodor of Iaroslavl, and Andrew of Gorodetz followed
Mangou Khan in a war against the tribes of the Caucasus, and
sacked Dediakof in Daghestan, the capital of the Iasses. The
Mongols scrupulously reserved to them their part of the booty.
The same Russian princes took part in an expedition against
an adventurer named Lachan by the Greek historians, formerly
a keeper of pigs, who had raised Bulgaria. The descendants
of Monomachus behaved still more dishonorably in the troubles

in the interior of Russia. They excited the Mongols against their countrymen and aided the invaders. Prince Andrew, son of Alexander Nevski, pillaged in 1281, in concert with the Tatars, the provinces of Vladimir, Souzdal, Mourom, Moscow, and Peréiaslavl, which he was disputing with Dmitri, his elder brother. He helped the barbarians to profane churches and convents. In 1327 it was the princes of Moscow and Souzdal who directed the military execution against Tver. In 1284, two Olgovitches reigned in the land of Koursk ; one of them, Oleg, put the other to death in the name of the Khan. Servitude had so much abased all characters, that even the annalists share the general degradation. They blame, not Oleg the murderer, but Sviatoslaf the victim. Was it not his unbridled conduct that caused the anger of the Khan ?

4. No prince could ascend the throne without having received the investiture and the *iarlikh*, or letters patent, from the Khan. The proud Novgorodians themselves rejected Michael, their prince, saying, " It is true we have chosen Michael, but on the condition that he should show us the *iarlikh*."

4. No Russian State dared to make war without being authorized to do so. In 1269 the Novgorodians asked leave to march against Revel. In 1303, in an assembly of princes, and in the presence of the Metropolitan Maximus, a decree of the Khan Tokhta was read, enjoining the princes to put an end to their dissensions, and to content themselves with their appanages, it being the will of the Grand Khan that the Grand Principality should enjoy peace. When the Mongol ambassadors brought a letter from their sovereign, the Russian princes were obliged to meet them on foot, prostrate themselves, spread precious carpets under their feet, present them with a cup filled with gold pieces, and listen, kneeling, while the *iarlikh* was read.

Even while the Tatars conquered the Russians, they respected their bravery. Matrimonial alliances were contracted between their princes. About 1272, Gleb, prince of Biélozersk, took a wife out the Khan's family, which already professed Christianity, and Feodor of Riazan became the son-in-law of the Khan of the Nogais, who assigned to the young couple a palace in Saraï. In 1318 the Grand Prince George married Kontchaka, sister of Uzbeck Khan, who was baptized by the name of Agatha. Towards the end of the 14th century, the Tatars were no longer the rude shepherds of the steppes. Mingled with sedentary and more cultivated races, they rebuilt fresh cities on the ruins of those they had destroyed ; Krym in the Crimea, Kazan, Astrakhan, and Saraï. They had acquired a taste for luxury and magnificence, honored the national poets who sang their exploits, piqued themselves on their chivalry and even on their gallantry. Notwithstanding the difference of religion, a reconciliation was taking place between the aristocracy of the two countries, between the Russian *kniazes* and the Tatar *mourzas*.

The Russian historians are not entirely agreed as to the nature and degree of influence exerted by the Mongol yoke on the Russian development. Karamsin and M. Kostomarof believe it to have been considerable. "Perhaps," says the former "our national character still presents some blots which are derived from the Mongol barbarism." M. Solovief, on the contrary, affirms that the Tatars hardly influenced it more than the Patzinaks or Polovtsi. M. Bestoujef-Rioumine estimates the influence to have been specially exerted on the financial administration and military organization. On one side the Tatars established the capitation-tax, which has remained in the financial system of Russia; on the other, the conquered race had a natural tendency to adopt the military system of the victors. The Russian or Mongol princes formed a caste of soldiers henceforth quite distinct from Western chivalry, to which the Russian heroes of the 12th century belonged. The warriors of Daniel of Galitch, it is said, astounded the Poles and Hungarians by the Oriental character of their equipment. Short stirrups, very high saddles, a long caftan or floating dress, a sort of turban surmounted by an aigret, sabres and poniards in their belts, a bow and arrows—such was the military costume of a Russian prince of the 15th century.

On the other side, many of the peculiarities in which the Mongol influence is thought traceable may be attributed as well or better to purely Slav traditions, or imitations of Byzantine manners. If the Muscovite princes inclined to autocracy, it was not that they formed themselves on the model of the Grand Khan, but that they naturally adopted imperial ideas of absolutism imported from Constantinople. It is always the Roman Emperor of Tzargrad, and not the leader of Asiatic shepherds, who is their typical monarch. If from this time the Russian penal law makes more frequent use of the pain of death and corporal punishment, it is not only the result of imitation of the Tatars, but of the evergrowing influence of Byzantine laws, and the progressive triumph of their principles over those of the ancient code of Iaroslaf. Now these laws so very easily admitted torture, flogging, mutilation, the stake, &c., that there is no need to explain anything by Mongol usages. The habit of prostration, of beating the forehead, of affecting the servile submission, is certainly Oriental, but it is also Byzantine. The seclusion of women was customary in ancient Russia, moulded by Greek missionaries, and the Russian *terem* proceeds more certainly from the Hellenic *gynæceum* than from the Oriental *harem*; all the more because the Tatar women, before the conversion of the Mongols to Islamism, do not appear to have been secluded. If the Russians of the 17th century seem strange to us in their long robes and Oriental fashions, we must remember that the French and Italians of the 15th century, dressed by Venetian merchants, displayed the same taste. Only in France fashions made advances, while in Russia, isolated from the rest of Europe they remained stationary.

From a social point of view, two Russian expressions seem to date from the Tatar invasion: *tcherne*, or the *black people*, to designate the lower orders; and *krestianine*, signifying the peasant, that is, the Christian *par excellence*, who was always a stranger to the Mongol customs adopted for a short time by the aristocracy. As to the amount of Mongol or Tatar blood mixed with the blood of the Russians, it must have been very small: the aristocracy of the two countries may have contracted marriages, a certain number of *mourzas* may have become Russian princes by their conversion to orthodoxy, but the two races, as a whole, remained strangers. Even to-day, while the autochthonous Finns continue to be Russified, the Tatar cantons, even though converted to Christianity, are still Tatar.

If the Mongol yoke has influenced the Russian development, it is very indirectly. 1. In separating Russia from the West, in making her a political dependency of Asia, it perpetuated in the country that Byzantine half civilization whose inferiority to European civilization became daily more obvious. If the Russians of the 17th century differ so much from Western nations, it is above all because they have remained at the point whence all set out. 2. The Tatar conquest also favored indirectly the establishment of absolute power. The Muscovite princes, responsible to the Khan for the public tranquillity and the collection of the tax, being all the while watched and supported by the *baskaks*, could the more easily annihilate the independence of the towns, the resistance of the second order of princes, the turbulence of the boyards, and the privileges of the free peasants. The Grand Prince of Moscow had no consideration for his subjects because no man had any consideration for him, and because his life was always at stake. The Mongol tyranny bore with a frightful weight on all the Russian hierarchy, and subjected more closely the nobles to the princes, and the peasants to the nobles. "The princes of Moscow," says Karamsin, "took the humble title of servants of the khans, and it was by this

means that they became powerful monarchs." No doubt the Russian principalities would always have ended by losing themselves in the same dominion, but Russian unity would have been made, like French unity, without the entire destruction of local autonomies, the privileges of the towns, and the rights of the subjects. It was the crushing weight of the Mongol domination that stifled all the germs of political liberty. We may say with Mr. Wallace, that " the first Tzars of Muscovy were the political descendants, not of the Russian princes, but of the Tatar khans."
3. A third indirect result of the conquest was the growth of the power and riches of the Church. In spite of the saintly legends about the martyrdom of certain princes, the Tatars were a tolerant nation. Rubruquis saw in the presence of the Grand Khan Mangou, Nestorians, Mussulmans, and Shamans celebrating their own particular worships.

Kouïouk had a Christian chapel near his palace; Khoubilaï regularly took part in the feast of Easter. In 1261 the Khan of Saraï authorized the erection of a church and orthodox bishopric in his capital. The Mongols had no sectarian hatred against bishops and priests. With a sure political instinct, the Tatars, like the Sultans of Stamboul, understood that these men could agitate or calm the people. After the first fury of the conquest was passed, they applied themselves to gaining them over. They excepted priests and monks from the capitation-tax; they received them well at the Horde, and gave pardons at their intercession. They settled disputes of orthodox prelates, and established the peace in the Church that they imposed on the State. In 1313 the Khan Uzbeck, at the prayer of Peter, Metropolitan of Moscow, confirmed the privileges of the Church and forbade her being deprived of her goods, " for," says the edict, "these possessions are sacred, because they belong to men whose prayers preserve our lives and strengthen our armies." The right of justice in the Church was formally recognized. Sacrilege was punished by death.

The convents also increased in numbers and riches. They filled enormously: were they not the safest asylums? Their peasants and servants multiplied: was not the protection of the Church the surest? Gifts of land were showered on them, as in France in the year 1000. It was thus that the great ecclesiastical patrimony of Russia, a wealthy reservoir of revenues and capital, was constituted, on which more than once in national crises the Russian sovereigns were glad to draw. The Church, which, even in her weakness, had steadily tended to unity and autocracy, was to place at the service of the crown a power which had become enormous. The Metropolitans of Moscow were nearly always the faithful allies of the Grand Princes.

CHAPTER XI.

THE LITHUANIANS: CONQUEST OF WESTERN RUSSIA (1240-1430).

The Lithuanians—Conquests of Mindvog (1240-1263), of Gedimin (1315-1340), and of Olgerd (1345-1377)—Jagellon—Union of Lithuania with Poland (1386)—The Grand Prince Vitovt (1392-1430)—Battles of the Vorskla (1399), and of Tannenberg (1410).

THE LITHUANIANS—CONQUESTS OF MINDVOG (1240-1263), OF GEDIMIN (1315-1340), AND OF OLGERD (1345-1377).

THE Lithuanian tribes had already been greatly broken up by the German conquest. Russians, Korsi, Semigalli, and Letts had been brought into subjection either by the Teutonic or Livonian knights. Two among the tribes, the Jmouds and the Lithuanians properly so called, had preserved in the deep forests and marshes of the Niemen their proud independence, their ferocity, and their ancient gods. A Russian tradition affirms that they formerly had paid the Russians the only tribute their poverty could afford—bark and brooms. Jmouds and Lithuanians were divided, like the ancient Slavs, into rival and jealous tribes. Although more than once they marched from their forests, blowing long trumpets, careering on rough ponies—though they had made many incursions into the Russian territory—they were not really dangerous. This old Aryan people, whom European influences had never modified, had preserved from the time they dwelt in Asia a powerful sacerdotal caste,—the *vaïdelotes* above whom were the *krivites*, whose chief, the *krive-kriveito*, was high-priest of the nation. Their principal divinity was Perkun, the god of thunder, analogous to the Perun of the Russians. The sacred fire, the *znitch*, burned constantly before this idol. They had also priestesses, the wild Velledas, like that Birouta who, captured by Kestout, became the mother of the great Vitovt. The time had come when the Lithuanians must perish like the Prussians or Letts, if they did not succeed in uniting against Germany. The emigrants from the countries already conquered would doubtless lend them new strength and energy. A wily barbarian, Mindvog, created Lithuanian unity at the beginning of the 13th century in much the same way as Clovis—by exterminating the princes. "He began," says a chronicle, "by slaying his brothers and his sons, chased the survivors from the country, and reigned alone over the land of Lithuania." Thence he led his savage warriors against the Russian principalities, now enfeebled by the Mongol invasions, and conquered Grodno and Novogrodek. Happily Western Russia had two great men at its head, Alexander Nevski and Daniel of Volhynia. Threatened on one side by these princes, on the other by the knights of Livonia, the Lithuanians bethought themselves of hastening to the Pope and embracing the Catholic faith. A legate of Innocent IV. and the *landmeister* of the Teutonic Order came to Grodno, escorted by a brilliant suite of cavaliers. In presence of an immense concourse of people, Mindvog received baptism with his wife, and was consecrated King of Lithuania (1252). The danger passed, and Rome was forgotten. He and his new co-religionists did not agree, and he was forced to cede the Jmoud country to the Livonian knights. Sharing the irritation of his subjects, he washed off his baptism as the unfortunate Livonians had done, re-established paganism, invaded Mazovia, ravaged the lands of the Order, and defeated the *landmeister* in person. He had taken the wife of one of his princes named Dovmont, and had married her. Dovmont awaited him on the road, and assassinated him (1263), and then fled from the vengeance of Mindvog's son to the Pskovians. He became their prince, was baptized, and defended them bravely against his pagan compatriots till he died, and was buried at the church of the Trinity. Voichel, son of Mindvog, in the first fervor of an ephemeral Christianity, had become a monk. When he heard of the murder of his father, he threw his cowl to the winds, and began a war of extermination with the confederates. Lithuania fell back into anarchy during the contest of the descendants of Mindvog with the rest of the princes who refused to accept their supremacy.

She recovered herself under the enterprising and energetic Gedimin (1315-1340), the real founder of her power. He turned the exhaustion and divisions of South Russia to his own profit; and to the conquests of his predecessors—Grodno, Pinsk, Brest, and Polotsk—soon added Tchernigof, and all Volhynia with Vladimir, under whose walls he defeated the Russians, aided though they were by an auxiliary army of Tatars (1321). As to Kief, it is not known in what year she fell under his power; in the universal disorder, this memorable event passed almost unnoticed. The old capital of Russia was, however, destined to remain for 400 years—up to the time of Alexis Romanof—in the hands of strangers. The Russian populations willingly received this new master, who would free them from the heavy yoke of the Mongols and the unceasing civil wars. As he respected their internal constitution and the rights of the orthodox clergy, it appears that many towns readily opened their gates to him. Gedimin sought to legalize his conquests by contracting alliances with the house of St. Vladimir, allowed his sons to embrace the orthodox faith, and authorized the construction of Greek churches in his residences at Wilna and Novogrodek. In the North he had a perpetual struggle to sustain against the deadly enemies of his race, the military monks of Prussia and Livonia. Like Mindvog, he addressed himself to the Pope, John XXII., and informed him that he wished to preserve his independence, that he only asked protection for his religion, that he was surrounded by Franciscans and Dominicans to whom he gave full liberty to teach their doctrine, and that he was ready to recognize the Pope as supreme head of the Church, if he would arrest the depredations of the Germans. The French Pope sent him Bartholomew, Bishop of Alais, and Bernard, Abbot of Puy. In the interval he had been exasperated by renewed attacks of the Teutonic knights, and forced the two legates to fly. He had transferred his capital to Wilna on the Wilia, and the ruins of his castle may still be perceived on the height which overlooks the citadel. He drew thither by immunities German artists and artisans, and granted them the rights of Riga and the Hanseatic towns. A Russian quarter was also formed in his capital. He died and was buried according to the pagan rite : his body was burned in a caldron with his war-horse and his favorite groom.

After his death his sons Olgerd (1345–1377) and Kestout deprived two of their brothers of their appanages, and together governed Lithuania, now re-united into a single State. Olgerd humiliated Novgorod the Great, which had received another of his fugitive brothers, ravaged her territory, and forced her to put to death the possadnik who had been the cause of the war. He extended his possessions to the east and south, and conquered Vitepsk, Mohilef, Briansk, Novgorod-Severski, Kamenetz and Podolia ; thus rendering himself master of nearly all the basin of the Dnieper, and obtaining a footing on the coast of the Black Sea, between the mouths of the Dnieper and the Dniester. With the republic of Pskof he maintained relations sometimes friendly, sometimes hostile ; gave her help against the Germans, and sent his son Andrew to govern her, and occasionally arrested her merchants and laid waste her territory. The Poles disputed Volhynia with him, oppressed the orthodox faith, and changed the Greek into Latin churches. Olgerd then made advances to Simeon the Proud, Grand Prince of Moscow, and, though a pagan, married Juliana, princess of Tver. Under Simeon's successors the Lithuanian army three times took the road to Moscow, and, without the check imposed on him by the Poles and the two German orders, Olgerd might have made the conquest of Eastern Russia. In 1368 he had annihilated the Mongol hordes which infested the Lower Dnieper, and, more destructive than even these barbarians, completed the ruin of Cherson in the Crimea.

JAGELLON—UNION OF LITHUANIA AND POLAND (1386).

Although Olgerd had reconstituted the Lithuanian unity, he fell back into the old error, and divided his States between his sons and his brother, the brave Kestout, who had been his faithful associate. One of his sons, *Iagaïlo* or *Jagellon* (1377–1434), cruelly repaired the fault of his father. He made his uncle Kestout prisoner by treachery, and caused him to be put to death. His brothers and cousins escaped a similar fate by flying to neighboring states. In spite of this the bloody pagan was the Apostle of Lithuania. For a long while Christianity had sought to penetrate by two different channels,—under the Latin form from Poland, and under the Greek form from Russia. The fierce war sustained by the Lithuanians against the military monks of the North had rendered Catholicism particularly hateful to them. Under Olgerd the people of Wilna had risen, and fourteen Franciscans were slain. On the other side the larger part of the Lithuanian conquests was composed of Russian territory, and Lithuania underwent the influence of the Russian religion as well as of the Russian language. Russian became the official tongue; it even seemed as if orthodoxy was to become the ruling faith, and the victors were to be absorbed by the vanquished, and Russified by their conquest. An unexpected event turned the natural course of history. The Angevin and French dynasty in Poland had lately been extinguished in the person of Louis of Hungary, whose only heir was his daughter Hedwiga. The Polish nobles felt that the best way of putting a stop to the eternal warfare with the Lithuanians was by marrying their queen to the powerful Prince of Wilna. The heart of Hedwiga is said to have been elsewhere engaged; but the Catholic clergy set forth her consent to this union as a duty, the fulfilment of which was to insure in Lithuania proper the triumph of the Latin faith, and thus to separate it from the Lithuanian Russian provinces which still remained orthodox.

In 1386 Jagellon went to Cracow and received baptism and the crown of Poland.

The conversion of the Lithuanians was then conducted after a fashion as summary as that of the Russians in the time of Vladimir. They were divided into groups, and the priest then sprinkled them with holy water, pronouncing, as he did so, a name of the Latin Calendar. To one group he gave the name of Peter, to another that of Paul or John. Jagellon overthrew the idol Perkun, extinguished the sacred fire that burned in the castle of Wilna, killed the holy serpents, and cut down the magic woods. The people, however, worshipped their gods for some time longer; like the Northmen who were converted by the Carolingians, many Lithuanians presented themselves more than once to be baptized, in order to receive again and again the white tunic of the neophyte. By transferring his capital to Cracow, in deference to his new subjects, Jagellon necessarily irritated his old subjects. To the determined pagans the orthodox allied themselves, provoked by the king's propaganda in favor of Catholicism. Lithuania believed that by her union with Poland she had forfeited her independence.

THE GRAND PRINCE VITOVT (1392-1430)—BATTLES OF THE VORSKLA (1399), AND OF TANNENBERG (1410).

Vitovt, son of the hero Kestout and the priestess Birouta, put himself at the head of the malcontents. He allied himself with the Teutonic knights, and twice besieged the Polish garrison in the Castle of Wilna. Weary of war, Jagellon ended by ceding him Lithuania with the title of Grand Prince (1392).

Vitovt (1392-1430), brother-in-law of the Grand Prince of Moscow (Vassili Dmitriévitch), took up the plans of Olgerd for the subjugation of the north-east of Russia. Sviatoslaf, the last prince but one of Smolensk, had made himself hated, even in that iron century, by his cruelties. Fighting in the Russian territory, he took pleasure in impaling and burning alive women and children. He was killed in 1387 in a battle against the Lithuanians, and his son Ioury was only the shadow of a Grand Prince of Smolensk, under the guardianship of Vitovt. The latter, who combined perfidy with the courage and energy of his father, made himself master of the town by a stratagem worthy of Cæsar Borgia. He contrived to induce the prince and his brothers to visit him in his tent, embraced and pressed them in his arms, and then declared them prisoners of war, while his army surprised and pillaged Smolensk. This queenly city on the Upper Dneiper was lost to Russia. The Lithuanian Empire now bordered on the ancient Souzdal and the principality of Riazan. These two countries, with Novgorod and Pskof, were the only ones which had preserved their independence. It seemed as if one campaign would suffice to annihilate the Russian name. But Vitovt cherished great projects, in which the conquest of Moscow was only an incident. He had already fought against the Mongols, and with the prisoners taken in the environs of Azof, had peopled many villages round Wilna, where their posterity still exist. He took under his protection the Khan Tokhtamych, whom Timour Koutlouï had expelled from Saraï, and resolved to subjugate the Golden Horde, to instal a vassal there, and finally add to the conquest of the Tatar Empire that of Moscow and Riazan. The army that he assembled under the walls of Kief was perhaps the most important that had marched against the infidels since the first crusade. To his Lithuanian troops he had united the Polish contingent sent by Jagellon under the famous voïevodes Spitko of Cracow, John of Mazovia, Sandivog of Ostorog, Dobrogost of Samotoul, and the *droujinas* of the Russian princes, Gleb of Smolensk, Michael and Dmitri of Volhynia, the Mongols of Tokhtamych, and five hundred knights, "iron men," richly armed, sent by the Grand Master of the Teutonic Order. He came up with the enemy on the banks of the Vorskla, an affluent of the Dnieper, that runs near Pultowa. It was almost the battle-field where fought in 1709 the heroes of the North. To Timour's proposals of peace, Vitovt answered that God had designed him to be master of the world, and that the Khan must recognize him as *his father*, pay him tribute, and place his armorial bearings on the Mongol coins. The Khan only negotiated to gain time till the bulk of the Tatar army, commanded by Ediger, came up. Ediger, in his turn, ironically summoned Vitovt to acknowledge him as father, and to place his arms on the Lithuanian coins. Vitovt, who hoped to make up for his deficiency in numbers by his artillery, gave the signal for battle. A manœuvre of the Tatars on the rear of the enemy assured them the victory. Two-thirds of the Lithuanian army, with the princes of Smolensk and Volhynia, remained on the field of battle. The remnant was pursued by Timour to the Dnieper. He levied war contributions on Kief and the Monastery of the Catacombs (1399). So fell the prestige of Vitovt. Even the princes of Riazan thought that they might safely insult his frontiers. But he was still formidable, and the Grand Prince of Moscow, after having tried to attack him, judged it more prudent to make peace.

When Vitovt began to recover from his disaster, he directed a still more famous expedition against the Teutonic knights. The Grand Prince of Lithuania had more than once found himself at issue with the two German orders. About this time the Teutonic knights had lost their early energy, thanks to the development of the system of fiefs, and to the progress of the commercial towns. In 1409 the Jmouds and Oriental Prussia, after having protested against the severity of the yoke imposed on them, revolted, counting on Vitovt to support them. A new Grand Master, the warlike Ulrich of Jungingen, refused the mediation of Vitovt's suzerain, the King of Poland. Upon this the united forces of Poland and Lithuania, with 40,000 Tatars and 21,000 Bohemian, Hungarian, Moravian and Silesian mercenaries, making a total of 97,000 infantry, 66,000 cavalry, and 60 cannons, entered Prussia. The Grand Master had only 57,000 infantry and 26,000 cavalry, with which to oppose them. The battle of Tannenberg (1410), gained chiefly by Vitovt, who broke the German centre and left wing, was a blow from which the power of the Teutonic Order never recovered. The Grand Master and nearly all the high dignitaries, 200 Knights of the Order, and 400 foreign knights, besides 4000 soldiers, were killed. Nearly all the princes of Western Russia took part in the combat, and the contingent of Smolensk especially distinguished itself. The Jmoud country was freed from the Teutonic rule and united to Lithuania.

Three years afterwards (1413) the Congress of Horodlo on the Bug, between Jagellon, accompanied by the Polish *pans*, and Vitovt, accompanied by his Lithuanian chiefs, took place. It was settled that the Lithuanian Catholics should receive the rights and privileges of the Polish *schliachta;* and that the representatives of the two countries should unite in a common diet to elect the Kings of Poland and the Grand Dukes of Lithuania, and decide important affairs. Vitovt soon had differences with his own subjects: the Jmouds, so refractory under the Teutonic rule, were pagans and Lithuanians at heart. They hated Catholicism and the Polish domination. They rose and expelled the monks. Vitovt could only govern them by force.

The Russian provinces of Lithuania were orthodox, and depended upon the Metropolitan of Moscow. Vitovt wished to shake off his religious supremacy, and demanded of the Patriarch of Constantinople a special metropolitan for Western Russia. In spite of the Patriarch's refusal, he convoked a council of orthodox prelates: a learned Bulgarian monk, Gregory Tsamblak, was elected Metropolitan of Kief. Thus Russia had two religious chiefs, as she had two Grand Princes—the Metropolitan of Eastern Russia, and the Metropolitan of Western Russia; one at Moscow, the other at Kief. Vitovt also wished to free himself on the western side, and deprive Poland of her supremacy over Lithuania. In 1429 he had an interview with the Emperor Sigismond, who promised to create him King of Lithuania. Vitovt, then eighty years of age, was at the height of his power. We see him at the fêtes of Troki and Wilna, attended by his grandson Vassili Vassiliévitch, Grand Prince of Moscow, who was accompanied by the Muscovite Metropolitan Photius, the Princes of Tver and Riazan, Jagellon, king of Poland, the Khan of the Crimea, the exiled Hospodar of Wallachia, the Grand Master of Prussia, the Landmeister of Livonia, and the ambassadors of the Emperor of the East. Daily were 700 oxen, 1400 sheep, and game in proportion, consumed. In the midst of these fêtes the ambitious old man had to swallow a bitter draught. The Poles had intrigued with the Pope, and he was forbidden to dream of royalty. The ambassadors of Sigismond were checked as they were bringing him the sceptre and the crown. Vitovt fell ill, and died of disappointment (1430).

After this Lithuania ceased to be formidable. We find it in turns governed by a Grand Duke of its own, united to Poland under Vladislas, separated again, then definitely placed under the Polish sceptre from 1501. Though henceforward it always had the same sovereign as Poland, it remained a State apart— the Grand Principality or Grand Duchy of Lithuania. Her Lithuanian and Russian provinces became steadily Polish, and the princely descendants of Rurik and St. Vladimir, or of Mindvog and Gedimin, assumed the manners and language of the Polish aristocracy.

CHAPTER XII.

THE GRAND PRINCES OF MOSCOW: ORGANIZATION OF EASTERN RUSSIA (1303-1462):

Origin of Moscow—Daniel—George Danielovitch (1303-1325) and Ivan Kalita (1328-1341)—Contest with the house of Tver—Simeon the Proud and Ivan the Débonnaire (1341-1359)—Dmitri Donskoï (1363-1389)—Battle of Koulikovo—Vassili Dmitriévitch and Vassili the Blind (1389-1462).

ORIGIN OF MOSCOW—DANIEL.

WHILST Western Russia grouped herself around the Lithuanian State, which had given the conquered Russian provinces a new capital in Wilna, and soon involved them in her own union with Poland, Eastern Russia grouped herself around Moscow. When this double concentration on the Moskowa and on the Wilna should be accomplished, Great Russia, proud of her national and religious unity, and Lithuanian Russia (or rather a foreign State composed of the Russian, Lithuanian, and Polish races, and of three religions, the Greek, Roman, and Protestant, besides the Jewish), would find themselves face to face. The contest of these two sister-enemies will fill many centuries of the history of the North. To other sovereigns, in other centuries, will fall the task of reconstituting the Russian unity in its fullest extent. The honor of the princes of Moscow is to have created the living germ which became Great Russia.

Around Moscow, under the Mongol yoke, a race was formed, patient and resigned, yet energetic and enterprising, born to endure bad fortune and profit by good, which in the long run was to get the upper hand over Western Russia and Lithuania. There a dynasty of princes grew, politic and persevering, prudent and pitiless, of gloomy and terrible mien, whose foreheads were marked by the seal of fatality. They were the founders of the Russian empire, as the Capetians were of the French monarchy.

The means used by the sovereigns of Russia were very

different. Here we shall find no sympathetic figures like that of Louis VI. careering proudly in the narrow domains of France, capturing rebel castles in the face of the sun—of a Louis IX., true mirror of chivalry, the noblest incarnation of the kingly ideal. The princes of Moscow gained their ends by intrigue, corruption, the purchase of consciences, servility to the khans, perfidy to their equals, murder, and treachery. They were at once the tax-gatherers and the police of the khans. But they created the germ of the Russian monarchy, and made it grow. Henceforward we have a fixed centre around which gathers that scattered history of Russia which we have had to follow in so many different places—in Novgorod and Pskof, in Livonia and in Lithuania, at Smolensk and in Gallicia, at Tchernigof and at Kief, at Vladimir and at Riazan. The mutilation of Russia, conquered on the west by the Lithuanians, enslaved on the east by the Mongols, was to facilitate the work of organization. In this diminished fatherland the sovereigns of Moscow could play more easily the part of Grand Princes.

The extent of country which had by the middle of the 15th century escaped the Lithuanian conquest was very small. Without counting Smolensk, whose days were numbered, there remained the following principalities:—1. Riazan, with its appanages of Pronsk and Peréiaslavl-Riazanski; 2. Souzdal, with the towns of Vladimir, Nijni-Novgorod, Souzdal, Galitch in Souzdal, Kostroma, and Gorodetz; 3. Tver, situated on the Upper Volga, and chiefly made up of bailiwicks taken from Novgorod by the Grand Princes of Souzdal, with the towns of Rjef, Kachine, and Zoubtsof; 4. Moscow, shut in on the north by Tver, on the east by Souzdal, on the south by Riazan, nearly stifled by its powerful neighbors, like the France of the Capetians between the formidable States of English Normandy, Flanders, and Champagne.

The name of Moscow appears for the first time in the chronicles at the date of 1147. It is there said that the Grand Prince George Dolgorouki, having arrived on the domain of a boyard named Stephen Koutchko, caused him to be put to death on some pretext, and that, struck by the position of one of the villages situated on a height washed by the Moskowa, the very spot whereon the Kremlin now stands, he built the city of Moscow. In the Capitol of ancient Rome the founder, Romulus, discovered the head of a man; the Capitol of Moscow, destined to become the centre of an empire, was sprinkled in its beginning by human blood. The name of a still-existing church, "St. Saviour of the Pines" (*Spass na Borou*), preserves the memory of the thick forests that then clothed both banks of the Moskowa.

on the space now covered by an immense capital. During the century following its foundation, Moscow remained an obscure and insignificant village of Souzdal. The chroniclers do not allude to it except to mention that it was burned by the Tatars (1237), or that a brother of Alexander Nevski, Michael of Moscow, was killed there in a battle with the Lithuanians. The real founder of the principality of the name was Daniel, a son of Alexander Nevski, who had received this small town and a few villages as his appanage. He increased his State by an important town, Peréiaslavl-Zaliesski, that belonged to one of his nephews, and by the addition of Kolomna, which he took from the Riazanese. At his death in 1303 he was the first to be buried in the church of Saint Michael the Archangel, which till the time of Peter the Great remained the burying-place of the Russian princes. He was followed, in due course, by his brothers George and Ivan.

GEORGE DANIELOVITCH (1303-1325) AND IVAN KALITA (1328-1341)—STRUGGLE WITH THE HOUSE OF TVER.

The first act of George Danielovitch (1303-1325) was to capture Mojaïsk from the Prince of Smolensk, and to take the latter prisoner. Almost at the same time began the bloody struggle with the house of Tver, which, transmitted from father to son, lasted for eighty years. When Andrew Alexandrovitch, Grand Prince of Souzdal, died in 1304, two competitors presented themselves—Michael of Tver, cousin-german of the deceased, and his nephew George of Moscow. The claim of Michael was incontestable; was he not the *eldest* of the family? The boyards of Vladimir and the citizens of Novgorod did not hesitate to acknowledge him as Grand Prince; at Saraï Tokhta the khan declared in his favor, and ordered him to be installed. Michael, who had on his side the national law and the sovereign will of the Mongols, could also use force; he twice besieged Moscow, and obliged the son of Daniel to leave him in peace. In this young man he had an implacable enemy. The chronicles, indignant at the revolt of George against the old hereditary custom, unanimously pronounced against him. While making due allowance for their efforts to blacken his character, we cannot help seeing that he was not a man to shrink from any crime. His father had taken the Prince of Riazan prisoner. He had him assassinated in his dungeon, and would have taken possession of his territories, if the Khan had not ordered the rights of the young heir to be respected. Then George caused himself to be recognized as Prince of Novgorod, to the prejudice of Michael, but the army of Tver and Vladimir defeated that furnished him by the republic. An unexpected event suddenly changed the face of things. The Khan Tokhta died; George managed to gain the good graces of his successor Uzbeck, so that the latter gave him his sister Lontchaka in marriage, and, reversing the decision of Tokhta, adjudged him the grand principality. The son of Daniel returned to Russia with a Mongol army, commanded by the *baskak* Kavgadi. Michael consented, say the chronicles, to cede Vladimir, if his hereditary appanage were respected; but George began to lay waste the country of Tver, and war was inevitable. Michael triumphed completely. The Tatar wife of George, his brother Boris, the Mongol general Kavgadi, and nearly all the officers of the Khan, fell into his hands. Michael covered his prisoners with attentions dictated by prudence. Kavgadi, released with honor, swore to be his friend, but, as the sister of the Khan died, the enemies of the Prince of Tver set on foot a report that he had poisoned her. The cause of the two princes was carried before the tribunal of the Khan. Whilst the indefatigable Muscovite went in person, with his hands full of presents, to the Horde, Michael had the imprudence to send his son, a boy of twelve years old, in his place. Finding George was occupied in accusing, intriguing, and corrupting, Michael at last made up his mind to follow him. Not unprepared for the lot that awaited him, he made his will, and distributed appanages among his children. He was accused of having drawn his sword against a *baskak*, envoy of the Khan, and of having poisoned Kontchaka. These accusations were so manifestly absurd, that Uzbeck deferred judgment. This, however, did not meet George's views, and, by means of intrigues, he obtained the arrest of his kinsman. The Khan now set out for some months' hunting in the Caucasus. Michael was dragged in the train of the court, loaded with irons, from the Saraï to Dediakof in Daghestan. One day he was put in the pillory in the market of a thickly-populated town, and the spectators crowded to see him, saying, "This prisoner was, a short time ago, a powerful prince in his own country." The boyards of Michael had told him to escape; he refused, not wishing his people to suffer for him. George was so energetic, and scattered about so much money, that, finally, the death-warrant was signed. One of Michael's pages entered the tent which served him as a prison, in great alarm, to tell him that George and Kavgadi were approaching, followed by a multitude of people. "I know the reason," replied the prince; and he sent his young son Constantine to one of the Khan's wives, who had promised to take him under her protection. His two enemies took their stand near his tent, dismissed the boyards of Tver, and sent their hired ruffians to assassinate the prince. They threw him down, and trampled him under their feet. As in the case of Michael of Tchernigof, it was not a Mongol that stabbed him and tore out his heart, but a renegade named Romanetz. When George and Kavgadi entered and contemplated the naked corpse, "What," said the Tatar, " will you allow the body of your uncle to be outraged?" One of George's servants threw a mantle over the victim (1319). Michael was bewailed by the Tverians. His body, incorruptible as that of a martyr, was afterwards deposited in a silver bier in the cathedral of Tver. He became a saint, and the patron of his city. On the walls of the cathedral, ancient and modern pictures recall his martyrdom, and condemn the crime of the Muscovite. All the contemporary chronicles warmly take his part against the assassin. Karamsin has made himself the echo of their apologies and curses. But at the same time that Michael became a saint, George became the all-powerful sovereign of Moscow, Souzdal, and Novgorod. The tragic fate of Michael foretold the ruin of Tver.

Some years afterwards, things were reversed at the Horde. Dmitri *of the terrible eyes*, son of the unhappy Michael, obtained the title of Grand Prince, and the *baskak* Seventch Bonga was charged to place him on the throne of Vladimir. George found himself obliged to go again to Saraï; there the two rivals, Dmitri of Tver and George of Moscow, met. Dmitri had his father to avenge; his sword leaped from the scabbard, and the Prince of Moscow fell mortally wounded (1325). All that his friends could obtain was that Dmitri should be put to death. The latter was succeeded in Vladimir by his brother Alexander.

Unluckily for the house of Tver, the following year the Tverians, exasperated by the *baskak* Chevkal, rose in rebellion and murdered him and all his suite. Alexander, instead of imitating the firm prudence of his Muscovite neighbors, allowed himself to be carried away by the popular passion. It was he who assaulted the palace of the *baskak*, and lighted the fire. After such an action, he had no pity to expect from the Khan; and if Uzbeck could have forgotten the insult to his majesty, the princes of Moscow would have kept him in mind of it. The brother of George, Ivan Kalita, offered to complete the ruin of Tver. Uzbeck promised him the title of Grand Prince, and gave him an army of 50,000 Tatars, to whom were joined the contingents of Moscow and Souzdal. Alexander, who had not had the wisdom to resist his people, had likewise not the courage to defend them and die with them. He fled with his brothers, to Pskof and Ladoga. Pitiless was the vengeance of the Khan, and the vengeance of Moscow. Tver, Kachine, and Torjok were sacked. Novgorod had to buy herself off by a war indemnity. Not content with exterminating the Tverians, Uzbeck put to death at the same time the Prince of Riazan, son of that Prince Iaroslaf whom George Danielovitch had murdered in prison. The Horde and Moscow seemed to have the same enemies—they struck in concert. It is remarkable that it was in the blood of the martyrs Michael of Tver and Dmitri " with the terrible eyes," that " holy Russia " came to her growth.

Ivan Kalita (1328-1341) became Grand Prince, and made the journey to the Horde with Constantine, son of Michael, who had replaced the fugitive Alexander on the throne of Tver. Ivan was well received, but Uzbeck commanded him to make Alexander appear before him. The ambassadors of the Grand Prince went to Pskof, to conjure Alexander to appear, or to summon the Pskovians to deliver him up. "Do not expose," they said, "a Christian people to the wrath of the infidels." But the Pskovians, touched by the prayers of the Prince of Tver, replied, "Do not go to the Horde, my lord; whatever happens, we will die with thee." As magnanimous as the Novgorodians at the time of Alexander Nevski, as heroically absurd, they ordered the ambassadors to be gone, took up arms, and built a new fortress near Izborsk. Ivan assembled an army and persuaded the Metropolitan Theognostus to place Alexander and the Pskovians under an interdict. Thus men saw a Christian prince persecute one of his kinsmen by order of the Tatars, and a metropolitan excommunicate the Christians to force them to obey the Khan. The Pskovians, though alarmed, would not yield an inch; but Alexander left them and took refuge in Lithuania. Then they said to the Grand Prince, " Alexander is gone; all Pskof swears it, from the smallest to the greatest, popes, monks, nuns, orphans, women, and children " (1329).

Alexander afterwards returned, and was again recognized by them as their prince, but still regretted his good city of Tver. The protection of the Lithuanian Gedimin was too dangerous and too burdensome. Alexander thought it would be easier to bend the terrible Uzbeck. He went to the Horde with his boyards. "Lord, all-powerful Tzar," he said to Uzbeck. "if I have done anything against you, I have come hither to receive of you life or death. Do as God inspires you; I am ready for either." The Khan pardoned him, and Alexander returned to Tver. Ivan Kalita had hoped he had forever got rid of him. In Alexander's absence he was the master of Russia, had interfered in the affairs of Tver, married one of his daughters to Vladimir of Iaroslavl and another to Constantine of Rostof, brother of the banished prince. The return of Alexander gave a chief to those who were discontented with Ivan. Instead of declaring war, Ivan preferred to resort to his ordinary means. He flew to the Horde, and there represented Alexander as the most dangerous enemy of the Mongols. In consequence of these insinuations, Alexander was summoned before the Khan; this time he was beheaded, with his son Feodor. The rivalry with Moscow had already cost four princes of the house of Tver their lives. Uzbeck, who had only confidence in Moscow, and who wished to govern the rest of Russia by terror, about this time put the Prince of Starodoub to death. The princes Constantine and Vassili of Tver, sons, brothers, and uncles of the victims, felt that they could only maintain themselves by obedience to their terrible father-in-law. As a proof of submission they sent to Kalita the great bell of the cathedral of Tver. The princes of Riazan and Souzdal were also obliged to fight under his standards. Novgorod, threatened by him, began the course which afterwards proved so fatal to her, and might have proved the ruin of Russia; she allied herself with Lithuania, accepted as prince, Narimond, a son of Gedimin, and gave him the Novgorodian possessions in Ingria and Carelia, as hereditary appanages. She tried also to make friends with the Grand Prince of Moscow, but Ivan only desired to restrict her liberties, and exacted, in the name of the Khan, a double capitation-tax.

This unwarlike prince, at the same time as he strengthened his supremacy, acquired by purchase the towns of Ouglitch, Galitch, Biélozersk, and lands in the neighborhoods of Kostroma, Vladimir, and Rostof. He was at once Prince of Moscow and Grand Prince of Vladimir; but Moscow was his inheritance, of which he could not legally be despoiled by the Khan, while Vladimir could be given to another house. It was thus that in Germany the archduchy of Austria was hereditary, whilst the imperial crown might legally pass to another family. It may therefore be imagined how Kalita chose to sacrifice Vladimir to Moscow, as the Hapsburgs sacrificed Frankfort to Vienna. His Tverian rivals, the two grand princes, his predecessors, had acted in the same way. Michael and Dmitri of Tver had hardly appeared at Vladimir, except to be crowned in the cathedral. They lived habitually in their appanage towns, one at Tver, the other at Peréiaslavl. Under Kalita, Vladimir remained the legal capital of Russia; Moscow was the real capital, and Kalita was working to make her the capital *de jure* as well as *de facto*. The Metropolitan of Vladimir, Peter, who had an affection for

Moscow, often resided there. His successor, Theognostus, established himself there completely. Then the religious supremacy which had first belonged to Kief, and next to Vladimir, passed to Moscow. Kalita did his best to give it the prestige of a metropolis. He built magnificent churches in the Kremlin, among others that of the Assumption, the *Ouspienski sobor*. The first Metropolitans of Moscow, thanks to him and his successors, were beatified. St. Alexis and St. Peter are reckoned among the patron-saints of Russia. It is related that the Metropolitan Peter himself marked out the place of his tomb in the new church, and that he said to Ivan, "God will bless thee, and elevate thee above all the other princes, and raise this town above all other towns. Thy race will reign in this place during many centuries; their hands will conquer all their enemies; the saints will make their dwelling here, and here shall my bones repose."

What made the chief glory of Kief the ancient metropolis was the famous Petcherski monastery, with its holy catacombs and the tombs of so many ascetics and wonder-workers. Moscow had also her heritage of virtues and glorious austerity. Under Kalita's successor, not far from the capital, in a deep forest, where he had at first no companion but a bear, on watercourses which were haunted only by the beavers, St. Sergius founded the Troïtsa monastery (the *Trinity*), which became one of the richest and most venerated of Eastern Russia. On its increase of wealth, it was obliged to be surrounded with ramparts; and its thick brick walls with a triple row of embrasures, its nine war-towers, and its still existing fortifications, were afterwards destined to brave the assaults of Catholics and infidels. The princes of Moscow, in spite of their perfidious and pitiless policy, were as pious as good King Robert—*dévots*, alms-givers, indefatigable in building churches and monasteries, in honoring the clergy, and in helping the poor. The surname of *Kalita* given to Ivan comes from the *kalita* or alms-bag he wore always at his girdle. This *kalita* may also have been Shylock's purse—the bag of a prince who was farmer-general and usurer who demanded from Novgorod double what he intended to pay on her behalf to Uzbeck. Ivan liked to converse with the monks in his Convent of the Transfiguration. Like all the other princes of the house, he took care, when at the point of death, to be tonsured and adopt the religious dress and a new name.

If the princes of Moscow labored with fierce energy to bind together the Russian soil, they continued to divide it into appanages among their sons. Many causes contributed to prevent the return of the former anarchy. These princes, as a rule, had few sons; they gradually got into the way of giving only very weak appanages to the younger ones, and these on condition of an absolute dependence on the eldest. Ivan, for example, had only three sons; he gave by far the larger share (Mojaïsk and Kolomna) to Simeon, and forbade Moscow to be divided. The idea of the State as one and indivisible was certain to end by gaining the day.

SIMEON THE PROUD AND IVAN THE DEBONNAIRE (1341–1359).

Simeon the Proud (1341–1353) and Ivan II. (1353–1359) succeeded one after the other their father Kalita. They were all three contemporaries of the early Valois. At the news of the death of Ivan, many princes at once disputed the throne of Vladimir with his sons. Constantine of Tver, and Constantine of Souzdal, especially, were supported by the other princes who did not desire the title of Grand Prince to be perpetuated in the house of Moscow. They went to the Horde at the same time as Simeon and his two sons travelled thither. Simeon owed his success neither to his eloquence nor his arguments, but to the treasure of his father, which won over the infidels. After being crowned in the Cathedral of Vladimir, he swore to live in harmony with his two brothers, and exacted from them the same oath. While pushing his submission to the Khan to the verge of baseness, he domineered over the Russian princes with a haughtiness that gained for him the surname of "the Proud." He forced Novgorod to pay him a contribution, and, in his capacity of supreme head of Russia, confirmed the liberties of the republic. He was the first who assumed the title of "Grand Prince of all the Russias," which was little justified by the facts, as in 1341 Olgerd of Lithuania besieged the town of Mojaisk, Simeon's own appanage. The friendship of St. Alexis, third Metropolitan of Moscow, gave him great moral aid. In his reign Boris, a Russian artist, cast bells for the cathedrals of Moscow and Novgorod; three churches of the Kremlin were adorned with new paintings—that of the *Assumption*, by Greek artists; that of *St. Michael*, by the Court painters; that of the *Transfiguration*, by a foreigner named Goiten. Paper replaced parchment: and it was on paper that Simeon's will was written. Russia then still maintained her old relations with Byzantium, and entered into new ones with Europe. Simeon died of the famous "black death" or "black pestilence," which at this time desolated the West.

Ivan II., brother and successor of "the Proud," deserves,

on the contrary, the surname of "the Débonnaire." He was of a different type from the sinister princes of Souzdal, and was pacific and gentle. The anarchy into which Russia fell during the six years of his reign, shows how little his virtues were those of his century. Without attempting to avenge himself, Ivan permitted Oleg of Riazan to insult his territory, burn his villages of the Lopasnia, and ill-treat his lieutenant. He allowed the Novgorodians to despise his authority and obey Constantine of Souzdal; he let the Grand Duke Olgerd occupy Rjef, and Andrew of Lithuania menace Pskof. He interfered neither in the civil wars of the princes of Riazan, nor in those of the principality of Tver, nor in the troubles excited at Novgorod by the rivalry of the Slavonian quarters and that of St. Sophia, nor in the storm raised in the Church by the Patriarch of Constantinople, who dared to consecrate metropolitan a rival of St. Alexis. The murder of one of his officers, Alexis, military governor of Moscow, remained unpunished. In this weakness of the prince, the churchmen naturally came to the front, and took up the part abandoned by him. Moses, Archbishop of Novgorod, quelled a revolt in the republic; St. Alexis reconciled the princes of Tver, and acquired, by a miraculous cure, great power in the Horde, by which he profited to protect his people and his prince. At the death of Ivan II., the title of Grand Prince, which his three predecessors had made such efforts to perpetuate in the house of Moscow, passed to that of Souzdal. Dmitri of Souzdal (1359-1362), furnished with the *iarlikh*, made his solemn entry into Vladimir. It was again St. Alexis who saved the supremacy of Moscow. After having blessed the Grand Prince in Vladimir, he returned to his care of the young children of Ivan II., and to Moscow, which had for a moment ceased to be the capital. It was by his counsel that Dmitri Ivanovitch, at the age of twelve, dared to declare himself the rival of Dmitri of Souzdal, and determined to appeal to the tribunal of the Khan. The Golden Horde was then a prey to civil wars; the ferocious Mamaï harassed Mourout, but as the latter reigned at Saraï, and seemed the legitimate successor of Bati, it was to him that the Souzdalian and Muscovite boyards addressed themselves. Mourout adjudged the Grand Principality to the grandson of Kalita, whom a Muscovite army led to be consecrated in Vladimir.

DMITRI DONSKOI (1363-1389)—THE BATTLE OF KOULIKOVO.

Dmitri Ivanovitch (1363-1389) is distinguished from nearly all the Souzdal princes by a warlike and chivalrous character

worthy of the West. He proves that the Russian soul had been
only repressed, not rendered depraved and servile by the Tatar
yoke, and that Slav chivalry only awaited an opportunity to
raise the cry of war, and make their swords flash like the *preux
chevaliers* of Louis IX. or of John the Good. Dmitri had at
once to sustain a series of wars against the neighboring princes;
notably against Dmitri of Souzdal, Michael of Tver, and Oleg
of Riazan. As changes took place at the Horde, Dmitri of
Souzdal obtained from the Khan Mourout a reversal of his first
decision, and returned to Vladimir. The Prince of Moscow,
who feared this feeble Khan no longer, did not hesitate to take
up arms, and to expel his rival from Vladimir. A treaty was
agreed on between them. The Souzdalian appanage of Nijni-
Novgorod having become vacant. Dmitri supported his ancient
enemy against his competitor Boris. Like his grandfather
Kalita, who had caused Novgorod to be excommunicated,
Dmitri Ivanovitch entreated St. Sergius, the founder of the
Troïtsa Monastery, to lay Nijni-Novgorod under an interdict.
Then Boris yielded, and Dmitri of Souzdal, now Prince of Nijni-
Novgorod, gave the Prince of Moscow his daughter Eudoxia in
marriage, and henceforward remained his friend. Dmitri Ivanovitch deprived the rebel princes of Starodoub and Galitch of
their appanages, and forced Constantine Borissovitch to recognize his supremacy. He made, under the guarantee of St.
Alexis, a treaty with his cousin, Vladimir Andriévitch, by which
he undertook to hand over to him the appanage that Kalita had
secured to his father, and by which Vladimir engaged to acknowledge him as his father and his Grand Prince. Vladimir
kept his word, and was always the bravest lieutenant and the
right arm of Dmitri.

The struggle now recommenced with the house of Tver.
Michael Alexandrovitch, whose father had been killed at the
Horde, disputed the throne with one of his uncles. The Grand
Prince and the Metropolitan of Moscow took the part of the
latter. Michael paid no attention to this decision, took Tver
with a Lithuanian army, besieged his uncle in Kachine, and
obliged him to renounce his claims. He then took the title of
Grand Prince of Tver. It was chiefly the alliance with Olgerd,
the husband of his sister Juliana, that rendered him formidable. Thrice—in 1368, in 1371, and in 1372—Olgerd conducted
his brother-in-law, burning and pillaging on his way, up to the
walls of the Kremlin on Moscow. Neither the Lithuanian nor
the Muscovite army on any of these occasions fought a decisive
battle. The boyards of Dmitri felt that a lost battle would be
the ruin of Russia; while Olgerd was too old and experienced to

stake all on a hazard. At last, in 1375, after the death of his brother-in-law, Michael found himself besieged in Tver by the united forces of all the vassals and allies of Dmitri and of the Novgorodians who had the sack of Torjok and the devastation of their territory to avenge. Reduced to extremities, and abandoned by Lithuania, he was constrained to sign a treaty by which he engaged to regard Dmitri as his "elder brother," to renounce all claim to Novgorod and Vladimir, not to disquiet the allies of Moscow, and to imitate Dmitri's conduct towards the Tatars, whether he continued to pay tribute or he declared war.

Another enemy, not less dangerous, was Oleg of Riazan who had formerly braved Ivan the Débonnaire. In 1371, the Muscovites defeated Oleg, and installed a prince of Pronsk in is capital, who was not, however, strong enough to maintain nis position. If Tver was sometimes supported by Lithuania, Riazan had often the Horde as an ally.

The empire of Kiptchak was gradually falling to pieces. Many competitors disputed the throne of Saraï. The Tatars acted after their kind, and invaded the Russian territory in disorderly style. It is true it was no longer a point of honor with the Christian princes to submit to them. Oleg of Riazan himself united with the princes of Pronsk and Kozelsk, and defied the *mourza* Tagaï, who had burnt Riazan. Dmitri of Souzdal, prince of Nijni-Novgorod, had defeated Boulat-Temir, who on his return to the Horde had been disavowed and put to death. Finally, Dmitri of Moscow had many times disobeyed the terrible Mamaï. He had, however, the courage to answer to the summons of the Khan, and the good fortune or the cleverness to return to Moscow safe and well (1371). In 1376 Dmitri sent a great expedition against Kazan by the Volga, and forced two Tatar princes to pay tribute. Conflicts multiplied between the Christians and the infidels. In this manner the princes of Souzdal exterminated a band of Mordvians, and delivered up their chiefs to be torn in pieces by the dogs of Novgorod ; in return, Mamaï ordered the town to be burnt. In 1378, Dmitri of Moscow gained a brilliant victory over the lieutenant of Mamaï on the banks of the Voja in Riazan. In the first intoxication of victory, he cried, " Their time is past, and God is with us ! " The Khan, in his blind fury, caused his anger to fall on Oleg of Riazan, the rival of Dmitri Ivanovitch, who fled, abandoning his lands to the ravages of the enemy.

It took Mamaï two years to mature his plans of vengeance, and he assembled in silence an immense host of Tatars, Turks, Polovtsi, Tcherkesses, Iasses, and Bourtanians or Caucasian Jews. Even the Genoese of Kaffa, settled in the Crimea and on the territory of the Khan, furnished a contingent. In these critical circumstances for Russia, Oleg of Riazan, forgetting his grievances against the Tatars, and only remembering his mistrust and jealousy of Moscow, betrayed the common cause. While keeping on good terms with Dmitri, even while warning him of what was preparing, he secretly negotiated an alliance between the two most formidable enemies of Russia—Jagellon of Lithuania and Mamaï. The Grand Prince's army would probably be crushed between them; but Dmitri did not lose heart. The desire of vengeance awakened in the Russians with the force of religious enthusiasm. At the call of the Grand Prince, the princes of Rostof, Biélozersk, Iaroslavl, Starodoub, and Kachine, with their *droujinas*; the boyards of Vladimir, Nijni-Novgorod, Souzdal, Perćiaslavl-Zaliesski, Kostroma, Mourom, Dmitrof, Mojaïsk, Zvenigorod, Ouglitch, and Serpoukhof, at the head of their contingents, successively made their entrance into the Kremlin, amid the acclamations of the Muscovites. At Kostroma Dmitri was to be joined by two Lithuanian princes—Andrew and Dmitri—who brought him troops from Pskof and Briansk. The grand Prince, with his cousin Vladimir, went to the hermitage of Troitsa to ask the benediction of Saint Sergius. The latter predicted that he would gain the victory, but that it would be a bloody fight. He sent two of his monks, Alexander Peresvet and Osliaba, formerly a brave boyard of Briansk, to accompany Dmitri. On their cowls he made the sign of the cross. "Behold," he cried, "a weapon which faileth never." The Prince of Tver had taken good care not to send his contingent, and the treason of the Prince of Riazan now became known. The hearts of the Russians beat with joy and enthusiasm at the throught of revenge. In spite of private jealousies, the princes were animated by the same ardor as the Spanish kings when they marched against the Moors, or the companions of Godfrey of Bouillon on the road for the Holy Land. Never had such an army been seen. Dmitri is said to have had 150,000 men.

They crossed the country of Riazan, then under a craven prince, and reached the banks of the Don. The princes debated as to whether it was necessary to cross the river immediately; but it was urgent to dispose of the Mongols before having on their hands Jagellon, who had already arrived at Odoef, fifteen leagues off. A letter which Dmitri received from Saint Sergius, recommending him to "go forwards," decided the matter. The Don was crossed, and they found themselves on the plain of Koulikovo (*the Field of Woodcocks*), watered by the Nepriadva. The centre was occupied by the princes of Lithuania and Smolensk, with the *droujina* of Dmitri; the right was commanded by the princes of Rostof and Starodoub, the left by those of Iaroslavl and Vologda; the reserve by Prince Vladimir, the brave Dmitri of Volhynia, and the princes of Briansk and Kachine. The Mongols soon came up, and the battle began. It was bloody and dubious. The enemy had already cut to pieces the *droujina* of the Grand Prince, when Vladimir and Dmitri of Volhynia, who had lain in ambush, suddenly attacked the Tatars. Mamaï, from the top of a *kourgan*, contemplated the flight of his army. His camp, his chariots, and his camels were all captured. The Mongols were pursued to the Métcha, in which many drowned themselves. If the barbarians lost, as they are said to have done, 100,000 men, the Russian loss was also very severe. They counted among the dead the two monks of Saint Sergius; one of them, Peresvet was discovered in the arms of a Patzinak giant, who had fought, with him hand to hand, and perished along with him. For a long while Dmitri could not be found; at last he was seen in a swoon, his armor bloody and broken. This memorable battle of Koulikovo has been related in more than one way by the Russian historians. With the annalists, properly so called, the official historiographers of the Grand Prince, Dmitri is the hero. In the poetical recitals which were inspired by the account of the pope Sophronius, it is Saint Sergius who at each moment supports the courage of Dmitri, whom they represent with rather too much humility for a general-in-chief. The battle of the Don, which gained for Dmitri the surname of *Donskoï*, and for Vladimir that of the Brave, is as celebrated in Russia as that of Las Navas de Tolosa in Spain. It showed the Russians that they could vanquish the invincible; and the Mongol yoke, even after they again fell under it, did not seem inevitable. Dmitri had heroically broken the tradition of slavery; he had proclaimed the future freedom (1380).

Unhappily the event showed the advantages of the policy of resignation over the policy of chivalry—of the patience of the hero of the Neva over the bravery of the hero of the Don. A man appeared at this moment at the head of the Mongols, who was as formidable as Genghis Khan—Tamerlane, the conqueror of the two Bokharas, of Hindostan, of Iran, and of Asia Minor. Tokhtamych, one of his generals, caused Mamaï to be put to death, and announced to Dmitri that he had triumphed over their common enemy; then he summoned the Russian princes to present themselves at the Horde. Dmitri refused. Was it in vain that the blood of the Christians had flowed at Koulikovo? The Khan assembled an immense army. Dmitri found no longer the same wisdom or energy among his councillors. Not knowing what to do, he left Moscow and went to assemble an army at Kostroma. Tokhtamych marched straight on the capital, and during three days tried to carry the walls of the Kremlin by assault. Then he had recourse to a *ruse*, and affected to enter in a negotiation. At last the Tatars surprised the gates, and delivered up Moscow to fire and sword. A tolerably exact calculation proves that 24,000 men perished, beside the precious documents and earliest archives of the principality.

Vladimir, Mojaïsk, Iourief, and other towns of Souzdal suffered the same fate. When Tokhtamych had retired, Dmitri came and wept over the ruins of his capital. "Our fathers," he cried, "who never triumphed over the Tatars, were less unhappy than we." Bitter morrow of victory! However, although Russia had to resign herself to her Tatar collectors, she felt that the Horde would never recover its former power.

Dmitri longed at least to revenge himself on the perfidious Oleg. The latter escaped him, but Riazan, which was regarded as a harbor for traitors, was sacked. Michael of Tver merited the same chastisement; he had refused to fight Mamaï, and was one of the first to fly to the Horde of Tokhtamych. The war continued with Oleg of Riazan, who ravaged the territory of Kolomna. Saint Sergius again intervened, entreated and threatened Oleg, and finally induced him to conclude a "perpetual peace" with Dmitri, and to cement it by the marriage of his son Feodor with Sophia, daughter of Dmitri.

The Novgorod adventurers, the "Good Companions," had about this time committed many ravages on the territories of the Grand Principalities. They insulted Iaroslavl and Kostroma in 1371, and Kostroma and Nijni-Novgorod in 1375, pillaging as far as Saraï and Astrakhan, sparing neither infidels nor Christians. Novgorod continued to furnish appanages to the Lithuanian princes, to despise the political authority of the Grand Prince, and the religious supremacy of the Metropolitan. Dmitri marched against the republic with the contingents of twenty-five provinces. Novgorod had to pay an indemnity for the glorious deeds of the Good Companions, and to engage to furnish a yearly tribute.

When Dmitri died, the principality of Moscow was by far the most considerable of the States of the North-east, since it extended on the south to Kalouga and Kasimof, and included on the north-east Biélozersk and Galitch. As to Vladimir, Dmitri, in his will, calls it his patrimony. He has been reproached for having limited himself to the sack of Tver and Riazan, without hastening their final annexation. If Dmitri gave appanages to his five younger sons, he at least established the principle of inheritance in a direct line instead of the ancient principle of collateral succession. He had signed a treaty with his cousin Vladimir, by which the latter renounced his rights as "eldest of the family," engaging to consider Vassili, eldest son of Dmitri, as his "elder brother." In the reign of Donskoï the monk Stephen founded the first church in the country of the Permians, confuted their priests and sorcerers, overthrew the idols of Voïssel and the *Old Golden Woman* who held two infants in her arms, put a stop to the sacrifice of reindeer, built schools, and died Bishop of Permia. A certain Andrew, probably a Genoese by birth, settled on the Petchora. Russia entered into relations with the West by means of the Genoese of Kaffa and Azof; coins of silver and copper, with the image of a knight, replaced the *kounes*, or marten-skins. About 1389 the first cannons appeared in the Russian army. Moscow continued to adorn herself, and the monasteries of the Miracle, of Andronii, and of Simeon were built.

VASSILI DMITRIEVITCH AND VASSILI THE BLIND (1389-1465).

Vassili Dmitriévitch (1389-1425), the contemporary of Charles VI. of France, succeeded his father without opposition as Grand Prince of Moscow and Vladimir. The preponderance of the first of these towns over the second became more and more marked. The situation of both was equally advantageous; the one on the Moskowa, the other on the Kliazma, affluents of the Oka. Vladimir, like Moscow, had its kremlin on a high hill, commanding a vast extent of country. Both cities were in communication with the great Russian artery, the Volga; but were far enough from it to escape the piracies of the Good Companions. Vladimir had been in other respects as favored as Moscow. Andrew Boglioubski had ornamented the former, as Ivan Kalita had embellished the second. Vladimir, to which the title of Grand Principality was attached, seemed even better fitted than Moscow to be the capital of Russia. It was almost an historical accident that decided in favor of the latter. At the present day Vladimir is merely a simple seat of government with a population of 14,000, while Moscow is a metropolis with 600,000 souls.

With regard to Novgorod, the Grand Prince of Moscow began to look upon it from the point of view of a sovereign, and called the city "his patrimony." The Novgorodians on their side appealed to the charter of Iaroslaf the Great, which formally conceded them the right to choose their princes. In the last reigns they had been accustomed to have recourse to a bargain. The republicans recognized the sovereign of Moscow as their prince, if the latter would consent to certain conditions,—the final homage rendered to the ancient Slav freedom. After the fall of Alexander of Tver (1328), no Russian prince could compete with the house of Moscow for the throne of Novgorod. The only possible rivals were the Grand Princes of Lithuania. Now with Lithuania it was not only a competition of candidates, but it was a great national and religious question. Moscow would prefer to ruin Novgorod rather than allow her to pass into the hands of the most dangerous enemy of Russian orthodoxy. We may say that after 1328 Novgorod had no longer a special prince, but only a boyard of Moscow, who represented the Grand Prince. The power of the latter was sometimes exerted with vigor. In 1393 Novgorod having revolted against Moscow, Vassili sent in his troops, and seventy inhabitants of Torjok, accused of having put to death one of his men, were cut to pieces.

Vassili Dmitriévitch then, on his accession to the throne, found his power considerably strengthened, as Vladimir on the Kliazma and Novgorod the Great, the objects of so many bloody contests with the Russian princes, had in some ways already become integral parts of his dominions. If he went to the Horde in 1392, it was less to obtain the confirmation of this triple crown than to acquire new territories. From the Khan Tokhtamych he bought a *iarlikh*, which put him in possession of the three appanages of Mourom, Nijni-Novgorod, and Souzdal. The boyards of Moscow and the ambassador of the Khan betook themselves to Nijni. Boris, the last titular prince of the two latter appanages, was betrayed by his men, who persuaded him to open the gates, and delivered him up to the soldiers of the Grand Prince. Then, with the ringing of all the bells in the town, Vassili of Moscow was proclaimed Prince of Nijni and Souzdal.

This prince, who lived on such good terms with the Horde, was witness, however, of two Tatar invasions of Russia. Tamerlane, conqueror of the Ottoman Turks at Anticyra, attacked his old favorite Tokhtamych, and pillaged the Golden Horde. He continued to move towards the West, putting the Russian territory to fire and sword. Moscow was threatened with an invasion as terrible as that of Bati. The famous Virgin of Vladimir, brought by Andrew Bogolioubski from Vychegorod, was taken solemnly to Moscow. The Tatars reached Eletz on the Don, and made its princes prisoners. There they stopped, and suddenly retreated. Accustomed to the rich booty of Bokhara and Hindostan, and dreaming of Constantinople and Egypt, they found, no doubt, that the desert steppes and deep forests only offered a very meagre prey. They indemnified themselves by the pillage of Azof, where Egyptian, Venetian, Genoese, Catalan and Biscayan merchants had accumulated great wealth, and by the destruction of Astrakhan and Saraï (1395.)

The irruption of Tamerlane resulted in the more rapid dissolution of the Golden Horde. We have seen that Vitovt took advantage of it to organize against the Mongols his great crusade of the Vorskla (1399). Vassili Dmitriévitch had taken good care not to interfere in the war between Lithuania and the Kiptchaks. His Western neighbors appeared to him more dangerous than those of the East; with the latter the payment of the tribute still sufficed, with the former the stake was the existence of Russia. Vassili profited by the defeat of the one and the disorganization of the other, and was careful to irritate neither party. As the Horde was then disputed by many competitors, he forbore to pay the tribute, affecting not to know which was the legitimate Khan. Ediger, the vanquisher of Vitovt, resolved to reduce the Russian vassals to obedience. He lulled the prudence of the Muscovites to rest by spreading the rumor that he was assembling troops for a war against Lithuania. Suddenly they heard that he had entered the Grand Principality. Vassili imitated the conduct of his father in similar circumstances. He retired to Kostroma to assemble an army, and confided the defence of Moscow to Vladimir the Brave. Defended by artillery, the Kremlin could withstand the attack of a large force, but the dense population caused fears of famine. Ediger burnt the towns in the flat country while blockading Moscow. Ivan, prince of Tver, showed on this occasion more greatness of soul and political wisdom than his father Michael. He abstained from coming to the help of the Tatars against his formidable suzerain. In these circumstances Ediger learnt that his master Boulat himself feared an attack at the Horde by his Oriental enemies. To cover his forced retreat he addressed a haughty letter to the Grand Prince, summoning him to pay tribute ; he obtained three thousand roubles from the Muscovite boyards as a war indemnity (1408).

Vitovt of Lithuania, whose daughter Sophia Vassili had married, was a still more dangerous enemy. Great caution was necessary in all dealings with him. Vassili saw the hand of his father-in-law, in the troubles of Novgorod, everywhere; at Pskof, where Vitovt had taken the title of Grand Prince ; at Smolensk, which he had united to Lithuania ; at Tver, where he supported Michael against the Grand Prince. Like Olgerd, Vitovt marched thrice against Moscow. Each of the two rivals had too many other enemies to dispose of, to risk in one battle **the fortunes of** Moscow or Lithuania. In 1408 they signed a treaty by which the Ougra was fixed on as the limit of the two Grand Principalities, leaving Smolensk to Vitovt, and restoring Kozelsk to Russia. Besides Mourom and Souzdal, Vassili had united to his domains many appanages of the country of Tchernigof, such as Toroussa, Novossil, Kozelsk, and Peremysl. In the quarrels with Novgorod, generally occasioned by the exploits of the Good Companions or by commercial rivalry, he had appropriated vast territories on the Dwina; among others, Vologda. In an expedition against the republic of Viatka he had reduced it to submission, and made one of his brothers its prince. He had imposed a treaty on Feodor Olgivitch, prince of Riazan, by which the latter undertook to look on him as a father, and to make no alliance to his hurt. Vassili on his side ceded to him Toula and the title of Grand Prince. The Oka formed the boundary of the two States. He made, no doubt, a similar treaty with Ivan, prince of Tver. One of his daughters had married the Emperor John Palæologus.

The reign of Vassili the Blind (1425-1462), contemporary with Charles VII. of France, marks a pause in the development of the Grand Principality. A civil war of twenty years broke out in the bosom of the family of *Donskoi*. One of his sons, George, or Iouri, whom he had made Prince of Roussa and Zvenigorod, attempted to revert to the ancient national law, and invoked his right as "eldest" against his nephew, Vassili Vassiliévitch. Vassili's other uncles declared in favor of the young prince. In 1431 it was necessary to carry the dispute to the Horde. Each of the two parties set forth his right to the Khan Oulou-Makhmet. Vsevolojski, a boyard of the Prince of Moscow, found the best of arguments for his master. "My Lord Tzar," he said to Makhmet, "let me speak—me, the slave of the Grand Prince. My master the Grand Prince prays for the throne of the Grand Principality, which is thy property, having no other title but thy protection, thy investiture, and thy *iarlikh*. Thou art master, and can dispose of it according to thy good pleasure. My lord the Prince Iouri Dmitriévitch, his uncle, claims the Grand Principality by the act and the will of his father, but not as a favor from the All-powerful." In this contest of baseness the prize was adjudged to the Prince of Moscow. The Khan ordered Iouri to lead his nephew's horse by the bridle. A Tatar *baskak* was present at the coronation of the Grand Prince, which took place, for the first time, not at Vladimir, but at the Assumption in Moscow. From this time Vladimir lost her privileges as the capital, although, in the enumeration of their titles, the Grand Princes continued to inscribe the name of Vladimir before that of Moscow.

Vassili owed his throne to the clever boyard, Vsevolojski. He had promised to marry his daughter, but his own mother, Sophia, the proud Lithuanian, daughter of the great Vitovt, made him contract an alliance with the Princess Maria, granddaughter of Vladimir the Brave. The irritated boyard left Vassili's service, and retired to his enemy, Iouri, whose resentment against his nephew he fanned. Another circumstance exasperated Iouri; his two sons, Vassili the Squinting, and Chemiaka, assisted at the marriage of the Grand Prince. The Princess Sophia recognized round the waist of Vassili the Squinting a belt of gold which had belonged to Dmitri Donskoï. She had the imprudence, publicly and with open scandal, to take it from the son of Iouri. On this affront, the two princes at once left the banqueting-hall, and retired to their father. The latter instantly took up arms, and departed for Peréiaslavl. The Prince of Moscow could hardly assemble any troops, and fell into the hands of his uncle at Kostroma, (1433). Vassili tried in vain to soften him by his tears. The Squinter and Chemiaka wished their prisoner to be put to death, but by the self interested counsel of the boyard Morozof, Iouri allowed his nephew to live, and gave him the appanage of Kostroma, while he took for himself the Grand Principality. The affection of the Muscovites for their prince was so great, that they abandoned their city *en masse*, and crowded into Kostroma. Iouri saw that his nephew was still powerful, reproached Morozof for his perfidious advice, and had him stabbed by his two sons. "Thou hast ruined our father," they said. The usurper was indeed unable to remain in Moscow, and sent to tell his nephew he might come and take possession of it. The boyards pressed around Vassili on his return to his capital, "as bees press around their queen." The war, however, continued : thanks to the cowardice of Vassili, Iouri again took the Kremlin, and made prisoners the wife and mother of the Grand Prince, while the Squinter and Chemiaka occupied Vladimir, and marched on Nijni-Novgorod.

Iouri had hardly been recognized as Grand Prince of Novgorod, when he died suddenly. His sons then made peace with Vassili, but immediately took up arms again. In one of the many reverses of this civil war, Vassili the Squinting fell into the hands of the Grand Prince, who had his eyes put out in an excess of fury (1436). Then, by one of those changes common to violent and impulsive natures, he passed from anger to dismay; and to atone for his crime against his cousin, set free Chemiaka, whom he had made prisoner at the same time.

Chemiaka promised to serve him, but served him very badly. In a battle with the Tatars, his desertion caused the rout of the Russian army (siege of Biélef, in Lithuania). In 1441 the war began again between the Grand Prince and Chemiaka. The latter, with some thousands of Free-lances and Good Companions, suddenly undertook the siege of Moscow. Zenobius, superior of the Troïtsa monastery, succeeded once more in reconciling them. Chemiaka displayed his ordinary duplicity on the occasion of a military incursion of the Tatars of Kazan. The Grand Prince waited in vain for the succors that had been promised him, and it was with only 1500 men that he finally took the field, so much had the discords between the descendants of Dmitri Donskoï weakened the Grand Principality, loosened the ties of obedience among the vassals, and degraded that Russia which had armed 150,000 men against Mamaï. Vassili, covered with fifteen wounds, fell into the hands of the barbarians, and was led prisoner to Kazan.

Moscow was in despair. The Prince of Tver insulted her territory; Chemiaka intrigued at the Horde to get himself nominated Grand Prince. All at once the Tzar of Kazan took it into his head to liberate his prisoners for a small ransom. Vassili re-entered his capital amid the acclamations of his people. Chemiaka had done enough to fear the vengeance of the Grand Prince; in the interests of his own safety, Vassili must be overthrown. Following the example of his father and grandfather, Vassili went to the Troïtsa monastery to return thanks to Saint Sergius for his deliverance. He had few companions and Chemiaka and his associates surprised the Kremlin in his absence, and captured his wife, his mother, and his treasures. Then he flew to Troïtsa, where his accomplice, Ivan of Mojaïsk, discovered the Grand Prince, who was hidden in the principal church near the tomb of Saint Sergius. He was brought back to Moscow, and ten years after the blinding of Vassili the Squinting, Chemiaka avenged his brother by putting out the eyes of the Grand Prince (1446).

During his short reign at Moscow, Chemiaka had made himself hated by the people and the boyards, who were faithful at bottom to their unhappy prince. In the popular language, a "judgment of Chemiaka" became the synonym for a crying wrong. Presently Vassili's partisans assembled troops in Lithuania, joined those of the two Tatar *tzarévitches*, and marched against the usurper. At this period, Russia was infested by armed bands, the relics of the great Tatar and Lithuanian wars, Lithuanian adventurers, *tzarevitches* banished from the Horde, Novgorodian Good Companions, Free-lances of all races. They ravaged the flat country, attacked the strongest towns, and their chiefs sometimes created ephemeral principalities for themselves. As the Asiatic element predominated in them, they might be termed *Great Mongol Companies*, analogous to the *Great English* or *the French Companies* that, about the year 1444, Charles VII. sent to Alsace and Switzerland. Serving Chemiaka or the Grand Prince indifferently, they did their best to perpetuate the quarrel. Chemiaka wished to march against his enemies. Hardly had he left Moscow when the city broke into revolt, and Vassili entered in triumph. Chemiaka fled, and accepted a reconciliation with his victim (1447). Incapable of repose, he again took up arms. was completely defeated near Galitch by the Muscovites and Tatars (1450), and fled to Novgorod, where he is said to have died three years after, by poison. All his appanages were reunited to the royal domain.

Disembarrassed of this dangerous enemy, Vassili the Blind hastened to take up the work of his predecessors. Novgorod had not ceased to give asylum to his enemies, to despise the authority of his lieutenants, to contest his right of final appeal and the supremacy of the Metropolitan. A Muscovite army reduced her to reason ; she was forced to annul all the acts of the *vetcha* which tended to limit the authority of the Grand Prince, to pay him a heavy indemnity, and to promise to set no seal but that of Vassili on her deeds. Pskof received one of his sons as her prince. The republic of Viatka had to pay tribute, and to furnish a military contingent. The Prince of Riazan having just died, Vassili took his young heir to Moscow, under pretence of bringing him up, and sent his lieutenant to govern the appanage. Vassili of Borovsk, grandson of Vladimir the Brave, had rendered him important services, but none the less was he imprisoned, and his possessions swallowed up in the Grand Principality. The authority of the Grand Prince began to be exercised on his subordinates with new rigor ; and the rebels, real or supposed, were subjected to the knout, tortures, mutilations, and refined cruelties. Vassili, who had suffered so much from the appanaged princes Iouri and Chemiaka—who was so energetic in destroying the appanages around him—could not free himself from the yoke of custom, and began to dismember the principality which he had aggrandized, in favor of his four younger sons. However, to avoid all contests about the title of Grand Prince, and to ensure the succession of the direct line, he had, since the year 1449, associated with himself his eldest son, Ivan.

Memorable events had agitated the orthodox world during

his reign. In 1439, Pope Eugenius IV. assembled the Council of Florence to discuss the union of the two Churches. The Greek Emperor, John Palæologus, who hoped to obtain the help of the Pope against the Ottomans, had sent the bishops of his communion; Isidore, Metropolitan of Moscow, was also present. It was in vain that the Emperor of Constantinople, three vicars of the Patriarchs of the East, seventeen metropolitans, and a multitude of bishops signed the act of union. The Greek world listened to the energetic protest of Mark, the old bishop of Ephesus, and rejected the union with Rome. Isidore announced at Kief and Moscow that he had signed the act of reconciliation; the appearance of the Latin cross at the Assumption in the Kremlin, the name of Pope Eugenius in the public prayers, and the reading of the formal document, astonished the Russians. Vassili, who piqued himself on his theology, also raised his voice, began a polemic against Isidore, and so overwhelmed him with insults, that the "false shepherd" thought it prudent to fly to Rome. This check to the union heralded the fall of the Greek empire. In 1453, Mahomet II. entered Constantinople. There was no longer a Christian Tzar; Moscow became the great metropolis of orthodoxy. She was heir of Constantinople. Soon the monks, the artists, the literary men of Constantinople were to bring to her, as to the rest of Europe, the Renaissance.

CHAPTER XIII.

IVAN THE GREAT, THE UNITER OF THE RUSSIAN LAND (1462-1505).

Submission of Novgorod—Annexation of Tver, Rostof, and Iaroslavl—Wars with the Great Horde and Kazan—End of the Tatar yoke—Wars with Lithuania—Western Russia as far as the Soja reconquered—Marriage with Sophia Palæologus—Greeks and Italians at the Court of Moscow.

SUBMISSION OF NOVGOROD—ANNEXATION OF THE PRINCIPALITIES OF TVER, ROSTOF, AND IAROSLAVL.

At the death of Vassili the Blind, Russia was all but stifled between the great Lithuanian empire and the vast possessions of the Mongols. To the north, she had two restless neighbors, the Livonian Order and Sweden. In spite of the labors of eight Muscovite princes, the little Russian State could not yet make its unity a fact; Riazan and Tver, though weakened, still existed. Novgorod and Pskof hesitated between the Grand Princes of Moscow and Lithuania. The heirs of Kalita, by creating new appanages, incessantly destroyed the unity after which they toiled, by means of a pitiless policy. Muscovy, which touches on no sea, had only intermittent relations with the centres of European civilization. It was, however, the time when the nations of the West began to be organized. Charles VII. and Louis XI. in France, Ferdinand and Isabella in Spain, the Tudors in England, Frederic III. and Maximilian in Austria, labored to build up powerful States from the ruins of feudal anarchy. European civilization made unheard-of strides; the Renaissance began, printing spread. Christopher Columbus and Vasco da Gama discovered new worlds. Was not Russia also going to achieve her unity, to take part in the great European movement? The man who was to restore her to herself, to free her from the Mongol yoke, to put her into relations with the West,—this man was expected. It had all been predicted. When a son named Ivan was born in 1440 to Vassili the Blind, an old monk had a revelation about it in Novgorod the Great.

He came and said to his archbishop: "Truly it is to-day that the Grand Prince triumphs; God has given him an heir; I behold this child making himself illustrious by glorious deeds. He will subdue princes and peoples. But woe to Novgorod! Novgorod will fall at his feet, and never rise up again."

Ivan III., whose reign of forty-three years was to permit him to realize the expectations of Russia, was a cold, imperious, calculating prince, the very type of the Souzdalian and Muscovite princes. Disliking war, he allowed doubts to be thrown upon his courage. He was victorious in Lithuania, in Livonia and Siberia, almost without leaving the Kremlin. His father had taken long journeys, which led him into many sad adventures, but Stephen of Moldavia said of Ivan: "Ivan is a strange man; he stays quietly at home and triumphs over his enemies, while I, though always on horseback, cannot defend my country." It was the verdict of Edward III. on Charles V. Ivan exhausted his enemies by negotiations and delay, and never employed force till it was absolutely necessary. His devotion was mixed with hypocrisy. He wept for his relatives whom he put to death, as Louis XI. bewailed the Duc de Guienne. Born a despot, "he had," says Karamsin, "penetrated the secret of autocracy, and became a formidable deity in the eyes of the Russians." His glance caused women to faint. When he slept after his meals, it was wonderful to see the frightened respect of the boyards for the sleep of the master. He inflicted cruel punishments and tortures on all rebels, even on those of the highest rank; he mutilated the counsellors of his son, whipped Prince Oukhtomski and the archimandrite of a powerful monastery, and burned alive two Poles in an iron cage on the Moskowa, for having conspired against him. He had already won the surname of "Terrible," which his grandson was to bear even more justly.

Ivan's first effort was directed against Novgorod the Great. The republic of the Ilmen was dying in the anarchy of the aristocracy, the dissensions of the people, the Church, and especially of the boyards. It is of this epoch that M. Biélaef has said, that "parties in Novgorod had become so complicated, that often it is difficult to perceive from what motive this or that faction excited troubles and revolts." They thought themselves able to despise the authority of a new prince, and had the imprudence to neglect the complaints and suggestions made in a tolerably moderate tone by Ivan III. He then signified to the Pskovians that they would have to second him in an expedition against the rebels. This the Pskovians did not wish to do, foreseeing that the fall of Novgorod would drag them down also

They offered their mediation to their "elder sister"—it was rejected, and they were obliged to proceed. Ivan III. often received, however, the Archbishop of Novgorod, Theophilus, in his palace at Moscow, and continued to negotiate. He had a large party in Novgorod, but the opposing faction was the bolder. Marfa, the widow of the possadnik Boretski, mother of two grown-up sons, put herself at the head of the anti-Muscovite party. Ready and eloquent speech, immense wealth, an audacity equal to everything, had given her a great influence with the people and the boyards. This intrepid woman was the last incarnation of Novgorodian liberty. To save the republic, Marfa wished to throw it into the arms of the King of Poland, Casimir IV. She contended also that the Archbishop of Novgorod should be nominated by the Metropolitan of Kief, not by the Metropolitan of Moscow. In her devotion to Novgorod, she thus betrayed the cause of Russia and orthodoxy. The sittings of the *vetché*, amid the opposition of the two parties, degenerated into violent tumults. Some cried, " The king ; " others, " Long live orthodox Moscow! long live the Grand Prince Ivan and our father the Metropolitan Philip!" The friends of Marfa finally won the day. Novgorod handed herself over to the King of Poland by a formal act in which she stipulated for the same rights as she had enjoyed under her ancient princes. Ivan III. tried once more to recall the citizens to obedience, and he sent them an ambassador, but the party of Marfa was always the more numerous or the more noisy. At last Ivan decided to begin the war. His voïevodes made the conquest of the territory of the Dwina ; the Muscovites, supported by the Tatar cavalry, cruelly ravaged the territory of the "perfidious" Novgorodians ; after the battle of Korostyne, they cut off the noses and lips of the prisoners. The republicans had fallen from their ancient valor ; Marfa had hastily enrolled ill-disciplined artisans. At the battle of the Chelona, 5000 Muscovites defeated 30,000 Novgorodians. At Roussa the Grand Prince caused many boyards to be beheaded, one of whom was a son of Marfa, and sent others as prisoners into Muscovy. Ivan III. always advanced, fighting and negotiating. Novgorod submitted, paid a war indemnity, and, if she still remained a republic, she was a republic dependent on the good pleasure of the Prince (1470).

From that time Ivan labored entirely to reduce the town, and his party in Novgorod increased. If the people complained of the injustice of his lieutenants, he blamed the insufficiency of the ancient laws of the city. He tried to excite the animosity of the lower classes against the boyards. It was by the invitation of the former that he came in 1475 to hold a solemn court in Novgorod. Great and small immediately crowded to his tribunal, to beg for justice one against the other. Ivan saw how much his own cause was strengthened by these divisions. An act of authority that he tried, succeeded completely. Marfa's second son, the possadnik, and many boyards were loaded with chains, and sent to Moscow. No one dared to protest. On his return to his capital, a multitude of complainants hastened after him; he forced them all to appear before him. Since Rurik, say the annalists, such a violation of Novgorod's liberty had never been known. Profiting by a documentary error made by the envoys of the town, he declared himself *sovereign* (goçoudar) of Novgorod, instead of *lord* (gospodine). Now if this interpretation were accepted, the subjection of the republic, which was only a matter of fact, would become a matter of law. The party of Marfa made a last effort to reject this *sovereignty;* the friends of the Grand Prince were massacred. Ivan declared that the Novgorodians, after having accorded him the title of *goçoudar*, had the effrontery to deny it. Then the Metropolitan, the bishops, the boyards, all Moscow, advised him to make war. Accordingly it was preached as a Holy War against the allies of the Pope and Lithuania. All the forces of Russia were put in motion, and many boyards of Novgorod appeared at the camp of the Grand Prince. The city was blockaded, and starved out. In vain the partisans of Marfa shouted the old war-cry: "Let us die for liberty and Saint Sophia!" They were forced to capitulate. Ivan guaranteed to them their persons and possessions, their ancient jurisdiction, and exemption from the Muscovite service; but the *vetché* and the possadnik were abolished forever. The belfry was reduced to silence. The Republic of Novgorod had ceased to exist (1478).

Marfa and the principal oligarchs were transported to Moscow, and their goods confiscated. Many times afterwards, there were party agitations, which were quelled by Ivan III. and his successor, by numerous transportations. In 1481 some boyards were tortured and put to death. Eight thousand Novgorodians were transplanted to the towns of Souzdal. Ivan III. struck another terrible blow at the prosperity of the city when, in 1495, after a quarrel with the people of Revel, he caused the merchants of forty-nine Hanseatic towns to be arrested at Novgorod, pillaged the "German market," and removed wares to the value of £40,000 to Moscow. The covetous Grand Prince doubtless did not see he was killing the hen with the golden eggs. A long while elapsed before the merchants of the West again made their appearance in Novgorod. Pskof, more docile, had preserved her *vetché* and her ancient institutions.

Whilst he was destroying the liberty of Novgorod, Ivan deprived her of her colonies, and undertook on his own account the conquest of Northern Russia. By this time Muscovy extended as far as Finland, the White Sea and the Icy Ocean, and had already obtained a footing in Asia. Ivan had conquered Permia in 1472, by which means he became master of the "silver beyond the Kama," which the Novgorodians had hitherto got in the course of trade. In 1489, Viatka, which had fallen for a short time into the power of the Tatars of Kazan, was reconquered, and lost her republican organization. In 1499 the voïevodes of Oustiougue, of the Dwina and of Viatka, advanced as far as the Petchora, and built a fortress on the banks of the river. In the depth of winter, in sledges drawn by dogs, they passed the defiles of the Ourals, in the teeth of the wind and snow, slew 50 of the Samoyedes, and captured 200 reindeer; invaded the territory of the Vogouls and Ougrians, the Finnish brethren of the Magyars; took 40 enclosures of palisades, made 50 princes prisoners, and returned to Moscow, after having reduced this unknown country, supposed by the geographers of antiquity to be the home of so many wonders and monsters. Russia, like the maritime nations of the West, had discovered a new world.

The cultivated provinces of Central Russia were more important than the deserts of the North. Here there were no immense territories to be conquered, but only the territories of the smaller appanaged princes to be grafted on to the already united mass. Ivan III. might have dethroned the young Prince of Riazan, whom his father had brought to Moscow, but he preferred to give him the hand of his sister, Anne Vassilievna, and send him back to his territories (1464). The absorption of the principalities of Riazan and Novgorod-Severski was reserved for his successor. He showed the same moderation about Tver, but in 1482 Prince Michael, who had only maintained his position on sufferance, had the imprudence to ally himself with Lithuania. Ivan hailed this pretext with joy, and marched in person against Tver, accompanied by the celebrated Aristotele Fioraventi of Bologna, grand master of his artillery. Michael took to flight; and Ivan began to organize his new subjects. A principality which could furnish 40,000 soldiers was united to Moscow without a blow. In like manner he obtained possession of Vereia and of Biélozersk, and deprived the princes of Rostof and Iaroslavl of their ancient rights of sovereignty.

His father, by giving appanages to his brothers, had prepared for him a new and ungrateful task, but Ivan undertook it without scruple. When his brother Iouri died, he wept much for him, but at once laid hands on his towns of Dmitrof, Mojaïsk, and

Serpoukhof, thereby causing his other brothers, who hoped to share the spoil, great discontent (1468). Andrew was accused of an understanding with Lithuania, and thrown into prison, where he died (1493). The Grand Prince convoked the Metropolitan and bishops to his palace, appeared before them with downcast eyes, his face sorrowful and bathed in tears, humbly accused himself of having been too cruel to his unhappy brother, and submitted to their pastoral admonitions; but he confiscated Andrew's appanage notwithstanding, and that of his brother Boris, who died a short time after, thus reuniting all the domains of his father. He acquired the surname of "Binder of the Russian Land," a name which his eight predecessors equally merited. It was owing to their earlier labors that Ivan was able to become the greatest and most powerful of these " Binders." He avoided their errors, and if later he gave appanages to his own children, it was only on condition that they should remain subjects of their eldest brother, and that they should neither have the right to coin money nor to exercise a separate diplomacy.

WARS WITH THE GREAT HORDE AND KAZAN—END OF THE TATAR YOKE.

The empire of the Horde was at last dissolved. The principal States which had risen from its *débris* were the Tazarate of Kazan, that of Saraï or Astrakhan, the Horde of the Nogaïs, and the Khanate of the Crimea. Kazan and the Crimea particularly presented strange ethnographical amalgamations. The Tzarate of Kazan had been founded in the reign of Vassili the Blind on the ruins of the ancient Bulgaria on the Volga, formerly so flourishing and civilized, by a banished prince of the Horde. It was the same Makhmet who had tried to establish himself at Belef, and had defeated Chemiaka. The Mongols had mixed with the ancient Bulgars, and reconstituted an important centre of commerce and civilization. The rule of the Tzarate extended over the Finnish tribes of the Mordvians, the Tchouvaches, and the Tcheremisses, as well as the Bachkirs and Metcheraks. The Khanate of the Crimea had been founded almost at the same date, by a descendant of Genghis Khan, named Azi. A peasant named Ghirei having saved him from death, Azi added his benefactor's name to his own, and henceforward the title belonged to all the khans of the Crimea. The Mongols, on arriving at the peninsula, found it occupied by the remains of the ancient Tauric, Hellenic, and Gothic races; by Armenians, Jews, and Jewish Kharaïtes, who pretended to have settled B.C. 500 on the rocks and in the Troglodyte cities of Tchoufout-Kalé and Mangoup-Kalé, and finally by the Genoese of Kaffa. The Jews and Italians excepted, a large part of the ancient population was absorbed by the Asiatic invaders. Thus while the Tatars of the steppes of the Northern Crimea are pure Mongols, those of the mountains of the south seem to be chiefly Taurians, Goths, and Islamized Greeks. As to the great Horde of Saraï, that was almost entirely composed of nomads, such as the Nogaïs and other Turco-Tatar races.

Anarchy and rivalry reigned in the heart of each of these States. The princes of Kazan, Saraï, and the Crimea came to seek an asylum from the Grand Prince, who made use of them to perpetuate these divisions. In 1473 Ivan constituted the town of Novgorod of Riazan into a fief for one Mustafa; others served in the armies, and aided Ivan against Novgorod and Lithuania. Towards the khans and the tzars, especially those of the Great Horde or Saraï, the sovereign of Moscow held himself on the defensive, repelling the attacks of adventurers, but taking care not to provoke them; avoiding the payment of the tribute, but disposed to send them presents. At the same time he schemed for alliances against the Khan of Saraï, and despatched to the Turkoman Oussoum-Hassan, master of Persia and enemy of the Mongols, his Italian ambassador, Marco Ruffo (1477). A more solid friendship united him with Mengli-Ghirei, Khan of the Crimea, and lasted all their lives. Mengli was as serviceable to him against Lithuania as against the Horde.

In 1478, having carefully taken all his measures, he openly rebelled. When the Khan Akhmet sent his ambassadors with his image to receive the tribute, Ivan III. trampled the image of the Khan under his feet, and put all the envoys to death, excepting one, who conveyed the news to the Horde. This act, so very little in accordance with the well-known prudence of Ivan, is not to be found in all the chronicles. When Akhmet took the field, Ivan occupied a strong position on the Oka, with a more numerous and better-organized army than that of Dmitri Donskoï. His 150,000 men and powerful artillery did not, however, prevent him from reflecting much on the hazard of battles. He even returned to reflect at Moscow, and it needed all the clamors of the people to induce him to leave it. "What!" exclaimed the Muscovites, "he has overtaxed us, and refused to pay tribute to the Horde, and now that he has irritated the Khan, he declines to fight!" Ivan wished to consult his mother, his boyards, and his bishops. "March bravely against the enemy," was the unanimous reply. "Is it the part of mortals to fear death?" said old Archbishop Vassian. "We cannot escape destiny." Ivan desired, at least, to send his young son Ivan back to Moscow, but the prince heroically disobeyed. The Grand Prince finally decided to return to the army, blessed by his mother and the Metropolitan, who promised him the victory as to a David or to a Constantine, reminding him that "a good shepherd will lay down his life for his sheep." Ivan, who did not feel himself made of the stuff of a Constantine, kept his army immovable on the Oka and the Ougra; the two forces contenting themselves with sending arrows and insults across the river. Ivan closed his ears to the warlike counsel of his boyards, and rather listened to the prudent advice of his two favorites—"fat and powerful lords," says the chronicle. However, he refused the proposition of the Khan, who offered to pardon him if he would either come himself or send one of his men to kiss his stirrup. At last monks and white-haired bishops lost all patience. Vassian addressed a bellicose letter to the Grand Prince, invoking the memories of Igor, Sviatoslaf, of Vladimir Monomachus, and Dmitri Donskoï. Ivan assured him that this letter "filled his heart with joy, courage, and strength; but another fortnight passed in inaction. On the fifteenth day the rivers were covered with ice; the Grand Prince gave the order to retreat. An inexplicable panic seized the two armies—Russians and Tatars both fled, when no man pursued. The Khan never stopped till he reached the Horde (1480). Such was the last invasion of the horsemen of the Kiptchak. It was in this unheroic way that Russia broke at last the Mongol yoke under which she had groaned for three centuries. Like Louis XI., Ivan III. had his battle of Montlhéry; but if he fought less, he gained far more. The Horde, attacked by the Khans of the Crimea, survived its decay but a short time. Akhmet was put to death by one of his own men.

Hostility increased between Kazan and Moscow. In 1467 and 1469 Ivan III. had organized two expeditions against Bulgaria. In 1487, seven years after having shaken off the supremacy of the Great Horde, the Muscovite voïevodes marched against the same Kazan, where the father of their Grand Prince had been held a captive. After a siege of seven weeks the city was taken, and the sovereign Alegam made prisoner. A tzar of Kazan was then seen a prisoner in Moscow! Ivan III. added the title of Prince of Bulgaria to those he already bore; but feeling that the Mussulman city was not yet ripe for annexation, he gave the crown to a nephew of his friend the Khan of the Crimea. The people were forced to take the oath of fidelity to him. The conquest of the land of Arsk, in Bulgaria itself, and the establishment of a Russian garrison in the fortress, allowed him to watch from close by all that passed in Kazan. The Khan of the Crimea did not care to protest against the captivity of the Tzar Alegam, his nephew's enemy, but the princes of the Chiban and the Nogaïs, who were related to him, and who beheld Islamism humiliated in his person, despatched an embassy to the Grand Prince. The latter refused to release his prisoner, but replied so graciously that the envoys could hardly be angry. He sent to those zealous kinsmen clothes of Flanders, fishes' teeth, and gerfalcons, and did not forget the wives of the *mourzas*, whom he called his sisters. At the same time, wishing to make these Asiatics feel that times had changed, he took care never personally to compromise himself with the Nogaï envoys, and only to communicate with them by means of treasurers, secretaries, and other officers of the second rank.

WARS WITH LITHUANIA—WESTERN RUSSIA UP TO THE SOJA RECONQUERED.

Lithuania and Poland united remained, after all, Ivan's great enemy. This composite State plays the same part in Russian history as the Burgundy of Philip the Good and Charles the Bold in that of France. Made up in a great degree of Russian as well as of Polish and Lithuanian elements, it was many times on the point of annihilating Russia, in the same way as Burgundy, composed of French, Batavian, and German provinces, had been on the point of annihilating the French nation. Lithuania was incorporated with Poland in the same manner as the States of Burgundy, unfortunately for France, were incorporated with Austria.

At the beginning of Ivan's reign the King Casimir IV. was sovereign of the two united States, and neglected no means of disquieting the Grand Prince. The latter, on his part, incited his ally Mengli to invade the Lithuanian possessions; and the Crimean Tatars pillaged Kief and the Monastery of the Catacombs (1482). When, ten years after, Casimir died (1492), leaving Poland to his eldest son Albert, and Lithuania to Alexander, the second son, Ivan III. resolved to turn the division to account. He had obtained the friendship of the Turkish Sultan Bajazet II., of Matthias Corvinus, king of Hungary, of the active Stephen of Moldavia, the determined enemy of the Lithuanians; but, above all, he counted on Mengli. Mengli had held Lithuania in check while Ivan had got rid of the Mongols; now he was to play the same part with the Horde, while the Grand Prince settled old scores with Alexander, but without interfering with the Tatar incursions in the Ukraine. The discovery at Moscow of a Polish plot against the life of the Grand Prince spread rumors of war. In the same way that he had been able to utilize the Mongol refugees against the Horde, he found the Lithuanian princes and other great personages entering into relations with him. It was then that Belski, afterwards so famous, obtained a footing in Russia, that the Prince of Mazovia sent an embassy to Ivan III., and the princes of Viazma, Vorotinsk, Belef, and Mezetsk did him homage.

The war was popular in Moscow, for its object was to break the yoke imposed by the Polish Catholics on the orthodox Russian people. In White Russia the Muscovites were to awake old national and religious sympathies. "Lithuania," said the ambassadors of Ivan III. to the plenipotentiaries of Alexander, "Lithuania has profited by the misfortunes of Russia to take our territory, but to-day things have changed." Peace was made after a short war (1494). The frontier of Muscovy was carried to the Desna, and comprehended the appanages of the princes who had taken service with Ivan, with Mstislavl, Obolensk, Kozelsk, Vorotinsk, Peremysl, &c.

The peace seemed to be cemented by the marriage of Alexander with Helena, daughter of Ivan III.; but, on the contrary, this union proved the germ of a new war. The sovereign of Moscow had stipulated that his daughter was under no circumstances to change her religion, that she was to have a Greek chapel in the palace, and an orthodox almoner. Ivan himself gave his daughter the most pressing injunctions never to appear in the Catholic church, and gave her minute directions as to her toilet, her table, her mode of travelling, and her way of conducting herself towards her new subjects. At her departure he bestowed on her a collection of various pious books. His policy agreed with his conviction; it was necessary that in Lithuania orthodoxy should raise her lowered head, and reign with his daughter. Soon afterwards, he complained that Helena was forced to offend her conscience, that she was made to wear the Polish costume, that her domestics and orthodox almoners were dismissed, and their places filled with Catholics—that the Greek religion was persecuted, that the assassination of the Metropolitan of Kief had remained unpunished, and that he was to be succeeded by a man devoted to the Pope. Lithuania, at the beginning of the war, was further enfeebled by new defections. The princes of Bielsk, of Mossalsk, of Khotatof, the boyards of Mtsensk and of Serpeïsk, and finally the princes of Tchernigof and Starodoub, of Rylsk and Novgorod-Severski, declared for the Grand Prince of Moscow. All the country between the Desna and the Soja passed into the hands of the Russians, to-

THE NEW PALACE

Russia, vol. one.

gether with Briansk, Poutivle, and Dorogbouge. They had only to show themselves to conquer. Alexander could not abandon the conquests of Olgerd, Vitovt, and Gedimin without striking a blow, but his army was cut to pieces at the battle of Vedrocha. Constantine Ostrojski, his voïevode, fell into the hands of the Muscovites, who tried to gain him over to their cause. The Lithuanians, however, kept the strongholds of Vitepsk, Polotsk, Orcha and Smolensk.

This prolonged struggle between Alexander and Ivan III. had set all Eastern Europe in a blaze. Alexander had made an alliance with the Livonian Order and the Great Horde. The Khan of the Crimea pitilessly devastated Gallicia and Volhynia. The Russian troops again defeated the Lithuanians near Mstislavl, but were forced to raise the siege of Smolensk. In the north, the Grand Prince of Moscow had stopped the Germans of Livonia from building the fortress of Ivangorod opposite Narva, and had seized the Hanseatic wares at Novgorod. The Grand Master, Hermann of Plettenberg, responded with joy to the appeal of the Lithuanians; and at the battle of Siritsa, near Izborsk, his formidable German artillery crushed an army of 40,000 Russians (1501). The latter took their revenge the following year on the *iron men* near Pskof. Schig-Akhmet, Kahn of the Great Horde, wished to make a diversion, but the Khan of the Crimea attacked him with fury, and in 1502 so completely extinguished his rule, that the ruins of Saraï, the capital of Bati, where the Russian princes had grovelled before the khans, were henceforward a home of serpents.

Alexander had just been elected King of Poland, and wished to finish this ruinous war. The celebrated Pope, Alexander VI., and the King of Hungary tried to mediate between the belligerent powers. As, however, neither of the two parties would abate any of their pretensions, a truce of six years only could be agreed on, during which time the Soja was to be the boundary, and the territories and towns of the princes who had gone over to Russia were to be abandoned to her (1503). What shows the good faith of Ivan III. is that, after the truce was signed, he obtained the promise from the Khan of the Crimea to continue his attacks against Lithuania.

MARRIAGE WITH SOPHIA PALÆOLOGUS (1472)—THE GREEKS AND ITALIANS AT THE COURT OF MOSCOW.

The acquisition of the Novgorodian possessions and the appanages, the capture of Kazan, the fall of the Horde, and the conquest of Lithuania up to the Soja, had doubled the extent of the Grand Principality, even without reckoning the immense territory it had gained on the north. An event not less important in its consequences was the marriage of Ivan III. with a Byzantine princess. Thomas Palæologus, a brother of the last Emperor, had taken refuge at the court of Rome. There he died, leaving a daughter named Sophia. The Pope wished to find her a husband, and the Cardinal Bessarion, who belonged to the Eastern Rite, advised Paul II. to offer her hand to the Grand Prince of Russia. A Greek named Iouri, and the two Friazini, relations of Friazine, minter of Ivan III., were sent on an embassy to Moscow. Ivan and his boyards accepted the proposal with enthusiasm; it was God, no doubt, who had given him so illustrious a wife; " a branch of the imperial tree which formerly overshadowed all orthodox Christianity." Sophia—dowered by the Pope, whose heart was always occupied with two things, the crusade against the Turks, and the re-union of the two Churches—went from Rome to Lübeck, from Lübeck by sea to Revel, and was received in triumph at Pskof, Novgorod, and the other towns subject to Moscow. This daughter of emperors was destined to have an enormous influence on Ivan. It was she, no doubt, who taught him to " penetrate the secret of autocracy." She bore the Mongol yoke with less patience than the Russians, who were accustomed to servitude. She incited Ivan to shake it off. " How long am I to be the slave of the Tatars?" she would often ask. With Sophia a multitude of Greek emigrants came to Moscow, not only from Rome, but from Constantinople and Greece; among them were Demetrios Ralo, Theodore Lascaris, Demetrios Trakhaniotes. They gave to Russia statesmen, diplomatists, engineers, artists and theologians. They brought her Greek books, the priceless inheritance of ancient civilization. These manuscripts were first beginnings of the present " Library of the Patriarchs."

Ivan III. was the heir of the Emperors of Byzantium and the Roman Cæsars. He took for the new arms of Russia the two-headed eagle which in its archaic form is still to be found in the " Palais à facettes " of the Kremlin. Moscow succeeded to Byzantium as Byzantium had succeeded to Rome. Having become the only metropolis of orthodoxy, it was incumbent on her to protect the Greek Christians of the entire East, and to prepare the revenge against Islamism for the work of 1453. With the Greeks came Italians: Aristotele Fioraventi of Bologna, who was Ivan III.'s architect, military engineer, and master of artillery; Marco Ruffo, his ambassador in Persia; Pietro

Antonio, who built his imperial palace ; the metal-founder, Paul Bossio, besides architects and arquebusiers.

Ivan entered into relations with Venice when Trevisani, envoy of the republic, on his way to the Horde, tried to traverse *incognito* the States of the Grand Prince, and was arrested and condemned to death. The Senate interfered, and the imprudent diplomatist was set at liberty. Ivan sent in his turn a Russian ambassador, Simeon Tolbouzine, charged to bind the two coun. tries in friendly ties, and to bring back some skilful architect from Italy. He was followed in 1499 by Demetrius Ralo and Golokhvastof. Contarini, the Venetian ambassador, returned from Persia with a French ecclesiastic named Louis, who called himself envoy of the Duke of Burgundy, and the Patriarch of Antioch. He stopped at Moscow, and was kindly received by Ivan. He himself was much struck by the Grand Prince. " When, in speaking, I respectfully stepped back," relates Contarini, "the Grand Prince always drew near, and gave particular attention to my remarks." Ivan III.—whether to secure himself allies against Poland, or to obtain from Germany artists and handicraftsmen — exchanged more than one embassy with Frederic III. and Maximilian of Austria, Matthias of Hungary, and the Pope. When attacked by Sweden, he nogotiated an alliance with Denmark. Plehtchéef was the first Russian ambassador at Constantinople under Bajazet II. From the East came envoys of Georgia and even of Djagatai (Turkestan and Tatar Siberia).

The prince who, born vassal of a nomad race, founded the greatness of Russia, may be compared with one of the greatest of French kings, Louis XI. What the latter accomplished in the case of appanaged feudalism, Ivan succeeded in doing in that of appanaged principalities. He was pitiless towards the smaller Russian dynasties, as the King of France was to Armagnac or Saint Pol. He detached a slice from Lithuania, as his Western contemporary managed to dismember Burgundy. He put an end to the Mongol invasions, as Louis did to the English wars. He repulsed, without striking a blow, the last incursion of the khans, as Louis XI. sweetly dismissed the last embarkation of the English under Edward IV. Both had the same taste for foreigners, especially industrious Italians, and for useful arts. Both explored the metallic riches of their States. They each created a diplomacy ; the one by means of Comynes, the other by means of Greeks, and Russians as supple as Greeks. They strengthened the national army, and gave it a permanent character ; they both owed the success against the minor princes to their artillery. Ivan III. had his brothers Bureau in Aristotele Fioraventi.

Louis XI., who wished to put an end to the anarchy of the law and to the thefts of chicanery, meditated a real code, or *grand costumier*, which would put the old laws in harmony with the new order of things. This is precisely what Ivan did in his *Oulogenia* (1497). In comparing it with the *Rousskaïa Pravda* of Iaroslaf, we are able to gauge the amount of change caused in the national laws by the influence of Byzantium, the example of the Tatars, and the progress of autocracy. Corporal penalties have notably increased: for homicide, death; for theft, whipping in a public place. Torture was making its way in the procedure. The judicial duel was still admitted, only now it could hardly become mortal; each of the combatants had a cuirass, and was armed only with a short club. Women, minors, and ecclesiastics were represented by a champion. In the same way as the end and aim of the policy of Ivan was the suppression of appanages, that of his code was to efface the privileges, the legal and judicial peculiarities of the different provinces.

For three generations the throne had been inherited in the direct line. When, however, Ivan, eldest son of Ivan III., died, the latter hesitated long between his grandson Dmitri Ivanovitch, and his second son Vassili. His wife supported Vassili; his daughter-in-law Helena, Ivan's widow, her own son. The court was divided, and both parties were absorbed in their intrigues. Ivan III. at first proclaimed Dmitri, threw Vassili in prison, and disgraced his wife. Then he changed his mind, imprisoned his daughter-in-law and his grandson in their turn, and proclaimed Vassili his heir. The hereditary right of the West was not established in Russia without many struggles.

CHAPTER XIV.

VASSILI IVANOVITCH (1505–1533).

Reunion of Pskof, Riazan, and Novgorod-Severski—Wars with Lithuania—Acquisition of Smolensk—Wars with the Tatars—Diplomatic relations with Europe.

REUNION OF PSKOF, RIAZAN, AND NOVGOROD-SEVERSKI—WARS WITH LITHUANIA—ACQUISITION OF SMOLENSK.

The reign of Vassili Ivanovitch may seem somewhat pale between those of the two Ivans—the two "*Terribles*,"—his father and son. It was likewise of shorter duration, lasting only twenty-eight years (1505–1533), but was the continuation of the one, and the preparation for the other: the movement which was bearing Russia towards unity and autocracy was not retarded under Vassili Ivanovitch.

There were still three States which had preserved a certain independence—the Republic of Pskof, and the Principalities of Riazan and Novgorod-Severski. The quarrels still continued at Pskof between the citizens and the peasants, the aristocracy and the lower classes. The whole of Pskof was in conflict with her *nameistnik*, or the royal lieutenant. Vassili came to hold his court at Novgorod, and summoned the magistrates of Pskof to appear before him. When they arrived, he arrested them. A merchant of Pskof, who was on his way to Novgorod, returned with the news to his compatriots. Instantly the bell of the *vetché* began to ring, and the cry was heard, "Let us raise the shield against the Grand Prince. Let us shut the gates of the town." The more prudent tried to restrain the people. "What can we do? Our brothers, our magistrates, our boyards, and all our chief men are in the hands of the Prince." The imprisoned Pskovians sent a messenger to implore their fellow-citizens not to attempt a useless resistance, and to avoid the shedding of blood. The latter then despatched one of their number to the Grand Prince, and charged him to say, "My lord, we are not your enemies. After God, it is you that have power over all your subjects." Vassili Ivanovitch sent them one of his *diaks*, or secretaries, who was admitted into the assembly of the citizens, saluted them in the name of the Grand Prince, and informed them that his master imposed on them two conditions: the first was that the towns subject to Pskof should receive his *maniestniks*; the second was the suppression of the *vetché* and its bell. For a long while they could give him no answer—their sobs and tears choked them. At last they demanded twenty-four hours to deliberate. The day and night passed in lamentations. "The infants at the breast," says the annalist, "alone could refrain from tears." Next day the people met for the last time, and the first magistrate of the city thus spoke to Dalmatof, *diak* of the Grand Prince: " It is written in our Chronicles that our ancestors took oaths to the Grand Prince. The Pskovians swore never to rebel against our lord who is at Moscow, never to ally themselves with Lithuania, with Poland, nor with the Germans, otherwise the wrath of God would be upon them, bringing with it famine, fires, floods, and the invasion of the infidels. If the Grand Prince, on his part, did not observe his vow, he dared the same consequences. Now our town and our bell are in the power of God and the prince. As for us, we have kept our oath." Dalmatof had the great bell, symbol of the independence of the republic, taken down, and carried to Novgorod, amid the general despair. Then Vassili Ivanovitch came to visit his " patrimony of Pskof." He installed his men and boyards in the upper town, transplanted 300 families of the aristocracy into the cities of the interior, and established 300 Muscovite families in their place. When he went away, he left a garrison of 5000 *dietiboyarskié*, and 500 Novgorod artillerymen (1510). "Alas!" cries the annalist, "glorious city of Pskof the Great, wherefore this lamentation and tears?" And the noble city of Pskof replies: " How can I but weep and lament? An eagle, a many-winged eagle, with claws like a lion, has swooped down upon me. He has taken captive the three cedars of Lebanon—my beauty, my riches, my children! Our land is a desert, our city ruined, our commerce destroyed. Our brothers have been carried away to a place where our fathers never dwelt, nor our grandfathers, nor our great-grandfathers."

Ivan, prince of Riazan, was accused about 1521 of having made an alliance with the Khan of the Crimea. He was summoned to Moscow, and imprisoned. He managed to escape into Lithuania, where he died in obscurity. This fertile country, whose rich harvests "looked like waving forests," was united to the Grand Principality. A certain number of Riazanese were transported to Muscovite soil. Vassili Chemiakine reigned at

Novgorod-Severski ; he was the grandson of the Chemiaka who had put out the eyes of Vassili Vassiliévitch. About 1523 he was thrown into prison, on the accusation of an understanding with Poland, where he died. There was now only one Russia A jester of the Grand Prince had predicted the fall of the last appanaged prince. He had gone through the streets of Moscow armed with a broom, crying "that it was time to clean the empire of what remained of this ordure." Vassili, like the most of his predecessors, had little tenderness for his family. His nephew Dmitri, whom his grandfather had for a moment destined to occupy the throne, and who by Western laws was the rightful heir, died in prison. One of Vassili's brothers, feeling the yoke press too heavily on him, tried to escape, but was brought back.

The son of Ivan the Great continued the struggle with Lithuania. He had attempted, at the death of Alexander, to get himself nominated Grand Prince of Wilna, and the reconciliation of Muscovite and Lithuanian Russia would have changed the destinies of the North. Sigismond I. reunited the two crowns of Wilna and Poland. An unimportant war ended in 1506 by a "perpetual peace," and Vassili renounced all claims on Kief and Smolensk. The perpetual peace lasted three years, which were filled by the recriminations of the two parties. Vassili accused Sigismond of never having sent back all the prisoners, of pillaging the Muscovite merchants, of maltreating the widow of Alexander, daughter of Ivan III.; of tempting Simeon, Vassili's brother, to fly to Poland ; and of inciting the Crimean Tatars to ravage Russia. He declared that " as long as his horse was in marching condition, and his sword cut sharp, there should be neither peace nor truce with Lithuania." Smolensk was instantly attacked ; part of her inhabitants were on the side of Russia, and offered to submit to the Grand Prince. A volley of artillery knocked down the ramparts of her Kremlin, which towers over the Dnieper. The Polish voïevode was compelled by the people to capitulate. " Spare your patrimony," said they to the Grand Prince. The Bishop of Smolensk blessed Vassili, and the inhabitants took the oaths of fidelity to him (1514). "The taking of Smolensk," says a Russian chronicler, " was like a brilliant fête-day for Russia ; for the capture of the property of another can only flatter an ambitious prince, but to gain possession of what is one's own is ever a cause of joy." Many of the Lithuanians, however, remained undecided ; the name of Russia and of orthodoxy brought them into communion with Moscow, but the Muscovites appeared very barbarous by the side of the Poles, and their turbulent nobility were better suited to Polish anarchy than to Russian autocracy. A Glinski, one of a Podolian family, who went over to Vassili at this time, played the traitor. Constantine Ostrojski, whom Vassili had tried to gain over to the cause of orthodoxy, fled from Moscow: and it was he who, in 1514, inflicted on the Russian voïevodes the bloody defeat of Orcha. "The next day," says Karamsin, "he celebrated the victory that he had won over a people of the same religion as himself, and it was in the Russian tongue that he gave thanks to God for having destroyed the Russians." Even the contemporaries felt vaguely that a struggle between Lithuanian Russia and Moscow was a kind of civil war. Had not Vassili tried to unite the two principalities?

As in the time of Ivan III., the duel of the two States made itself felt throughout Europe, and occasioned a great diplomatic movement. Now, Sigismond had the Tatars of the Crimea on his side; Vassili opposed them with the Tatars of Astrakhan. Sigismond reckoned on Sweden. Vassili negotiated with Denmark. The King had gained over to his cause the Dnieper Cossacks, whose name already began to be heard in history, and who had been powerfully organized by Dachkovitch. But Vassili secured the friendship of the Teutonic Order, who even consented to invade Polish Prussia; of Maximilian of Austria, who signed a treaty of partition of the Polish territory; of the Hospodar of Wallachia; and finally of the Sultan Selim, to whom he sent embassy after embassy. Negotiations were set on foot in consequence of the defeat of Constantine Ostrojski before Smolensk, in the battle of Opotchka. Maximilian of Austria undertook the office of mediator; his ambassador, Herberstein, the same who has left us the curious book entitled 'Rerum Moscovitarum Commentarii,' promised that Vassili should cede Smolensk, and quoted to him the disinterestedness of King Pyrrhus and other great men of antiquity. Pope Leo X. intervened without greater success, though he counselled Vassili to leave Lithuania alone, and to turn his thoughts to Constantinople, the inheritance of his mother, Sophia Palæologus. At last in 1522, the negotiations opened and terminated in the truce of 1526. Vassili pronounced a discourse on the subject, in which he expressed his friendship for his noble mediators, the Pope, the Emperor, and the Archduke of Austria (Clement VII., Charles V., and Ferdinand), but Russia kept Smolensk.

WARS WITH THE TATARS—DIPLOMATIC RELATIONS WITH EUROPE.

The Tatars were still dangerous. Mengli-Ghirei, the ancient ally of Ivan III., had declared for Lithuania against Vassili.

Perhaps the old Khan might have lost the authority necessary to restrain his sons and mourzas, who only wished to pillage the Russian territory. Under his successor, Makhmet Ghirei, the Crimea became a deadly enemy of Russia. Kazan, on expelling the *protégé* of Ivan III., had elected a prince hostile to Moscow. Two expeditions directed against the rebel city failed completely. At the death of the Tzar of Kazan, the principality became the apple of discord between the Khan of the Crimea and the Grand Prince. The Russians, however, had succeeded, and installed their client, Schig-Alei, a Mussulman brutalized by idleness and pleasures, whose enormous stomach gave him a grotesque appearance ; but he was overthrown by the intrigues of the Khan of the Crimea, and a kinsman of the Ghirei was placed on the throne. In support of their candidate, the Taurians prepared, in 1521, a great invasion of Russia. They crushed the Russian voïevodes on the banks of the Oka, ravaged the Grand Principality, looked on Moscow from the Hill of Sparrows, and made themselves drunk with hydromel found in the cellars of the Grand Prince. At the Kremlin there was a formidable array of artillery, but no powder. Herberstein assures us that the powerful son of Ivan III. humiliated himself, as in the time of Ivan Kalita, to save his capital, sent presents to the Khan, and signed a treaty by which he professed himself his tributary ; but that in his retreat, Makhmet Ghirei was received with cannonballs by the voïevode of Riazan, who took from him the humiliating treaty. Though the Russian honor was saved by the cannonade of Riazan, this invasion cost Russia dear. All the flat country was a prey to the flames. A multitude of people, especially women and children, had been carried off by the barbarians. Many perished on the journey ; the rest were sold in whole troops in the markets of Kaffa and Astrakhan. The following year Vassili assembled on the Oka a formidable army, with an imposing artillery, and sent a challenge to the Khan of the Crimea summoning him to accept an honorable fight in the open country. The Tatar answered that he knew the way to Russia, and never consulted his enemies as to when he was to fight. A short time after, Makhmet conquered the Tzarate of Astrakhan, but was assassinated by Mamaï, Prince of the Nogaïs.

The Tatars of the Crimea were, thanks to the vast southern steppes, nearly beyond Russian enterprises ; but it was still possible to attain Kazan. In order to profit by the dissensions of the Hordes of the South, two new expeditions were fitted out in 1523 and 1524 against this town, but both were unsuccessful. Vassili discovered a more certain way of ruining his enemies—he established a fair at Makarief on the Volga, and by this means destroyed that of Kazan. It was this fair of Makarief that was afterwards transported to Nijni-Novgorod, and draws more than 100,000 strangers from Europe and Asia.

Day by day Russia took a more important place in Europe. Vassili exchanged embassies with all the sovereigns of the West, except those of France and England. He was the correspondent of Leo X. and Clement VII.; of Maximilian and Charles V.; of Gustavus Vasa, founder of a new dynasty; of Sultan Selim, conqueror of Egypt; and of Suleiman the Magnificent. In the East, the Great Mogul of India, Baber, descendant of Tamerlane, sought his friendship. Autocracy daily became stronger. Vassili governed without consulting his council of boyards. "*Moltchi smerd!*" (Be silent, rustic!) he said one day to a great lord, who dared to raise an objection. Prince Vassili Kholmaski, who was married to one of his sisters, was thrown into prison for indocility. The boyard Beklemychef having complained that "the Grand Prince decided all the questions alone, shut up, with two others, in his bed-chamber," had his head cut off. The Metropolitan Varlaam was deposed and banished to a monastery. Herberstein asserts already, that no European sovereign is obeyed like the Grand Prince of Moscow. This growing power was manifested externally by the splendor of the court, which naturally did not preclude the worst barbaric taste. In the reception of his ambassadors, Vassili displayed unheard-of luxury; many hundreds of horsemen accompanied him when he hunted. The throne of the Prince was guarded by young nobles, the *ryndis*, with their head-dresses of high caps of white fur, dressed in long caftans of white satin, armed with silver hatchets. The lists of his masters of the horse, his cup-bearers, chamberlains, &c., are already very long. Strangers continued, though in small numbers, to come to Moscow. The most illustrious of them was Maximus, surnamed the Greek, a monk of Mount Athos, and a native of Arta, in Albania. In his youth he had studied at Venice and at Florence, and been the friend of Lascaris and Aldus Manutius. He had remained the sincere admirer of Savonarola. Vassili had sent for him with other Greeks to translate the Greek books into Slavonic, and put his library in order. Maximus is said to have been astonished to find in the Kremlin such a large number of ancient manuscripts; he vowed that neither Italy nor in Greece was to be found such a rich collection. After having finished the translation of the Psalter, he wished to return to Mount Athos. Vassili retained him, made him his favorite, and often granted him the lives of condemned boyards. His works, his science, as well as his favor, gained him the hatred of ignorant and fanatical monks. The Metropolitan Daniel declared against him. When Vassili repudiated against her will his wife Solomonia, because of her sterility, the *philosopher*, it seems, ventured to blame the prince, who then abandoned him to his enemies. Denounced before an ecclesiastical tribunal, accused of heresy and of false interpretation of the sacred books, he was banished to a monastery at Tver. Later he obtained leave to retire to that of Troïtsa, where there is still shown the tomb of the man who was, in Russia, one of the apostles of the Renaissance.

CHAPTER XV.

IVAN THE TERRIBLE (1533-1584.)

Minority of Ivan IV.—He takes the title of Tzar (1547)—Conquest of Kazan (1552), and of Astrakhan (1554)—Contests with the Livonian Order, Poland, the Tatars, Sweden, and the Russian aristocracy—The English in Russia—Conquest of Siberia.

MINORITY OF IVAN IV.—HE TAKES THE TITLE OF TZAR (1547).

THE *rôle* and the character of Ivan IV. have been and still are very differently estimated by Russian historians. Karamsin, who has not subjected to a criticism sufficiently severe the narratives and documents from which he has drawn his information, has seen in him a prince who was born cruel and vicious, but was miraculously brought back into the paths of virtue. Under the guidance of two excellent ministers he gave some years of repose to Russia; then abandoning himself to his passions—astounded Europe and the empire with what the historian calls the "seven periods of massacres." M. Kostomarof supports the verdict of Karamsin. Another school represented by M. Solovief and M. Zabiéline, has shown more mistrust of the partial accounts of Kourbski, leader of the oligarchic party, of Guagnini, courtier of the King of Poland, of Taube and Kruse, traitors to the sovereign whom they served. Above all, they have taken into consideration the time and the environment of Ivan the Terrible. This party concerns itself less with his morality as an individual, than with the part he played as the agent of the historical development of Russia. Did not the French historians for a while refuse to recognize the immense services rendered by Louis XI. in the great work of consolidating the unity of France, and the creation of a modern State? He has been justified at last by an attentive examination of documents and facts.

At the time that Ivan IV. succeeded his father, the struggle of the central power with the forces of the past had changed its character. The old Russian States which had for so long held in check the new power of Moscow—the principalities of Tver,

Riazan, Souzdal and Novgorod-Severski—and the republics of Novgorod, Pskof, and Viatka, had lost their independence; their possessions had gone to swell those of Moscow. All North and East Russia is now united under the sceptre of the Grand Prince. To the perpetual contests with Tver, Riazan, and Novgorod succeed the great foreign wars; the crusades against Lithuania, the Tatars, the Swedes, the Livonian knights.

Precisely because the work of Great Russian unity was accomplished, the internal resistance to the authority of the Prince became stronger. The descendants of the princely families which had been dispossessed by money or force of arms, and the retainers of these ancient reigning houses, enlisted in the service of the master of Moscow. The Court of the latter was full of uncrowned nobles, Belskis, Chouïskis, Kourbskis, Vorotinskis, descendants of the appanaged princes, proud of the blood of Rurik which ran in their veins. Others sprang from Gedimin, the Lithuanian, or from baptized Tatar *mourzas*. All these, as well as the powerful boyards of Tver, Riazan, and Novgorod, became the boyards of the Grand Prince. There was only one Court for all to serve—that of Moscow. When Russia was divided into sovereign States, discontented boyards were free to change their master, to pass from the service of Tchernigof to that of Kief, or from the service of Souzdal to that of Novgorod. Now, where could they go? Outside of Moscow there was nothing but foreign sovereigns, the enemies of Russia. To make use of the ancient right of changing your master, was to pass over to the enemy to be a traitor. To change and betray became synonyms. From the Russian word *izmiéni* (change) is derived the word *izmićnik* (to betray). The Russian boyard could go neither to the Germans, to the Swedes, nor to the Tatars : he could only go to the Grand Duke of Lithuania, but that was exactly the worst sort of *change* the blackest of treasons. The Prince of Moscow knew well that the war with Lithuania—that State which was Polish in the west, and exercised, by means of its Russian provinces in the east, a dangerous fascination on the subjects of Moscow—was a struggle for existence. Lithuania, was an internal as well as an external enemy, with links and sympathies with the heart of the Russian State, even in the palace of the Tzar himself, and her formidable hand is found in all intrigues and conspiracies. The external struggle with Lithuania, and the internal struggle with the Russian oligarchy, are different phases of the same contest, the heaviest and most perilous of all sustained by the Grand Princes of Moscow. The dispossessed princes, the boyards of the ancient independent States, had renounced the strife with him on the battle-field, but they continued to combat his authority in his own Court. There are no more wars of States against State; henceforth the war is intestine, that of oligarchy against autocracy. Resigned to being sovereign princes no longer, the boyard princes of Moscow were not yet content to be only subjects. The narrower area intensified the violence of the contest. The Court of Moscow was a fenced-in field, from which none could go out without changing the Muscovite for the Lithuanian master —without *betraying*. Hence the passionate character of the struggle between the two principles under Ivan IV. Besides, the sovereigns of Moscow who had destroyed, after so many efforts, the Russian States that held Moscow in check, committed the same fault as the Capetians or the early Valois. In constituting appanages for the younger branches, they built up with one hand what they pulled down with the other; to the sovereign princes of the 11th century succeeded the princes of the blood the appanaged princes of the 15th and 16th centuries. These also had their domain, &c., their boyards, their *dieti boyarskie* (men-at-arms.) They were the brothers, uncles, cousins of the Grand Prince, who became the chiefs of the vanquished oligarchy and organized the coalition of the forces of the past against him. They stood to him as the Capetians of Burgundy, Berri, Bourbon, and Orleans, stood to the Capetian kings, Charles VII., Louis XI., and Charles VIII.

Vassili Ivanovitch left two sons, Ivan and Iouri, under the guardianship of his second wife, Helena Glinski. She had come into Russia with a family of Podolian nobles, proscribed by Sigismond, and accused of having plotted against his life. Helena Glinski had subdued her old husband Vassili, not only by her beauty, but by her free and attractive manners, an independence of spirit and character, and a variety of accomplishments not to be found among the Russian women of that day, condemned as they were to seclusion. She was almost a Western. Vassili was able to leave her, on his death-bed, with the guardianship of her sons, and the care of strengthening his work and that of his ancestors. This energetic woman knew how to put down all attempts of princely and oligarchic reaction against the autocracy of the Grand Prince. One of her husband's brothers, Iouri Ivanovitch, convicted of rebellion, was thrown into prison, where he died. Helena's own uncle, Michael Glinski, an ambitious and turbulent Podolian, after having enjoyed her confidence for some time, was likewise arrested and died in confinement. Andrew Ivanovitch, another brother of the late Tzar, tried to escape into Poland to obtain the support of Sigismond; he was stopped on the way, and imprisoned. Lithuania attempted to come to his aid, by taking up arms for the rebels of the interior. This unimportant war was ended in 1537 by a truce. The Tatars of Kazan and the Crimea suffered many defeats; and to place Moscow beyond the possibility of being seized by a *coup de main*, Helena enclosed with ramparts the quarter known by the name of Katai-gorod. As she could not entirely rely either on the boyards or on the princes, nor even on her own relations, she gave all her confidence to the master of the horse, Telepnef, whom the public voice charged with being her lover. A government as energetic against its internal as against its foreign enemies, gave little satisfaction to the oligarchic party. In 1538 Helena died, the victim of poison.

The boyards then took possession of the government, after having put to death the master of the horse, and imprisoned his sister Agrafena, Ivan's nurse. The chief power was disputed specially by two families—the Chouïskis and the Belskis. Russia became a prey to anarchy, the governments and the voïevodies were given by turns to the creatures of these two families, and the people were cruelly oppressed; the two factions even elevated and deposed at will the Metropolitan of Moscow. At last, Andrew Chouïski overthrew the government of the Belskis, and finally deposed the Metropolitan.

Whilst the nobles were thus intriguing for the supreme power, Vassili's two sons were left by themselves. Iouri, the younger, was feeble in intellect, but Ivan, like Peter the Great, whom in many points he resembled, was a highly-gifted boy. He suffered keenly from the contempt in which his turbulent subjects held him. "We and our brother Iouri," he afterwards writes, "were treated like foreigners, like the children of beggars. We were ill-clothed, we were cold and hungry." They saw the boyards pillage the treasures and luxurious furniture of the palace; Chouïski even threw himself in Ivan's presence on the bed of the late Tzar. The empire was plundered as well as the palace. "They wandered everywhere," continues Ivan IV., "in the towns and villages, cruelly tormenting the people, inflicting all kinds of evils on them, exacting fines without mercy from the inhabitants. Of our subjects they have made their slaves; of their slaves, the nobles of the State." He had seen all whom he loved torn from him—his nurse Agrafena; the master of the horse, Telepnef, who had been put to death; and his favorite Voronzof, who was roughly handled and nearly killed by the boyards. It was enough for a courtier to take pains to please him, for him instantly to become an object of mistrust to the oligarchs. Ivan, like a neglected child, badly educated, never disciplined, had to be his own master. He read much, without method—the Bible, the Lives of the Saints, the Byzantine Chroniclers translated into Slavonic—whatever came in his way. Above all, he thought. He had imbibed from his reading a high idea of what it was to be a king, and knew well that he was the rightful master. These very boyards, so insolent towards him in private—did he not see them in public ceremonials, at receptions of ambassadors, rival each other in affected respect and servility? It was he who, seated on his throne, received the compliments of the foreign envoys; his signature was necessary to give the force of law to actions the most contrary to his will. These were no vain forms, but involved real power. Ivan, however, dissembled. After the Christmas fêtes of 1543, he suddenly summoned his boyards before him, addressed them in a menacing tone, and reproached them sternly for their manner of governing. "There were among them," he added, "many guilty ones; but this time he would content himself with making one example." He then ordered his guards to seize Andrew Chouiski, the chief of the government, and there and then had him torn to pieces by hounds. Some of the most turbulent and the most compromised were banished to distant towns. The author of this *coup d'état* was thirteen years old.

According to the invariable custom of Muscovite sovereigns, Ivan surrounded himself by his maternal relations, those on his father's side being naturally objects of suspicion. Then began what was called a *vremia*; that is a *season* of favor." The relatives of the Prince, the men of the *season* (*vremenchtchiki*), the Glinskis, were charged to provide for the administration of the empire. In January 1547, Ivan ordered the Metropolitan Macarius to proceed with his coronation. He assumed at the ceremony not only the title of Grand Prince, but that of Tzar. The first title no longer answered to the new power of the sovereign of Moscow, who counted among his *domestics*, princes and even Grand Princes. The name of Tzar is that which the books in the Slavonic language, ordinarily read by Ivan, give to the kings of Judæa, Assyria, Egypt, Babylon and to the emperors of Rome and Constantinople. Now, was not Ivan in some sort the heir of the *Tzar* Nebuchadnezzar, the *Tzar* Pharaoh, the *Tzar* Ahasuerus, and the *Tzar* David, since Russia was the sixth empire spoken of in the Apocalypse? Through his grandmother Sophia Palæologus, he was connected with the family of the Tzar of Byzantium; through his ancestor Vladimir Monomachus, he belonged to the Porphyrogeniti; and through Constantine the Great, to Cæsar. If Constantinople had been the second, Moscow was the third Rome—living heir of the Eternal

City. We may imagine what prestige was added to the dignity of the Russian sovereign by this dazzling title, borrowed from Biblical antiquity, from Roman majesty, from the orthodox sovereigns of Byzantium. It recalled at the same time the recently acquired freedom of Russia ; the Slavonic authors likewise bestowed this august title on the Mongol khans, suzerains of the Muscovite princes. Now that fortune smiled upon Russia, it well became her prince to call himself " Tzar." Shortly after, Ivan, whose deserted youth had been soiled by debauchery, confirmed his return to virtue by his marriage with Anastasia, of that family of Romanof whose future destiny was to be so brilliant. His Court was increased by *vrémenchtchiki* chosen from the relatives of the Tzarina.

The vanquished party naturally would not consent to be set aside without a struggle for revenge. Fortune soon gave them an opportunity. For four years Ivan had governed absolutely, supported by his connections, the Glinskis and the Romanofs, and it was many years since Russia had been so tranquil. Suddenly, in 1547, a terrible fire broke out and destroyed a great part of Moscow, and 1700 people perished. The Tzar took refuge at Vorobief, and thence contemplated with terror the destruction of his capital. An inquiry was made, and the boyards took advantage of it to insinuate to the people that it was the Glinskis who had burnt Moscow. " It is the Princess Anne Glinski," repeated voices among the crowd, " who, with her two sons, has made enchantments ; she has taken human hearts, and plunged them in water, and with this water has sprinkled the houses. This is the cause of the destruction of Moscow." The enraged multitude burst into the palace of the Glinskis. One of them, Iouri, was stabbed in the porch of the Assumption. Then the rioters proceeded to Vorobief, and demanded Ivan's uncle, the old Glinski. The sovereign's own life was in danger ; it was necessary to use force to disperse the rebels.

The events which followed are unintelligible from the dramatized recital of Karamsin, but very clear if we keep to the logic of facts. Ivan could hardly be ignorant who had raised this revolt, and he was not the man to give himself up to his ancient guardians. But his nervous, impressionable nature had been greatly struck by the spectacle under his eyes. Under the influence of this terror he examined his conscience, and resolved to amend his life. He took the priest Silvester, who had dwelt in his palace for nine years, and had a great reputation for virtue, as his spiritual director ; he gave him at the same time the administration of ecclesiastical affairs. Alexis Adachef, one of the smaller nobility, was charged with receiving petitions, and the supervision of the interior and of the war. As long as the two new favorites confined themselves to their offices, the Court was tranquil. It was the happiest period of the reign of Ivan IV. The municipal administration was reorganized in the interior (1551). A new code (*Soudebnik*) was prepared, and a council assembled, whose hundred articles (*Stoglaf*) were occupied with Church reforms. In foreign affairs Russia conquered her ancient masters.

CONQUEST OF KAZAN (1552), AND OF ASTRAKHAN (1554).

The kingdom of Kazan continued to be distracted by two opposing influences—that of Russia and that of the Khan of the Crimea. The latter seemed the stronger, and Safa-Ghirei, candidate for the Crimea, distinguished his accession by ravaging the Russian territory; the Khan supported him in these incursions by advancing with the whole Crimean horde as far as the ka. When Safa died, leaving a son who was a minor, the Muscovite party took the upper hand in Kazan and bestowed the crown on Schig-Alei. He made himself detested by his new subjects, and things came to such a pass that the Kazanese appeared to prefer the direct rule of Moscow to this disguised subordination. At the request of the inhabitants Ivan recalled Schig-Alei, and sent them a viceroy, Mikoulinski. Suddenly a rumor was spread in Kazan that Mikoulinski was approaching with Russian troops with the object of exterminating the population. A rebellion broke out. The gates of Moscow were shut on the Muscovites, and men demanded a prince of the Nogaï Tatars. Ediger-Makhment was proclaimed Tzar of Kazan.

Ivan determined to make an end of this Mussulman city. In June 1552, the same year that Henry II. obtained possession of the three bishoprics, the Tzar took the field. He was at once checked by the news that the Khan of the Crimea, wishing to save Kazan by a diversion, had invaded Moscow. Ivan advanced against him as far as the Oka; there he learnt that the barbarians, not being able to take Toula, had hastily retired. Upon this, Ivan's infantry, with 150,000 men and 150 pieces of cannon, descended the Volga in boats, while the cavalry followed along the banks, and directed their course to Kazan. The creation of advanced posts had diminished the distance that separated Kazan from Nijni-Novgorod. His father had founded Makarief and Vassilsoursk on the Volga; and he himself had established in 1551 the warlike colony of Sviajsk on the Sviaga. Later he founded those of Kosmodemiansk and Tcheboksary.

At the beginning of September Ivan encamped under Kazan and surrounded it by a line of circumvallation, which cut off all communication between the town and the cavalry of the Mourza Iapantcha, which had taken the field. The garrison of Kazan, numbering 30,000 Tatars and 2500 Nogaïs, defended themselves energetically and incessantly, and managed by their *sorties* to hinder the work of the assailants. The Tzar repeatedly offered them honorable terms; he even hung up his prisoners on gibbets to frighten the Kazanese into surrendering, but the besieged only shot arrows against these unhappy wretches, crying that "it was better for them to receive death from the clean hands of their countrymen than to perish by the impure hands of Christians." The Russian army had to struggle with the unchained elements as well as with their enemies. The fleet, which bore their provisions and powder, was destroyed by a tempest. The voïevodes wished to raise the siege, but Ivan reanimated their failing courage. Prolonged rains flooded the Muscovite camp, caused, it was said, by the sorcerers of Kazan, who stood on the walls, their robes girt up, insulting the besiegers by their words and gestures. Ivan sent to Moscow for a miraculous cross, which dispersed the enchantments.

Ivan had secured the services of a German engineer, who laid mines under the very walls of the town. The ramparts of wood and bricks at many points fell with a great noise, and the Russian army entered the town by the breaches. A fierce hand to-hand fight took place in the streets and around the palace. The bravest of the Kazanese, after having tried to defend their prince, cut their way through, but, pursued by the light cavalry, few escaped. In the town numbers were massacred: those only were spared who could be sold to slave-merchants. When the Tzar made his triumphal entry into the middle of these bloody ruins, he was moved, like Scipio at Carthage, by a feeling of pity for this great disaster. "They are not Christians," said he, weeping, "but yet they are men." The town was re-peopled by Russians, and even at the present day the Tatar population is confined to the faubourgs. In the Kremlin Ivan annihilated all the monuments of the Mongol past, and replaced them by churches and monasteries which attested his gratitude towards God and the triumph of the Cross over Islam.

The date of these events is already far distant, but they still live in the memory of the Russian people. Many epics are consecrated to this great victory. It is not only, as Karamsin says, because Kazan was the first fortress taken by the Russians after a siege according to the rules of war; it is because the capture of Kazan marks the culminating point in the history of the long struggle of the Slavs against the Tatars—a struggle which began by the total subjugation of Russia by the Mongols, but which has continued to our own day, and probably will only end with the conquest of the Tatar races by the Russian Empire. The victory of Ivan the Terrible is the first great revenge of the vanquished over the vanquishers, the first triumph at the expense of the conquerors, the first stage reached by European civilization in taking the offensive towards Asia. In the Russian annals the expedition of Kazan occupies the same glorious place as the defeat of Abderahman in the history of the Franks, or Las Navas da Tolosa in the chronicles of Spain. It was more than a conquest—it was a crusade. During the assault Ivan did not cease to display the standard of the holy faith. It was remarked that the day the ramparts fell the Tzar was at church, and the deacon read the following verse from the Gospel for the day : "There shall be one flock, one shepherd." It was with the cry of "God with us!" that the Russians precipitated themselves into the town. The triumph of Moscow mingled with that of Christianity and orthodoxy.

The political consequences of the taking of Kazan were considerable. The five Finnish or Mongol tribes who had been subject to this royal city—the Tcheremisses, the Mordvians, the Tchouvaches, whom M. Radlow considers the descendants of the Bulgars of Bolgary, the Votiaks and the Bachkirs—after a resistance of some years, were obliged to do homage to Moscow. Ivan sent them missionaries at the same time as his voïevodes.

The fall of the kingdom of Astrakhan soon followed that of Kazan. This great city was also divided between two parties. In 1554 Prince Iouri Pronski descended the Volga with 30,000 men, and established Derbych, the *protégé* of Russia, on the throne. Derbych, after a short time, was accused of having an understanding with the Khan of the Crimea; and Astrakhan was conquered a second time, and finally united to Russia. The Nogaïs, who wandered over the neighboring steppes, were forced to accept the Muscovite protection. Thus the Volga—that famous river whose banks sustain so many ruined cities, Itil capital of the Khazars, Bolgary capital of the Bulgars, Saraï capital of the Golden Horde—that keep the memory of the ancient races who have vanished from history; the Volga—that grand artery of Eastern commerce—now flowed in the whole of its course from its source to its mouth through the land of the Tzars.

Persian Asia was thrown open to Russian influence by means of the Caspian; and already the petty princes of the Caucasus, always fighting either among themselves or with the Tatars of the Crimea, sought the alliance of the successors of the Greek Cæsars. In order to keep a firmer hold on the Horde of the Taurid, Ivan took under his protection one of the two warlike republics which had been formed in the neighborhood of the Crimea: the Cossacks of the Don declared themselves subjects of Moscow, the Cossacks of the Dnieper remained Poles.

WARS WITH THE LIVONIAN ORDER, POLAND, TATARS, SWEDEN, AND ARISTOCRATIC RUSSIA.

Russia, which felt the growth of her forces, felt equally the need of throwing open the Baltic at the same time as the Black Sea. The Baltic was even the more necessary to the Russians, as by it only could they communicate with Western Europe, and receive vessels, artillery, and engineers. Thence Muscovy awaited the increase of power that civilization could alone give her. Between Muscovy and the Baltic lay more than one enemy: Sweden, the Livonian knights, Lithuania, and Poland. In 1554 a war broke out about the rectification of the frontiers between Ivan the Terrible and the great Gustavus Vasa; but as the founder of the Swedish dynasty was not supported by his neighbors, the war was a short one. It terminated by a commercial treaty which opened India and China to the Swedish merchants by way of Russia; and to those of Russia, Flanders, England, and France, by way of Sweden. Moscow could not yet communicate with the West except through a jealous intermediary.

Ivan the Terrible, inspired by the same political and civilizing ideas as Peter the Great, wished to "open a window" into Europe. For this purpose he coveted the ports of the Narva, Revel and Riga, then in the hands of the Livonian Order, against which Ivan had some grievances. About 1547 Ivan had sent the Saxon Schlitte into Germany to engage for him a certain number of engineers and artizans, and Schlitte had managed to collect about a hundred people. The jealousy of the Germans then awoke; they feared that, as she became civilized, Russia would also become strong. The Livonian Order demanded of the Emperor Charles VI. the right to stop these strangers on their road. None ever reached Moscow. Ivan, then occupied with Kazan, was unable to avenge himself; but when in 1554 the envoys of the Order came to Moscow to solicit a renewal of the truce, he summoned them to pay tribute for Iourief, the ancient patrimony of the Russian princes. Such a demand meant war. In 1558 the Russian army took Narva, Neuhausen,

Dorpat, and seventeen other places. The Grand Master Kettler asked help of his neighbors. Poland alone responded to his appeal, and Sigismond Augustus II. concluded an offensive and defensive alliance with the Livonian Order.

At this juncture an important revolution took place in the palace of the Tzar. Ivan's relations with his two counsellors Silvester and Adachef had singularly altered. They had disagreed with respect to the war with Livonia; they had desired that after the capture of Kazan and Astrakhan Ivan should turn in preference to the third Mussulman State, the Khanate of the Crimea. M. Kostomarof gives excellent reasons for this preference, but the reasons in favor of the opposite opinion are not less good. By conquering the Crimea the safety of the empire would be secured, and the conversion to Islamism, the complete Tatarization of the ancient Taurian tribes still professing Christianity, would be prevented; but by conquering Livonia an ancient patrimony of the Russian princes would be recovered and it would become possible to enter into direct relations with civilized Europe. The chances of success were equal. The Horde was then decimated by an epidemic, but the Livonian Order was in the act of dissolution by the result of the contest between Catholicism and Protestantism. The difficulties were equal. In attacking Livonia, Russia would come in contact with Sweden, Denmark, Poland, and Germany; but behind the Crimea were the Turks, then at the height of their power, and much irritated by the conquest of 'Kazan and Astrakhan. Peter the Great did not conquer Livonia till after twenty years hard fighting with the Powers of the North; but how many Russian expeditions against the Crimea have not been stopped by the distance, the difficulty of communication, the sandy deserts, and the extreme temperatures? Catherine the Great only conquered the Taurid in the decadence of the Turkish Empire, and after many campaigns, when she not only brought into play her armies of the Danube, but sent a fleet to the Archipelago. In reality both enterprises were premature; Russia had not yet strength to carry them through. Neither the Tzar nor his counsellors were completely in the right, but the obstinacy of the latter had a fatal result. To content everybody two wars were declared —which was to run the certain risk of a double check.

The misunderstanding between the Tzar and his two ministers dated from further back. Silvester abused his spiritual influence with the Tzar to multiply jobs of his own. He had ended by leaving him no liberty; and when Ivan's favorite son died, he told him brutally that it was a chastisement from Heaven for his indocility. He had entered into relations with

boyards whom Ivan justly suspected; he took their part against
the Tzarina Anastasia, whom he represented as a second Empress Eudoxia, the persecutor of Chrysostom; against the Glinskis, and against the Romanofs. Adachef followed the same
path. Like Haroun-al-Raschid's favorites, the Barmecides,
these two ministers had ended by appropriating all the power of
their master. Ivan had patience with them, believing them to
be faithful; but in 1553 he fell dangerously ill, and was thought
to be at the point of death. Then the boyards resumed their
old arrogance; they obstinately refused to swear allegiance to
the son of the Tzar, the young Dmitri, declaring that they would
not obey his maternal relations, the Romanofs. The noisy discussions reached the bed of the sick man, and his entreaties
were despised. The boyards approached Vladimir, cousin of
Ivan IV., who had also refused to take the oaths, and it was
known that the mother of this ambitious prince was distributing
largesses to the army. Silvester took the part of Prince Vladimir against those boyards who remained faithful, and the family
of Adachef joined with the mutineers. The faithful boyards
even feared for the life of the Tzar; Ivan could not be under
any delusions as to the fate awaiting his wife and his son in case
of his death.

"When God shall have worked His will on me," said Ivan
to the few boyards gathered round him, "do not, I pray you,
forget that you have sworn an oath to my son and to me; do
not let him fall into the hands of the boyards; fly with him to
some strange land, whithersoever God will conduct you. And
you," he continued, addressing the Romanofs, "wherefore these
terrors? Do you think that the boyards will spare you? You
will fall the first: die then rather—since die you must—for my
son and for his mother; do not abandon my wife to the fury of
the boyards." Ivan IV. recovered, but he preserved a lasting
impression of these days of anguish. When we see him, later
in his reign, give himself up to revenge, and to apparently inexplicable fury, we must think of the terrible vigils of 1553, of the
scenes of rebellion and violence that troubled the peace of his
sick chamber, of the obstinate refusals to take the desired vow
of the delcarations of hatred against the Tzarina and her relations, and of the intrigues woven round Vladimir against the
Tzarévitch Dmitri.

He had no more confidence in his favorites; both were banished from the Court. Silvester retired to the monastery of
Saint Cyril, and was afterwards exiled to Solovetski. Adachef
was appointed voïevode at Fellin in Livonia, and later was
forced to live at Dorpat. But they left behind them **a complete**
Vol. '

administration, a perfect army of clients. They had peopled the Court, the governments, and the voïevodies with their creatures. Their partisans were certain to agitate and plot for the return of their chiefs. Who knew how far these plots might go? A short time after Adachef's disgrace, that Anastasia whom he detested died suddenly. Ivan alleged that she was poisoned. Since the publication of M. Zabićline's careful studies on the 'Private Life of the Tzarinas of Russia,' this allegation and others like it do not appear as inconceivable as they seemed to Karamsin. The intrigues of the friends of Adachef forced Ivan IV. many times to have recourse to severity, but at this epoch he was comparatively merciful.

"When the treachery of that dog Alexis Adachef and his accomplices was discovered," Ivan afterwards writes, "we let our anger be tempered with mercy; we did not condemn the guilty to capital punishments, but only banished them to our different towns. . . . Then we put no one to death. Those who belonged to the party of Silvester and Adachef we commanded to separate from them, and no longer to recognize them as chiefs. This promise we made them confirm by a vow, but they paid no heed to our injunction, and trampled their oath under foot. Not only did they not separate from the traitors, but they aided them by all possible means, and schemed to render them back their ancient power, and to set on foot against us a perfidious plot. Then only, seeing their wicked obstinacy and unconquerable spirit of rebellion, I inflicted on the guilty the penalty of their faults." Capital punishment was indeed rare at this epoch. Ivan usually contented himself with demanding a fresh oath from those who were arrested on the road to Lithuania, and exacted surety from them and their friends that they would not seek again to pass into Poland. Sometimes he condemned them to the easy durance of the monasteries.

What finally decided the Tzar to be more severe in his treatment was the defection of Prince Andrew Kourbski, who belonged to a family once royal, and descended from Rurik. He had distinguished himself against the Tatars on the Oka and at Kazan, and, being a zealous partizan of Adachef and Silvester, he was deeply irritated by their fall. Nominated general-in-chief of the army in Livonia, his carelessness allowed the Russians to suffer a shameful defeat. · 15,000 Russians were beaten by 4000 Poles; and even, if the Polish historian Martin Belski is to be believed, 40,000 Russians by 1500 Poles. Kourbski had reason to fear the anger of the Tzar. He had been for some time negotiating with the King of Poland, being desirous of obtaining in Lithuania a command, lands, and advantages

equal to those he would lose. At last, abandoning his wife and
children to the vengeance of the Tzar, he left Wenden and
crossed into the Polish camp. Thence he sent to Ivan a letter
by his servant Chipanof, whose foot, according to the tradition,
Ivan nailed with his iron staff on to a step of the *red staircase*,
while the message was being read to him.

"Tzar formerly glorified by God!" wrote Kourbski, "Tzar
who formerly shone like the torch of orthodoxy, but who, for
our sins, art now revealed to us in quite a different aspect, with
a soiled and leprous conscience, such as we could not find even
among barbarian infidels! Exposed to thy cruel persecution,
with a heart filled with bitterness, I wish notwithstanding to say
a few words to you. O Tzar, why hast thou put to death the
strong ones of Israel? Why hast thou slain the valiant voïevodes given thee by God? Why hast thou shed their victorious
blood, their only blood on the profaned pavement of the churches
of God, during the sacred ceremonies? Why hast thou red-
dened the porch of the temple with the blood of the martyrs?
In what were they guilty towards thee, O Tzar? Was it not
their valor which overthrew, which laid at thy feet, those
proud kingdoms of the Volga, before which thine ancestors
were slaves? Is it not their zeal, their intelligence, to which,
after God, thou owest the strong towns of the Germans? And
behold thy gratitude to these unhappy ones! Thou hast exterminated whole families amongst us. Dost thou think thyself
then immortal, O Tzar? or dost thou think (seduced by some
heresy) that thou canst escape the incorruptible Judge, Jesus
our God? No; He will judge the whole world, and chiefly such
proud persecutors as thou art. My blood, which has already
flowed for thee like water, will cry against thee to our Lord.
God sees all consciences!" Kourbski then invokes the victims
of Ivan, and shows them standing before the throne of God, demanding justice against their executioner. "Is it that in thy
pride thou trustest in thy legions to keep thee in this ephemeral
life, inventing against the human race new engines of torture
to tear and disfigure the body of man, the image of the angels?
Dost thou reckon on thy servile flatterers, on thy boon companions, on thy turbulent boyards, who make thee lose thy soul
and body, entice thee to the debaucheries of Venus, and sacrifice their children to the vile rites worthy of Saturn? When my
last day comes, I wish that this letter, watered with my tears,
should be placed on my coffin." He ended by declaring himself a subject of Sigismond Augustus, "my sovereign, who, I
hope, will load me with favors and consolations for my misfortunes." Thus Kourbski spoke "in the name of the strong ones

of Israel, of the living and the dead," that is, in the name of all
the friends of Adachef; he made himself the organ of their
wrath and complaints; he formulated their grievances, and exaggerated them; he demanded an account of the Tzar of his
conduct towards them, threatening him with a higher tribunal,
and dared to ask if he thought himself immortal; he refused
Ivan all participation in the glory acquired at Kazan, insulted
the boyards who surrounded him, and boasted of the crime
which was the most unpardonable in the eyes of the Tzar—the
recognition of the Polish sovereignty.

Kourbski's letter was a manifesto. It helped to irritate the
suspicions of the Tzar, already only too disposed to imagine
plots. Ivan, who thought himself a man of letters, and was
really one of the most learned men in his empire, conceived it
necessary to answer the letter of Kourbski with a long vindica-
tion, adorned with quotations from sacred and profane authors.
The Tzar and his rebel subject exchanged many epistles of this
kind. Ivan, who had begun by this time to justify his surname
of Terrible, gave, besides, another answer to Kourbski's manifesto—the punishment of his supposed accomplices.

Ivan felt that he could no longer govern with a Court, a
council of state (*douma*), and an administration which were filled
with the friends of Adachef and Kourbski. Kourbski's conduct
shows to what depths of treason their rancor could bring them.
He was to return to devastate Russia with a Polish army! Was
the life of the Tzar safe in the midst of such men? In Decem-
ber 1564 Ivan quitted Moscow with all his friends, servants, and
treasures, and retired to the Slobode Alexandrof. He then wrote
two letters to Moscow—one to the Archbishop, complaining of the
plots and infidelity of the nobles, and the complicity of the clergy,
who, abusing the *right* of *intercession*, prevented the sovereign
from punishing the guilty; in the other he reassured the citizens
and people of Moscow, by informing them that they were not
included in his censure. The terror of the capital was great;
the people trembled at the thought of falling again under the
government of the oligarchs; the boyards feared what the people
might do to them. Neither the one nor the other could resign
themselves to the anger of the sovereign. The boyards and the
clergy resolved to ask pardon, and, if necessary, to "carry their
heads" to the Tzar. They went in procession to the Slobode
Alexandrof, to beseech him to recall his abdication. Ivan consented to resume the crown, but on his own conditions. As he
could neither govern with the actual administration nor destroy
it, as he was forced to respect its vested interests, he made a
sort of partition of the monarchy. The greater part of the

empire continued to be governed by the *douma* of the boyards, and constituted the *zemchtchira*, that is, the " rule of the country." Over this part of Russia Ivan only reserved a surveillance, and the right of punishing treason. The other part was placed under the "personal and individual" government of the Tzar, and formed the "*opritchnina.*" Leaving the ancient Court, the ancient *douma*, and the ancient administration still in existence, Ivan IV. formed with his own creatures a new Court, a new council, and a new administration to which he confided the towns and villages that had fallen to his share. He surrounded himself with a special guard, called " the thousand of the Tzar," or the *opritchniki* who had adopted, as *armes parlantes*, a dog's head, and a broom suspended from their saddles. They were ready to bite the enemies of the Tzar, and *to sweep treason off the Russian soil.* This singular *régime* lasted seven years (1565-1572).

Ivan made great use of his right to punish traitors, or those whom he regarded as such. A perfect reign of terror hung over the Russian aristocracy, with alternations of calm and renewed fury. We know the names of his victims, but we do not always know their crimes. The writers hostile to Ivan IV., Kourbski, the Italian Guagnini, then in the service of the King of Poland, and the German refugees Taube and Kruse, are not always agreed on the subject.

About the facts which can be clearly proved, we can see that Ivan had real grievances against the nobles whom he put to death. On the side of the oligarchs the strife, though quiet and noiseless, was not less bloody. We ought not to be deceived by their demonstrations of humility and submission With their foreheads in the dust, they could still conspire. We must beware of thinking Ivan's enemies were any better than himself. They were as cruel towards their inferiors as the Tzar was towards them. This aristocracy of slave-masters, habituated under the Tatar yoke to an insolent disdain of human life and feeling, was not superior in morality to its tyrant. It presented more than one type similar to the French monsters Gilles de Retz and the Sieur de Giac. Under very different colors, it was the same battle that raged in Russia and in France. But in France men fought in open day on the battle-fields of the Praguerie or of the League of the Public Good ; in Russia the contest was carried on by silent plots, by noiseless attempts to poison or slay by magic, met by the axe of the executioner. In this sinister dialogue between the master and his subjects, it was naturally the master who spoke the loudest. In the absence of a sufficient number of authentic documents, we risk nothing by being a little more sceptical than Karamsin.

The principal episodes of this autocratic reign of terror are: 1. The deposition and perhaps the murder of St. Philip, Archbishop of Moscow, guilty of having nobly interceded for the condemned, and of hating the *opritchniki*. 2. The execution of Alexandra, widow of Iroui and sister-in-law of Ivan; of Prince Vladimir and his mother, the ambitious Euphrosyne, who thus expiated their intrigues of 1553. We must remark that Ivan, whatever Kourbski may say, spared Vladimir's children, and largely provided for them. 3. The chastisement of Novgorod, where the aristocratic party had entertained, it seemed to Ivan, the project of opening the gates to the King of Poland, and where the Tzar, according to his own testimony, put to death 1505 persons. 4. The great execution in the Red Place in 1571, where a certain number of Muscovites and Novgorodians were slain, and where many of Ivan's new favorites, notably Viazemski and the Basmanofs, underwent the same penalty as his old enemies.

A curious memorial has been left us of the vengeance of "the Terrible"; it is the synodical letter of the Monastery of St. Cyril, in which Ivan asks for each of his victims by name the prayers of the Church. This list shows a total of 3470 victims, of whom 986 are mentioned by name. Many of these names are followed by this sinister statement,—" with his wife," " with his wife and children," " with his daughters," " with his sons." It was this that Kourbski called "the extermination of entire families" (*vsiorodno*). The constitution of the Russian family at this epoch was so strong, that the death of the head necessarily involved that of the other members. Other collective indications are not less significant. For example: " Kazarine Doubrovski and his two sons, with ten men who came to their help." "Twenty men of the village of Kolmenskoé;" "eighty of Matveiché;" these were no doubt peasants and *dieti-boyarskie* who tried to defend their masters. There is this mention relative to Novgorod: "Remember, Lord, the souls of thy servants, to the number of 1505 persons, Novgorodians." Had not Louis XI. tender feelings of this nature? He prayed with fervor for the soul of his brother, the Duke de Berri.

Other records demonstrate that Ivan the Terrible thought he had serious reasons to fear for his life. His curious correspondence with Queen Elizabeth of England proves this, as he obtains of her the formal promise that in case of misfortune he is to find in England a safe asylum and the free exercise of his worship (1570). There is besides his will of 1572, which contemplates the case of his being "proscribed by his boyards and expelled by them from the throne, and being obliged to wander from country to country," and recommends to his sons to live on good terms with each other after his death, to learn how to restrain and reward their subjects, and above all to be on the watch against them.

During this terrible intestine strife, the war with Livonia and her ally the King of Poland continued. Notwithstanding the help of the latter, the Knights were everywhere beaten, and their fortresses taken by the Russian troops.

At last, ruined by so many blows, this famous Order dissolved. The Isle of Œsel sold itself to Denmark; Revel gave itself to the Swedes; Livonia was ceded by the Grand Master to Poland; Kettler reserved to himself Courland and Semigallia, which were erected into a hereditary duchy. There were no more Livonian knights, but Poland, as heir of the quarrels of Livonia, became more than ever ardent in the struggle. The Russians sustained their new reputation. In 1563 Ivan the Terrible, with a numerous army and many guns, besieged and took Polotsk, a very important position from its proximity to Livonia and its situation on the Dwina, the grand commercial route to Riga. In spite of a victory at Orcha, the King of Poland demanded a truce (1566).

Ivan at this moment offered a strange spectacle to Russia. To deliberate on the request of Sigismond he assembled a counsel, composed of the higher clergy, the territorial boyards on the frontiers of Lithuania (and well acquainted with the local topography), and finally the merchants of Moscow and Smolensk. This despot, who founded autocracy in blood, convoked real States-general; he made an appeal to their opinion, as he had many times before, when from the stone tribune of *Lobnoe miesto* he harangued the three orders. The Assembly decided that the King of Poland's conditions could not be accepted, and offered men and money for the continuation of the war. This was prolonged for four years, and ended in a truce. The Tzar, who saw difficulties accumulating in Livonia, conceived an expedient to enable him to escape them. No longer hoping to be able directly to unite the Baltic ports to his empire, he offered the title of King of Livonia to the Danish Prince Magnus, and made him marry a daughter of the same Prince Vladimir whom he had put to death. Magnus, nominal King of Livonia, soon perceived that he was only an instrument of Muscovite policy. He intrigued against the Tzar and was dethroned, Ivan the Terrible took Wenden in person, which Magnus had garrisoned, and massacred the German soldiers to the last man.

Unfortunately the war with Poland was complicated by the raids of the Tatars of the Crimea. Sigismond did not cease to work upon the Khan, who well understood that his cause was allied with that of Poland. The Tzar, however, overpowered the Khan, took Kief, and established towns on the Dnieper. And what could the Tatars gain there, after all? Had not Ivan overthrown two Mongol kingdoms? The Sultan of Stamboul, Selim II., was ready to join in the Holy War for Kazan and Astrakhan. In 1569, 17,000 Turks, commanded by Kassim Pacha, and 50,000 Tatars, led by the Khan, besieged Astrakhan. The operations dragged on; the Pacha wished to pass the winter there, but a sedition broke out in the army. He was obliged to raise the siege, and lost many of his men in the steppes of the desert. Two years after, the Khan Devlet-Ghirei invaded Russia with 20,000 men. Was he aided by the treachery of the voïevodes? He crossed the Oka, and suddenly appeared under the walls of Moscow. He burned the faubourgs and the fire spread to the town, which, except the Kremlin, was completely reduced to ashes. A foreign author gives the evidently exaggerated number of 800,000 victims. The Khan retired with more than 100,000 prisoners, and despatched the following insolent message to Ivan: " I burn, I ravage everything because of Kazan and Astrakhan. I came to you and I burnt Moscow. I wished to have your crown and your head, but you did not show yourself; you declined a battle, and you dare to call yourself a Tzar of Moscow. Will you live at peace with me? Yield me up Kazan and Astrakhan. If you have only money to offer me, it would be useless, were it the riches of the whole world. What I want is Kazan and Astrakhan. As to the roads to your empire, I have seen them—I know them." He returned the following year (1572), but Prince Michael Vorotinski met him on the banks of the Lopasnia, and inflicted on him a complete defeat.

The same year (that of the Massacre of St. Bartholomew) died Sigismond Augustus II., king of Poland. His reign was especially memorable for the union of Lublin (1569), in virtue of which Poland and Lithuania were henceforth to form only one State under an elective prince. Thus Poland enfeebled royal power at home, just when it acquired in Russia an extraordinary degree of energy. A party of nobles was formed at Warsaw who wished to elect the son of Ivan the Terrible as King of Poland. This was to prepare for the reunion of the two great Slav empires, separated less by language than religion, whose growing antagonism could only terminate in the ruin of one of them, to the great advantage of the German race. Ivan coveted the crown, not for his son, but for himself. Let us see him court the Polish ambassadors, and try to defend himself against the accusations of cruelty and tyranny which the banished Muscovites brought against him.

"If your *pans*, who are now without a king," said he to the Polish envoy Voropaï, "desire me for their sovereign, they will see what a good protector and kind master they will find in me. Many among you say that I am cruel. It is true that I am cruel and irascible—I do not deny it; but to whom, I ask you, am I cruel? I am cruel towards anyone that is cruel to me. The good! ah, I would give them in a moment the chain and the robe that I wear! It is nothing wonderful that your princes love their subjects, if their subjects love them. Mine have delivered me over to the Tatars of the Crimea. My voïevodes did not even warn me of the arrival of the enemy. Perhaps it was difficult for them to vanquish a force so superior to them in numbers; but even if they had lost some thousands of men, and only brought me a whip or a cane of the Tatars, I should have been grateful. Think of the enormity of their treason towards me. If some of them were afterwards chastised, it was for their crimes they were punished. I ask you—do you spare traitors?" Ivan then spoke of his grievances against Kourbski, and ended by promising "to observe the laws, to respect and even to extend the liberties and franchises of Poland."

The ambassador of France at Warsaw finally carried the day, and Henri de Valois, duc d'Anjou, was proclaimed king. He did not stay long in Poland, and, after his flight to the West, a new Diet assembled, and the intrigues of the rival Courts began again.

Stephen Batory, voïevode of Transylvania, was elected king. He was a young, ambitious, and energetic prince, and no more formidable enemy to Ivan the Terrible in his old age could have been chosen. It was now not only a question of the conquest of Livonia which was pursued so laboriously in the face of so many obstacles, but, in placing the crown on his head, Batory had sworn to give back to Poland the towns conquered from her by the Muscovite princes. It was now a contest between the semi-barbarous army of Russia, her almost feudal soldiery, her Tatar cavalry, her tactics of routine, and her feeble artillery, and a really European army, a well-directed artillery, compact regiments of German mercenaries, and Hungarian veterans, seasoned by many combats. Ivan awaited his enemy in Livonia, when suddenly Batory appeared before Polotsk and took it, in spite of a vigorous resistance. The Russian gunners hung themselves by their guns in despair. This and the following years were marked by the capture of many Russian fortresses. Batory, the hero of the North—the Charles XII. of the century of Ivan the Terrible—seemed ready to annihilate the work of a long reign, and to check the first effort of Russia to escape from a state of barbarism. The Swedes on their side, commanded by De la Gardie, took Kexholm in Carelia, and invaded Esthonia. Old Pskovian and Novgorodian Russia was invaded. In 1581 Batory besieged Pskof, whilst De la Gardie captured Narva, Ivangorod, Iam, and Koporié. But Pskof marked the limit of Batory's successes. This little town was defended with so much energy by Ivan Chouïski, that, after a three months' siege and many assaults, Poles and Hungarians had to confess themselves vanquished.

Ivan had ceased to appear at the head of his troops, thinking that a prince who is not sure of his peers would be foolish if he risked himself in a battle; a conclusion to which Louis XI. had come at Montlhéry. There still remained diplomacy to direct. Threatened by Batory, he had recourse to an expedient. He implored the mediation of Pope Gregory XIII. between the Catholic king and himself. The Pontiff sent to Moscow the Jesuit Antonio Possevino, with orders at the same time to negotiate the union with the two Churches. The account of Possevino shows us Ivan the Terrible in his true colors; almost freethinking, curious, and sometimes humorous, with ideas of tolerance remarkable for his time. If the Pope's envoy failed in the religious part of his mission, he at least succeeded in concluding a truce between the two sovereigns, by which Ivan had to cede Polotsk and all Livonia. This bold enterprise for opening the Baltic Sea, which preceded by 150 years that of Peter the Great, had fallen miserably to the ground. The fruit of thirty years' efforts and sacrifices was lost (1582).

THE ENGLISH IN RUSSIA—CONQUEST OF SIBERIA.

Writers hostile to Ivan love to contrast the end of his reign —his *personal* government—with his early years, when Silvester and Adachef were in power. In the first period there was nothing but success; Kazan and Astrakhan were conquered. In the second period the Russians were vanquished by the Poles and Swedes; were expelled from Livonia; they lost Polotsk, and saw Moscow burnt by the Khan of the Crimea. The meaning of these facts really is that the Russian arms were triumphant in the East against barbarians ignorant of the military art, and unfortunate in the West, where they had to contend with the artillery, the tactics, the discipline, and the troops of Europe. Ivan needed more wit to be defeated as he was in Livonia, than to win as he did in Kazan. It is no dishonor for the Russia of the 16th century to have failed in this great undertaking, since Peter, with all his genius, spent twenty-five years in the same task. This unlucky period of the reign of Ivan was not without fruit for the grandeur and civilization of Russia. The Germans closed to her the Baltic, the English opened for her the White Sea.

Under Edward VI. a company of merchant venturers was formed for the discovery of "regions, kingdoms, islands, and places unknown and unvisited by the highway of the sea." Sebastian Cabot, chief pilot of England, was nominated governor for life. Three vessels, under the command of Sir Hugh Willoughby and Chancellor, set sail towards the north-east, towards that strange sea spoken of by Tacitus—"a sluggish mere and motionless—which forms the girdle of the world, where you hear the sound of sun-rising!" That sea must lead, men thought, to China. On the coasts of Scandinavia near Vardehuus, a frightful tempest arose and dispersed the squadron. Willoughby disappeared with the 'Buona Speranza' and the 'Buona Confidenza.' Some fishermen afterwards found the two ships in a bay of the White Sea, where they had been nipped by the ice, and all the sailors who manned them were dead of cold and hunger. Chancellor, with the 'Edward Bonaventura,' succeeded in doubling Laponia and the Holy Cape, penetrated first into an unknown sea, and then into the mouth of a river, near which was a monastery. The sea was the White Sea, the river the Dwina, the monastery that of St. Nicholas. Chancellor learned with astonishment that he was on the territory of the Tzar of Moscow; he had found Russia beneath the North Pole (1553). Further off was the monastery of St. Michael, near which was afterwards to be built in this desert, chiefly thanks to the English, the commercial city of St. Michael the Archangel, or, more shortly, Arkhangel. Chancellor at once left for Moscow, and delivered to Ivan the Terrible the letters which Edward VI., not knowing where his subjects might land, had addressed vaguely "to all the princes and lords, to all the judges of the earth, to their officers, to whoever possesses any high authority in all the regions under the vast sky." Ivan IV. admitted the English "to see his majesty and his eyes," feasted them in the Golden Palace, and gave them a letter for their king, in which he authorized the English to trade with his dominions, and made them promise to send ships to the Dwina.

Mary Tudor succeeded her brother, and shared the throne with her Spanish husband, Philip II. They confirmed the privileges of the company of merchant venturers, and in 1556 Chancellor, accompanied by Richard Gray and George Killingworth, again set sail for the mouth of the Dwina, and arrived successfully at Moscow. This time they obtained from the Tzar letters-patent formally authorizing the members of the company to establish themselves at Kholmogory and at Vologda, and to trade east and west. During this time Stephen Burroughs, in the 'Search-thrift,' navigated the east, gained the shores of the country of the Samoyedes, touched on the islands of Nova Zembla and Vaigatz, and was only checked by the approach of the dark Polar winter.

Chancellor's two vessels—the 'Edward Bonaventura' and the 'Philip and Mary'—which had discovered the missing ships of Willoughby, departed for England. The former had on board Osip Nepei, governor of Vologda, the first Russian ambassador that had been seen in England, accompanied by a suite of sixteen Russians, and carrying a letter and presents from Ivan IV. A tempest scattered the fleet, sent the 'Philip and Mary' as far as the coast of Norway, sunk the 'Speranza' and the 'Confidenza,' and threw the 'Bonaventura' on the inhospitable rocks of Inverness. Chancellor succeeded in saving the Russian envoy, but perished himself with his son and nearly all the crew. The cargo and the presents of the Tzar were plundered by the savage natives of the country.

Twelve miles from London Osip Nepei was received by eighty merchants of the company, mounted on magnificent horses, and adorned with heavy chains of gold. He now became acquainted with "all the solid respectability of old England." His *cortége* was increased by new squadrons of merchants and gentlemen as they approached the town, and he made his triumphal entry on February the 28th 1557. Harangued by the Lord Mayor, received by the Queen and the King, feasted by the corporation of drapers he departed for Russia with letters-patent according to Russian merchants in England a reciprocity of privileges. England did not bind herself down to much.

Nepei this time was accompanied by Jenkinson, an admirable type of an English sailor,—bold, indefatigable, ready for anything; a merchant, an administrator, a diplomat at need, who had already visited all the seas of Europe, and, in despair at England not being able to contest the Mediterranean with her Venetian rival, wished to secure her a new passage by Russia to the East. His open character and wide knowledge were wonderfully seductive to Ivan. He obtained from the Tzar a letter of recommendation to the Asiatic princes, descended the Volga, flew the first English flag on the Caspian, landed on the coast of Turkestan; plunged with camels loaded with merchandise into regions infested with brigands, and ravaged by the wars of the khans; was very nearly massacred, reached Bokhara, and was lucky enough to return before the city was sacked by the Sultan of Samarcand (1558–1559). In another voyage (1562) he again crossed the Caspian, and presented specimens of English manufacture and the letters of Elizabeth to Shah Thamas, King of Persia, who, warned by the friends of the Turks and Venetians, received Jenkinson with an insulting mistrust and coldness. When he retired from the Court, a domestic followed him carrying a basin of sand, and scattered it to efface the impure footsteps of the *giaour* on the soil of the sacred palace. Jenkinson brought back to Ivan IV. messages from many small princes, notably from those of Chirvan and Georgia, who wished to place themselves under the Muscovite protection. The results of these voyages were negative. Seeing the instability of the Asiatic regions, the English had for the present to confine themselves to trading in the territories of the Tzar. The latter, in acknowledgment of the services rendered him by Jenkinson, authorized them to trade on all the rivers of the north, from the Dwina to the Obi, and to establish themselves in the principal Russian towns—Pskof, Novgorod, Nijni-Novgorod, Kazan, Astrakhan, and Narva, which had just fallen into the power of the Russians.

In 1568 Ivan wished to conclude with Elizabeth a treaty of alliance, offensive and defensive, against Poland and Sweden. He offered her in exchange a monopoly of commerce with Russia, though this right, by his own showing, weighed more heavily on his empire than a tribute would have done. He also requested her to sign an engagement, reciprocal for the two sovereigns, to furnish each other with an asylum in the event of the success of an enemy, or the rebellion of their subjects, obliging them to fly from their States. Elizabeth declined the offer of alliance, and refused to accept for herself the offered asylum, " finding, by the grace of God, no dangers of the sort in her dominions." It was in 1570 that she signed the treaty mentioned above, and had it countersigned by Bacon and the principal statesmen. This, however, was far from contenting Ivan, as Elizabeth persisted in declining a refuge in Russia. The discussion on this " great affair," as Ivan calls it in his letters, was prolonged for some time longer. Elizabeth sent Randolph, Jenkinson, and Daniel Silvester to Russia. Ivan was represented in London by Andrew Sovine, Pisemski, and the English merchant, Horsey.

The last envoy of England in the reign of Ivan was Jerome Bowes, charged to explain to the Tzar the difficulties in the way of his project of marriage with Lady Mary Hastings, cousin of Elizabeth. Notwithstanding his heaviness and want of tact, Bowes obtained great credit with the Tzar, who sometimes said to him, " May it please God that my servants prove as faithful!" Bowes profited by his favor to get the privileges of the English augmented, but he made himself many enemies at Court, and was greatly maltreated during the reaction that followed the death of Ivan. The relations were renewed in Feodor's reign by Horsey, and above all, by Fletcher, author of a curious account of Russia.

French merchants had also brought to Ivan a letter of Henry III., and had settled themselves in Moscow. Other envoys arrived from Holland, Spain, and Italy, to try to rival the English; but the latter, who had been the first to reach Russia, kept the pre-eminence.

In 1558 the Tzar had yielded to Gregory Strogonof ninety-two miles of desert land on the banks of the Kama. Here the Strogonofs created many centres of population, and began to explore the mineral wealths of the Ourals. Their colonists even passed the " mountain girdle," and came in contact with the kingdom of Siberia. The Strogonofs, as audacious as the Spaniards, dreamed of the conquest of this vast empire, and requested authority of the Tzar to take the offensive against the Tatars. To fight, an army was necessary. Russia was so full of vigor, that the most impure elements often became the agents of her security and progress. The Good Companions of the Don had more than once excited the anger of the Tzar by pillaging the travellers and boats on the royal road of the Volga. They had not always respected the possessions of the Crown. One of these brigand chiefs, the Cossack Irmak Timoféevitch, obtained the pardon of the Tzar, and took service with the Strogonofs. At the head of 850 men—Russians, Cossacks, Tatars, German, and Polish prisoners of war—he crossed the Ourals, terrified the natives by the novelty of fire-arms, traversed the immense untrodden forests of Tobol, defeated the Khan Koutchoum in many battles, took Sibir, his capital, and made his cousin Mametkoul prisoner. Then he subjugated the banks of the Irtych and the Obi, and consoled the last years of the Tzar by the news that he had conquered him a new kingdom, and added to all his other crowns that of Siberia. Ivan also sent bishops and priests into his new dominions. Irmak, after having finished his conquest and thrown open the communications with the rich Bokhara, only survived Ivan a short time. One day he allowed himself to be surprised by his enemies, and sank in trying to swim the Irtych, from the weight of the cuirass given him by the

Tzar (1584). This rival of Pizarro and Cortez, the *conquistador* of a new world, was reckoned a hero by the people, and is honored as a saint by the Church. Miracles were accomplished at his tomb; epic songs celebrated his exploits. The Tatars have composed a whole legend about him.

If Adachef had given to Russia in 1551 her first municipal liberties, Ivan had assembled in 1556 the first States-general, composed of the three orders. The reformation of the Church under Silvester was completed by the Council of 1573, which forbade rich convents to acquire new lands; and, by the Council of 1580, extending the prohibition to all convents. The Church could no longer acquire property. Ivan the Terrible restrained an abuse which troubled all the public ceremonies, and more than once imperilled the success of battles. We know how powerful, in the Russia of the 16th century, was the constitution of the family. When a noble rose or fell, his whole family rose or fell with him; even the memory of his ancestors and the future of his youngest nephews were concerned. This is the reason why a Russian noble never consented to occupy an inferior place, if no precedents on the subject existed. Court and camp were constantly disturbed by the "quarrels of precedence" (*miestnitchestvo*). Neither the knout nor the executioner's axe could subdue their resistance. They would rather die than dishonor their ancestors. The 'Books of Rank' were consulted on all occasions, to know the respective precedence of the different families. Ivan IV. forbade all disputes of rank to any noble who was not the head of his family. This was only to restrain the evil; it had yet to be extirpated.

Ivan the Terrible may be considered as the founder of the National Guard of the *streltsi* or *strelitz*, who during two hundred years rendered great services to the empire.—He also organized, on the frontiers threatened by the Tatars, a series of posts and camps where the soldiers of the country might be exercised.

He gathered strangers about him. He authorized the minister Wettermann, of Dorpat, to preach at Moscow, listened to Eberfeld, and refused a discussion with Rosvita, saying that he would not "cast pearls before swine." He permitted the erection of the first Calvinist and Lutheran churches at Moscow, thus anticipating the toleration of the 18th century; but, on seeing the people's dislike to them, he had them removed two versts from the capital.

Ivan's character was a strange compound of greatness and barbarism. Cruel, dissolute, superstitious, we see him by turns yielding himself, with his favorites, to the most shameful excesses, or, covered with a monkish garment, heading them in processions and other pious exercises. Like Henry VIII., he had many wives. After Anastasia Romanof he married a barbarian, the Tcherkess Maria; next, two legitimate wives; then two more whose union the Church refused to sanction. By his seventh wife, Maria Nagoi he had a son, another Dmitri. At the close of his days we see him seeking an alliance with foreigners, and asking first the sister of the King of Poland, and then a cousin of Elizabeth of England, in marriage. His brutal habits and the facility with which he used his iron staff, had a tragic conclusion. In an altercation with his son Ivan he struck him, and the blow was mortal. Great and fierce was the sorrow of the Tzar. In slaying his beloved son, he had slain his own work. He had no longer a successor, since Feodor, the elder of his remaining sons, was feeble in body and mind; and the second Dmitri was only an infant. It was for foreign successors—for one of the detested boyards—that, at the price of so much blood and so many perils, he had founded autocracy. He only survived his son three years, and died in 1584. Without allowing himself to be biassed by Ivan's numerous cruelties, the historian ought fairly to compare him with men of his own time. He ought not to forget that the 16th century is the century of Henry VIII., of Ferdinand the Catholic, of Catherine de Medici, of the Inquisition, of Saint Bartholomew, and of *strapados*. Was the Europe of this era indeed so far advanced beyond Asiatic Russia, newly escaped from the Mongol yoke? Ivan the Terrible, in decimating, in suppressing, in tyrannizing over the aristocracy, at least put it out of their power to establish after him that anarchic *noblesse*, the hidden danger of Slav nations, which in Poland, under the name of *pospolite*, began by enfeebling royalty, and ended by enfeebling the nation.

CHAPTER XVI.

MUSCOVITE RUSSIA AND THE RENAISSANCE.

The Muscovite government—The *kin* and the *men* of the Tzar--The *prikazes*—Rural classes—Citizens—Commerce—Domestic slavery— Seclusion of women—The Renaissance ; Literature, popular songs, and cathedrals—Moscow in the 16th century.

MUSCOVITE GOVERNMENT—THE RELATIONS AND MEN OF THE TZAR—THE PRIKAZES.

THE Russia of the 16th and 17th centuries is an Oriental state, almost without relations with Europe. The Livonian knights, the Poles, the Swedes, and the Danes, who understood that it was only her barbarism which ensured her inferiority to her weaker neighbors, took good care that neither the men, the arms, nor the sciences of the West should reach her. Sigismond threatened the English merchants of the Baltic with death. He did not intend that " the Muscovite, who is not only our present adversary, but the eternal enemy of all free States, should provide herself with guns, bullets, and munitions ; and, above all, with artisans who continue to make arms, hitherto unknown in this barbaric country." Moscow, thanks to those jealous precautions, thanks also to the hatred of the Russians for the " Mussulmans " and " heretics " of the West, remained what the Tatar invasions had made her—an Asiatic Empire. The patriarchal rule of ancient Slavonia and the example of the Oriental sovereigns contributed to maintain in her the despotic principle in all its force. The Tzar was at once the father and the master of his subjects, more absolute than the Khan of the Tatars or the Sultan of Constantinople. The persons and the goods of his subjects were his property ; the greatest lords, the princes descended from Rurik, were only his slaves (*kholopy*). A petition in Russian signifies a " beating of the forehead " (*tchélobitié*). The nobles of the empire signed their requests not with their names, Ivan or Peter, but with a lackey's nickname, a servile diminutive, Vania or Pétrouchka. The Byzantine formula, " May I speak and live ? " is exaggerated in the Russian, " Bid me not to be chastised; bid me to speak a word." Men approached the Tzar in fear and trembling; the people prostrated themselves before that terrible iron staff with which Ivan was always armed. He considered the empire as his private property; he administered it with his own "people," who had succeeded to the *droujina* of former princes; he governed it by the help of his own relations or those of his wife. The sons of the greatest lords gloried in serving him in the capacity of *spalniki* or gentlemen of the bedchamber, and *stolniki* or waiters at the royal table. These domestic functions led to the rank of boyards or *okolnitchié* (surrounders of the prince.) The principal boyards formed the *douma* or council of the empire, assembled in the chamber of the prince, and were presided over by him. On solemn occasions the *sobor* or general assembly was convoked, which was composed of deputies from all the orders, and was a sort of States-general of ancient Russia. The proud Russian aristocracy did not allow itself tamely to be reduced to this state of independence; but the *kniazes* scattered as provincial or municipal governors through Siberia, Kazan, or Astrakhan, or subjected in the capital to rigorous surveillance, had become powerless. To ensure the results of their cruel policy, the successors of Ivan IV. forbade the bearers of certain too illustrious names to marry.

When the Tzar desired to marry, he addressed a circular to the governors of the towns and provinces, commanding them to send to Moscow the most beautiful maidens of the empire, or at all events those of noble birth. Like Ahasuerus in the Bible, like the Emperor Theophilus in the chronicles of Byzantium, like Louis the Débonnaire in the narrative of the 'Astronomer,' he made his selection out of all these beauties. Fifteen hundred young girls were assembled for Vassili Ivanovitch to choose from; after the first meeting, 500 of these were sent to Moscow. The Grand Prince then made a fresh selection of 300, then of 200, then of 100, then of 10, who were examined by the doctors and midwives. The most beautiful and the healthiest became the Tzarina; she took a new name, as a sign that she was going to begin a new existence. Her father, on becoming father-in law of the Tzar, also changed his name; her relations became the nearest relations (*proches*) of the prince, constituted his companions, undertook the care of everything, and governed the empire like the house of their imperial relative. The dispossessed ministers and friends tried in secret to reconquer their lost power by putting the new sovereign to death, and did not hesitate to have recourse to magic and poison. Many of these imperial brides never survived their triumphs, and, suddenly attacked by mysterious maladies, died before their coronation day. All the successors of Vassili Ivanovitch, even including Alexis Mikhaïlovitch, instituted these assemblages of beauty for the choice of their wives. It was the privilege of the sovereigns of Moscow and of the princes of their blood.

The men of the *droujina* or of the *surrounding* of the prince thought it beneath their dignity or above their power to serve him otherwise than in war or justice. The work of the pen had to be confided to the sons of the priests and merchants—the *diaki* whose beginnings were as humble as those of the Capetian lawyers, seated at the feet of the peers of France; like them, they ended by taking the place of the great lords. The administration of the State was entrusted to twenty or thirty *prikazes* or bureaux, whose numbers and functions varied at different times. There was notably the *prikaz* of provisions, that of drinks, and that of the pantry, which were all concerned with the commissariat of the Court. The duties were very heavy, as not only the Tzar, the Tzarina, and the princes of the blood kept an open table, but, in accordance with patriarchal and family ideas, the prince was supposed to feed from his own table the nobles and functionaries lodged beyond the palace. He was obliged to send them daily, cooked meats, wines, and fruits. There was the *prikaz* of the gold and silver cup, that of the wardrobe, of pharmacy, of horses, of the falconry, of games, to which belonged comedians buffoons, dwarfs, fools, keepers of bears and dogs ready to fight with the bears, the menagerie of rare animals, chess, cards, and in general everything that served to amuse the Tzar. The *prikaz kazennyi*, or " of the crown," had under its control the manufactures fabricating the golden and silken stuffs, of which the prince had a monopoly, and the depot of the precious Siberian furs. It furnished the presents to be distributed among the clergy, the boyards, the ambassadors of foreign powers, and the Greek monks who came from Byzantium or Mount Athos, to ask for alms. The *prikazes* of the great palace, of the *quarter*, of the revenue, and of the tax on liquors, were concerned with the finances. There were also those of the imperial family, of secret affairs, of petitions, posts, and police; of the buildings of the Tzar, slaves, monasteries, streltsi, embassies, and artillery. The *prikazes* of Oustiougue, of Kazan, of Galitch, of Kostroma, of Little Russia, and Siberia, had a territorial competence. Usually the expenses of such and such a bureau were defrayed by the produce of taxes on a given town or province.

The State revenues were composed: 1. Of that of the demesne, including thirty-six towns and their territory, the inhabitants of which paid their dues either in kind or in money. 2. Of the *tagla*, an annual impost on every 60 measures of corn.

3. Of the *podate*, a fixed tax on every *dvor* or fire. 4. The produce of the custom-houses, and of the excess of the municipal dues. 5. The tax on the public baths. 6. The farming-out of the Crown taverns. 7. The fines and expenses of justice, the confiscations pronounced by the "tribunal of the brigands." Fletcher, who visited Russia in the time of Boris Godounof, valued the whole of these revenues at 1,223,000 roubles of their money. The Tzar annually received besides, furs and other things from Siberia, Permia, and the Petchora; he exchanged them himself with the Turkish, Persian, Armenian, Bokharian, or Western merchants, who came to the fairs or landed at the ports of the empire. Further, the Crown, after having allowed the officers to gorge themselves some time at the expense of the people, reserved to itself the power of calling them to justice, and of depriving them of part, or the whole, of their booty. The Tzar, who, like the ancient despots of Egypt and the East, had already monopolized certain branches of commerce, kept up an undignified rivalry with his own subjects. He sent agents into special provinces, who seized on all the productions of the country, furs, wax, and honey; forced the proprietors to sell them to them at a low price, and then obliged the English of Arkhangel or the merchants of Asia to buy them at a high rate; he even laid hands on the goods brought by these merchants, and made the Russian tradesmen pay dear for them, forbidding them to purchase from others till the warehouses of the Tzar were emptied. Fletcher exposes many other means of extortion, to which the Tzarian government periodically had recourse.

The grades of courts of civil justice were three: 1. The tribunals of the starost of the district, and of the hundred men, a magistrate established for every hundred ploughs. 2. The tribunal of the voïevode, in the head-city of each province. 3. The Supreme Court of Moscow. In spite of the Codes of Ivan III. and Ivan IV., the law was so confused and uncertain that Fletcher said of it, "There is no written law in Russia." The mode of procedure was that of the Carolingian age; if a man could neither produce witnesses nor written proofs, the judge could take the oath of one of the parties. Often the value of an oath was confirmed by a judicial duel. The champions, says Herberstein, loaded themselves with arms and heavy armor. They were so embarrassed by all this weight of iron, that a Russian was invariably overcome by a foreigner, and Ivan III. forbade foreigners to fight with his subjects. Often the parties had themselves represented by hired champions, and then the combat became a comedy, the mercenaries only thinking how to spare themselves.

The legislation in the matter of debts equalled in rigor that of the Roman law of the Twelve Tables. The insolvent debtor was subjected to the *pravége;* that is, tied up half-naked on a public place, and beaten three hours a day. This punishment was repeated for thirty or forty days. If by that time no one was moved by his lamentations and cries to pay his debt for him he was allowed to be sold, and his wife and children let out to hire; if he had none, he became the slave of the creditor. The penal legislation was frightful. In cases of accusation of theft, murder, or treason, the accused was subjected to tortures worthy of a Spanish Inquisitor. The punishments were infinitely varied: a man might be hung, beheaded, broken on the wheel, impaled, drowned under the ice, or knouted to death. A wife who had murdered her husband "was buried alive up to her neck;" heretics went to the stake; sorcerers were burned alive in an iron cage; coiners had liquid metal poured down their throats. We must not forget the death of "ten thousand pieces," the torment in which the sides were torn away by iron hooks, and all the varieties of mutilation. On the other hand, a noble who slew a mougik was only fined or whipped. The noble who killed his slave suffered no penalty; he could do what he liked with his own.

Before the creation of the patriarchate, the highest dignity in the Russian Church was that of the Metropolitan of Moscow. Then came the six Archbishops of Novgorod, Rostof, Smolensk, Kazan, Pskof, and Vologda; the six Bishops of Riazan, Tver, Kolomenskoé, Vladimir, Souzdal, and Kroutiski or Saraï, whose dioceses were immense. This Church was as dependent on the Tzar as that of Byzantium had been on the Emperors; at the expense of a few formalities he could create a prelate or a new see. The bishops were selected from the Black Clergy; that is, the monks who had taken the vow of chastity. Their revenues were large and their ceremonies imposing. "As for exhorting or instructing their sheep," says Fletcher, "they have neither the habit of it nor the talent for it, for all the clergy are as profoundly ignorant of the Word of God as of all other learning." With the secular or White Clergy, marriage was not only a right, but a duty. Their manners and education hardly distinguished them from the peasants, and like them, they were sometimes subjected to the most degrading chastisements. The convents were numerous, very full, and very rich; that of St. Sergius, at Troïtsa, possessed 110,000 souls,—that is, male peasants. All broken men took refuge there; on the other hand, the councils fulminated against the vagabond monks who infested the country. More than once the monasteries served as prisons for disgraced nobles, who there led a gay and noisy life, like the Frank nobles of other days in the cloisters of the Merovingian churches. Delicate meats were sent them from the table of the Tzar—sturgeons, sterlets, figs, dry raisins, oranges, pepper, and saffron.

In a letter to the monks of St. Cyril on the White Lake, Ivan IV. blames with a mixture of severity and irony their lenity towards the imprisoned boyards. "In my youth," he writes, "when we were at St. Cyril, if dinner happened to be late, and if the intendant asked a sterlet or any other fish of the cellarer, he would reply, 'I have no orders about it; I have only prepared what I was ordered. Now it is night, and I can give you nothing; I fear the sovereign, but I fear God more.'" "See," continues Ivan, "what was the severity of the rule. They fulfilled the word of the prophet : ' Speak the truth, and have no shame before the Tzar.' To-day my boyard Cheremetief reigns in his cell like a Tzar; my boyard Khabarof pays him visits with the monks. They drink as if in lay society. Is it a wedding ? is it a baptism ? The captive distributes pieces of iced fruits, spiced bread, and sweetmeats. Beyond the monastery there is a house filled with provisions. Some say that strong drinks are gradually smuggled into the cell of Cheremetief. Now in monasteries it is against the rules to have foreign wines ; how much more, then, strong waters?"

The orthodox faith, deprived of the stimulus of liberty and instruction, tended to become mere routine. Salvation was gained by hearing long liturgies, by multiplying Slavonic orisons, by making hundreds of prostrations and genuflexions, by telling rosaries, and by frequenting shrines. The most celebrated centres were the catacombs of Kief, where slept the incorruptible bodies of the saints, and where dwell their successors without ever seeing the light of day ; the monastery of St. Cyril, on the White Lake ; of St. Sergius, at Troïtsa; and the cathedral of St. Sophia, at Novgorod. Men prostrated themselves at the tombs of St. Peter and St. Alexis of Moscow ; before the wonder-working virgins of Vladimir, Smolensk, Tischvin, and Pskof. The most pious journeyed as far as the sacred Mount Athos, and the city of Constantinople, full of blessed relics, though polluted by the presence of the Turk ; nay, further still, to the tomb of Christ, to Golgotha, to Mount Sinai, wherever orthodox communities disputed possession with Catholic communities.

The national army was, like the Tatar army, chiefly composed of cavalry. The *stolniki*, *spalniki*, and other young courtiers, formed an Imperial Guard of about 8000 men. All the gentlemen of the empire, *dvoriane*, or *dieti-boyarskii*, were confined to the mounted ranks ; the revenues of their lands were counted as pay for these *men of service (sloujilii lioudi)*; the ancient distinction between the *pomestie* (fiefs) and the *votchiny* (free allods) was almost abolished. It was nearly the *régime* of the fiefs of the West, or of the *ziams* and *timars* of Turkey. This noble cavalry could reckon 80,000 horsemen; with the levy of free peasants, it mounted up to 300,000. To this we must join the irregular cavalry, composed of the Cossacks of the Don and the Terek, of Tatars and Bachkirs. The national infantry was constituted—1, by the *datotchnié lioudi*, peasants of the monasteries, churches, and domains; 2, by the *streltsi*, free archers, or communal soldiers, organized in the time of Ivan IV., and who, in Moscow alone, formed a body of 12,000 men. Then came the artillery, and the soldiers told off to the *gouliaïgorod*, the "city that walks," movable ramparts of wood, which were used both in sieges and in the open country, where the Russian troops, if they were not protected, showed little firmness. In the 15th century, foreign mercenaries began to be enlisted—Poles, Hungarians, Greeks, Turks, Scotch, Scandinavians, armed and disciplined after the European fashion, and enrolled under the names of *ritters*, soldiers, and dragoons. History has preserved the names of some of their leaders: Rosen the German, and Margeret the Frenchman, who has left us some curious memoirs of the False Dmitri.

The equipment of the national troops was completely Oriental. They had long robes, high saddles, short stirrups, rich caparisons, scale or ring armor. The Tzar himself went into battle with his lance, bow and quiver. The army was always divided into five divisions—the main army, the right and left wings, the van and rear guards. Each was commanded by two voïevodes of unequal rank, without counting the voïevode of the artillery or of the movable camp, and the *atamans* of the streltsi and of the Cossacks. The grades of the regular army were those of the *tysatski* or chiliarch, the centurion, the commander of fifty, and the *deciatski*, or commander of ten. All obeyed the grand voïevode, or general-in-chief. Each soldier brought provisions for four months, and the Tzar furnished nothing, except occasionally some corn. The men lived almost entirely on biscuit, dried fish or bacon, and proved capable of enduring much fatigue. The campaigns never lasted long, and only part of the army was permanent.

From this time Russia sought to enter into regular relations with foreign Powers. Her diplomatic traditions were those of the East or Byzantium. Her first ambassadors were the Greek Dmitri Trakhaniotes, and the Italian Marco Ruffo, sent into Persia. They treated with most deference the neighboring

States, not those which were most powerful. Whilst they sent a simple courier (*gonets*) to the Emperor, and the kings of France, England, and Spain, they despatched boyards, accompanied by *diaks*, to Sweden, Denmark, and Poland. The *prikaz* of the embassies, which had under its orders fifty translators and seventy interpreters of all languages, gave them their safe conduct, detailed instructions, letters for the foreign sovereign, presents, two years' pay, and a certain number of furs of costly materials from the *prikaz* of the Crown, which they were to do their best to sell at a high price. The Russian ambassador, like those of the Greeks and Tatars, was also a commission agent for the benefit of the Tzar. The envoys were recommended to avoid all insolence, and to watch their men, but to display the greatest luxury, to exact due payment of all honors, and, at the peril of their lives, never to suffer the Tzar's titles to be diminished—titles which were rather complicated, as he enumerated all his subject States. The mercantile preoccupations of the Russian ambassadors, and their eternal quarrels about etiquette, rendered them unbearable at all the European Courts. On their return they were summoned before the Tzar, gave him a detailed account of their mission, and handed over to him the journal of their tour and the notes of all that they had observed in the distant countries. From the 16th century a shrewd and observant spirit is noticeable in their relations, which is not unworthy of the wisdom of their masters, the Byzantines.

When foreign ambassadors arrived in Russia, they were treated with magnificence and distrust. From the time they crossed the frontier, they and their people were fed, housed, and provided with carriages, but a *pristaf* attached to their persons watched carefully that they obtained no interviews with the natives, nor information about the state of the country. They were taken through the richest and most populous provinces; the citizens were everywhere required to meet them on their route, dressed in their costliest clothes. At Moscow a palace of the Tzar was assigned them as a residence, and they were fed from his table. Their first interview took place with great pomp in the Palace of Facets (*Granavitaia palaïa*). The walls of the hall were hung with magnificent tapestries; gold and silver vessels, of Asiatic form, shone on the daïs. The Tzar, crown on head, sceptre in hand, seated on the throne of Solomon, supported by the mechanical lions, which roared loudly, surrounded by his *ryndis* in long white caftans and armed with the great silver axe, by his sumptuously-dressed boyards, and by his clergy in their simple costume, received their letters of credit. He asked the ambassador for news of his master, and how he had travelled. If the Tzar were not contented with him, the ambassadors' palace became a prison where no native might penetrate, and carefully-studied humiliations were practised to extract from him concessions or to abridge his stay.

THE RURAL CLASSES—CITIZENS OF THE TOWNS—COMMERCE.

The lower classes of Muscovy were composed of three elements :—1. The slave, or *kholop*, properly so called, the *mancipium* of the Romans, a man taken in war, sold by himself or some one else, or son of a *kholop*. 2. The *peasant inscribed* on the lands of a noble, the *colonus adscriptius* of the Roman Empire, whose person was legally free, but who was to be reduced by means of a more and more rigorous legislation to the condition of *krepostnyi* or serf of the glebe. 3. The free cultivator, who lived like a farmer on the lands of another, and had the right to change his master, but who was soon to be mingled with the preceding class.

It was the *inscribed peasants* who constituted almost the whole of the rural population. In the ancient provinces the peasant might consider himself as the primitive inhabitant of the soil. He was only made subject to the gentleman in order to secure to the latter an income sufficient for military service; he therefore continued to look on himself as the true proprietor. In these rural masses, the primitive features of the Slav organization were preserved in all their vigor. It was the commune, or *mir*, and not the individuals, who possessed the land ; it was the commune that was responsible to the Tzar for the tax, for the *corvée* and dues to the lord. This responsibility armed the commune with an enormous power over its members, and this power embodied itself in the *starost*, assisted by elders. In the bosom of the commune the family was not organized less severely, less tyrannically than the *mir*. The father of the family had over his wife, his sons, married or single, and their wives, an authority almost as absolute as that of the starost over the commune, or the Tzar over the empire. The paternal authority became harder and more stern from the contact with serfage and the despotic rule. Ancient barbarism was still intact among these ignorant people : the graceful customs or the savage manners, the poetic or cruel superstitions of the early Slavs, were perpetuated by them. The Russian peasant remained a pagan under his veneer of orthodoxy. His funeral songs seem destitute of all Christian hope. His marriage songs preserve the tradition of the purchase or capture of the bride. The sad lot of the rustic was yet to be aggravated during the three centuries of progress which the upper classes had still to accomplish. In view of the State, as of the proprietor, he tended more and more to become a beast of burden, a productive force to be used and abused at pleasure.

The Russian towns were composed first of a fortress or *kreml*, where at need a garrison of "men of the service" could be sent, the walls being generally of wood; next of faubourgs or *possads*, inhabited by the citizens or *possadskie*. They were governed by voïevodes nominated by the prince, or by a *starost* or mayor who was elected by an assembly of the inhabitants, nobles, priests, or citizens, but was always a gentleman. The starost governed the town and the district depending on it. As the citizens paid the heaviest taxes, they were forbidden to quit the town; they were, as during the last days of the Roman Empire, bound to the city glebe. Alexis Mikhaïlovitch was afterwards to attach the pain of death to this prohibition. To assess the impost, the starost convoked at once both the deputies of the town and those of the rural communes. The impost of the *tagla* was paid by the town collectively, in proportion to the number of fires, and all the people were collectively responsible for each other to the State.

In the burgess class may be counted the merchants, whose Russian name of *gosti* (guests and strangers) shows how far commerce still was from being acclimatized in this land and under this *régime*. Muscovy produced in abundance leather from oxen; furs from the blue and black fox, the zibeline, the beaver, and the ermine; wax, honey, hemp, tallow, oil from the seal, and dried fish. From China, Bokhara, and Persia, she received silks, tea, and spices. The Russian people are naturally intelligent and industrious, but still commerce languished. Fletcher, the Englishman, has assigned as the reason for this decay, the insecurity created by anarchy and despotism. The mougik did not care either to save or to lay by. He pretended to be poor and miserable, to escape the exactions of the prince and the plunder of his agents. If he had money, he buried it, as one in fear of an invasion. "Often," says the English writer, "you will see them trembling with fear, lest a boyard should know what they have to sell. I have seen them at times, when they had spread out their wares so that you might make a better choice, look all round them, as if they feared an enemy would surprise them and lay hands on them. If I asked them the cause, they would say to me, 'I was afraid there might be a noble or one of the "sons of boyards" here; they would take away my merchandise by force.'" "The merchants and the citizens," says M. Leroy-Beaulieu, "could with difficulty become a powerful class in a country cut off from Europe and the sea, and cut off, too, from all great commercial routes by the Lithuanians, the Teutonic Order, and the Tatars." The citizen, like the inhabitant of the French towns of the 14th century, was only a sort of villain ; he wore the costume of a peasant, and lived almost like him. The merchants were really what they were called by Ivan the Terrible—the mougiks of commerce.

DOMESTIC SLAVERY—THE SECLUSION OF WOMEN.

Only two more facts were needed to give to Russian society the same Asiatic character which we noted already in the despotism of the Tzars and the communism of the people : domestic slavery, and the seclusion of women.

Besides the peasants more or less attached to the glebe, all Russian proprietors kept in their castles, or in their town-houses at Moscow, a multitude of servants like those who encumbered the senators' palaces in imperial Rome. A great lord always gathered round him many hundreds of these *dvorovié*, both men and women, bought or born in the house, whom he never paid, whom he fed badly, and who served him badly in return, but whose numbers served to give an idea of the wealth of their master. The *cortége* of a noble on his way to the Kremlin may be compared to that of a Japanese daimio. A long file of sledges or chariots, a hundred horses, outriders who made the people stand back by blows with their whips ; a crowd of armed men, who escorted the noble ; and behind a host of *dvorovié*, often with naked feet beneath their magnificent liveries, filled with their stir and noise the streets of *Biélyi-gorod*. These domestic slaves were subjected, without distinction of sex, to the most severe discipline, and were forced to submit to all the cruel or voluptuous caprices of their masters, and, like the slaves of antiquity, were exposed to the most frightful chastisements. Whilst the registered colon was attached to the land, the *kholopy* could be sold, either by heads or by families, without compunction. Wives were separated from their husbands, and children from their parents.

The custom of secluding women is older than the Tatar invasion. The Russian Slavs were Asiatics, even before they were subdued by the Mongols. Byzantium had likewise far more influence than Kazan on Russian manners. Now, in ancient Athens, and in the Constantinople of the Middle Ages, the matron and the young girl were alike obliged to remain in the *gynæceum*, which became in Moscow the *terem* or *verkh* (upper apartment). In Russia, as in the Rome of the Twelve

Tables, the woman was always a minor. This was one consequence of the patriarchal organization of the family. She always remained under the guardianship of her father, her husband's father, an uncle, an elder brother, or a grandfather. The Russian monks translated for her use the sermons of the monks of the Lower Empire, which enjoined the wife " to obey her husband as the slave obeys his master ; " to consider herself only as the " property of the man ; " never to allow herself to be called *gospoja*, or mistress, but to look on her husband as her gospodine or lord. The father of the family had the right to correct her, like one of his children or slaves. The priest Silvester, in his ' Domostroï,' only advises him not to employ too thick sticks, or staffs tipped with iron ; nor humiliate her unduly by whipping her before his men, but, without anger or violence, to correct her moderately in private. No woman dared to object to this chastisement ; the most robust would allow herself calmly to be beaten by a feeble husband.

The Russian proverb says, " I love thee like my soul, and I dust thee like my jacket." Herberstein mentions a Muscovite woman who, having married a foreigner, did not believe herself loved, as he never beat her. At home the Russian woman was hid behind the curtains of the *terem* ; in the street, by those of her litter. Over her face fell the *fata*, a sort of nun's veil. It was an outrage even to raise the eyes to the wife of a noble, and high treason to see the face of the wife of the Tzar. A stranger might have thought himself at Stamboul or Ispahan. It appeared so highly necessary that this fragile being should remain at home, that she was allowed to dispense even with going to church. Her church was her own house, where she had to occupy herself with prayers, pious reading, prostrations, genuflexions, and alms, and was surrounded by beggars, monks, and nuns. The priest Silvester also wished her to superintend her house, be the first to rise, to watch over her men and maidservants, to distribute their tasks, and work herself with her own hands, like Lucrece of old, or the wise women of the Proverbs. In reality she had many other ways of occupying her time The toilette of the Russian boyarines was very complicated. " They paint themselves all colors," says Petreï ; " not only their faces, but their eyes, neck, and hands. They lay on white, red, blue, and black. Black eyelashes they tint white, and white ones black, or some dark color, but they put on the paint so badly that it is visible to every one. At the time of my visit to Moscow the wife of an illustrious boyard, who was exceedingly beautiful, declined to paint herself, but she was an object of scorn to all the other women. ' She despises our customs,' said they. They induced their husbands to complain to the Tzar, and obtained an imperial order to make her paint." Stoutness was the ideal of Turkish and Tatar beauty, so the Russians did all in their power to deform their slender figures, and, by means of idleness and drugs, managed to succeed. As to the men, they always wore a long beard and long dresses. To shave the beard like the European nations, was, said Ivan the Terrible, " a sin that the blood of all the martyrs could not cleanse. Was it not to deface the image of man, created by God?"

The influence of Byzantine monachism is also to be found in the objection to all innocent amusements. Cards, and even chess, were forbidden; music and songs glorifying the ancient heroes of Russia were condemned as " diabolic " ; the noble exercises of the chase and dancing were not allowed. " If they give themselves up at table," says the ' Domostroï," " to filthy conversation; if they play the lute or the goussla ; if they dance, or jump, or clap their hands, then, as smoke chases the bees, the angels of God are made to fly from that table by those devilish words, and demons take their place. Those who give themselves up to diabolic songs ; those who play the lute, the tambourine, or the trumpet ; those who amuse themselves with bears, dogs, and falcons—with dice, chess, or tric-trac, will together go to hell, and together will be damned."

Thanks to the general ignorance, there was no intellectual life in Russia ; thanks to the seclusion of women, there was no society. Compared with the gallant and witty society of Poland, Russia seems a vast monastery. The devil lost nothing in the long run. The nobles, living in the midst of slaves subjected to their caprices, degraded themselves while they degraded their victims. Debauchery and drunkenness were the national sins. Rich and poor, young and old, women and children, often dropped down dead drunk in the streets, without surprising anyone. The priests, in their visits to their sheep, got theologically drunk. " Even at the houses of the great lords," says M. Zabiéline, " no feast was gay and joyous unless every one was drunk. It was precisely in drunkenness that the gayety consisted. The guests were never gay if they were not drunk." Even to-day, " to be merry " signifies to have been drinking. The preachers, even, while attacking the national vice, touched it delicately. " My brothers," says one of them, " what is worse than drunkenness ? You lose memory and reason, like a madman, who knows not what he does. Is this mirth, my friends, mirth according to the law and glory of God ? The drunkard is senseless. He lies like a corpse. If you speak to him, he does not answer, He foams, he stinks, he grunts like a brute. Think of his poor soul which grows foul in its vile body, which is its prison. Drunkenness sends our guardian angels away, and makes the devil merry. To be drunk, is to perform sacrifices to Satan. The devil rejoices, and says, ' No ; the sacrifices of the pagans never caused me half so much joy and happiness as the intoxication of a Christian.' Fly, then, my brothers, the curse of drunkenness. To drink is lawful, and is to the glory of God, who has given us wine to make us rejoice. The Fathers were far from forbidding wine, but we must never drink ourselves drunk."

Their only diversions were, in spite of the 'Domostroï,' the jests of the buffoons, who, like the writers of the French *fabliaux*, never spared Churchmen ; the coarse pleasantries of court fools and *folles*, who were the inseparable companions of the great, and were to be found even in the monasteries ; hunts with falcons and hounds, and bear fights. All these festivities were accompanied with music, and sometimes a blind singer would come and celebrate the *bogatyrs* of Old Russia. The rich never willingly went to sleep without being lulled by tales told by some popular story-teller. Ivan the Terrible always had three, who succeeded each other at his bedside. Soon, under Alexis Mikhaïlovitch, theatrical representations in imitation of Europe were to begin.

All Western superstitions were current in Russia, which also added follies of her own. The people believed in horoscopes, diviners, sorcery, magic, the miraculous virtues of certain herbs or certain formulæ, the evils produced by "lifting the footmarks" of an enemy, in bewitched swords, in love philtres, in were-wolves, ghosts and vampires, which play such a terrible part in the popular tales of Russia. Their terror of sorcerers is shown by the horrible deaths they made them die. The most enlightened Tzars shared this weakness, and Boris Godounof made all his servants swear "never to have recourse to magicians, male or female, or to any other means of hurting the Tzar, the Tzarina, or their children ; never to cast spells by the traces of their feet or of their carriages." They had more confidence in the receipts of a wise woman, in holy water in which the relics had been dipped, than in doctors, whom they only regarded as another variety of sorcerers. Nothing was more difficult and dangerous than the early exercise of this profession. If the doctor did not succeed in curing his patient, he was punished as a malicious magician. One of these unfortunate people, a Jew, was executed under Ivan III. in a public place for having allowed a Tzarévitch to die. Anthony, another, a German by nation, was accused of having put a Tatar prince to death, and delivered to his relatives to suffer by the *lex talionis*. He was stabbed. Towards the end of the 16th century the situation of doctors was somewhat ameliorated; but when a Tzarina or a great lady had to be attended, whose face they were never allowed to see, and whose pulse they might only touch through a muslin covering, what proper means had they of taking a diagnosis?

Such was ancient Russia,—that European China discovered and described by the European travellers of the 16th and 17th centuries, by Herberstein, Mayerberg, Cobenzel, envoys of Austria; Chancellor, Jenkinson, and Fletcher, envoys of England; the Venetians Contarini and Marco Foscarini; the Roman merchant Barberini; Ulfeld the Dane; Petreï the Swede; the Germans Heidenstein, Eric Lassota, Olearius; Possevino the Jesuit; the French captain Jacques Margeret; the English doctor Collins, &c. It now remains to speak of literature and the arts.

THE RENAISSANCE: LITERATURE, POPULAR SONGS, AND CATHEDRALS—MOSCOW IN THE 16th CENTURY.

Ecclesiastical literature was chiefly composed of a collection of ideas borrowed from the Fathers of 'Readings for Every Day in the Year,' called 'Waves of Gold,' 'Months of Gold,' 'Emeralds,' &c.; or of collections of Lives of the Saints of the Greek or Russian Churches. The most considerable monument belonging to this last group is the 'Tchetiminéi,' a vast compilation of the Metropolitan Macarius, one of the directors of the conscience of Ivan the Terrible. The chronicles are still produced, among others the 'Stepennyïa knigi,' a history of the Russian princes after Vladimir. Besides the great legal collection of the 'Code' and of the 'Stoglaf,' we must mention the 'Domostroï' of the Pope Silvester, Minister of Ivan IV. This is a collection of precepts instructing readers in the arts of keeping house and securing salvation. It enumerates the days on which swans, cranes, capons, egg-pasties, and cheese are to be eaten. It gives receipts for making hydromel, kvass, beer gruel, and sweetmeats. It gives bills of fare, and at the same time teaches the master of the house how he ought to govern his wife, his children, and his servants: avoid the sin of wicked conversation; please God, honor the Tzar, the princes, and all persons of rank; how he should conduct himself well at table, "to blow his nose, and to spit without noise, taking care to turn

away from the company, and put his foot over the place." The
'Domostro' gives the characteristics of the Russian civilization,
as the *De Re Rustica* of the elder Cato gives those of the ancient Roman civilization. From Cato to Silvester there is an
evident progress. Whilst the Roman advises that the old oxen,
the old iron, and the old slaves should be sold, the Pope Silvester enjoins that "the old servants who are no longer good for
anything, be fed and clothed, in consideration of their former
services: this ministers to the salvation of the soul, and we must
fear the anger of God." "Masters," he says again, "ought to
be benevolent towards their servants, and give them to eat and
drink, and warm them properly; for, if they keep their *dvorovie*
by force around them, and do not nourish them sufficiently,
they turn them into bad servants, who lie, steal, are dissipated,
spoil everything, and get drunk at the tavern. These foolish
masters sin against God, are despised by their slaves, and contemned by their neighbors."

"When a man sends his servant to honest people, he should
knock softly at the great door; when the slave comes to ask
him what he wants, he should reply, 'I have nothing to do with
thee, but with him to whom I am sent.' He should only say
from whom he comes, so that the other may tell his master. On
the threshold of the chamber he will wipe his feet in the straw;
before entering he will blow his nose, spit, and say a prayer. If
no one says *amen* to him, he will say a second prayer; if they
still keep silence, a third prayer, in a louder voice than the preceding ones. If they still do not speak, he will knock at the
door. On entering, he must bow before the holy images; then
he will explain his mission to the master, and during this time
he must take care not to touch his nose, nor to cough, nor spit;
he must conduct himself with propriety, without looking to the
right or the left. If he is left alone, he must examine nothing
belonging to the master of the house and touch nothing
neither to eat nor drink. If he is sent to carry anything, he
must not look to see what it is; and if it should be eatable,
neither his tongue nor his fingers are to know it."

At the head of the literary movement of the time, Ivan the
Terrible and his enemy Kourbski occupy a place of honor.
They exchanged many letters, in which the one displayed a great
knowledge of sacred and profane literature, close reasoning, and
bitter irony; the other an indignant and tragic eloquence.
Besides these letters, Ivan addressed an admonition to the monks
of St. Cyril, full of vigor and mocking gravity. The same
Kourbski has written, in eight books, a passionate history of the
Tzar who persecuted "the strong ones of Israel, the high-born

heroes of Russia"; in his exile in Lithuania he defended orthodoxy against the encroachments of Jesuitism and Protestantism, compiled the 'History of the Council of Florence,' and learnt Latin in order to translate into Russian the Fathers of the Church.

Like his rival Louis XI. in France, Ivan the Terrible was in Russia the protector of printing, abhorred by the people as an impious art. Mstislavets and the deacon Feodorof printed the Acts of the Apostles, and a 'Book of Hours;' but later they were obliged to fly into Lithuania to escape from accusations of heresy and the hate of the people.

There existed a literature which could do without the art of Gutenberg, and which at this time attained its most splendid development. This was the literature which from the earliest centuries of Russian history had been kept alive on the lips of the people, in the memory of the peasants, and which, perpetuated by oral tradition, has at last been collected in our own day by Rybnikof, Afanasief, Schein, Sakharof Kiriéevski, Bezsonof, Hilferding, Kostomarof, Koulich, Tchoubinski, and Dragomanof. The people had their lyric poetry, marriage-songs, funeral dirges, rural dance-songs, hymns for Christmas (*koliadki*), Epiphany, Easter, and the Feasts of St. George and St. John,— hymns in which they celebrated the death of winter, the birth of spring, the harvest, and preserved the recollections of the ancient religions and ancient Slav gods. There were epic songs which glorified the legendary exploits of the early heroes of Russia. the demi-gods of primitive paganism : Volga Vseslavitch, Sviatogor, Mikoula Selianinovitch, Polkane, Dounaï, &c. In these songs Vladimir, the "Beautiful Sun" of Kief, groups around him, like the Charlemagne of the *chansons de gestes* and the King Arthur of the Breton romances, a whole pleiad of *bogatyrs*. They have immortalized Ilia of Mourom, the hero-peasant; Dobryna Nikititch, the hero-boyard; Alécha Popovitch, conqueror of the gigantic dragon, Tougarine; Soloveï Boudimirovitch, navigator of the falcon-ship Potyk, whom the perfidy of an enchantress caused to descend alive into the tomb; Diouk Stépanovitch, who crossed the Dnieper at one leap of his horse; Stavre Godinovitch, the warrior-musician, released by a *ruse* of his wife from the prisons of Vladimir; Thomas Ivanovitch, whom the Princess Apraxie calumniated like another Joseph, but for whom God worked a miracle; Vassili, the hero-drunkard, who went from a tavern to save Russia; Sadko, the rich merchant of Novgorod, whose maritime adventures form an Odyssey; the Princess Apraxie, who is seated on the throne by the side of Vladimir her husband; the heroines Nastasia and Marina, the Penelope and

Circe of the Russian epopee; Maria the White Swan, who belongs to the cycle of bird-women; and Vassilissa, who passed herself off as a *bogatyr*, and beat all the athletes of Vladimir Such were the heroes of Kief and Novgorod.

Historical heroes belong to the cycle of Moscow: Dmitri, the vanquisher of the Tatars; Michael of Tchernigof, Alexandei Nevski, and Ivan the Terrible, around whom are grouped the songs of the taking of Kazan, the conquest of Siberia, and the famous by-lines entitled 'The Tzar wishes to kill his Son,' 'The Tzar sends the Tzarina to a Convent,' and 'How Treason was introduced into Russia.' This epic current flows on up to the 19th century; and others, born of the shock of events on the popular imagination, celebrate the deeds of Skopine Chouïski, the wars of Peter the Great, the victories of Elizabeth and Catherine II., the campaigns of Souvorof, and even the invasion of Russia by the "King Napoleon."

Narratives, sometimes in prose and sometimes in poetry, glorify the heroes of the Eastern epopee: Akir of Nineveh, Solomon the Wise, Alexander of Macedon, and Rousslan Lazarévitch. Wonderful stories are told by the peasants of Helen the Fair, of the Tzar of the Sea, and of Vassilissa the Wise; of the Seven Simeons; of the adventures of Ivan, Son of the King, and of the lovely Nastasia; of the Baba-Yaga, and of the King of the Serpents. There were religious verses, which were carried by the blind *kalicki*, who sang the praises of the Russian saints from village to village—St. George the Brave, and St. Dmitri of Solun, vanquishers of dragons and infidels; Boris and Gleb, sons of Vladimir the Baptist; St. Theodosius, founder of the catacombs of Kief; Daniel the Pilgrim, who visited Jerusalem; and others who belong almost as much to the Slav mythology as to the Christian hagiography. Lastly, there are satirical tales, light and biting as French fables, turning into ridicule the greed of the popes, and the interested calculations of their wives.

Thanks to the Greeks who fled from Constantinople, and their pupils the Italians, Russia had a sort of artistic Renaissance from the 15th to the 17th century, under the same influences as the West. The revolution was, however, less complete in Muscovy than in Russia; there was no need to substitute the round for the pointed arch, since Russia had no Gothic churches, and the Roman Byzantine style, borrowed in the 11th century by St. Sophia at Novgorod and St. Sophia at Kief from St. Sophia at Constantinople, was perpetuated, under the influence of religious ideas and unbroken traditions, as a legacy from Byzantium. There was no sort of change in painting; and even in the present day, in the Russian convents, the hieratic usage causes the saints and the Mother of God to be painted as they might have been painted by Pansélinos in the 10th century in the churches of Mount Athos. The Renaissance chiefly manifests itself by the number and magnificence of the orthodox churches with which Italian artists then "illuminated" Old Russia, and by the greater perfection of their modes of building. It was then that Moscow became worthy by her new monumental splendors to be the capital of a great empire; it was then that she became the "Holy City," with forty times forty churches, with innumerable cupolas of gold, of silver, and of blue, which the Russian pilgrim, kneeling on the Hill of Prostrations, salutes from afar off.

Moscow was at that time composed: 1. Of the *Kreml* or Kremlin, a fortified enclosure in the form of a triangle, of which the smallest side rests on the Moskowa, and the apex is turned towards the north. 2. Of the *Kitaï-gorod*, not, as so many travellers translate it, the China City, but perhaps derived from Kitaï-gorod in Podolia, the birthplace of Helena, mother of Ivan IV., foundress of the Kitaï-gorod of Moscow, which encloses the bazaars and the palaces of the nobles, and is separated from the Kremlin by a vast space that they call the Red Place or Beautiful Place. 3. Of the *Biélyi-gorod*, or White City, which surrounds this double centre of the Kremlin and the Kitaï-gorod as the outer skin of an almond encloses the two cotyledons. 4. Of the *Zemlianyi-gorod*, or City of the Earthen Ramparts, enveloping in its turn the White City, enclosing the faubourgs, gardens, woods, lakes, and vast unbuilt-on spaces, then occupied by the *slobodes* of the *streltsi*. 5. On the outer circle of Moscow, like detached forts, stood the fortified convents with white walls, which more than once sustained the assault of the Poles and the Tatars. This huge Asiatic town was a city of contrasts. The buildings grouped themselves almost by accident along the wide, marshy, tortuous, hardly marked-out streets. *Isbas* of pine, like those of the Russian villages, stood by the side of the palaces of the nobles. The people either chose them ready made from the yards, or ordered them according to their measure. The carpenters built them in two days on the place pointed out: they only cost a few roubles.

Moscow is situated in that part of Russia which is totally lacking in stone, and where the forests were formerly thickest. In point of fact, it is a city of wood, which a spark might set on fire. It had been burned almost entirely under Dmitri Donskoï, and twice under Ivan the Terrible; it was to burn again during the Polish invasion of 1612, and the French invasion of 1812.

The oukazes of the Tzars ordered certain precautions under the most severe penalties: all the fires had to be put out at nightfall; in summer it was absolutely forbidden to have lights in the houses, and cooking had to be done in the open air. There were no means of extinguishing the fires, and, when one broke out, the Muscovites showed themselves as passively fatalistic as the people of the East.

It was chiefly the Kremlin that profited by the embellishments undertaken by the two Ivans and their successors. The enclosure—of wood before the burning of Tokhtamych—was now of solid white stones, cut in facets (thence was derived the poetical name of " Holy mother Moscow with the white walls "); it was surmounted by high and narrow battlements in the form of teeth. Eighteen towers protected it, and five gates led into the interior. These five gates present much originality and variety. That of the Saviour was built in 1491 by Pietro Solario of Milan. It is the sacred gate, that cannot be entered covered; formerly obstinate people were forced to kneel down before it fifty times. Criminals were allowed to make their last prayer before the image of the Saviour, and the new Emperor always made his entrance through it on his way to his coronation at the Assumption. Another Italian built at the same date the gate of St. Nicholas of Mojaïsk, avenger of perjury, before whose image the suitors made oath. That of the Trinity was built in the 17th century by Christopher Galloway.

The wall of the Kremlin, like that of the old imperial palace of Byzantium, encloses a quantity of churches, palaces, and monasteries. The most celebrated of these churches is the *Ouspienski Sobor*, or the Cathedral of the Assumption, in which since the 15th century the Tzars have always made a point of being crowned It is their Cathedral of Rheims. Its architect was Aristotele Fioraventi, who had already worked for Cosmo de Medici, Francis I., Gian Galeazzo of Milan, Matthias Corvinus, and the Pope Sixtus IV., and whom Tolbousine, ambassador of Ivan III., met at Venice, and engaged for the service of the Tzar. One can hardly believe that the Assumption is of the same date as the luminous churches of the Renaissance. The architect, or those who inspired him, has here tried to reproduce the mysterious obscurity of the old temples of Egypt and the East. The cathedral has no windows, but only close-barred shot-holes in the walls, which admit into the interior a doubtful light, like that which filters through the hole of a dungeon. This pale glow touches the massive pillars covered with a tawny gold; on the tarnished background stand out, severe and grave, the faces of the saints and doctors; it dwells here and there on the *relief* of the golden *iconostase*, covered by miraculous images, sprinkled with diamonds and jewels; it hardly lights the representations of the ' Last Judgment ' and the ' End of the World,' painted on the walls of the church. All the upper part of the temple is partly enveloped in shadows, like the crypts of the Pharaohs ; the pictures which cover the vault can hardly be distinguished. The artist has evidently made them for the eye of God, not for that of man ; for the eye of man can only contemplate them on the rare occasions, such as the Feast of the Assumption or a coronation-day, when the whole cathedral is illumined to its furthest corners by innumerable wax tapers. It seems that Aristotele built this church according to a former plan of some other architect, only it is said that, finding the constructions already begun not sufficiently solid, he with a battering-ram, perfected by himself, overthrew the walls; that he caused new foundations to be dug ; finally, that he taught the Russians a better way of baking bricks. At the Assumption is the tomb of St. Peter, the first Metropolitan of Moscow, and people come here to worship before the holy images of Vladimir and Iaroslavl. The Cathedral of St. Michael the Archangel, built in 1505, is the St. Denys of the Tzars of Russia : here, in a coffin of pine covered with red cloth, sleep Ivan the Terrible and his two sons. In the Church of the Annunciation with the agate pavement, the marriages of the princes are celebrated. In that of the Ascension are the tombs of the sovereigns. The Tower of Ivan the Great, 325 feet high, surmounted with a golden cupola, with Slavonic inscriptions in letters of gold which may be distinguished from afar, with thirty-four bells in the *carillon*, was built in 1600 by Boris Godounof.

Of the imperial palace built in 1487, only a few fragments still remain : the little " Golden Palace," where the Tzarinas received the members of the clergy ; the " Palace of Facets," where the solemn audiences of ambassadors were held ; the " Red Staircase," from the top of which the Tzar allowed the people to contemplate "The light of his eyes;" finally the " Terem," with the painted roof, where we still find the dining-hall, the hall of council, and that of the oratory—vaulted halls still complete, where shine on golden backgrounds the images of the saints who protect the Tzar. The Palace of Facets was begun in 1487 by the Italian Mario, and finished by Pietro Antonio. The other palaces are the work of the Milanese Aleviso. In the Tzarian apartments, rarities imported from the West already mixed with the ancient Russian furniture. In 1594 the German ambassador presented the Tzar Feodor with a gilt clock, on which were marked the planets and the calendar ; and in 1597 with another clock, where little figures played on trumpets, Jews' harps, and tambourines each time the hour struck.

The most curious edifice in Moscow is perhaps the Church of Vassili the Blessed, on the Red Place. It was built by Ivan the Terrible in 1554, in memory of the taking of Kazan, and is the work of an Italian artist. The legend insists that Ivan put out the eyes of the artist, to prevent his building a similar marvel for others. We must imagine a church surmounted by six or eight round cupolas, all of different heights and forms, "some beaten into facets, others cut; these carved into diamond points, like the ananas, those in spirals; others, again, marked with scales, lozenge-shaped, or celled like a honeycomb."* A powerful imagination has defied all symmetry. From the base to the summit the church is covered with colors, which are glaring, and even crude. This many-colored monster has the gift of stupefying the most *blasé* traveller. "You might take it," says Haxthausen, "for an immense dragon, with shining scales, crouching and sleeping." Conceive the most brilliant bird of tropical forests suddenly taking the shape of a cathedral, and you have *Vassili-Blagennoï*.

It was not only architects that Russia owed to Italy. Aristotele Fioraventi coined money for Ivan III., built him a bridge of boats over the Volkhof during the expedition to Novgorod, cast the cannons which thundered against Kazan, and organized his artillery. Paolo Bossio of Genoa cast for him the *Tzarpouchka*, the king of guns, the giant piece of the Kremlin. Pietro of Milan made him arquebuses. The art of the founder shed its greatest brilliancy under Boris Godounof, whose effigy adorns the queen of bells (*Tzar-kolokol*), subsequently re-cast under Alexis and Anne Ivanovna, the bronze Titan whose weight of 288,000 pounds could be contained in no belfry, which broke every scaffolding, and rests voiceless like a pyramid of bronze on its pedestal of masonry, constructed in the beginning of this century by Montferrand.

* Théophile Gautier, 'Voyage en Russie.'

CHAPTER XVII.

THE SUCCESSORS OF IVAN THE TERRIBLE: FEODOR IVANOVITCH AND BORIS GODOUNOF (1584-1605).

Feodor Ivanovitch (1584-1598)—The peasant attached to the glebe—The patriarchate— Boris Godounof (1598-1605)—Appearance of the false Dmitri.

FEODOR IVANOVITCH (1584-1598)—THE PEASANT ATTACHED TO THE GLEBE—THE PATRIARCHATE.

FEODOR, son of Ivan IV. and of Anastasia Romanof, resembled his father in nothing. He had neither his instinctive love of cruelty and debauchery, nor his lively intelligence, nor his iron will. The throne of the Terrible was occupied by a saint— a monk. The power passed naturally to the chamber of the boyards. Five among them had special influence over the government—Prince Ivan Mstislavski, a descendant of Gedemin; Prince Ivan Chouïski, a descendant of Rurik, a member of a family disgraced in the early years of Ivan IV., but himself celebrated as the defender of Pskof; and Prince Bogdan Belski, another descendant of Rurik. After these three heads of princely families came two chiefs of boyard families. Both became sovereigns, and both owed their elevation to their wives. The importance of Nikita Romanof came from his sister, the first wife of Ivan IV.; Boris Godounof owed his to his sister Irene, wife of the Tzar Feodor. Minister of Ivan IV., brother of the reigning Tzar, Godounof was devoured by an insatiable ambition. Sorcerers who had escaped from Ivan the Terrible are said to have prophesied that he should become Tzar, but that his reign was only to last for seven years. From that time his policy consisted in putting aside all rivals—in overcoming all the obstacles that lay between him and the throne.

The Tzar Feodor had a brother, Dmitri, son of Ivan's seventh wife. The *douma* of boyards feared the intrigues of which this infant might be made the centre, and, by the advice of Godounof, sent him to his appanage Ouglitch, with his mother and her relations, the Nagoïs. Belski, another descendant of Gedemin, an intelligent and ambitious man, irritated the people, who besieged the Kremlin, and demanded his head. Boris took advantage of such a good opportunity, and despatched this rival to Nijni-Novgorod. When Feodor at his coronation had placed on his head the crowns of Russia, Kazan Astrakhan, and Siberia, it was his maternal uncle, Nikita Romanof, who governed in his name; but at his death the power passed to the natural chief of a new *vrémia*, Boris Godounof. There still remained in the council two rivals to Boris. Mstislavski allowed himself to be implicated in a plot, and was forced to become a monk; Prince Chouïski, who had tried to make himself a party among the merchants, was accused of treason, arrested with all his family, and all were banished to different distant towns. The Metropolitan Dionysius, who had taken his part, was deposed, and replaced by Job, a man completely at the disposal of Godounof, who was now supreme. He induced his brother-in-law to grant him the title of Allied Chief Boyard, the viceroyalties of Kazan and Astrakhan, and immense territories on the Dwina and the Moskowa. His revenues were enormous, and he is said to have been able to put a hundred thousand men in the field. Nothing could be obtained from the sovereign except through Boris; more powerful than even Adachef had been, he had an army of clients. It was he who replied to the ambassadors, and who received the presents of the Emperor, of the Queen of England, and of the Khan of the Crimea. His enemies were the enemies of the prince. He lacked nothing that is royal but the title.

In foreign affairs, the regency of Godounof strengthened the prestige of Russia. Batory, who had never ceased to threaten revenge, died in 1586. A new danger appeared in this quarter. Sigismond, son of the King of Sweden, had schemed successfully for the suffrages of the Polish electors. It was to be feared that he would one day unite under the same sceptre the two nations whom Russia had most cause to dread in Europe. Rodolph of Austria, the other candidate, was less dangerous. Austria and Russia had the same interests with regard to Turks and Tatars, and this identity was one day to result in the almost perpetual alliance between the two Powers. Boris put forward Feodor as a candidate for the crown of Poland, and the idea of the union of the two Slav monarchies under one prince. The Poles refused to obey any prince who was not a Catholic; they feared that, instead of a fraternal union, the Muscovite would only "join their monarchy to that of Moscow, like a sleeve to a coat." The interests of caste were added to national and religious prejudices; the nobles, who only had in view the weakening of the royal power, were not likely to give themselves as master a sovereign as absolute as the Tzar of Muscovy. Finally, nothing could be done without money in the Polish diets; Boris was so mistaken as to spare it. The negotiations fell to the ground, and the prince of Sweden was elected.

The war with Sweden began again vigorously; Russia recaptured what had been taken from Ivan the Terrible—Iam, Ivangorod, and Koporié. The Poles, who, since they had a Swedish king, did not care to augment the Swedish power, gave no assistance. Sigismond Vasa, on his father's death in 1592, did indeed see himself for a moment king of both countries; but his zeal for Catholicism, which made him dear to the Poles, caused him to be detested by the Swedes. The latter wished for a separate government, under the regency of Charles Vasa, and they soon after offered him the crown. This union, so much dreaded by the Russians, soon ended in a rupture. The Poles and Swedes had never before been such bitter enemies, and the hatred of the two peoples and the two religions was complicated still further by that of the two kings. The occasion was favorable for Russia to undertake the conquest of Livonia. Boris Godounof had never abandoned this great scheme of Ivan the Terrible, only he failed to take the proper means for realizing it. Instead of openly allying himself with Sweden against Poland, or with Poland against Sweden, he negotiated with both, tried to play off one against the other, and ended by alienating both equally. The former minister of Ivan the Terrible, the intriguing Grand Boyard, was too fond of hidden paths.

To clear his way to the throne, it was not sufficient for him to be master of the palace and the Court; he must create himself a strong party in the nation. Boris, who felt himself to be hated by the princes and boyards, sought the support of the small *noblesse* and the clergy. Hence resulted two of the most important actions of the reign of Feodor—the binding of the peasant to the soil, and the institution of the patriarchate.

The Russian peasant was in fact delivered over to the will of his master. In law, he remained a free man, as he was allowed to pass from the service of one proprietor to that of another. This right brought with it an abuse. The large proprietors, who, being the richest, could also be the most generous, tried to attract to their lands the peasants of the smaller landowners, by insuring them privileges and immunities. We must remember that at this epoch the population was very scanty, and land had of itself no value. It was precious according to the number of laborers who could be induced to settle on it. Thus the lands of the smaller proprietors ran the risk of being depopulated for the benefit of the great lords ; if they lost their laborers, the value of the land became proportionately depreciated. Now the class of small landowners was at this period almost the only military class of Russia ; the national cavalry was recruited almost entirely from it alone. If the source of their revenues were cut off, where would they get the money to equip themselves, to answer to the call of the Tzar, according to the text of the ordinances, " mounted, armed, and accompanied " ? Their interest thus became confounded with that of the empire, which was soon to become unable to support its armies. Boris Godounof found means to save the rights of the State, and gain for himself the gratitude of a numerous and powerful class. The comfort of the peasant did not trouble any one at this epoch. He was an instrument of agriculture, a force—nothing more. An edict of Feodor forbade the peasants henceforth to go from one estate to another. The free Russian *krestianine* was now attached to the glebe, like the Western serf. In the name of the interest of the State and that of the military nobles, an immemorial right was extinguished. We must not think that these silent masses were insensible. The day of the " St. George," when the ancient laws permitted the peasant to pass yearly from one domain to another, remained for centuries a day of bitter regret. He cursed for long the authors of this oukase, and even protested when he had the opportunity; but his protestation took more the form of flight than of revolt. The development of Cossack life has a close relation to the change in the rural *régime;* and the more men sought to bind the peasant to the soil, the more his spirit revolted, and the more the camps of the Don and the Dniester were filled. The Russian peasant never allowed the prescription of this new form of slavery to be established ; in one way or another he has constantly resisted it. Boris Godounof afterwards partially repealed this oukase : while still forbidding them to pass from the service of the small to the great proprietor, they were allowed to change the mastership of one small landowner for that of another. The feeling of the time was not in favor of liberty ; the more Russia tended to become a modern State, the more her expenses increased, and the more the Government was conscious of the need of assuring the revenues by fixing to the soil the population which was subject to the tax and *corvée*. It was the crushed peasant who bore the weight of the reform. awaiting the day, still very distant, when he also would profit by the progress accomplished.

The other innovation made in the name of Feodor was the

establishment of the patriarchate. The Russian ecclesiastics complained with reason of having to obey patriarchs who were themselves only slaves of the infidels. Ancient Rome was polluted by the Pope; Constantinople, the second Rome, was profaned by the Turk: had not Moscow, the third Rome, a right at least to independence? Boris encouraged these murmurs: it was his interest that at the death of the Tzar there should be a great ecclesiastical authority standing alone, and that this great authority should owe all to him. He profited by the arrival at Moscow of Jeremiah, Patriarch of Constantinople, to induce him to found the Russian patriarchate and consecrate Archbishop Job, who was a tool of Boris. The latter had now a powerful friend.

Boris had need to create for himself a strong party. Many eyes began to turn towards Ivan's second son, Dmitri. His mother's kindred, the Nagoïs, from their exile at Ouglitch, watched carefully all the variations in the health of the Tzar, and the movements of Boris. The death of Feodor would give the throne to Dmitri, and power to his relatives—power to avenge themselves for all. It would deliver Boris up to the reprisals of his enemies. He knew this only too well. In 1591, it was suddenly announced that the young Dmitri had been slain. The public voice denounced Boris. To stifle suspicion he ordered an inquest, and his emissaries had the audacity to declare that the young prince cut his own throat in a fit of madness, and that the Nagoïs and the people of Ouglitch had put to death innocent men as murderers. The result of the inquiry was the extermination of the Nagoïs and the depopulation of Ouglitch. Seven years after, the pious Feodor died, and in the person of this vague and virtuous sovereign the race of bloody and violent men of prey who had created Russia was extinguished. The dynasty of Andrew Bogolioubski had accomplished its mission—it had founded the Russian unity. The task of obtaining the entrance of this semi-Asiatic State into the bosom of civilized Europe was reserved for another dynasty.

BORIS GODOUNOF (1598-1605)—APPEARANCE OF THE FALSE DMITRI.

Boris Godounof had reached the aim of his desires—but at what a price! The murder of Dmitri, the last offshoot of St. Vladimir, of Monomachus, of George and the Ivans, was no ordinary crime. Russia had seen many horrors, but never one like this. The Tzar might have put the Russian princes to

death, but they were his enemies, they were often guilty, and
then he was the Tzar. Now a simple boyard sacrificed to his
own ambition the son of his benefactor, the heir of his master,
the last descendant of the founders of Russia. It was one of
those crimes that ever deeply agitate the people. Boris believed
vainly he had buried all in the earth with the corpse of the
Tzarévitch.

After the death of Feodor, his widow Irene entered the
Dievitchi Monastyr, and took the veil there, mourning her sterility, and lamenting that " by her the sovereign race had perished." The nobles and the people took the oaths to her, so
that there should be no interregnum. A woman had the crown
at her disposal, and that woman was the sister of Godounof.
As she refused to govern, the *douma* had to discharge affairs
under the presidency of the Patriarch Job, who owed everything to Godounof. It was impossible that the throne should
escape Godounof; yet it seemed strange that a simple boyard,
a creature of Ivan IV., should take precedence of all the princes
descended in direct line from Rurik. However, the Patriarch
and his clergy, the boyards and citizens of Moscow, appeared
before the *Dievitchi Monastyr*, in which Godounof was shut up
with his sister. Job entreated him to accept the crown. Godounof refused, apparently from an excess of modesty—in reality,
because he wished to receive it from the hands of the nation.
The States-general were then assembled; the lesser nobility
and the clergy, that is, the friends of Boris, formed the majority.
After the despotism of Ivan, it was a strange sight to see this
assembly dispose of the crown. The Russia of the Terrible
had, like Poland, her elective diet, but the lesson of obedience
had been so well learnt, that there was no fear of anarchy. They
were told that Ivan IV. on his death-bed had confided to Boris
his family and his empire, and that Feodor had put around his
neck a chain of gold. Men made the most of the experience of
government that he had acquired under two reigns; they
boasted of his skilful dealings with Sweden, Poland, and the
Crimea. The national voice decreed to him the crown, and the
States sent him a deputation. He still feigned to hold back,
and cast out " the tempters"; but his sister " blessed him for
the throne," and thus consecrated the wish of the people.
Boris reigned.

His reign was not without glory. He took up the designs of
his master, Ivan IV., on Livonia; and as the Terrible had his
puppet king Magnus, Boris sought first a Swedish prince Gustaf,
and then a Danish prince John, to play the part of King of
Livonia. John was to marry Xenia, daughter of the new Tzar,

when he died suddenly. Denmark declared that he was poisoned; and in the Russia of that date everything is conceivable. The Khan of the Crimea, who had vainly tried to make two incursions, and who had then a quarrel with the Turks, sought the friendship of Boris. Affairs in the Caucasus were less happy. Alexander, prince of Kachetia, who had acknowledged himself vassal of Boris, was assassinated, and succeeded by his son, who was on the side of the King of Persia (Shah Abbas), and Islamism. In Daghestan a body of Russians sent to occupy the country were exterminated by the Turks. Russia had not yet approached near enough to the Black Sea to be able to take the field with assurance in those distant regions. In Siberia, Koutchoum, the dethroned khan, was vanquished; the battle was decisive, though the Russian voïevodes only had 400 men, and Koutchoum 500; but none the less did it decide the fate of Asia.

Boris continued to be sought by the Powers of the West, beginning with Austria. In 1600 he sent Gregory Mikouline to Queen Elizabeth. "He had learnt," says the letter of the Tzar, "that the Queen had furnished help to the Turks against the Kaiser of Germany. We are astonished at it, as to act thus is not proper for Christian sovereigns; and you, our well-beloved sister, you ought not for the future to enter into relationships of friendship with *Bousourman* (Mussulman) princes, nor to help them in any way, whether by men or silver; but on the contrary should desire and insist that all the great Christian potentates should have a good understanding, union, and strong friendship, and make one against the Mussulmans, till the hand of the Christians rise, and that of the Mussulmans is abased."

Mikouline was received in London with great honors. In the audience given him by the Queen, "she arose from her throne and advanced some distance" to listen to his compliments; after which she bowed her head and asked for news of the health of the Tzar, the Tzarina, Maria Gregorievna, and of the Tzarévitch Feodor Borissovitch. She received "with great joy" the credentials, and, being seated, listened to the message of Mikouline. She replied to the passage touching on her relations with Turkey by protestations of friendship and union with all the Christian princes, gave her hand to be kissed by the envoy and also by the secretary of the embassy, Ivan Zinovief, and sent them to talk over their affairs with Lord Robert Cecil. The commercial interests of the two peoples were guaranteed anew. During his visit to London, Mikouline was present at the revolt of 1601, led by Essex, and saw the citizens rush through the streets with armed cuirasses and arquebuses to defend the Queen.

He gives in his account many curious details of the Court of England at this epoch—the most brilliant of the reign of Elizabeth,—quitted London in May 1601, and arrived at Arkhangel in July.

The firm government of Boris gave confidence, and he continued to be sought by the Powers of the West, especially by Austria and England. Sweden and Poland could do him no hurt. He surrounded himself with soldiers, learned men, and artists. With their help he raised monuments, built the tower of Ivan the Great at the Kremlin, and had the "queen of bells" cast. It was he who first sent young Russians to Lübeck, England, France, and Austria, to study European arts. The fashions of the West penetrated to Moscow, and some of the nobles began to shave their beards.

This prosperity was all unreal. His services—even his charities—turned against him. "He presented to the poor," says a contemporary, "in a vase of gold, the blood of the innocents. He fed them with unholy alms." The oligarchic party, ashamed of obeying a simple boyard, began to agitate. After having pardoned his ancient rival Belski, Boris was obliged to throw him into prison. He acted with severity towards the Romanofs, who were exiled, many of them having been previously tortured. Feodor, the eldest, was forced to become a monk under the name of Philarete, and his wife took the veil under the name of Marfa. From the son of this monk and this nun, emperors were to spring.

Feeling himself surrounded by plots, Boris Godounof did not hesitate before any means of security, and received the denunciations of slaves against their masters. From 1601 to 1604 a frightful famine devastated Russia, and was followed by a pestilence. The famished peasants joined the servants of the disgraced nobles, and formed themselves into bands of brigands who infested the southern provinces, and even insulted the environs of Moscow. It was necessary to send a regular army against them. To these calamities was added the universal presentiment of others yet greater. The term of seven years assigned by the astrologers to the reign of Boris was approaching. The crime of Ouglitch, still unexpiated, had left a strange uneasiness throughout Russia. Suddenly there arose a rumor that the murdered Dmitri was living, and with arms in his hands was making ready to reconquer the empire.

At the Monastery of the Miracle a young monk, Gregory Otrépief, had brought himself into notice. After having for a long while wandered from convent to convent at his own pleasure, he finally reached the Monastery of the Miracle; and the Patriarch Job discerning his intelligence, made him his secretary. In discharge of these functions, he became acquainted with more than one State secret. "Do you know," he used to say to the other monks, "that I shall be one day Tzar of Moscow?" They spat in his face, and the Tzar Boris Goduonof ordered him to be confined in the Monastery of the White Lake. He succeeded in escaping: again became a wandering monk, and, being well received at Novgorod-Severski, had the temerity to write to the inhabitants: "I am the Tzarévitch Dmitri, and I will not forget your kindness." Then he threw his frock to the winds, enrolled himself among the Zaporogues, and became a bold rider and a brave Cossack. He passed into the service of Adam Vichnevetski, a Polish *pan*; he fell ill, or feigned to do so, summoned a priest, and revealed to him, under the seal of confession, that he was the Tzarévitch Dmitri, who had escaped from the hands of the assassins at Ouglitch, by another child being substituted in his place. He showed a cross, set with jewels, that hung round his neck, given him by Mstislavski, godfather of the Tzarévitch. The Jesuit did not dare to keep such a secret to himself. Otrépief was recognized by his master, Vichnevetski, as the son of the Terrible. Mniszek, palatine of Sandomir, promised him his support and the hand of his daughter, Marina, who consented with joy to be Tzarina of Moscow. The strange news spread throughout the kingdom. The Pope's nuncio took the Tzarévitch under his protection, and presented him to King Sigismond. Were they really deceived? It is more probable that they saw in him a formidable instrument of agitation, which the king flattered himself he would be able to use against Russia, and the Jesuits against orthodoxy. Sigismond feared to take on himself the rupture of the truce he had concluded with Boris, and expose himself to Russian vengeance. He treated Otrépief as Tzarévitch, but only in private; he refused to put the royal troops at his disposal, but he authorized the nobles, who were touched by the misfortune of the prince, to help him if they wished. The *pans* did not need the royal authority; many of them, with the levity and love of adventure which characterized the Polish nobility, took up arms in favor of the Tzarévitch. Then Boris recognized, says Lévêque, that the weakest enemy can make a usurper tremble.

No revolution, even if it were the wisest and most necessary, could be accomplished without putting in motion the dregs of society—without the clashing of a mass of interests, and the creation of a multitude who are outcasts from all classes. The transformation which was then taking place in Russia for the formation of the modern united State, had engendered all these elements of disorder. The peasant whom the laws of Boris had attached to the glebe, was everywhere sullenly hostile. The smaller nobility, for whose profit this law had been made, were scarcely able to live on their lands ; the service of the Tzar had become ruinous, and many were inclined to supplement the insufficiency of their revenues by brigandage. The boyards and the great nobility were profoundly demoralized—they were ready for any treason. The warlike republics of the Cossacks of the Don and the Dnieper, the bands of serfs, of fugitive peasants, who infested the Russian territory, only waited for an opportunity to lay waste the country. The ignorance of the masses was profound, and their minds greedy of wonders and change ; no other nation has allowed itself to be deceived so often by the same fable, the sudden apparition of a prince whom all believed dead. Adventures like those of Otrépief the false Dmitri, and of Pougatchef the false Peter III., could not be reproduced in any other European country. These two adventurers rendered themselves particularly famous, but the secret archives show us that in the Russia of the 17th and 18th centuries there were hundreds of impostors, of false Dmitri's, false Alexis, false Peters II., and false Peters III. We might almost think that the Russians, the most Asiatic of all European nations, had not renounced the Oriental dogma of re-incarnations and avatars. The Government was powerless, in a country so utterly without communication, to put a stop to the most absurd rumors. Besides, the ignorant and superstitious masses were hostile to it, and delighted to allow themselves to be deceived. So many elements of rebellion only required to be set in motion by the hand of a skilful agitator. The entrance of the impostor into Russia was the signal of dissolution.

As long as the power lay in the hands of the clever and energetic Godounof, he was able to maintain order, to restrain the authors of revolt, and to discourage the false Dmitri. The Patriarch Job and Vassili Chouïski, who had conducted the inquest at Ouglitch, made proclamations to the people affirming that Dmitri was really dead, and that the impostor was none other than Otrépief. Similar declarations were sent to the King and the Diet of Poland. Finally, troops were put in marching order, and a line of communications established with the Western frontier. But already the towns of Severia revolted at the approach of the Tzarévitch, and the boyards publicly announced "that it was hard to bear arms against your lawful sovereign." At Moscow the health of the Tzar Dmitri was drunk at feasts. In October 1604, the impostor crossed the frontier with an army of Poles, of Russians banished in the preceding reign, and German mercenaries. Severia at once rose, and Novgorod-Severski opened her gates to him. Prince Mstislavski tried to check his progress by a battle, but the soldiers were struck by the idea that the man whom they fought was the real Dmitri. "They had no hands to fight, but only feet to fly." Vassili Chouïski, Mstislavski's successor, did his best to rally their courage, and this time, in spite of his intrepidity, the impostor was defeated at Dobrynitchi. Boris believed the war finished; but in reality it had only begun. After Severia the Ukraine rebelled, and 4000 Cossacks of the Don came to rejoin " the brigand." The inaction of the Muscovite voïevodes proved that the spirit of treason had already penetrated the nobility.

In 1605 Boris died, commending his innocent son to the care of Basmanof, the boyards, the Patriarch, and the people of Moscow. But hardly had Basmanof taken the command of the army of Severia, than he understood that neither the soldiers nor the leaders were going to fight for a Godounof. Rather than be the victim of treason, he preferred being the author of it. The man in whom the dying Boris had placed all his confidence united with Galitsyne and Soltykof, secret adherents of the impostor. He solemnly announced to the troops that Dmitri was in truth the son of Ivan the Terrible and the lawful master of Russia, and was the first to throw himself at the feet of the Pretender, who was at once proclaimed by the troops. Dmitri marched to Moscow; at his approach his partisans rose, and the wife and son of Godounof were massacred. Such was the end of the dynasty which Boris had thought to found in the blood of a Tzarévitch!

CHAPTER XVIII.

THE TIME OF THE TROUBLES (1605-1613).

Murder of the false Dmitri—Vassili Chouïski—The brigand of Touchino—Vladislas of Poland—The Poles at the Kremlin—National rising—Minine and Pojarski—Election of Michael Romanof.

MURDER OF THE FALSE DMITRI—VASSILI CHOUISKI—THE BRIGAND OF TOUCHINO.

THE event that had taken place in Russia is one of the most extraordinary in the annals of the world. A runaway monk entered Moscow in triumph as her Tzar, among the joyful tears of the people, who thought they beheld a descendant of their long line of princes. Only one man had the courage to affirm that he had seen Dmitri assassinated, and that the new Tzar was an impostor. This was Vassili Chouïski, one of those who had directed the inquest at Ouglitch, and who had defeated the Pretender at the battle of Dobrynitchi. Denounced by Basmanof, he was condemned to death by an assembly of the three orders, and his head was actually on the block, when he received a pardon from the Tzar. Men did not recognize the son of Ivan the Terrible in this act of clemency, and Otrépief had afterwards cause to repent of it. Job, the tool of Godounof, was replaced in the patriarchate by a favorite of the new prince, the Greek Ignatius. The Tzar had an interview with his pretended mother, Maria Nagoï, widow of Ivan IV. Whether because she wished to avenge her injuries, or merely to recover her honors, Maria recognized Otrépief as her son, and publicly embraced him. He loaded the Nagoïs, whom he regarded as his maternal relations, with favors; the Romanofs were likewise recalled from exile, and Philarete made Metropolitan of Rostof.

The Tzar presided regularly at the *douma*, where the boyards admired the clearness of his apprehension and the variety of his knowledge. As a monk he was a man of letters, and as a pupil of the Zaporogues an accomplished horseman, bold and skilful in all bodily exercises. He was fond of foreigners, and even spoke of sending the Russian nobles to be educated in the West. This taste for strangers went hand in hand with a certain contempt for the national ignorance and grossness. He offended the boyards by his raillery, and alienated the people and the clergy by his disdain of Russian customs and religious rites. He ate veal, never slept after dinner, did not take baths, borrowed money from the convents, turned the monks into ridicule, fought with bears, visited jewellers and foreign artisans familiarly, and took no heed of the severe Court etiquette. He pointed cannons with his own hand; organized sham fights between the national troops and the foreign mercenaries; was pleased to see the Russians beaten by the Germans; and surrounded himself by a European guard, with Margeret, Knutsen, and Van Dennen at its head. On his entry into Moscow a struggle took place between the clergy and the papal legate, and two bishops were exiled. He got no thanks for resisting the legate and Poland— for declining to help the one to effect the union of the two Churches, and refusing to cede to the other an inch of Russian land. The arrival of his wife, the Catholic Marina, with a suite of Polish gentlemen, who assumed an insolent demeanor towards the Russians, completed the irritation of the Muscovites. Less than thirty days after his entrance into the Kremlin, men were ripe for a revolution.

Vassili Chouïski, pardoned by Otrépief, was the head of the conspirators. The extreme confidence of the Tzar was his ruin. One night the boyards attacked the Kremlin, which had been left unguarded. Otrépief was thrown out of a window, and stabbed in the court of the palace; Basmanof, who defended him, being killed by his side. They took the two corpses, put ribald masks on their faces, and exposed them on the place of executions between a flute and a bag-pipe. The widow of Otrépief, and the Polish envoys sent to assist at the wedding, were spared, but kept prisoners by the boyards. The corpse of the "sorcerer" was burned, and a cannon was charged with his ashes, which were blown to the winds (1606).

It was now necessary to elect a new Tzar. Two candidates, two chiefs of princely families, presented themselves, Vassili Chouïski and Vassili Galitsyne. Chouïski had signalized himself by his hatred of the usurper, had defeated him in battle, had been condemned by him to death, and had been foremost in the conspiracy. The boyards would have preferred assembling the States-general, as in 1598, but Vassili would not await their decision. More impatient and less wise than Boris Godounof, he chose to owe his crown to the Muscovites alone, and not to the delegates of the whole nation. It was the original sin of the new administration. Vassili had on his side neither hereditary right, like the ancient Tzars, nor the vote of the three orders, like Boris. His claim to the throne thus remained dubious in times of the greatest disturbance. The Patriarch Ignatius, the nominee of the impostor, was replaced by Hermogenes. Thus, at each change in the government, a corresponding change took place in the first dignity of the Church.

On ascending the throne, Vassili swore a solemn oath to put no boyard to death without trial, not to confiscate the goods of criminals, and to chastise calumniators. True Russians felt profound sorrow when they saw the Tzar thus despoil himself of his sovereign rights, and alienate part of his autocratic power for the benefit of the boyards. He was entering, indeed, on the path of the *pacta conventa*, which, at every new election in Poland, deprived the king of some of his attributes, and led to the enfeebling of the crown, and the triumph of the aristocratic anarchy of the nobles.

The provinces were discontented at not being consulted in the choice of a sovereign. They learnt almost at the same moment that Dmitri had regained the throne of his forefathers; then that Dmitri was an impostor, who had usurped the throne by the aid of the devil; finally, that a new Tzar reigned over Russia. They did not know what to believe, or in whom to trust; everything seemed doubtful. The Russian conscience was greatly troubled, and, in the universal demoralization, adventurers found an easy road to success.

Vassili, who was fifty years old, wanted both energy and prestige. He had specially distinguished himself by his talents for intrigue, and even his partisans reproached him with avarice. The elements of disorder put in motion by the last two revolutions, were not yet appeased. Neither ambitious boyards, nor felonious nobles, nor insurgent peasants, nor brigands, nor the Cossacks and Zaporogues, nor the companies, nor the foreign mercenaries were satisfied. In such a situation it was inevitable that a new impostor should take the place of the former, and again furnish the worst passions with an outlet. Instead of one, there were two Pretenders: on one side a Cossack of Terek gave himself out to be the Tzarévitch Peter, a pretended son of the chaste Feodor; on the other, it was announced that Dmitri had, for the second time, escaped his murderers. The same transparent fable was always received with the same credulity, real or feigned. At Moscow the people recalled the fact that the face of the corpse exposed on the Red Place was covered with a mask. Vassili tried in vain to disabuse the people; he was not more successful than Boris. Had not Boris overwhelmed the Muscovites and the King of Poland with evidence? Severia and the turbulent cities of the South again rose; the discontented masses armed again for a new Otrépief against a new Godounof. In the South, a certain Bolotnikof, by birth a serf, called all the brigands, all slaves and peasants to his standard, and began a servile war. By his side, Prince Chakovskoï Pachkof, one of the *diéti-boyarskié*, the voïevode Soundoulof, and the aristocratic Procopius Lapounof, organized the war of the nobles. On the banks of the Volga, the Tatars and Finnish tribes, under pretext of sustaining the son of Ivan the Terrible, proclaimed their national independence. The empire was menaced with total dissolution by the reaction of all the forces till then repressed by the strong hand of the Tzars.

The reappearance of the false Dmitri was announced throughout Russia. In reality no one had dared to take up this *rôle;* but the impostor was so universally necessary that he was everywhere recognized even before he existed. Bolotnikof and his peasants threatened the capital, and agitated the lower classes of Moscow. The Tzar Chouïski seemed lost, when he was saved by the military talents of his nephew, Skopine Chouïski. Lapounof and two other leaders took fright, and were disgusted with their popular allies; they separated from Bolotnikof, offered to submit to the Tzar, and were received at Moscow with caresses. Bolotnikof, left alone, fell back on Toula, and was so closely pressed that he wrote to Mniszek that all was lost if he could not produce the false Dmitri. At last the desired one, expected by all the rebels, appeared. His real name is undivulged; his origin is uncertain; he is only mentioned by the title of the "second false Dmitri." All we know of him is that he was a clever, intelligent man, tolerably educated, and very brutal. He came too late to save Toula. Bolotnikof was drowned, and the false Peter hanged.

Lissovski and Rojinski, two Polish nobles of great repute, soon came to the aid of the false Dmitri. The Zaporogues and the Cossacks of the Don, under Zaroutski, hastened to take part in the expected booty. It is a curious fact that there were in their ranks five or six impostors, who all gave themselves out as being sons or grandsons of Ivan the Terrible. With all these forces the impostor marched on Moscow, defeated the detachments of the Tzar's army, and established himself twelve versts from the capital, at the village of Touchino. This encampment has remained celebrated in the history of the troubles; it has gained for this second impostor the surname of the brigand of Touchino, and for his Russian partisans the designation of Touchinists. Thus in face of the Tzar of Moscow—the nominee of the Muscovites, who hardly seemed the Tzar of Russia—stood the Tzar of Touchino. He, like his rival, had his Court, his army, his administration. He distributed titles and dignities; and—evidence of profound popular degradation—an ambitious crowd was to be seen passing from one court to the other, falling at the feet of both Tzars, receiving double pay, and, loaded with honors by Vassili, flying to Dmitri, to return again to Vassili. A *sobriquet* was invented to designate these refugees. They were called "birds of passage" (*pérélêti*).

Whilst Touchino menaced and braved Moscow, Polish reinforcements flocked to the camp of the brigand, in spite of the promises and assurances of the perfidious Sigismond. The celebrated voïevode, John Sapieha, came to join Lissovski, and they both tried to capture the Troïtsa monastery. This famous convent tempted them by its riches. With its ramparts and towers, it was a strong place of arms for the partisans of the Tzar; its monks were convinced that they knew how the country was to be saved, and did not cease to call all the neighboring cities to take up arms "for faith and the Tzar." These warlike monks, who were like the "Church militant" of the French League—though they, to be sure, defended at once the national and the orthodox cause—repelled all the assaults of the Catholic adventurers. After a siege of sixteen months, Sapieha had to acknowledge himself beaten. Abraham Palitsyne, treasurer of the convent, has narrated the exploits of his brethren. Souzdal, Vladimir, Peréiaslaf, Rostof, and eighteen other northern towns, not being able to decide which was the legitimate sovereign, opened their gates to the Touchinists. Chouïski was still disliked at Moscow, but they knew what they had to expect from the second false Dmitri. Honest people who did not look forward to the triumph of the brigand, and who saw no possible Tzar but Vassili, forced themselves to support him. What saved the capital was the bad discipline that reigned in the enemy's camp; new rebellions broke out against the rebel. Serfs and mougiks threatened their masters and ravaged the country, and the brigand was forced to employ part of his forces to suppress this brigandage.

About this time the Tzar Chouïski turned for help to Sweden; he ceded the town of Karela to Charles IX., contracted with him an offensive and defensive alliance against Poland, and received in return a body of 5000 Swedes, under the command of De la Gardie. With this reinforcement, Skopine Chouïski expelled the Touchinists from the cities of the North, advanced on Moscow, and obliged the brigand to evacuate Touchino. The perfidious policy of the Polish government, which armed the impostors against the Tzar and allowed their voïevodes to attack a friendly country, amply justified Chouïski in seeking an ally in Sweden. But this foreign intervention gave rise to another: the King of Poland, affecting to think himself endangered by the Tzar's alliance with his worst enemy, decided to drop the mask and openly interfere. It was thus that under the most fatal auspices the long rivalry began between these two Slav nations, whom statesmanship had once tried to unite under the same sceptre. Poland, governed by an instrument of the Jesuits, inflicted on Russia a frightful wrong. Sigismond disloyally affected zeal for a pretender whom he knew to be an impostor; he violated treaties and all the rights of nations; allowing Russia to be attacked by his armies, all the while that he was asserting his peaceful disposition. His invasion of Russia filled up the measure of his iniquities. This conduct necessarily left ineffaceable memories in the hearts of the Russians.

By taking up arms, Sigismond intended to assure to his son the throne of Russia, and restore to Poland the places she had lost in the 15th century. He besieged Smolensk, and wrote to announce to the inhabitants that he did not come to shed the blood of the Russians, but, on the contrary, to protect them; and that he was prepared to guarantee to them the maintenance of their worship and liberties. The people of Smolensk, who knew the ardor with which Sigismond persecuted orthodoxy in his own dominions, repelled all his advances, and the voïevode Cheïn made ready to defend the town to the last. Sigismond wrote from his camp at Smolensk to the Polish voïevodes who were serving under the impostor, with orders to abandon him. The Polish Touchinists obeyed with regret, complaining that the king would appropriate the reward of their toils; the Russian Touchinists, not knowing what to do, followed their allies, and, already accustomed to every sort of treason, made their submission to the king, and offered to recognize his son Vladislas as Tzar of Russia. At the head of these refugees were the boyard Michael Soltykof and the currier Andronof.

Chouïski had now two enemies equally formidable—the King of Poland and the false Dmitri, who, himself threatened by the ambition of his royal rival, had to retreat to the South. Vassili's nephew, Skopine, who had saved him by his victories, and won him popularity by his frank manners, died in the midst of his successes. The people then revived their old dislike of the Tzar, and accused him of poisoning his nephew. Another of the Chouïskis, the ambitious Dmitri, was also involved in the accusation. Dmitri Chouïski, as unpopular with the army as he was with the capital, was betrayed in battle by the foreign regiments, and this defeat completed the ruin of Vassili. The people rose in Moscow; a great assembly of the populace and the boyards was held in the plains of Serpoukhof. The Tzar was "humbly requested" to vacate the throne, because he caused Christian blood to be shed, and was not successful in his government. The southern frontier towns also refused to obey him. Vassili Chouïski yielded, and abdicated; a short time afterwards he was forced to become a monk.

VLADISLAS OF POLAND—THE POLES AT THE KREMLIN.

Everyone was obliged to take an oath of obedience to the *douma* of boyards, who naturally seized the executive power during the interval before the election of a new Tzar. There were two candidates for the vacant throne—Vladislas, son of the King of Poland, and the false Dmitri. Now the latter was evidently an impostor. He ruled the upper and middle classes by terror alone, and had only the populace on his side. As they could not at once get rid of both the Poles and the brigand of Touchino, they chose the lesser of the two evils.

A Polish army, under the hetman Zolkiewski, had arrived at Mojaïsk: the impostor occupied Kolomenskoé. The boyards invited Zolkiewski to approach Moscow, and they began to negotiate. The hetman promised in the name of the young prince to maintain orthodoxy, the liberties and privileges of the orders, the partition of legislative power between the king and the *douma*. No one was to be executed without a trial, nor deprived of his dignities without a reason; all Muscovites might go, if they wished, to be educated abroad. The Russians began to like the Polish system of the *pacta conventa*. The inhabitants of Moscow vowed fealty to the Tzar Vladislas. One point still remained to be decided—the Russians desired that Vladislas should embrace orthodoxy. Zolkiewski reserved the decision to the King of Poland. He induced the boyards to send ambassadors to Sigismond, and Prince Vassili Galitsyne and the Metropolitan Philarete Romanof left immediately for the camp at Smolensk. This terrible crisis seemed at the point of disentangling itself in a way that was tolerably advantageous for Russia. She was to have a foreign sovereign, but one already acquainted with Slav manners, and his being a foreigner was even a gage for the partisans of reforms and Western civilization. Poland and Russia, which might have united under Ivan and under Feodor, had another chance of doing so under a Polish prince. Such was the confidence of the boyards, that, finding the security of Moscow troubled by the neighborhood of the impostor, they proposed to Zolkiewski to enter into the town and even the Kremlin. This unpatriotic resolution, dictated to the nobles by their mistrust of the lower classes, was to bring fatal consequences on Moscow. Zolkiewski wished to take his guarantees against the chiefs of the nation : Galitsyne and Philarete were already under Smolensk at the discretion of the king ; he sent for the fallen Tzar also and his two brothers as hostages.

Sigismond meditated a new treachery against Russia. His object was to conquer Muscovy, not for his son, but for himself. He stipulated with the ambassadors that Smolensk should be ceded to Poland, but they courageously repelled this proposition. They demanded on their own part that Vladislas should leave immediately for Moscow, as being the only means for allaying the suspicions to which the conduct of the king had given rise. Sigismond refused. He wished to be Tzar himself. In despair of conquering the scruples of the two chief ambassadors, he addressed himself to their inferior colleagues. The Secretary Tomila, on being asked to open the gates of Smolensk, replied : " If I were to do it, not only would God and the Muscovites curse me, but the earth would open and swallow me. We are sent to negotiate in the interests of our country, not of ourselves." All the Russians did not show this probity. The disgusting spectacle of the camp of Touchino was repeated at Smolensk. Men crowded round the king, as formerly around the brigand, to wring from him dignities, land, and money. Soltykof, Mstislavski, and the currier Andronof especially distinguished themselves by their baseness. At Moscow the boyards denounced each other to the commandant of the Polish garrison. By the suggestion of Soltykof they wrote to the king to beg him to make his entry into Moscow. The Patriarch Hermogenes refused to sign the letter, and the people, more patriotic than the boyards, supported the Patriarch. Some few nobles, like Andrew Galitsyne and Ivan Vorotinski had the honor of being suspected by the Poles, and were arrested by Leo Sapieha, successor of Zolkiewski. By permitting the Poles to enter the towns, the oligarchs had put Russia in the power of the King of Poland.

About this time the second impostor died, assassinated by one of his private enemies. His death had grave consequences. It healed misunderstandings, as, since the false Dmitri was dead, Sigismond had no longer any pretext for keeping his troops in Russia. The nobles had now no motive for distrusting the people, and could unite with them against the strangers. Whispers were heard in the streets of Moscow that it was necessary to combine against the Lithuanians. Soltykof and Andronof denounced these generous intentions to the enemy. The Patriarch Hermogenes, suspected of patriotism, was thrown into prison, where he afterwards died of hunger. The provinces were agitated, and the inhabitants of Smolensk and Moscow wrote to all the towns entreating them not to accept the perfidious enemy of orthodoxy as their prince. The citizens did their part, the *diéti-boyarskié* made their preparations for war, and Lapounof collected an army at Riazan. At his approach Moscow began to fill with reinforcements, and the Poles fortified the rampart of the Kremlin. Suddenly a quarrel broke out between the people and the soldiers. In the first heat the Poles and Germans are said to have massacred 7000 men; but resistance was organized in the streets of the Biélyi-gorod, and the foreigners, repulsed by Prince Pojarski, had to intrench themselves in the Kremlin and the Kitaï-gorod. To clear the neighborhood, the Poles set fire to the neighboring streets. Moscow was almost entirely in flames.

On hearing of the preparations of Lapounof and the revolt of Moscow, Sigismond caused the Muscovite ambassadors, Galitsyne and Philarete, to be arrested, and sent them prisoners to Marienburg, in Prussia. A short time afterwards Smolensk fell, after a resistance compared by the Poles themselves to that of Saguntum, though the king was not ashamed to torture the brave voïevode Cheïn, who had dared to resist him. He entered Warsaw in triumph, and the unhappy Vassili Chouïski, a Tzar of Russia, was dragged a prisoner through the streets in triumph. Lapounof was now reinforced by Prince Troubetskoï and Ivan Zaroutski, at the head of the Cossacks of the Don. A hundred thousand men besieged the Poles, who were shut up in the Kremlin, but the elements composing this large army were too conflicting and corrupt for the enterprise to succeed. The three leaders were mutually jealous of each other. Lapounof had committed more than one treason, Zaroutski had been one of the first to declare for Otrépief, and the others were hardly more loyal. The soldiers of Lapounof hated the Cossacks, who on their part only sought occasions for pillage. The Poles managed to raise the men of the Don, by inventing a pretended letter of Lapounof, saying, "Wherever you take them, slay them or drown them." A revolt broke out in the camp: Lapounof was assassinated, many of his adherents were murdered, and this great army was miserably dispersed.

Russia, a prey to civil war, as was France of the 16th century to the wars of religion, suffered, like her, from foreign intervention. In France, English and Spaniards watched the tides of party success, and profited by them all to gain some place or some province. Russia became the theatre of war for two rival Powers, Catholic Poland and Lutheran Sweden. When Vladislas was proclaimed Tzar, Sweden considered herself offended, and acted as an enemy. De la Gardie took the ports of the Baltic; and the boyards of Novgorod the Great, imitating those of Moscow, opened the gates to the foreigners. It was under the protection of Poland that the first two impostors had arisen in the west and south; under the protection of Sweden a third false Dmitri started up in the country of Pskof. Marina Mniszek on her side, who after the death of Otrépief had thrown herself into the arms of the brigand Touchino, acknowledged the Cossack Zaroutski as guardian of her son.

NATIONAL RISING—MININE AND POJARSKI—ELECTION OF MICHAEL ROMANOF.

The situation of Russia, like that of France during the English wars, or the wars of the League, was frightful. The Tzar was prisoner, the Patriarch captive, the Swedes at Novgorod the Great, the Poles at the Kremlin, and the higher nobility bought by the strangers. Everywhere bands of brigands and highwaymen pillaged towns, tortured peasants, and desecrated churches. Famine increased: in certain districts men were driven to eat human flesh. This country, accustomed to be governed autocratically, had no longer any government. In her supreme need, who was to save Russia? It was the people, by a movement similar to that which in France produced Joan of Arc; it was the people, in the largest acceptation of the word, including the honest nobility and the patriotic clergy. Already miraculous rumors showed the excitement that possessed all minds. At Nijni-Novgorod, at Vladimir, apparitions were seen. The monks of Troïtsa, with the hegumene Dionysius and treasurer-historian Palitsyne at their head, sent letters to all the Russian cities. The citizens of Kazan raised the distant Russia of the Kama. When the despatches from Troïtsa reached Nijni, and the protopope read them to the assembled people, a citizen of the town, the butcher Kouzma Minine, rose. "If we wish," he said "to save the Muscovite Empire, we must spare neither our lands nor our goods; let us sell our houses, and put our wives and children to service; let us seek a man who will fight for the orthodox faith, and march under his banner." To give up all, and to arm themselves, such was the word that was handed round. Minine and others gave the third of their possessions; one woman who had 12,000 roubles gave 10,000 of them. Those who hesitated to contribute had to do it by force. Minine only accepted the office of treasurer of the insurrection on condition that his fellow-citizens should place themselves absolutely at his discretion. A chief was necessary; the people saw that he must be a noble. Now at Starodoub lived Prince Dmitri Pojarski, still weak from wounds he had received in the revolt of Moscow. Minine went to seek him, and besought him to take the command of the army. Their preparations then began, and they fasted and prayed. Russia felt herself in a state of sin; she had taken and violated so many oaths—to Godounof, to his son Feodor, to Otrépief, to Chouïski, to Vladislas. Three days of fast were commanded. Everyone took part in it, even the infants at the breast. With the money collected they organized the *streltsi*, and equipped the *diéti-boyarskié*; but they refused to admit those impure elements which had imperilled the national cause. They would have none of the help of Margeret, the mercenary who had perjured himself so many times, nor of the pillaging and murdering Cossacks. They remembered the assassination of Lapounof.

With the army marched the bishops and monks; the holy images were borne at the head of the columns. This enthusiasm did not exclude political wisdom; they wished at least to secure the support of Sweden against Poland, so they amused de la Gardie by negotiating for the election of a Swedish prince. When the troops had completely assembled at Iaroslavl, they marched on Moscow. The Cossacks of Zaroutski and Troubetskoï were still encamped under its walls; but these two armies, though fighting for the same object, could not act together. An attempt to murder Pojarski had increased the mistrust of the men of the Don. When, however, the hetman Chodkiewitz tried to throw a detachment into Moscow, he was defeated on the left bank of the Moskowa by Pojarski, on the right bank by the Cossacks. It is true that the latter, at the decisive moment, refused to fight; it needed the prayers of Abraham Palitsyne to bring them into line, and the intervention of Minine and his troops to decide the victory. The Polish garrison of the Kremlin were then pressed so close that they were reduced to eat human flesh. They capitulated, on condition that they were to have their lives. They gave up their prisoners, among whom was young Michael Romanof.

The Kremlin and the Kitaï-gorod had opened their gates, when men learned that Sigismond was advancing to the help of the Polish garrison. It was too late. At the news of these events he had to retrace his steps; the devotion of the people of Russia had freed their country. This year of 1612 remained for long in the memory of the nation; and when the invasion of 1812 came to refresh their recollections, they raised on the Red Place a colossal monument to the two liberators, the butcher Minine and the Prince Pojarski.

Russia, once more herself, could proceed freely to the election of a Tzar. A great National Assembly gathered at Moscow. It was composed of the great ecclesiastical dignitaries, of delegates nominated by the nobles, by the *diéti-boyarskié*, the merchants, the towns and districts. The delegates had to be furnished with special powers. They all agreed they would have no stranger, neither Pole nor Swede. When it became a question of choosing among the Russians, scheming and rivalry commenced; but one name was pronounced which gained all the votes, that of Michael Romanof. He was elected not for his own sake, for he was only fifteen years old, but for that of his ancestors the Romanofs, and his father, the Metropolitan Philarete, then prisoner at Marienburg. The name of Romanof, of the kin of Ivan IV., was the highest expression of the national feeling (1613).

The new dynasty had better chances of stability than that of Godounof or that of Chouïski. There were no crimes to reproach it with; it had its origin in a national movement, it dated from the liberation, and had only glorious memories. No phantom, no recollection, no regret of the past, stood before it. The house of Ivan the Terrible had been the cause or the occasion of too much suffering to Russia; the false Dmitris had stifled the regrets for the true. The accession of the Romanofs coincided with a powerful awakening of patriotism, with the passion for unity, with universal longing for order and peace. Already they inspired the same devotion as the oldest dynasty. It is said that the Poles, on hearing of the election of Michael, sent armed men to seize him in Kostroma. A peasant, Ivan Soussanine, misled the Poles through deep woods in the darkness of the night, and died under their blows. This is the subject of the beautiful opera by Glinka, of 'Life for the Tzar.' The time of troubles had ended.

CHAPTER XIX.

THE ROMANOFS : MICHAEL FEODOROVITCH AND THE PATRIARCH PHILARETE (1613-1645).

Restorative measures—End of the Polish war—Relations with Europe—The States-general.

RESTORATIVE MEASURES—END OF THE POLISH WAR.

Russia had at last a sovereign, but she was in the situation in which Henry IV. found France at his accession. The great civil and foreign war was finished, but it had left everywhere its evil traces. Henry IV., when he became king, had been obliged to reconquer all his kingdom, province by province, town by town, half by arms and half by negotiations, to win it from chiefs of the bands, leaguers, great governors who had become independent, and foreigners. In the same way, in Russia, Zaroutski, leader of the Don Cossacks, ruled in Astrakhan, with Marina and the son she had borne to the brigand of Touchino ; the Polish partisan Lissovski ravaged the country of the southwest ; the Zaporogian Cossacks infested the regions of the Dwina: scarce a province but was a prey to some robber-band. No doubt the Poles had been expelled from the Kremlin as the Spaniards were expelled from reconquered Paris, but an offensive movement of the enemy might be expected ; moreover they still retained many places, notably the important town of Smolensk. Sweden had profited by the state of Russia to lay hands on the cities of Carelia and on Novgorod the Great. In the interior of the country, the towns and cities were in ruins, the population diminished and impoverished, and brigandage had become a habit. At the Court, the Russian lords had learned to disobey, and were not less turbulent than the Leaguers who surrounded Henry IV. What Russia needed was a reign of restoration.

Michael Romanof had not the genius of the restorer of France. He was almost a child, and the boyards turned his authority against himself : the silent and bloody intrigues that Ivan IV. had only restrained by capital punishment broke forth again, and the ferocious depravity of the nobles was the shame of Russia. Quiet men and foreigners regretted Ivan the Terrible. "Oh that God would open the eyes of the Tzar as he opened those of Ivan!" wrote a Dutchman at this time, "otherwise Muscovy is lost." Happily the good will of the nation was equal to every emergency. The day of the coronation the men-at-arms presented a request for pay, as their devastated fiefs no longer gave them any revenue. The Tzar and the clergy sent letters to the Russian towns to entreat them to help the State to pay the troops, and to aid her with men and money against the foes within and without. Zaroutski was the first who was attacked. The inhabitants of Astrakhan, outraged by his barbarities, had rebelled and imprisoned him in the Kremlin, whence he attempted to escape at the approach of the Russian voïevodes. He was captured, and condemned to be impaled; the son of the brigand of Touchino, in spite of his youth, was hung, and his mother, Marina the Pole, died in prison. By the advice of the clergy and the boyards, the Tzar tried to negotiate with Baloven, another brigand chief, who, by way of answer, attacked Moscow, but was defeated and his band destroyed. The people of the Dwina themselves executed justice on the Zaporogues. Lissovski was eagerly pursued by Pojarski, but this clever partisan outwitted all the efforts of the liberator. Peace with Poland had to be concluded before he could be quieted.

In 1615 a Congress assembled beneath the walls of Smolensk under the mediation of Erasmus Handelius, envoy of the Emperor of Germany. It was impossible to come to an understanding: the Poles refused to admit the election of Michael Romanof, and wished to recognize Vladislas as Tzar of Russia. "You might as well," said Handelius, "try to reconcile fire and water." The negotiations were broken off. With Sweden, however, they were more successful; here the mediators, England and Holland, showed more zeal and energy than the house of Austria had done. The troubles and the impoverished state of Muscovy reacted on their commerce. By pacifying the North, they hoped to re-open Russia to their merchants, and secure for themselves greater advantages.

In May 1614, Ouchakof and Zaborovski had been sent to ask help from Holland in men and money. The Dutch gave them a thousand gulden, but said that they had themselves only lately ended a great war, that they could give the Tzar no substantial aid, but would do their utmost to induce the King of Sweden to make peace. Alexis Ziousine had been despatched to London in June 1613; he was ordered to narrate all the excesses committed by the Poles in Moscow, and to say to King

James, "After the destruction of Moscow, the Lithuanians seized your merchants—Mark the Englishman, and all the others—took away all their wares, subjected them to a rigorous imprisonment, and ended by massacring them." If by chance he discovered that the English were aware that it was not the Poles, but the Cossacks and the lower classes who had put Mark to death and seized on the merchandise, he was to have other excuses ready. The Tzar entreated help in money to pay the men-at-arms, and not in soldiers, as he could give them no pay. They would think themselves happy if the King of England would send the Tzar money, provisions, powder, lead, sulphur, and other munitions, to the value of about 100,000 roubles; but would content themselves with 70,000 roubles' worth, or in case of absolute necessity with 50,000. James received the envoy and his suite courteously, informed them that he was aware of the wrongs the Poles and the Swedes had inflicted on them, and ordered them three times following to cover themselves. The Russians declined to do this. "When we see thy fraternal love and lively friendship for our sovereign, when we hear thy royal words which glorify our prince, and contemplate thine eyes thus close at hand, how can we, *kholopys* as we are, put our hats on our heads at such a moment?" In August 1614, the year following this embassy, there appeared at Moscow John Merrick, who had for long traded with the holy city, but who came this time as ambassador from James I., qualified with full powers, as prince, knight, and gentleman of the bedchamber. In an interview with Prince Ivan Kourakine he began by demanding, on the part of the English merchants, a direct communication with India by the Obi, and with Persia by the Volga and Astrakhan. Kourakine alleged that this route was unsafe, that Astrakhan had only lately been delivered from Zaroutski, and that numerous brigands still infested the Volga. When security should be established, they would open the question with King James. They then passed to the subject of mediation. John Merrick declared that the King of England had assembled his Parliament to consider the best means of helping the Tzar, but that the Parliament had as yet decided nothing, and that he had no instructions on this head. "But," said Kourakine, "can you not assure us that your sovereign will send us help in the spring?" "How can I guarantee it? The journey is long, and there is no way save that by Sweden. . . . . I believe, however, he will give you aid." Merrick, having contented himself with causing the Russians to hope, returned to commercial matters: liberty of trade by the Obi and the Volga, concessions of iron and jet mines on the Soukhona, concessions of territory about Vologda.

for new establishments, &c. The Russian boyards continued to expatiate on the difficulty of the situation, and John Merrick went to Novgorod to negotiate with the Swedes, where he was joined by the envoys of Holland. Gustavus Adolphus, King of Sweden, had obtained some successes over the voïevodes, but he had not contented the Novgorodians, nor been able to take Pskof. The kings of Denmark and Poland were his enemies, and he may have felt a presentiment of the splendid career that awaited him in Germany. He consented to open a congress, and in 1617 concluded with Russia the Peace of Stolbovo, by which he received an indemnity of 20,000 roubles, and kept Ivangorod, Iam Koporié, and Oréchek (Schlüsselburg), but ceded Novgorod, Roussa, Ladoga, and some smaller places.

Russia was now able to concentrate all her forces against her worst enemy—the instigator of all her troubles. The Poles took the offensive, under the command of Vladislas and the hetman Khodkévitch. Dorogobouge and Viasma were surrendered by the treachery or weakness of their voïevodes; but Mojaïsk and Kalouga (which was defended by Pojarski) resisted and arrested the progress of the enemy. Vladislas, who had all the instincts of a soldier, resolved in 1618 to march on Moscow. Michael Romanof dreaded treason more than the arms of the enemy, and determined to exact a new oath of allegiance from his subjects. He assembled the Estates, and informed them that he was ready once more to suffer hunger in besieged Moscow, and to fight Lithuania, but he asked in return that the nobles should do as much for him, and that they should resist the seductions of "the king's son." Everyone made the required promise, and fresh letters went out from Moscow, calling all the towns to a holy war. Vladislas, however, had stopped at Touchino, where the hetman of Little Russia, after having ravaged the frontiers of the south-west, had joined him with his Cossacks. The days of the second impostor and of Touchinism seemed to have come back. The Poles having been defeated in an attack on Moscow proposed a congress, which met at Devulino, not far from the Troïtsa monastery, lately the victim of a new siege. A truce of fourteen years and six months was agreed on. Poland kept Smolensk and Severia, and Vladislas did not even renounce the title of Tzar of Russia, leaving this difficulty to be solved by the judgment of God. Such a peace was only an armistice (1618); there was, however, an exchange of prisoners: the brave voïevode Cheïn and the Metropolitan Philarete returned to Russia, and the latter was at once made Patriarch.

By the return of his father the young Tzar obtained the counsellor his inexperience had hitherto needed, and even more than a counsellor—a colleague, and almost a master. Philarete was in some sort associated with the throne. The empire had two chief nobles, two sovereigns, the Tzar of all the Russias and the Patriarch of all the Russias. They figured together in all public acts, and together received the reports of the boyards and foreign ambassadors. It was time that a master was given to the boyards. The Soltykofs, Michael's favorites, had distributed the empire among their partisans, and plundered the treasury and the nation. They were charged with having falsely accused Michael's first bride, who was expelled from the palace, and having poisoned the second. This was a common practice with the nobles of Muscovy, those who were in favor fearing a new Tzarina above everything. They shrank from no means of removing her from their path; and their reputation on this head was so firmly established that the King of Denmark had refused Michael the hand of his niece, because, " in the reign of Boris Godounof, his brother, *fiancé* of the Princess Xenia, had been poisoned; and this would also be the fate of this young girl." Philarete made the boyards feel the weight of the Tzar's hand, and exiled the most guilty.

RELATIONS WITH EUROPE—THE STATES-GENERAL.

Russia had begun at last to be a European nation. Everywhere her political or commercial alliance was sought. Gustavus Adolphus, who was making preparations to play his part as the champion of Protestantism in Germany, wished to assure himself of the friendship of Russia against Poland. He represented to Michael, with much truth, that the Catholic League of the Pope, the King of Poland, and the house of Hapsburg were as dangerous to Russia as to Sweden; that if Protestantism succumbed it would be the turn of orthodoxy, and that the Swedish army was the outpost of Russian security. " When your neighbor's house is on fire," writes the King, " you must bring water and try to extinguish it, to guarantee your own safety. May your Tzarian majesty help your neighbors to protect yourself." The terrible events of late years had only too well justified these remarks. The intrigues of the Jesuits with the false Dmitri, and the burning of Moscow by the Poles, were always present to the memory of the Russians. A treaty of peace and commerce was concluded with Sweden, and a Swedish ambassador appeared at the Court.

England had rendered more than one service to Russia. In her pressing need James I. had lent her 20,000 roubles, and

British mediation had led to the Peace of Stolbovo. John Merrick considered he had the right to demand that Russia should open to English commerce the route to Persia by the Volga, and to Hindostan by Siberia. The Tzar consulted the merchants of Moscow. They unanimously replied that such a concession would be their ruin, for they could never hope to rival the wealthier and more enterprising English. They were, however, ready to sacrifice their interests to those of the empire, if the dues paid by the foreigners were essential to the treasury. John Merrick declined to pay any dues, and the negotiation was broken off. They paid him, however, the 20,000 roubles, as he assured them the King had need of them for the help of his son-in-law, the Elector Palatine.

In 1615 the Tzar sent an envoy into France, to announce to Louis XIII. his accession to the throne, and to ask his aid against Poland and Sweden. In 1629 there appeared at Moscow the ambassador Duguay Cormenin, who was commissioned to solicit for French commerce what had been refused to English trade—free passage into Persia. He also spoke of a political alliance. "His Tzarian majesty," he said, "is the head of Eastern countries and the orthodox faith; Louis. King of France, is the head of Southern countries; and the Tzar, by contracting a friendship and alliance with him, will get the better of his enemies. As the Emperor is closely allied to the King of Poland, the Tzar must be allied to the King of France. These two princes are everywhere glorious; they have no equals either in strength or power; their subjects obey them blindly, while the English and Brabançons are only obedient when they choose. The latter buy their wares in Spain, and sell them to the Russians at a high price, but the French will furnish them with everything at a reasonable rate." This negotiation for the first Franco-Russian treaty spoken of in history had no result. As to the route to Persia, it was refused by the boyards, who said that the French might buy the Persian merchandise from the Russians.

Another ally against Poland offered itself to Muscovy. The Sultan Osman sent to Moscow the Prince Thomas Cantacuzene, to announce that Turkey had already declared war against the king. The Russians asked no more than to help him, and Philarete and Michael assembled the States-general. The deputies "beat their foreheads" to the sovereigns, beseeching them to "hold themselves firm for the holy churches of God, for their Tzarian honor, and for their own country against the enemy. The men-at-arms were ready to fight, and the merchants to give money." The troops were already assembling when news was received that Turkey had been defeated, and war was postponed. The preparations had revealed certain faults existing in the national army, and it was decided to enlist foreign mercenaries, and instruct the native soldiers in Western tactics. Orders were accordingly given to buy arms, and to attract into Russia gun-founders and artillerymen. The Russia of Michael and Philarete already announced the Russia of Peter the Great; the era of reform had begun. Each day Muscovy strengthened herself against her European enemies, by turning against them the weapon of their own civilization.

She remained quiet for eight years. In 1632 Sigismond III. died, and the Elective Diet assembled at Warsaw. Michael was determined not to let this opportunity slip, and the second war with Poland began. It did not turn out as well as had been hoped. The vices of the old organization and institutions showed themselves anew. The two voïevodes commanding the army suddenly became possessed with the old mania of disputing precedence. They were deprived of their command, and replaced by Cheïn and Ismaïlof, who crossed the frontier with 32,000 men and 158 guns. Twenty-three towns surrendered to the Muscovites, but Smolensk held out for eight months, and, just as it showed signs of capitulating, the Polish army under Vladislas, now King of Poland, made its appearance. On the rumor of a Tatar invasion in the south, part of the Russian nobles at once hastened to the defence of their own lands, and Cheïn, thus enfeebled, was attacked by the king, and his communications cut. Famine obliged him to surrender in the open field, and he obtained leave to retreat, though forced to abandon both his baggage and his artillery. His only fault lay in not understanding as well as his Western adversaries the strategy of modern warfare. He was only guilty of being a Russian of unreformed Russia. His enemies, however, accused him of treason in a council of war, and he was condemned with his colleague to be beheaded. Philarete was no longer there to force the boyards to live at peace with each other. He died in 1633. Vladislas, successful at Smolensk, was defeated at Bielaïa, and a congress was held on the Polianka. The conditions of the truce of Devulino were confirmed. The Russians paid 20,000 roubles, and Vladislas renounced all claim to the throne of Moscow, and recognized for the first time the Tzarian title.

Shortly after there arose a new occasion for war. In spite of the treaties of peace concluded by Poland and Russia with Turkey, the Cossacks of the Dnieper, who were subjects of Poland, and the Cossacks of the Don, who were subjects of Russia, still continued to fight against Islam. To them, besides being a holy war, it was the means of procuring *zipouns*,—wide trousers of a beautiful scarlet cloth. Determined partisans and pirates, both on land and sea, they were thorns in the sides of the Khan of the Crimea and the Grand Turk, attacking with their light boats the heavy Ottoman galleys, and insulting the coasts of the Bosphorus and Anatolia. They were disavowed by their respective governments, and were the subjects of perpetual recrimination between the Porte and the two Slav States. They were the brigands and corsairs of Christianity, as the Tatars were of Islamism.

In 1627, 4400 Cossacks of the Don, aided by 1000 Zaporogues of the Dnieper, surprised Azof, and offered to make a gift of it to the Tzar of Moscow. The acquisition of such an important place, which would secure the command of the mouth of the Don and access to the Black Sea, was very tempting to Russia. Again Michael Romanof assembled his Estates. We must observe that since Ivan IV. first assembled them the meetings had become more and more frequent. The parliamentary history of Russia dates from the reign of "the Terrible." This time the nobles declared themselves ready to fight if they had money given them for their equipment, and begged the Tzar to exact it from the clergy and merchants. The latter alleged that the robberies of the public functionaries, the prolongation of the wars, and the rivalries with the Germans and Persians, had ruined them. The officers sent by the Tzar to Azof reported that it was in too bad a state for defence. In fact the conquest of Azof, like that of the Crimea in the time of Ivan, was premature, Russian colonization not having as yet extended itself sufficiently towards the South. The Tzar gave orders accordingly to the *Dontsi* for its evacuation, and they did not leave one stone upon another.

Western influence made considerable progress during this reign. The merchants entreated that access into the interior might be forbidden to those strangers whose rivalry was their ruin; but the latter were, on the contrary, so necessary to the State and to the general progress that they had to be invited into the country by all possible means. Under Michael, more foreigners than ever came into Russia. Vinius the Dutchman established foundries at Toula for guns, bullets, and other iron weapons. Marselein the German opened similar ones on the Vaga, the Kostroma, and the Cheksna. Privileges were granted to other foreign merchants or artisans, and the only condition imposed on them was not to conceal the secrets of their industries from the inhabitants of the countries. This is another point of resemblance between this reign of reform and that of Henri IV., who also summoned to his kingdom Flemish, English, and **Venetian** artisans. One European import did not however, find favor in Russia—the usage of tobacco was forbidden, and snuff-takers had their noses cut off.

Learned men were also sought from Europe. Adam Olearius of Holstein, a celebrated astronomer, geographer, and geometer, was invited to Moscow. Already the Academy of Sciences of Peter the Great was foreshadowed. A cosmographical treatise was translated from Latin into Russian. The Patriarch Philarete had established at Moscow an academy where Greek and Latin, the languages of the Renaissance, were taught. The Archimandrite Dionysius of Troïtsa, who had distinguished himself in the struggle with the Poles, undertook to correct the text of the Slavonian books—a hazardous enterprise, which cost Dionysius himself a short period of persecution. Native historians continued to re-edit their chronicles, and Abraham Palitsyne, cellarer of Troïtsa, narrated the famous siege of the convent.

CHAPTER XX.

WESTERN RUSSIA IN THE 17TH CENTURY.

The political union of Lublin (1509), and the religious union (1595)—Complaints of White Russia—Risings in Little Russia.

POLITICAL UNION OF LUBLIN (1509), AND THE RELIGIOUS UNION (1595).

SPAIN in the 16th century had taken a large share in the troubles of France; France in the 17th century dismembered the Spanish Empire. In like manner Poland expiated her part in the civil wars of Russia. After the reforming reign of Michael Romanof, his son Alexis was to inaugurate the era of reprisals. Russia had almost fallen before Poland, like France before Burgundy or Austria, but she grew strong at Poland's expense, and on the ruins of Poland founded her own greatness. A glance at the constitution of the Polish Empire will show us what internal difficulties prepared the way for the external enemy—the Muscovite, the *Moskal*, as he was called by the men of the West.

White Russia and Little Russia had been conquered by the Lithuanians, and formed with them part of the Polo-Lithuanian State. They kept for a long while Russian manners and habits. The Russian language was used in the acts of legislation till the 16th, and even till the 17th century. For a short time, under the early Jagellons, it had even been the language of the Court. Soon, however, Polish influence predominated in the ruling class. The Russo-Lithuanian nobility were divided, like the Polish nobility, into *magnates*, who possessed large territories and occupied the high offices, *schliachtas* or lesser nobles, who formed the retainers and almost the servants of the *magnates*. The military class assembled in the *diets* and *diétines*. The king's officers bore the titles of *voïevodes*, *castellans*, and *starosts*. The Russo-Lithuanian towns, like those of Poland, received what was called "the law of Magdeburg." They were governed by a *vogt* of the king, who administered justice, assisted by the *burgomaster* and by *rathmänner*. The trading classes organized themselves, after the German fashion, into *zėche*, tribes or corporations.

Up to that time Russo-Lithuania and Poland had formed two States, distinct in law; and at the extinction of the Jagellons, who had always maintained them in a personal union, it was feared they would again separate. Ivan IV. founded great hopes on this expected separation, but the Poles in the reign of Sigismond made a great effort to accomplish a definite union. A diet was held at Lublin. The Russo-Lithuanian aristocracy were much averse to the union; difference of religion, national self-love, and corporate interests created a barrier between them and Poland. The Government shrank from no means of overcoming their resistance. It threatened not to defend Lithuania against the incursions of the Tzar, and to resume the Crown lands held by the refractory nobles. Notwithstanding, the Polish party were almost checkmated; rather than yield, the Lithuanian deputies left the diet in a body. At last the king contrived to gain two of the most influential members—Constantine Ostrojski, voïevode of Kief, and Alexander Czartoryski, voïevode of Volhynia. Nicholas Radziwill, who had so long held the Polish tendencies in check, and who was the last representative of independent Lithuania, was dead. The king managed also to win over the Little Russian nobility, less hostile to Catholic Poland than the Protestant nobility of Lithuania. The *Union of Lublin* provided that the two crowns should be united on the same head, with equal rights; that there should be only one general diet and one senate; that they should sit at Warsaw, a Mazovian town, which was to become the capital of the new State; and that Poland and Lithuania should preserve each its great dignitaries—chancellor, vice-chancellor, marshals, and hetmans—their own army and their laws. The Russian countries, properly so called, underwent a fresh dismemberment. Little Russia was specially united to Poland.

The natural result of the Union of Lublin was the growth of Polish influence in the Russian territory. On one side, the Polish nobles had obtained the right of acquiring lands and holding offices in Lithuania; on the other, the Russian nobility, by mingling more completely with the nobility of the neighboring country, adopted its ideas, habits, fashions, and even its language. It began to be *Polonized*, thus widening the breach that separated it from the masses of the people, profoundly attached to their tongue and their nationality. The division between the aristocracy and the people increased still further, when the Catholic propaganda penetrated among the nobility of the Russian territory.

A special article of the Union of Lublin ensured respect to the orthodox religion. Poland and Lithuania had not, however, been able to escape from the great religious struggles that then divided Western Europe, and which sent a wave even into Poland. A certain number of lords had embraced Protestantism (Lutheranism, Calvinism, and Socinianism). The Jesuits, who were everywhere at the head of the reaction against reform, and whose hand may be traced in all the civil wars of the 16th and 17th centuries, soon made their appearance in Poland. Protestantism only took a feeble root in the country, and did not occupy them long; they then turned their attention to orthodoxy, the real national religion of the Russo-Lithuanian provinces. They employed the same means by which they had hitherto succeeded everywhere in Europe: founded colleges, obtained a hold on the young people, insinuated themselves into the confidence of the women, gained the ear of the kings, and reckoned yet more surely on their worldly cleverness than on the purely ecclesiastical means of preaching, confession, and pilgrimages. The brave Batory, who specially occupied himself with all that concerned the public peace and national greatness, kept them at a distance. They found a monarch more to their taste in Sigismond III., a feeble copy of the Philips of Spain and the Ferdinands of Austria, and well fitted to draw on the East the calamities that desolated Germany and the West. He protected the Jesuits, and exhausted all the influence and seductions that the throne put at his disposal, to convert the orthodox nobility of his oriental provinces to Catholicism. In order to enlarge the field of conversions, the Jesuits invented a compromise, which was to obtain from the Russian clergy and people their submission to the Holy See, while their Slavonic liturgy and special usages were guaranteed them; this is what is called the Union of the two Churches. In fact, the *union* once obtained, they thought it but a step to unity, and even uniformity. Peter Skarga the Jesuit, who published the book of 'The Unity of the Church of God,' wished to exclude the teaching of Slavonic, and only admit that of Greek and Latin. In order to make their plan more easily accepted by Government, they represented to it that the effect of their religious "union" would be consolidation of the political union of Lublin, and that a true Polish Estate would not exist till the subjects held the same faith as their prince.

Now orthodoxy, menaced by the King of Poland, found a powerful support in the Russian princes descended from Rurik and Gedimin. We have seen Prince Kourbski, in the time of Ivan IV., and later, Constantine Ostrojski, defend by their pen, their word and their influence, the faith of their fathers, and translate, compile, and disseminate books in favor of orthodoxy. Little by little the nobles yielded to the influence of the Court; in their struggle with the Roman religion, the people saw themselves abandoned almost entirely by their natural chiefs, and even by their bishops. The king filled the Lithuanian sees with prelates who were great princes, wholly indifferent to theological questions, and proud of their immense riches, of their numerous villages, and their strong castles bristling with artillery. Still the people did not give up all hope. From Novgorod the Great, from Pskof, from Germany, the principle of association had spread widely among the cities of Western Russia. Societies were formed for mutual assistance, which had their roots in the most distant Slavonic, German, or Scandinavian past; they were at the same time religious confraternities, and took an energetic part in the strife with the Jesuits. They had their elected chiefs, their common treasury, and they began to found schools, to set up printing-presses, and to disseminate polemical or pious books. They entered into mutual relations, and formed ties with the patriarchs of the East; to the royal bishops they opposed a democratic force, watching them, reprimanding them, and denouncing the carelessness of their religion or manners to orthodox Christendom. The most celebrated of these confraternities were those of Lemberg in Gallicia, of Wilna in Lithuania, and of Loutsk in Volhynia; that of Kief founded the great ecclesiastical academy of Little Russia.

Under the stimulus of these popular societies, the bishops could no longer remain indifferent. It was necessary to take up a position at the head of the believers, or pass over to the ranks of the enemy. The orthodox prelates were in a very difficult position; they were in disgrace with the Government as the defenders of orthodoxy, and at the same time were harassed as lukewarm by the orthodox demagogy. Terletski, Bishop of Loutsk, was in this trying situation—the *starost* of Loutsk, a convert to Catholicism, directed a fierce persecution against his ancient bishop. Terletski was taken, imprisoned, and starved in his dungeon; he complained, but an orthodox bishop could expect no justice. He saw only one means of escaping from this humiliation, to disarm the violence of the Catholic nobles, and to enjoy in peace his episcopal revenues: this was to pass over to the Union. His neighbor, Ignatius Potieï, Bishop of Vladimir in Volhynia, and Michael Ragoza, Metropolitan of Kief, Primate of Western Russia, who was discontented with the Patriarch of Constantinople, followed his example. Sigismond III. received these first defections with joy; Terletski and Potieï

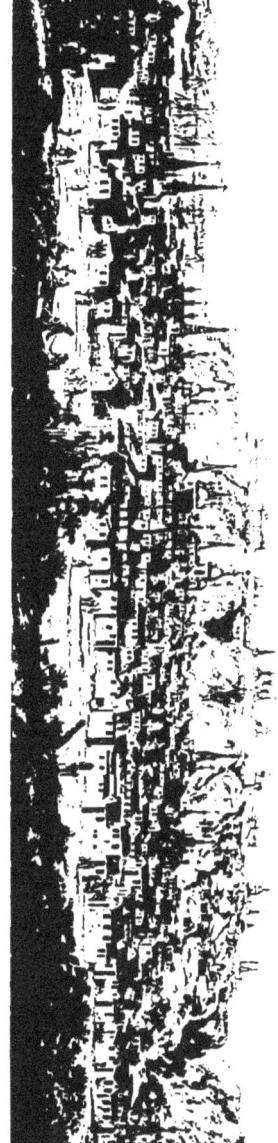

CITY OF TOBOLSK

Russia, vol. one.

left for Rome ; and placed the Russian Church at the feet of Clement VIII. The Pope celebrated this success by pompous solemnities(1595); but the projected union could not be realized without the consent of all the Russian bishops, of whom only three, the Metropolitan and the two Volhynians, were as yet gained over. Balaba, Bishop of Lemberg—who, although he was always at war with the confraternity, had not sacrificed the national cause to his private enmity—remained with a layman, Constantine Ostrojski, the soul of orthodoxy. A council was held at Brest, in Lithuania (1596), under the presidency of Nicephorus, envoy of the Patriarch of Constantinople. The three dissidents refused to attend. Then the bishops formulated the anathema and the sentence of deposition. The Uniates hastened to retaliate by an excommunication, but their attempt in favor of the cause of Rome failed piteously. The people everywhere declared against them. At Wilna Bishop Potieï was assassinated by the citizens. At Vitepsk, Bishop Kountsévitch, who, from a renegade, had become a persecutor, gave occasion for a terrible riot; he was stabbed and thrown into the Dwina. Many of the citizens were punished, and the city deprived of "the law of Magdeburg." The Uniates fished out of the Dwina the body of the prelate, and his tomb shortly became famous for its reputed miracles. At Kief, Veniamine Routski, a successor of Ragoza, re-organized the convents on the model of Latin monasteries: the monks took the name of Basilians. They did not gain in popularity. A Little Russian saying attributes to them the following catechism :—" Wherefore did God create thee and put thee in the world?" "To do the seigneurs' dirty work."

The Eastern Church did not allow itself to be defeated so easily as the Jesuits had hoped. It opposed schools with schools, propaganda with propaganda ; it preached and it printed. The Uniate Routski was replaced even at Kief by Peter Mohila, a zealous partisan of orthodoxy. He was a rough prelate, such as was needed in those hard times, and an old soldier, ready to meet force with force. A monastery of the diocese resisted his authority ; he marched to it instantly with troops and guns, and chastised the rebels. He made the school founded by the confraternity into a college, like those of the Jesuits; instituted professors of Latin, Greek, and philosophy, and made it the intellectual centre of Western Russia, and one of the points of departure of the Russian Renaissance (1633).

COMPLAINTS OF WHITE RUSSIA—RISINGS IN LITTLE RUSSIA.

In the diets of Warsaw, the complaints of the orthodox clergy, and of the country people, more completely enslaved, more cruelly oppressed since they no longer held the religion of their masters, did not remain without an echo. A deputy from Volhynia, Lawrence Drevninski, exclaimed at the Diet of 1620: "When your Majesty makes war on Turkey, from whom do you obtain the greater part of your troops? From the Russian nation, which holds the orthodox faith; from that nation which, if it does not receive relief from its sufferings and an answer to its prayers, can no longer continue to make itself a rampart for your kingdom. How can you beg it to sacrifice all to secure for the country the blessings of peace, when in its homes there is no peace? Everyone sees clearly the persecutions that the old Russian nation suffers for its religion. In the large towns our churches are sealed up, and our goods are pillaged; from the monasteries the monks have departed, and cattle are shut up in them. Children die without baptism; the ashes of the dead, deprived of the prayers of the Church, are carried out of the city like dead beasts; men and women live together without the benediction of the priest; they die without confession, without communion. Is not this to offend God himself, and will not God avenge His people? At Lemberg no one, not a Uniate, can live in the city, trade freely, and enter into the *zèche* of artisans. . . . For twenty years in each *diétine*, in each diet, we have asked for our rights and liberties with bitter tears, and for twenty years we have not been able to obtain them. We shall have to cry with the prophet, 'O God, judge me, and judge my actions.'" The situation of the serfs had become specially intolerable: to the Polish or Polonized lord, to the Latin missionary, was added a third scourge, the Jew, whom the noble had made steward of his lands, and to whom he had given the right of life and death over his subjects, and farmed out the fishing and hunting, the roads and taverns, even the orthodox Church, so completely, that the peasant could neither marry nor baptize his child without having bought from this miscreant the access to the sanctuary.

The populations of White Russia had suffered, and were still to suffer long, without rebellion. It was not the same with the Little Russian populations of the Ukraine. They had colonized the steppes of the south, and reconquered the desert from the Tatars. To attract emigrants to fill the royal grants, the Polish lords offered twenty or thirty years of absolute liberty. Thanks to this, the desert was peopled with unheard-of rapidity, and on this virgin soil a nation was formed, ignorant of slavery, that spoke not of thirty years' liberty, but perpetual freedom. The King of Poland favored this race of hardy pioneers—these intrepid soldiers. The Ukraine was for him a sort of military frontier, a strong rampart for Poland against the Tatar and the Turk.

These warlike populations were organized in twenty *polks* of Cossack—those of Peréiaslaf, Tcherkask, Mirgorod, Pultowa, &c. Each *polk* had its *polkovnik* or colonel; all obeyed one supreme chief, the *hetman* of Little Russia nominated by the king, who presided over the *starchina* * or council of elders. In time the Cossacks became formidable to Poland herself; they incessantly embroiled her with her formidable neighbor, the Ottoman Empire. Batory was forced to punish with death more than one Cossack chief for having violated a truce or a treaty of peace, and he also limited the number of the military population, only recognizing as Cossacks those who were inscribed on the register, to the number of six thousand, condemning the others to the cultivation of the soil: that is, to serfage. But the Cossacks would have nothing to do with the *corvée* of the *pans*, nor admit the limitations of the king. Notwithstanding the register, they remained in arms, a formidable force, who in the religious struggle were all enlisted on the side of orthodoxy, and who caused royalty and the Uniate hierarchy and aristocracy to tremble.

Besides the Cossacks of the sedentary populations or the Cossacks of the towns, there were also the Zaporogues "beyond the *porogs*" or cataracts of the Dnieper. They stood in the same relation to the Little Russian Cossacks as those did to the Russo-Lithuanian population; they were the vanguard of the vanguard, the forlorn hope of the Russian nationality. Entrenched in the "Large Meadow," a fortified island of the Dnieper, they had built a fort or *setcha* surrounded by a palisade. They recognized no authority; like the Knights of Rhodes and Malta, they encamped on the land wrested from the Mussulmans, and continued the holy war with Turk and Tatar, when Christendom was at peace with him. They neither gave nor asked quarter, existed on the plunder of the infidel, courted dangers and "martyrdom," and received no women in their camp. They

---

* The *starchina* was composed of the *oboznvi*, the head of the baggage department; of the judge; of the *pisar*, or chancellor; of the *esaoul*; of the standard-bearer; of the *polkovniks*; of the *stoniks*, or centurions; of the *atamans*. When the king invested the *hetman*, he handed to him the *boundchouk* (or banner), like a horse's tail, the stick or mace, and the seal.

were a race of warrior-monks, a Church militant, the **Templars** and Hospitallers of the Dnieper. More than one Polish noble of high rank came to join them in their life of adventure and heroic poverty, and learnt from them lessons of courage and chivalry. All were equal, all brothers, and ate like the Spartans at a common table ; the offices of the *ataman* of the *camp*, and of the ten *atamans* of the *kourenes*, were obtained by election. In close union with the Cossacks of the Don, they were on land and sea the scourge of Islamism—the Barbary Christians of the Black Sea.

The ill-feeling between the aristocratic government of Poland and the orthodox population of Little Russia continued to increase. When the Polish nobles wished to treat the free husbandmen as serfs, they deserted in crowds to the countries of the Ukraine ; the boldest went to reinforce the hordes of the Dnieper Cossacks, or the *setcha* of the Zaporogues. The *Kobzars* (blind bards) hastened from village to village, singing the song of the *parvada* (justice) : " In this world there is no justice, justice is not to be found here ; now justice lives under the laws of injustice. To-day justice is imprisoned by the nobles ; injustice is seated at her ease by the *pans* in the hall of honor. To-day justice stands near the threshold, and injustice is throned with the *pans*, and hydromel is poured out into cups for injustice. O justice ! our mother with the wings of an eagle, where shall we find thee ? May God send the man who will perform justice —days of prosperity." These wandering poets sang so persistently, that the villages were emptied for the benefit of the Cossack camps, and justice ended by spreading her " eagle's wings," and the men " who were to perform justice " showed themselves openly.

The orthodox religion persecuted by the Uniates, the threatened serfage, the insolence of the nobles, the robberies of the Jews, the register and its limitation, gave rise in the 16th and 17th centuries to a series of revolts, in which the Zaporogues, zealous adherents of orthodoxy, in spite of their brigandage, played a great part. Specially distinguished among the Cossack chiefs were Nalivaïko, Pavliouk, Ostranitsa, and many others, whose memory has been retained by the wandering singers of the Ukraine. The Government wished after each victory to give satisfaction to the Little Russians, but their authority was not sufficient to restrain either the exigencies of the *pans* or the intolerance of the Jesuits. To the horrible atrocities perpetrated on the insurgents, the latter retaliated at each insurrection by atrocities still greater. Each time the Government was **victorious, and after each defeat the yoke** pressed more heavily on Little Russia. From these successes sprang a new danger for Poland. The eyes of the oppressed turned towards an orthodox sovereign—the Tzar of Russia ; the democratic populations of the Ukraine surmounted their repugnance to authority, on seeing the anarchic violence produced by Polish liberties. The Cossacks imagined they could conquer if they had an ally, and this ally was only to be found at Moscow.

CHAPTER XXI.

ALEXIS MIKHAILOVITCH (1645-1676) AND HIS SON FEODOR.

Early years of Alexis—Seditions—Khmelnitski—Conquest of Smolensk and the Eastern Ukraine—Stenko Razine—Ecclesiastical reforms of Nicon—The precursors of Peter the Great—Reign of Feodor Alexiévitch (1676-1682)

EARLY YEARS OF ALEXIS—SEDITIONS.

THE reign of Alexis Mikhaïlovitch may be summed up in three facts : the reaction against Poland and the union with Little Russia ; the struggle between the empire and the Cossacks ; the first attempt at religious reform, and the growth of European influence.

The new Tzar, the son of Michael and Eudoxia Strechnef, was good and easy, like his father. In his most violent rages, say the contemporary writers, he never allowed himself to go beyond kicks and cuffs. Though his mind was quicker than his father's, he gave himself up to anyone who took the trouble to influence him, even to the point of permitting himself to be ruled entirely; unlike Ivan the Terrible, who, as we have seen, never long retained the same favorites. The extreme good-nature of the prince towards his relations had grave consequences. The people were oppressed with impunity, and were allowed to make no complaint. Alexis gave all his confidence to the boyard Morozof, who had taken charge of his education, and for thirty years had never left him. Morozof was proud, ambitious, and unscrupulous ; but learned, intelligent, and full of *finesse*. He excelled above all in disentangling the diplomatic complications bequeathed to him by the last reign. When Alexis was about to marry, Morozof did not disturb himself at seeing the young bride, Maria Ilinitchna Miloslavski, arrive with a whole new dynasty of relations and " men of the time." Instead of conspiring, as was usual, against the health or beauty of the Tzarina, he preferred to associate her family with his power, and take from them a surety. He married a sister of Maria Ilinitchna, and became the brother-in-law of his sovereign. He thus added to the old title of favorite the new one of a kinsman by his wife and was strengthened in his power instead of being ejected from it. His influence with his master was greater than Richelieu's with Louis XIII., and he had the honor of beginning the revenge for the civil wars—the war with Poland.

Affairs in the interior were always too complicated for Alexis to be able to act very energetically in his relations with foreign Powers. The Russian people in the " time of the troubles " had unlearnt the passive and resigned obedience that had formerly distinguished them; they knew no longer how to suffer uncomplainingly, and complaint soon led to revolt. We must also recognize the fact that they suffered more than formerly. Russia had come exhausted out of her civil wars, her agriculture and commerce were ruined, and her population diminished by emigrations and flight into the Cossack country. The state, which already began to feel the heavy expenses of a modern empire, which had to keep up an army, foreign troops, all the machinery of war, diplomacy, and an administration, saw itself forced to increase the taxes, which fell more heavily than ever on the thinned population. The Russian Government united the vices of the past with those of modern times; the corruption of its agents, the impunity of the favorites and their creatures, and the defective organization of justice, tried to the utmost the diminished patience of the people.

The year 1648, which saw the breaking-out of the Fronde in France, witnessed a terrible revolt in Moscow. The Tzar, powerless to stem the torrent, had to deliver the judge Plechtchéef over to the people, who dealt him summary justice. They then demanded the *okolnitchii* Trakhaniotes, who was likewise handed over to them; finally, their fury turned against Morozof, but the Tzar aided his brother-in-law to escape and take refuge in the convent of St. Cyril, whence he emerged quietly, like another Mazarin, when the public emotion was appeased. At Pskof the people rose on pretence that the Government had given money and corn to the *Niemtsi* (Germans)—that is, the Swedes—in accordance with the last treaty with this Power. Nummens, the Swede, was maltreated and imprisoned by the populace; the voïevode and the Prince Volkonski, envoy of Moscow, expected to be put to death, and Archbishop Macarius was twice put in chains. From Pskof the revolt spread to Novgorod, where the Danish ambassador was attacked by the people, and left for dead in the streets. Archbishop Nicon, who tried to quell the rebellion by spiritual arms, was met by blows, and the *streltsi* made common cause with the people. Novgorod only submitted at the approach of Prince Khovanski at the head of his troops. These troops were insufficient for the reduction of Pskof, which, behind her tried ramparts, prepared to resist the Muscovites, as she had resisted the Poles. The Pskovians made many successful sorties, and only capitulated under the promise of a general amnesty. Khovanski's troops were too few to enable him to refuse their conditions, and it was time to turn against external enemies the spirit of turbulence that the civil war had left in the masses.

Happily for Russia, Poland was still more profoundly agitated, and a revolt more considerable than those of Moscow, Pskof, or Novgorod, was to open to the Muscovite armies the entrance into the Ukraine.

KHMELNITSKI—CONQUEST OF SMOLENSK AND THE EASTERN UKRAINE—STENKO RAZINE.

We have seen that Little Russia, after many partial risings, only awaited a chief to break out into a general insurrection. This chief was found in Bogdan Khmelnitski,—a brave, clever, energetic, and even educated Cossack. He was owner of Soubbotovo, near Tchigirine, and had been ill-treated and imprisoned by one of his neighbors, the Pole Tchaplinski, who also seized on Khmelnitski's son, a boy of ten years, and had him whipped in the public streets by his men. Khmelnitski could obtain no redress, either for himself or for his countrymen, against the Jews and the taxes. King Vladislas is said to have told him that the senators would not obey him, and, drawing a sword on paper, he handed it to Bogdan, observing, "This is the sign royal: if you have arms at your sides, resist those who insult and rob you; revenge your wrongs with your swords, and when the time comes you will help me against the pagans and the rebels of my kingdom." In the Polish anarchy of that date it is quite possible that the king may have held this language, and himself placed the sword in the hands of those whom he could not protect. Vladislas acknowledged Bogdan ataman of the Zaporogues, and in return Bogdan promised him the following year a body of 12,000 men.

Konetspolski, the gonfalonier of the Crown, and Potoçki, tried to get rid of Bogdan, but he fled to the Zaporogues, and then passed over to the Khan of the Crimea, and returned to the heroes of the Dnieper with a Mussulman army. To Tatars and Zaporogues were soon added all the malcontents of Little Russia. Cossacks and people were alike determined to finish with it. Bogdan defeated the Polish generals Potoçki and

Kalinovski; first at the "Yellow Waters," where the registered Cossacks abandoned the Polish banners after having stabbed their hetman Barabbas, and then at Korsoun, where the Poles lost 8000 men and 41 guns. The two generals fell into the hands of Bogdan, who delivered them up to the Khan of the Crimea. This double victory was the signal of a general insurrection. The orthodox clergy everywhere preached a crusade against the Jesuits and Uniates, and everywhere the peasants rose against the Polish or Polonized *pans*. The castles were demolished, the governors put to death. The Jews were in a sad strait. According to a popular song they only asked one thing—to be allowed "to escape in their shirts beyond the Vistula, abandoning their wealth to the Cossacks, and promising to teach their children to live honestly, and to covet no more the land of the Ukraine" (1648).

At this critical moment for Poland. King Vladislas died, and the Diet met at Warsaw for the new election, with all its accustomed turbulence. At this news the revolt in Little Russia increased. Wherever the nobles could defend themselves they gave back cruelty for cruelty. Jeremiah Vichnevetski, a powerful Polonized Russian lord, took a town belonging to him by assault, and exercised the most horrible reprisals. "Make them suffer," he cried to the executioners, "they must be made to feel death;" and his Cossack prisoners were impaled. The Cossacks, who in the absence of a king expected justice from no one, broke out more violently than ever. Khmelnitski pursued his course of success; he defeated the Poles near Pilava, and penetrated into Gallicia as far as Lemberg, a rich, half-Jewish city, which had to pay a war indemnity. He was besieging Podmostié when he learned that John Casimir was elected in the place of his brother Vladislas. The new king at once sent envoys to negotiate his submission. The commissioners promised him satisfaction for his own grievances and those of the Cossacks on condition that the insurgents were abandoned to them. "Let the peasants return to their ploughs, and the Cossacks alone bear arms," said the Poles. Bogdan could neither abandon the Cossacks, who would not hear of the register, nor the country people, whose revolt had given him the victory, to be again placed, as was proposed, under the yoke of the *pans*. "The time for negotiations is past," he said to the commissioners; "I must free the whole Russian nation from the yoke of the Poles. At first I took up arms for my own injuries—now I fight for the true faith. The people will stand by me as far as Lublin, as far as Cracow; I will not betray them." The war continued, and Bogdan summoned the Khan of the

Crimea to his aid, and marched to meet the Polish army, commanded by the king in person. John Casimir found himself at Zborovo surrounded by the innumerable cavalry of the enemy. It would have been all over with him had he not purchased the defection of the Khan of the Crimea by a large sum, and the promise of an annual tribute. The Khan then retired, recommending his ally to the clemency of the king. Khmelnitski was driven to treat; the register was re-established, but the number of Cossacks enrolled was raised to 40,000; Bogdan was recognized hetman of Little Russia, and the town of Tchigirine assigned to him as a residence. It was agreed that there should be neither Crown troops nor Jews in the localities inhabited by the Cossacks, and no Jesuits where orthodox schools existed. The Metropolitan of Kief was to have a seat in the senate of Warsaw.

What Bogdan had foreseen when he refused to treat really happened; the treaty could not be executed. The number of fighting men who had taken part in the election exceeded 40,000 —were those in excess to be relegated to the work of the fields, to the seignorial *corvée?* The people had helped the Cossacks, were they then to be surrendered to their *pans?* Bogdan soon found himself involved in inextricable difficulties: on one side he violated the treaty by enrolling more than 40,000 men in his register; on the other hand, if he executed it, he would have to begin by inflicting death on the rebels. He wore out his popularity in performing this ungrateful task. He preferred to take up arms, accusing the Poles of having broken certain clauses of the treaty. This war was less successful than the first; the Khan of the Crimea, who a second time came to the aid of the Cossacks, a second time betrayed them, and the Cossacks were beaten at Berestechtko. The conditions of the Peace of the White Church (*Belaïa Tcherkof*) were more severe than those of the first peace. The number of registered Cossacks was reduced to 20,000; and 20,000 more, thus finding themselves excluded from the army, were thrown back upon the people. The greater part chose rather to emigrate to Russian soil, to wander to the Don, or to live by brigandage on the Volga.

A peace such as this was only a truce, and the Cossacks were certain to break it as soon as they could find an ally. Bogdan wrote to entreat the Tzar to take Little Russia under his protection. The Government of Alexis had sought for some time a pretext for rupture with Poland. The Polish Government, in writing to the Tzar, had not used the full royal title. Moscow never missed an opportunity for remonstrance; Warsaw assured them that it was pure inadvertence. "Then," said the

Russians, "an example must be made of the guilty." No example was made, and the diminution of title was used at every interchange of notes. The Court of Russia kept up this *casus belli*, waiting for a moment to profit by it ; this was found in the appeal of Khmelnitski. The Estates were convoked, and to them were reported the repeated insults to his Tzarian Majesty, and the persecution of the true faith in Little Russia. It was added, that the Little Russians, if repulsed by the Tzar, would have to place themselves under the protection of the Sultan. On this occasion the Estates declared for war. Alexis sent the boyard Boutourline to receive the oath of the hetman, the army, and the people of Little Russia.

It was time that the Tzar decided. Bogdan, betrayed a third time by the Khan, had been defeated at Ivanetz on the Dniester, but on the receipt of the news from Moscow he called the General Assembly at Peréiaslavl to announce to them the fact. "Noble colonels ; *esaouls*, and centurions, and you army of Zaporogues, and you orthodox Christians," cried the hetman, "you see it is no longer possible to live without a prince. Now we have four to choose from : the Sultan of Turkey, the Khan of the Crimea, the King of Poland, and the Tzar of orthodox Great Russia, whom for six years we have not ceased to entreat to become our Tzar and lord. The Sultan is a Mussulman ; we know what our brethren the orthodox Greeks suffered at his hands. The Khan is also a Mussulman, and our alliances with him have brought us nothing but trouble. It is needless to remind you of what the Polish *pans* have made us endure. But the Christian and orthodox Tzar is of the same religion as ourselves. We shall not find a better support than his. Whoever thinks otherwise may go where he likes—the way is open." The air rang with applause, the oath demanded by Boutourline was taken, and an embassy set out for Moscow, to ask the maintenance of Ukranian liberties. The Tzar freely granted all their conditions : the army was to be raised permanently to the number of 60,000 ; the Cossacks were to elect their hetman ; the rights of the *schliachta* and the towns were to be maintained ; the administration of the towns and the imposition of taxes were to be entrusted to the natives ; the hetman was to have the right of receiving foreign ambassadors, but was to signify the fact to the Tzar ; and he was forbidden, without special leave, to receive the envoys of Turkey and Poland.

In May 1654 the Tzar Alexis solemnly announced in the *Ouspienski Sobor* that he had resolved to march in person against his enemy the King of Poland. He commanded that in this campaign no occasion should be given for the generals to dispute precedence. The Polish voïevodes affirm that on this occasion "Moscow made war in quite a new way, and conquered the people by the clemency and gentleness of the Tzar." This humanity, so well timed in a war of deliverance, contributed greatly to the success of the Muscovites. Polotsk, Mohilef, and all the towns of White Russia opened their gates one after the other, and Smolensk only resisted five weeks (1654). The following year the Prince Tcherkasski defeated the hetman Radziwill and began the conquest of Lithuania proper; Wilna, the capital, Grodno, and Kobno, fell successively. During this time Khmelnitski and the Muscovites invaded Southern Poland and took Lublin. All the East resounded with the Russian victories: it was said at Moscow that the Greeks prayed for the Tzar and refused obedience to any but an orthodox emperor, and that the Hospodars of Wallachia and Moldavia implored Alexis to take them under his protection.

Poland seemed reduced to the last extremity; and there was still a third enemy to fall on her. Charles X., King of Sweden, arrived and captured Posen, Warsaw, and Cracow, the three Polish capitals. This conflict of ambitions was, however, the salvation of the *pospolite;* the Swede threatened the Russian conquests, and claimed Lithuania. He entered into relations with Khmelnitski, who forgot the oath he had taken; it was Charles XII, and Mazeppa enacted half a century before. The Tzar Alexis feared he had only shaken Poland to strengthen Sweden, and would not risk the reunion of these two formidable monarchies under the same sceptre. He hastened to negotiate with the Poles, who promised to elect him after the death of their present king; then he turned his arms against Sweden. The latter was the heir on the Baltic of the Livonian Order. Alexis trod in the steps of Ivan the Terrible; like him, his successes were rapid, but they as rapidly evaporated in smoke. He took Dünaburg and Kokenhusen, two old castles of the Knights; but the Russians besieged Riga in vain, and succeeded no better at Oréchek or Kexholm. The occupation of Dorpat terminated the first campaign (1656); after that, hostilities languished, and Alexis concluded a truce of twenty years, which secured him Dorpat and a part of his conquests. The affairs of Poland and Little Russia became, however, so terribly complicated, that the truce became the Peace of Cardis, by which Alexis abandoned all Livonia (1661).

The hetman Khmelnitski had more than once given his new sovereign cause for discontent. In spite of his oath, he had negotiated with Sweden and Poland. In fact, now that he had got rid of his former master, he did not want to become the vassal of a new sovereign, but to create a third Slav State between Poland and Russia, and to remain its independent sovereign. This hope was shared by the Cossacks. They had revolted against Poland because the king was weak and could not make himself respected by the aristocracy; they feared the Tzar of Muscovy would be only too strong. All government. all authority, was a burden to the free Cossack.

Bogdan, however, kept up the appearances of submission. His death was the signal of disorder. Vygovski, chancellor of the Cossack army, took the mace of the hetman, but Martin Pouchkar, the *polkovnik* of Pultowa, and the Zaporogues, refused to recognize him. Vygovski, Pouchkar, and the Zaporogue ataman denounced each other at Moscow. Vygovski caused Pouchkar to be assassinated, and made advances to Poland, to secure himself an ally against the Tzar; he also applied to the Khan of the Crimea, and defeated Prince Troubetskoï at Konotop; but after the retreat of the Khan, the majority of the Cossacks declared for Moscow, and obliged the rebel to fly to Poland. George Khmelnitski, son of the liberator, was elected hetman.

The troubles of Little Russia revived the courage of the Poles. They succeeded in expelling the Swedes, and refused to execute the treaty of Moscow. The war recommenced, and the Russians were unfortunate. The very extremity of their misfortunes seemed to have bound the Poles together. After some slight successes, one Russian army was defeated at Polonka by the voïevode Tcharnetski, the conqueror of the Swedes; another, commanded by the boyard Cheremetief and the hetman George Khmelnitski, allowed itself to be surrounded near Tchoudnovo by the Tatars and Poles, and being deserted by the Cossacks, was forced to lay down its arms. In the north they lost Wilna and the whole of Lithuania.

Khmelnitski, had become a monk. Teteria, his successor, had done homage to the king; but the country on the left bank of the Dnieper refused to recognize him as hetman, and elected Brioukhovetski, who was devoted to Russia. John Casimir crossed the river, and was on the point of reconquering the whole Ukraine; but having been repulsed at the siege of Gloukhof, he lost all his best troops through hunger and cold in the steppes of the desert. The two empires were exhausted by a war which had already lasted ten years. The whole of Poland had been overrun by Swedes, Russians, and Cossacks. Russia had no longer money with which to pay her army, and she had recourse to a forced currency, by which a bronze coinage was given the fictitious value of silver. Everywhere were heard bitter complaints of the famine. At Moscow a riot broke out against the Miloslavskis, the kinsmen of the Tzarina, and the multitude marched to the palace of Kolomenskoé to drag them out by force. The soldiers had to fire on the rebels, and 7000 of them were killed or taken.

Notwithstanding all this, neither the Poles nor the Russians would lay down arms without being assured the possession of all that they had conquered with so many sacrifices. Poland was now attacked by two new misfortunes—the revolt of Prince Lubomirski, who had some grievance against the queen, and the death of Teteria, whose successor, Dorochenko, went over to the Sultan, and by so doing involved the Government in a war with both Turks and Tatars. It was necessary to treat with Russia, and a thirteen years' truce was concluded at Androussovo. Alexis renounced Lithuania, but kept Smolensk and Kief on the right bank of the Dnieper, and all the Little Russian left bank (1667).

The treaty with Poland did not give peace to Little Russia. Neither the Dnieper Cossacks nor the Don Cossacks could exist under the obedience and regularity essential to a modern State. The more Russia became civilized and centralized, the more she became separated from the men of the Steppe; the further the frontier of this civilized Russia advanced to the South, the nearer approached the inevitable conflict. The reign of Alexis, troubled at first by the revolts of the Muscovite cities, was now vexed by the revolts of the Cossacks.

The hetman Brioukhovetski was a devoted adherent of Russia, but he was surrounded by many malcontents. As usual, the people had not got all they had hoped by the revolution; he saw, however, in the absolute authority of the Tzar, a bulwark against the Little Russian oligarchy of the *starchina* and the *polkovniks*, and against the turbulence of the Cossacks. "God," he said to the latter, "has delivered us from you; you can no longer pillage and devastate our houses." The Cossacks and the *starchina*, or in other words, the military and aristocratic party, were still more displeased to see the Muscovite voïevodes establish themselves in the towns. The Republic of the Zaporogues already feared that it had given itself a master. Methodius, Metropolitan of Kief, encouraged the resistance of a party of the clergy who wished to remain subject to the Patriarch of Constantinople, and not to be transferred to the Patriarch of Moscow. It was Methodius who organized the rebellion; he made advances to the hetman, who opened a negotiation with Dorochenko, the ataman of the right bank, who promised to resign his office and to recognize as chief of Little Russia the man who would deliver her. The weak Brioukhovetski allowed himself to be persuaded, and at the Assembly of Gadatch, in 1668, it was decided to revolt against the Tzar, and to take the oath to the Sultan, as the men of the right bank had already done. Two voïevodes and 120 Muscovites were put to death. A short time after, Brioukhovetski was slain by order of Dorochenko, who became hetman of both banks. But of the two parties which divided Little Russia, the party of independence or the Polish and Turkish Party, and the party of Moscow, the latter was predominant on the left bank. It did not hesitate to make terms with the Tzar, and, at the price of a few concessions, a second time submitted to him entirely. Mnogogrechnyi, the new hetman, took up his abode at Batourine.

The right bank had no reason to pride itself on the policy to which it was committed by Dorochenko. It became the theatre of a terrible war between Turkey and Poland, and was cruelly ravaged by Mahomet IV. Abandoned for a moment by the weak King Michael Vichnevetski, it was conquered by his energetic successor, John Sobieski. The left, or Muscovite bank, had less to suffer, although the Sultan claimed it equally as his own possession, but the inhabitants had only to fight with their old enemies the Tatars.

The Cossacks of the Don at this period were, on the whole, tolerably quiet; but one of their number, Stenko Razine, overturned all Eastern Russia. The immigration of Cossacks of the Dnieper, expelled from their native land by war, had created a great famine in these poor plains of the Don. Stenko assembled some of these starved adventurers, and formed a scheme for the capture of Azof; but on being hindered by the *starchina* of the Dontsi, he turned towards the East, towards the Volga and the Jaïk (Oural). His reputation was wide-spread: he was said to be a magician, against whom neither sabre, balls, nor bullets could prevail, and the brigands of all the country crowded to his banner. He swept the Caspian, and ravaged the shores of Persia. The Russian Government, powerless to crush him, offered him a pardon if he would surrender his guns and boats stolen from the Crown. He accepted the offer; but his exploits, his wealth acquired by pillage, and his princely liberality created him an immense party among the lower classes, and among the Cossacks and even the *streltsi* of the towns. The lands of the Volga were always ready for a social revolution; hence the success of Razine, and later of Pougatchef. There brigands were popular and respected: honest merchants, come to the Don for trading purposes, and learning that Stenko had **begun the career of a pirate,** did not hesitate to join him.

In 1670, Stenko having spent all the money he had gained by pillage, went up the Don with an army of vagabonds, and thence crossed to the Volga. All the country rose on the approach of a chief already so famous. The inhabitants of Tzaritsyne opened their gates to him. A flotilla was sent against him, but the sailors and the *streltsi* surrendered, and betrayed to him their commanders. Astrakhan revolted, and delivered up its two voïevodes, one of whom was thrown from the top of a bell-tower. Ascending the Volga, he took Saratof and Samara, and raised the country of Nijni-Novgorod, Tambof, and Pensa. Everywhere in the Russia of the Volga the serfs revolted against their masters—the Tatars, Tchouvaches, Mordvians, and Tcheremisses against the domination of Russia. It was a fearful revolution. In 1671 Stenko Razine was defeated, near Simbirsk, by George Baratinski. His prestige was lost; he was pursued into the steppes, arrested on the Don, and sent to Moscow, where he was executed (1671).

His death did not immediately check the rebellion. The brigands still continued to hold the country. At Astrakhan, Vassili Ouss governed despotically, and threw the archbishop from a belfry. Finally, however, all these imitators of Razine were killed or captured, the Volga freed, and the Don became as peaceful as the Dnieper.

ECCLESIASTICAL REFORMS OF NICON—THE PRECURSORS OF PETER THE GREAT.

If Alexis, father of Peter the Great, was not himself a reformer, his whole reign was a preparation for reform. Who can tell how much Peter owed to the example of his father—and of his mother Natalia, the pupil of Matvéef—to the ideas of Nicon, Polotski and Nachtchokine? Nicon was the son of a simple peasant of the Government of Nijni-Novgorod. The Church drew the young man from obscurity, and gave him little by little a place among those who were great. A priest at Moscow, a recluse renowned for his piety on the banks of the White Lake, and later an archimandrite of the *Novospasski Monastyr*, he was at last nominated Metropolitan of Novgorod, where we have seen him appease a sedition at the peril of his life. The Tzar loved and admired him, and made him Patriarch, and allowed him to take the title of Chief Noble and Sovereign, once borne by Philarete. A man who had raised himself to such a height from such a depth was not capable of mastering his ambition. Proud and imperious, he made himself a multitude of enemies among the clergy and the nobles, and despised them.

Nicon took up the correction of the holy books began by Dionysius of Troïtsa. A number of gross mistakes and even interpolations had slipped into the Slavonic manuscripts, and thence passed into print. On being informed of these mistakes by some Greek prelates who had come to Moscow, Nicon assembled a council, where it was decided that the printed books must be corrected according to the ancient Slavonic or Greek manuscripts. Nicon collected these texts from all parts, and, with the help of learned ecclesiastics, set to work. This attempt, which denotes a truly modern and scientific spirit, was the cause of a schism. To the people, and to a large party of the clergy and monks, everything in the holy books, even the mistakes of the copyists, was sacred. Certain altered or interpolated texts had in their turn consecrated usages opposed to those generally followed by the Church. The sectaries relying on these texts forbade the beard to be shaven under the penalty of committing a mortal sin, and ordered the sign of the cross to be made with two fingers and not with three, and the liturgy with seven *prosphires* and not with five. Fanatics were ready to die sooner than read *Iisous* for *Isous* (Jesus). Besides those whom an excessive respect for ancient texts and customs drove into schism, we must reckon true heretics, who adopted falsified or apocryphal renderings, and who, after having been for long hidden and ignored in the bosom of the orthodox Church, were all at once unmasked. Thus the reforms of Nicon brought to light the *raskol* latent in the Russian Church, with all its multiplicity of sects—Old Believers, Drinkers of Milk, Champions of the Spirit, Flagellants, Skoptsi, or voluntary eunuchs, and many others, whose origin may be traced to Alexandrine Gnosticism, Persian Manichæism, and perhaps even to Hindu Pantheism (1654).

The Tzar energetically supported his patriarch. He diligently sought out the *religious madmen* (*iourodivié*) and the wandering prophets who led the people astray, disgraced the men and women of his Court who persisted in crossing themselves with two fingers, imprisoned rebellious monks and ecclesiastics, and hunted down assemblies of non-conformists. One of Nicon's enemies was burnt alive. The most curious episode of this religious war was the revolt of the holy monasteries of the White Sea. The monks, passionately attached to their ancient customs, won over the *streltsi* and the *diéti-boyarskié* who formed the garrison of the fortified convent of Solovetski. An army had to be sent against them (1668), but the monastery only capitulated after a siege of eight years. It was then taken by assault, and the rebels hung.

At the same time that Alexis enabled Nicon to subdue his religious foes, he delivered him up to his political enemies. The proud and imperious character of the Patriarch had ended by rendering him insupportable to the Tzar. It was a reproduction of the rivalry of the Patriarch Keroularios and the Emperor Isaac Comnenus in the 11th century (Byzantine). The courtiers did their best to foment this misunderstanding. Nicon, instead of combating their arts, treated them with disdain. At last his enemies put upon him a public insult, which made him beside himself. In the midst of the tears of the people, he solemnly placed his pontifical insignia on the altar, and retired to a convent he had founded near Moscow. This was to relinquish the field of battle to his adversaries. He expected that the Tzar would beseech him to resume his office, but the Tzar did not trouble himself about his old favorite. His voluntary exile lasted eight years (1658–1666), when a council was assembled on the occasion of the arrival of the Patriarchs of Antioch and Alexandria at Moscow. The council approved of Nicon's reforms and his corrections of the sacred books; but for his voluntary desertion of the patriarchate, his audacious attacks on the Tzar and the bishops, and the abuse of his power over the inferior clergy, he was condemned to be imprisoned in a monastery on the White Lake.

By the side of Nicon among the reformers, we must mention Simeon Polotski, tutor of the sons of Alexis, who published against the *raskolniks* the 'Rod of Government;' wrote light verses, panegyrics, sermons, dramatic compositions, maxims, and examples drawn from the Scriptures, and never ceased to remind the Tzar of a French king. "There was once," he wrote, "a King of France called Francis I. As he loved literature and science, though his ancestors hated them and lived in ignorance like barbarians, the sons of illustrious families sought instruction, in order to please the monarch. Thus knowledge spread through the country, for it is the custom of subjects to imitate the prince; all love what he loves. Happy is the kingdom whose king gives a good example to all!" Simeon was a White Russian; others, like Slavinetski and Satanovski, who were charged by Nicon with the translation of foreign books, were natives of Little Russia, of Kief the learned. These two western divisions of Russia served as a link between Muscovy and Europe.

Two writers of this epoch merit special mention. Gregory Kotochikhine, under-secretary of the *Prikaz of Embassies*, was obliged, in consequence of a quarrel with the voïevode Dolgorouki, to fly first into Poland and then into Sweden, where he wrote a curious treatise, called ' Russia under the reign of Alexis Mikhaïlovitch,' which appeared about 1666. He does not concern himself either with the clergy or the inferior classes, but gives a frightful picture of the ignorance, sensuality, and brutality of the boyards and nobles. So graphic is it that, as Polévoï remarks, we are forced involuntarily to ask, " In what state could the lower orders have been ? " He speaks with horror and disgust of the administration of justice, compares foreign institutions with those of his own country to the advantage of the former, and regrets that his compatriots did not send their sons to be educated abroad.

Iouri Krijanitch, a Servian by birth and a Catholic priest, was one of those learned Slavs who now came into Russia to seek employment for their talents. He had proposed to himself three aims in coming to Moscow: 1. To elevate the Slavonic tongue by compiling a grammar and a lexicon, so that the Slavs might learn to speak and write correctly; and to place a larger number of words and phrases at their disposal, so that they might be able to express all the thoughts common to the human mind, and also political and general ideas. 2. To write the history of the Slavs, and to refute the falsehoods and calumnies of the Germans. 3. To unmask the tricks and sophisms made use of by foreign nations to deceive the Slavs. In his work entitled ' The Russian Empire in the middle of the 17th Century, dedicated to Alexis Mikhaïlovitch, and lately republished by M. Bezsonof, he touches on all points of manners and customs, politics, and political economy. Like Kotochikhine, he attacks ignorance and barbarism, and advocates instruction, study, and civilization, as being the only remedies for the misfortunes of Russia.

Krijanitch is the first of the Slavophiles, or the Pan-Slavists, as they are at present called. He appeals to all the Slav nations —" Borysthenites, or Little Russians, Poles, Lithuanians, and Serbs. He advises the Russians to mistrust equally Germans and Greeks. It was probably his philippics against the Greek clergy established in Russia that caused him in 1660 to be exiled to Tobolsk.

Ordine-Nachtchokine, son of a gentleman of Pskof, distinguished himself as a diplomatist in the negotiations for the Peace of Androussovo, which gave Kief and Smolensk to Russia. Summoned to take part in the councils of the Tzar, he applied his activity to all branches of the administration; to the army, that needed reform; to commerce, that must be freed from the interference of the voïevodes; to diplomacy, for which men skilled in languages, representatives worthy of the Court of Russia, must be found. His object was to make Muscovy the centre of Asiatic and European trade; he instituted an Armenian Company for the purchase of Persian silks, dreamed of a fleet on the Caspian, constructed the first Russian vessel on the Oka, had extracts from foreign news-letters regularly translated for the enlightenment of the sovereign, and thus founded, though for the Tzar's benefit alone, the Russian press.

As he had necessarily to praise the usages of foreign countries, and to find fault with those of Russia, Nachtchokine could not but make himself many enemies. His morality was equal to his talent: incorruptible, indefatigable, and master of himself, he was the first great European that Russia had produced. While praising Europe he still remained a Russian. In his old age he become a monk.

When Nachtchokine had to leave his post, the boyard Matvéef, a familiar friend of Alexis, was appointed his successor. One day, when the Tzar was dining with Matvéef, he noticed a young girl who was serving at table, and who pleased him by her modest and intelligent air. This was a motherless girl, Natalia Narychkine, to whom her uncle Matvéef had been a second father. "I have found a husband for her," said the Tzar to Matvéef some days after. This husband was the Tzar himself. The marriage drew closer still the ties that bound him to Matvéef. Now the latter was, like Nachtchokine, full of European ideas. His house was furnished and ornamented according to Western notions. His chosen guests did not give themselves up to the orgies authorized by national custom; they behaved as courteously as if they were in a French *salon*. His Scotch wife, a Hamilton by birth, was the only lady of the Court who did not paint herself, and, instead of keeping herself secluded in her apartments, took part in the conversation of men. We may conceive the influence of the boyard and his wife on their adopted daughter; and is it surprising that Natalia was the first Russian princess who drew back the curtains of her litter, and allowed her face to be seen by her subjects? Matvéef protected foreign artists,—"masters in perspective writings," as they were called. In the German *Slobode* of Moscow he established a sort of dramatic academy, where twenty-five merchants' sons learnt to act comedies. The Tzar acquired a taste for theatrical entertainments. Likatchof, his envoy at the Court of Florence, wrote to his sovereign enthusiastic letters full of the marvels which he had seen at the opera—of palaces which came and went, of a sea that rose and fell and filled itself with fish, of men who rode on monsters of the deep, or pursued each other into the clouds.

Moscow undertook to rival Florence. In a wooden theatre. ballets and dramas, adapted from the Bible, were represented before the Tzar : ' Joseph sold by his Brethren,' ' The Prodigal Son,' and ' Esther,' which preceded that of Racine by seventeen years. At Moscow, as at St. Cyr, the piece gave scope to many allusions. Here Esther was Natalia Narychkine ; Mordecai was Matvéef, the protector of her youth ; and the *vrémianchtchik* Haman, who was hung on the *tchélobitié* of Queen Esther, was, no doubt, Khitrovo, the former favorite. These pieces were enlivened by somewhat rough pleasantries. In ' Holofernes,' when Judith has cut off the head of the Assyrian voïevode, the servant cries "Here is a poor man who will be much astonished, on awaking, to find his head carried away ! "

During this reign, when Russia was trying to assimilate herself to Europe, diplomacy naturally took rapid strides. Muscovy had entered into more or less close relations with all the Cou.ts of the West.

In 1645, Alexis sent Gerasimus Doktourof to notify his accession to the King of England, Charles I. The Russian envoy arrived in England in the midst of the Revolution. Being received at Gravesend with great honors and the firing of guns by the company of merchants that traded with Russia, he at once inquired " where was the king ? " They replied, they did not know exactly where he was, because for three or four years there had been a great civil war, and instead of the king they had now the Parliament, composed of deputies from all the orders, who governed London as well as the kingdoms of England and Scotland. " Our war with the king," said the merchants, " began for the sake of religion, when he married the daughter of the King of France. She, being a Papist, persuaded the king into various superstitious practices ; it was by her counsel that the king instituted archbishops and called in the Jesuits. Many people, in order to follow the example of the king, made themselves Papists too. Besides this, the king wished to govern the kingdom according to his own will, as do the sovereigns of other States. But here, from time immemorial, the country has been free : the early kings could settle nothing : it was the Parliament, the men who were elected, that governed. The king began to rule after his own will, but the Parliament would not allow that, and many archbishops and Jesuits were executed. The king, seeing that the Parliament intended to act according to its own wish, as it had done from all time, and not at all according to the royal will, left London with the queen, without being expelled by anyone, saying that they were going away into other towns. Once out of London, he sent the queen to France, and began to fight us, but the Parliament was the stronger. The Parliament is composed of two *palaty* (chambers): in one of them sit the boyards, in the other the men elected by the commons—the *sloujilié liouili* and the merchants. Five hundred men sit in the parliament, and one orator speaks for all."

These l...ons in the English Constitution could not penetrate the brain of the Russian envoy. He only recognized the king, and persisted, according to the text of his instructions, in trying to deliver his letters of credit to the king himself. "Hast thou a letter from thy sovereign, and a mission to the Parliament?" they asked him. He replied, "I have neither a letter nor a mission to the Parliament. Let the Parliament send me immediately before the king, and give me an escort, carriages, and provisions. Let the Parliament present me to him—it is to him that I will speak." His demand was naturally refused, and he wished instantly to leave for Holland, but this was not allowed.

The following year Charles I. was brought a prisoner into London. Doktourof insisted on being presented to him. His request was ill-timed. "You cannot be brought before him," they said to him; "he no longer governs anything." Doktourof then refused a dinner given to him by the Russian Company, and only yielded when the dinner was served at his own house. The Parliament, however, did not wish to interrupt the friendly relations with Russia.

Doktourof was summoned before the House of Lords on the 13th of June. At his entrance all the "boyards" took off their hats, and Lord Manchester, the "chief boyard," rose. Then Doktourof, to the general consternation, made the following speech:—"I am sent by my sovereign to your king, Charles King of England. I have been sent as a courier (*gonets*) to negotiate important affairs of State, which offer great advantages to both sovereigns and to all Christendom, and may help to maintain peace and concord. It is the 13th of June, and, since I arrived in London on the 26th of November last, I have never ceased to show you the letter of the Tzar and to beg you to allow me to go before the king. You have kept me in London without permitting me either to have an interview with the king or to return to the Tzar; and yet in all the neighboring countries the route is free to all ambassadors, envoys, and couriers of the Tzar."

Manchester replied that they would explain to the Tzar by letter their reasons for acting thus. They gave him a chair, and the English "boyards" likewise seated themselves; and he began to look about the House, of which he gives a minute description in his report. He was then conducted to the House of

Commons, and the dignitaries came to meet him preceded by the royal sceptre. He renewed his declarations, and then retired ceremoniously. In June 1646 he left England much discontented. Alexis could understand no more of the English Revolution than his envoy. He maintained, like Catherine II., the cause of kings against the liberty of the subjects. In May 1647 he received at Moscow Nawtingall, envoy of Charles I., who denounced the captivity of the king, and said Charles would see with pleasure the English Company deprived of its privileges, and everyone allowed to trade freely with Russia. Alexis listened to his request, and granted him, as aid to the king 30,000 *tchetverts* of corn, out of the 300,000 that were asked of him. But the English merchants settled in Russia accused Nawtingall of imposture, saying that the king's letter was apocryphal, and that the dog he had brought as a present to Alexis had never been bought by Charles I. Nawtingall was expelled in disgrace, and avenged himself by accusing his compatriots of a project of attacking Arkhangel, and of pillaging the Russian merchants. His honors as ambassador were then given back to him, but he quitted Russia.

When Alexis heard of the execution of Charles I., he published the oukase of June 1649, which, as a punishment to the regicides, forbade the English merchants to live in the cities of the interior, and confined them to Arkhangel. The Tzar furnished help in money and corn to Charles, Prince of Wales, who in 1660 became Charles II., and resumed relations with him when he ascended the throne of the Stuarts.

At the opening of the war with Poland, it occurred to Alexis to notify the fact to the sovereigns of the West. In 1653 he sent to Louis XIV. a certain Matchékine, who was also presented to Anne of Austria. In 1668 Peter Potemkine was accredited first to the Court of Spain, and then to that of France. It was just after the Peace of Aix-la-Chapelle, and it was not difficult for Russia to guess that the war would soon recommence. The object of the embassy was to induce Louis XIV. to enter into regular relations with Russia, and to send French vessels to Arkhangel. Potemkine had conferences with Colbert and the six merchant guilds of Paris. But the results of this embassy were hardly greater than those of the preceding one. The account of Potemkine contains some curious details and quaint reflections on the Spain and France of the 17th century, but is chiefly occupied with difficulties raised by him on questions of etiquette.

REIGN OF FEODOR ALEXIEVITCH (1676-1682).

On the death of Alexis, his eldest son Feodor succeeded to the crown. The Miloslavskis, Feodor's maternal relatives, profited by his accession to ruin their enemy, Matvéef who was accused of magic, deprived of his property and his title of boyard, and banished to Poustozersk. In this reign the Little Russian question received a solution. The hetman Samoïlovitch and Prince Romodanoviski defeated Dorochenko, and obliged him to resign the office of ataman. They then had to fight the Turks and Tatars, who twice invaded the Ukraine and advanced to Tchigirine.

The country, according to a contemporary account, was covered with ruined towns and castles, and heaps of human bones that whitened in the sun. Finally the Sultan concluded at Bakhtchi-Seraï a truce of twenty years, which ceded to Russia Zaporogia and the Ukraine. In 1681 Feodor sent a new embassy to Louis XIV.; his envoy being the son of the old Potemkine, who managed, according to the diplomatic historian Flassans, to give by his own wisdom and learning a favorable idea of the nation which he represented.

It was in this reign that an assembly was held of the higher clergy and the boyards, to legislate on the question of precedence (*miestnichestvo*), which continued to be one of the plagues of Russia. The assembly commanded that there should be no more disputes, and in its presence and that of the Tzar the 'Books of Rank' were solemnly burnt. In future whoever " disputed " was to be deprived of his nobility and his wealth.

In order to defend the orthodox Church against the heresies of the West, and to connect it more closely with the Eastern Church, Feodor founded the Slavo-Græco-Latin Academy of Moscow. Greek and Latin, Christian philosophy and theology, were taught there. The brothers Likhoudi were brought from Greece to be professors there. This school, although ecclesiastical, was an advance on all other establishments of the kind in Russia, and produced some brilliant pupils. Among them we may mention the mathematician Magnitski under Peter the Great, and the historian Bantych-Kamenski and the Metropolitan Plato under Catharine II. The school was afterwards transferred to the Monastery of Troïtsa.

CHAPTER XXII.

PETER THE GREAT: EARLY YEARS (1682-1709).

Regency of Sophia (1682-1689)—Peter I.—Expeditions against Azof (1695-1696)—First journey to the West (1697)—Revolt and destruction of the *strel'tsi* Contest with the Cossacks : revolt of the Don (1706) ; Mazeppa (1709).

REGENCY OF SOPHIA (1682-1689) PETER I.

ALEXIS MIKHAILOVITCH had by his first wife, Maria Miloslavski, two sons (Feodor and Ivan) and six daughters; by his second wife Natalia Narychkine, one son (who became Peter I.) and two daughters. As he was twice married, and the kinsmen of each wife had, according to custom, surrounded the throne, there existed two factions in the palace, which were brought face to face by the death of Feodor. The Miloslavskis had on their side the claim of seniority, the number of royal children left by Maria, and above all, the fact that Ivan was the elder of the two surviving sons; but unluckily for them, Ivan was notoriously imbecile both in body and mind. On the side of the Narychkines was the interest excited by the precocious intelligence of Peter, and the position of legal head of all the royal family, which, according to Russian law, gave to Natalia Narychkine her title of "Tzarina Dowager." Both factions had for some time taken their measures and recruited their partisans. Who should succeed Feodor? Was it to be the son of the Miloslavski, or the son of the Narychkine? The Miloslavskis were first defeated on legal grounds. Taking the incapacity of Ivan into consideration, the boyards and the Patriarch Joachim proclaimed the young Peter, then nine years old, Tzar. The Narychkines triumphed: Natalia became Tzarina-Regent, recalled from exile her foster-father, Matvéef, and surrounded herself by her brothers and uncles.

The Miloslavskis' only means of revenge lay in revolt, but they were without a head; for it was impossible for Ivan to take the lead. The eldest of his six sisters was thirty-two years of age, the youngest nineteen; the most energetic of them was

Sophia, who was twenty-five. These six princesses saw themselves condemned to the dreary destiny of the Russian *tzarevni*, and were forced to renounce all hopes of marriage, with no prospects but to grow old in the seclusion of the *terem*, subjected by law to the authority of a stepmother. All their youth had to look forward to was the cloister. They, however, only breathed in action; and though imperial etiquette and Byzantine manners, prejudices, and traditions forbade them to appear in public, even Byzantine traditions offered them models to follow. Had not Pulcheria, daughter of an emperor, reigned at Constantinople in the name of her brother, the incapable Theodosius? Had she not contracted a nominal marriage with the brave Marcian, who was her sword against the barbarians? Here was the ideal that Sophia could propose to herself; to be a Tzardiévitsa, a woman-emperor. To emancipate herself from the rigorous laws of the *terem*, to force the "twenty-seven locks" of the song, to raise the *fata* that covered her face, to appear in public and meet the looks of men, needed both energy, cunning, and patience that could wait and be content to proceed by successive efforts. Sophia's first step was to appear at Feodor's funeral, though it was not the custom for any but the widow and the heir to be present. There her litter encountered that of Natalia Narychkine, and her presence forced the Tzarina-Mother to retreat. She surrounded herself with a court of educated men, who publicly praised her, encouraged and excited her to action. Simeon Polotski and Silvester Medviédef wrote verses in her honor, recalled to her the example of Pulcheria and Olga, compared her to the virgin Queen Elizabeth of England, and even to Semiramis; we might think we were listening to Voltaire addressing Catherine II. They played on her name Sophia (wisdom), and declared she had been endowed with the quality as well as the title. Polotski dedicated to her the 'Crown of Faith,' and Medviédef his 'Gifts of the Holy Spirit.' The *terem* offered the strangest contrasts. There acted they the 'Malade Imaginaire,' and the audience was composed of the heterogeneous assembly of popes, monks, nuns, and old pensioners that formed the Courts of the ancient Tzarinas. In this shifting crowd there were some useful instruments of intrigue. The old pensioners, while telling their rosaries, served as emissaries between the palace and the town, carried messages and presents to the turbulent *streltsi*, and arranged matters between the Tzarian ladies and the soldiers. Sinister rumors were skilfully disseminated through Moscow: Feodor, the eldest son of Alexis, had died, the victim of conspirators; the same lot was doubtless reserved for Ivan. What was to become of the poor *tzarévni*, of the blood of kings? At last it was publicly announced that a brother of Natalia Narychkine had seized the crown and seated himself on the throne, and that Ivan had been strangled. Love and pity for the son of Alexis, and the indignation excited by the news of the usurpation, immediately caused the people of Moscow to revolt, and the ringleaders cleverly directed the movement. The tocsin sounded from 400 churches of the "holy city"; the regiments of the *streltsi* took up arms and marched, followed by an immense crowd, to the Kremlin, with drums beating, matches lighted, and dragging cannon behind them. Natalia Narychkine had only to show herself on the Red Staircase, accompanied by her son Peter, and Ivan who was reported dead. Their mere appearance sufficed to contradict all the calumnies. The *streltsi* hesitated, seeing they had been deceived. A clever harangue of Matvéef, who had formerly commanded them, and the exhortations of the Patriarch, shook them further. The revolt was almost appeased; the Miloslavskis had missed their aim, for they had not yet succeeded in putting to death the people of whom they were jealous. Suddenly Prince Michael Dolgorouki, chief of the *prikaz* of the *streltsi*, began to insult the rioters in the most violent language. This ill-timed harangue awoke their fury; they seized Dolgorouki, and flung him from the top of the Red Staircase on to their pikes. They stabbed Matvéef, under the eyes of the Tzarina; then they sacked the palace, murdering all who fell into their hands. Athanasius Narychkine, a brother of Natalia, was thrown from a window on to the points of their lances. The following day the *émeute* recommenced; they tore from the arms of the Tzarina her father Cyril, and her brother Ivan; the latter was tortured and sent into a monastery. Historians show us Sophia interceded for the victims on her knees, but an understanding between the rebels and the Tzarévna did exist; the *streltsi* obeyed orders. The following days were consecrated to the purifying of the palace and the administration, and the seventh day of the revolt they sent their commandant, the prince-boyard Khovanski, to declare that they would have two Tzars—Ivan at the head, and Peter as coadjutor; and if this were refused, they would again rebel. The boyards of the *douma* deliberated on this proposal, and the greater number of the boyards were opposed to it. In Russia the absolute power had never been shared, but the orators of the *terem* cited many examples both from sacred and profane history: Pharaoh and Joseph, Arcadius and Honorius, Basil II. and Constantine VIII.; and the best of all the arguments were the pikes of the *streltsi* (1682).

Sophia had triumphed: she reigned in the name of her two brothers, Ivan and Peter. She made a point of showing herself in public, at processions, solemn services, and dedications of churches. At the *Ouspienski Sobor*, while her brothers occupied the place of the Tzar, she filled that of the Tzarina; only *she* raised the curtains and boldly allowed herself to be incensed by the Patriarch. When the *raskolniks* challenged the heads of the orthodox Church to discussion, she wished to preside and hold the meeting in the open air, at the *Lobnoé Miésto* on the Red Place. There was however so much opposition, that she was forced to call the assembly in the Palace of Facets, and sat behind the throne of her two brothers, present though invisible. The double-seated throne used on those occasions is still preserved at Moscow; there is an opening in the back, hidden by a veil of silk, and behind this sat Sophia. This singular piece of furniture is the symbol of a government previously unknown to Russia, composed of two visible Tzars and one invisible sovereign.

The *streltsi*, however, felt their prejudices against female sovereignty awaken. They shrank from the contempt heaped by the Tzarévna upon the ancient manners. Sophia had already become in their eyes a "scandalous person" (*pozornoé litzo*). Another cause of misunderstanding was the support she gave to the State Church, as reformed by Nicon, while the *streltsi* and the greater part of the people held to the "old faith." She had arrested certain "old believers," who at the discussion in the Palace of Facets, had challenged the patriarchs and orthodox prelates, and she had caused the ringleader to be executed. Khovanski, chief of the *streltsi*, whether from sympathy with the *raskol*, or whether he wished to please his subordinates, affected to share their discontent. The Court no longer felt itself safe at Moscow. Sophia took refuge with the Tzarina and the two young princes in the fortified monastery of Troïtsa, and summoned around her the gentlemen-at-arms. Khovanski was invited to attend, was arrested on the way, and put to death with his son. The *streltsi* attempted a new rising, but, with the usual fickleness of a popular militia, suddenly passed from the extreme of insolence to the extreme of humility. They marched to Troïtsa, this time in the guise of suppliants, with cords round their necks, carrying axes and blocks for the death they expected. The Patriarch consented to intercede for them, and Sophia contented herself with the sacrifice of the ringleaders.

Sophia, having got rid of her accomplices, governed by aid of her two favorites—Chaklovity, the new commandant of the *streltsi*, whom she had drawn from obscurity, and who was completely devoted to her, and Prince Vassili Galitsyne. Galitsyne has become the hero of an historic school which opposes his genius to that of Peter the Great, in the same way as in France Henry, Duke of Guise, has been exalted at the expense of Henry IV. He was the special favorite, the intimate friend of Sophia, the director of her foreign policy, and her right hand in military affairs. Sophia and Galitsyne labored to organize a Holy League between Russia, Poland, Venice and Austria against the Turks and Tatars. They also tried to gain the countenance of the Catholic Powers of the West ; and in 1687 Jacob Dolgorouki and Jacob Mychetski disembarked at Dunkirk, as envoys to the Court of Louis XIV. They were not received very favorably : the King of France was not at all inclined to make war against the Turks ; he was, on the other hand, the ally of Mahomet IV., who was about to besiege Vienna while Louis blockaded Luxemburg. The whole plan of the campaign was, however, thrown out by the intervention of Russia and John Sobieski in favor of Austria. The Russian ambassadors received orders to re-embark at Havre, without going further south.

The government of the Tzarévna still persisted in its warlike projects. In return for an active co-operation against the Ottomans, Poland had consented to ratify the conditions of the Treaty of Androussovo, and to sign a perpetual peace (1686). A hundred thousand Muscovites, under the command of Prince Galitsyne, and fifty thousand Little Russian Cossacks, under the orders of the hetman Samoïlovitch, marched against the Crimea (1687). The army suffered greatly in the southern steppes, as the Tatars had fired the grassy plains. Galitsyne was forced to return without having encountered the enemy. Samoïlovitch was accused of treason, deprived of his command, and sent to Siberia; and Mazeppa, who owed to Samoïlovitch his appointment as Secretary-at-war, and whose denunciations had chiefly contributed to his downfall, was appointed his successor. In the spring of 1689 the Muscovite and Ukranian armies, commanded by Galitsyne and Mazeppa, again set out for the Crimea. The second expedition was hardly more fortunate than the first : they got as far as Perekop, and were then obliged to retreat without even having taken the fortress. This double defeat did not hinder Sophia from preparing for her favorite a triumphal entry into Moscow. In vain Peter forbade her to leave the palace ; she braved his displeasure and headed the procession, accompanied by the clergy and the images and followed by the army of the Crimea, admitted the generals to kiss her hand, and distributed glasses of brandy among the officers. Peter left Moscow in anger, and retired to the village of Preobrajenskoé. The foreign policy of the Tzarévna was marked by another display of weakness. By the Treaty of Nertchinsk, she restored to the Chinese Empire the fertile regions of the Amour, which had been conquered by a handful of Cossacks, and razed the fortress of Albazine, where those adventurers had braved all the forces of the East. On all sides Russia seemed to retreat before the barbarians.

Meantime Peter was growing. His precocious faculties, his quick intelligence, and his strong will awakened alike the hopes of his partisans and the fears of his enemies. As a child he only loved drums, swords, and muskets. He learned history by means of colored prints brought from Germany. Zotof, his master, whom he afterwards made " the archpope of fools," taught him to read. Among the heroes held up to him as examples, we are not surprised to find Ivan the Terrible, whose character and position offer so much analogy to his own. "When the Tzarévitch was tired of reading," says M. Zabiéline, "Zotof took the book from his hand, and, to amuse him, would himself read the great deeds of his father, Alexis Mikhaïlovitch, and those of the Tzar Ivan Vassiliévitch, their campaigns, their distant expeditions, their battles and sieges : how they endured fatigues and privations better than any common soldier ; what benefits they had conferred on the empire, and how they extended the frontiers of Russia." Peter also learnt Latin, German, and Dutch. He read much and widely, and learnt a great deal, though without method. Like Ivan the Terrible, he was a self-taught man. He afterwards complained of not having been instructed according to rule. This was perhaps a good thing. His education, like that of Ivan IV., was neglected, but at least he was not subjected to the enervating influence of the *terem*—he was not cast in that dull mould which turned out so many idiots in the royal family. He "roamed at large, and wandered in the streets with his comrades." The streets of Moscow at that period were, according to M. Zabiéline, the worst school of profligacy and debauchery that can be imagined ; but they were, on the whole, less bad for Peter than the palace. He met there something besides mere jesters ; he encountered new elements which had as yet no place in the *terem*, but contained the germ of the regeneration of Russia. He came across Russians who, if unscrupulous, were also unprejudiced, and who could aid him in his bold reform of the ancient society. He there became acquainted with Swiss, English, and German adventurers—with Lefort, with Gordon, and with Timmermann, who initiated him into European civilization. His Court was composed of Leo

Narychkine, of Boris Galitsyne (who had undertaken never to flatter him), of Andrew Matvéef (who had marked taste for everything European), and of Dolgorouki, at whose house he first saw an astrolabe. He played at soldiers with his young friends and his grooms, and formed them into the "battalion of playmates," who manœuvred after the European fashion, and became the kernel of the future regular army. He learnt the elements of geometry and fortification, and constructed small citadels, which he took or defended with his young warriors in those fierce battles which sometimes counted their wounded or dead, and in which the Tzar of Russia was not always spared. An English boat stranded on the shore of Yaousa caused him to send for Franz Timmermann, who taught him to manage a sailing boat, even with a contrary wind. He who formerly, like a true boyard of Moscow, had such a horror of the water that he could not make up his mind to cross a bridge, became a determined sailor: he guided his boat first on the Yaousa, then on the lake of Peréiaslavl. Brandt, the Dutchman, built him a whole flotilla; and already, in spite of the terrors of his mother, Natalia, Peter dreamed of the sea.

"The child is amusing himself," the courtiers of Sophia affected to observe; but these amusements disquieted her. Each day added to the years of Peter seemed to bring her nearer to the cloister. In vain she proudly called herself "autocrat"; she saw her stepmother, her rival, lifting up her head. Galitsyne confined himself to regretting that they had not known better how to profit by the revolution of 1682, but Chaklovity, who knew he must fall with his mistress, said aloud, "It would be wiser to put the Tzarina to death than to be put to death by her." Sophia could only save herself by seizing the throne—but who would help her to take it? The *streltsi*? But the result of their last rising had chilled them considerably. Sophia herself, while trying to bind this formidable force, had broken it, and the *streltsi* had not forgotten their chiefs beheaded at Troïtsa. Now what did the emissaries of Sophia propose to them? Again to attack the palace; to put Leo Narychkine, Boris Galitsyne, and other partisans of Peter to death; to arrest his mother, and to expel the Patriarch. They trusted that Peter and Natalia would perish in the tumult. The *streltsi* remained indifferent when Sophia, affecting to think her life threatened, fled to the *Dievitchi Monastyr*, and sent them letters of entreaty. "If thy days are in peril," tranquilly replied the *streltsi*. "there must be an inquiry." Chaklovity could hardly collect four hundred of them at the Kremlin.

The struggle began between Moscow and Preobrajenskoé,

the village with the prophetical name (the *Transfiguration* or *Regeneration*). Two *streltsi* warned Peter of the plots of his sister, and, for the second time, he sought an asylum at Troïtsa. It was then seen who was the true Tzar ; all men hastened to range themselves around him : his mother, his armed squires, the " battalion of playmates," the foreign officers, and even the *streltsi* of the regiment of Soukharef. The Patriarch also took the side of the Tzar, and brought him moral support, as the foreign soldiers had brought him material force. The partisans of Sophia were cold and irresolute ; the *streltsi* themselves demanded that her favorite Chaklovity should be surrendered to the Tzar. She had to implore the mediation of the Patriarch. Chaklovity was first put to the torture and made to confess his plot against the Tzar, and then decapitated. Medviédef was at first only condemned to the knout and banishment for heresy, but he acknowledged he had intended to take the place of the Patriarch and to marry Sophia ; he was dishonored by being imprisoned with two sorcerers condemned to be burned alive in a cage, and was afterwards beheaded. Galitsyne was deprived of his property, and exiled to Poustozersk. Sophia remained in the *Diévitchi Monastyr*, subjected to a hard captivity. Though Ivan continued to reign conjointly with his brother, yet Peter, who was then only seventeen, governed alone, surrounded by his mother, the Narychkines, the Dolgoroukis, and Boris Galitsyne (1689).

Sophia had freed herself from the seclusion of the *terem*, as Peter had emancipated himself from the seclusion of the palace to roam the streets and navigate rivers. Both had behaved scandalously, according to the ideas of the time—the one haranguing soldiers, presiding over councils, walking with her veil raised ; the other using the axe like a carpenter, rowing like a Cossack, brawling with foreign adventurers, and fighting with his grooms in mimic battles. But to the one her emancipation was only a means of obtaining power ; to the other the emancipation of Russia, like the emancipation of himself, was the end. He wished the nation to shake off the old trammels from which he had freed himself. Sophia remained a Byzantine, Peter aspired to be a European. In the conflict between the Tzarévna and the Tzar, progress was not on the side of the *Diévitchi Monastyr*.

EXPEDITIONS AGAINST AZOF (1695-1696) — FIRST JOURNEY TO
THE WEST (1697).

The first use the Tzar made of his liberty was to hasten to Arkhangel. There, deaf to the advice and prayers of his mother, who was astounded at this unexpected taste for salt water, he gazed on that sea which not Tzar had ever looked on. He ate with the merchants and the officers of foreign navies; he breathed the air which had come from the West. He established a dockyard, built boats, dared the angry waves of this unknown ocean, and almost perished in a storm, which did not prevent the " skipper Peter Alexiévitch " from again putting to sea, and bringing the Dutch vessels back to the Holy Cape. Unhappily, the White Sea, by which, since the time of Ivan IV., the English had entered Russia, is frostbound in winter. In order to open permanent communications with the West, with civilized countries, it was necessary for Peter to establish himself on the Baltic or the Black Sea. Now the first belonged to the Swedes, and the second to the Turks, as the Caspian did to the Persians. Who was first to be attacked ? The treaties concluded with Poland and Austria, as well as policy and religion, urged the Tzar against the Turks, and Constantinople has always been the point of attraction for orthodox Russia. Peter shared the sentiments of his people, and had the enthusiasm of a crusader against the infidel. Notwithstanding his ardent wish to travel in the West, he took the resolution not to appear in foreign lands till he could appear as a victor. Twice had Galitsyne failed against the Crimea ; Peter determined to attack the barbarians by the Don, and besiege Azof. The army was commanded by three generals, Golovine, Gordon, and Lefort, who were to act with the " bombardier of the Preobrajenski regiment, Peter Alexievitch." This regiment, as well as three others which had sprung from the " amusements " of Preobrajenskoé—the Semenovski, the Botousitski, and the regiment of Lefort—were the heart of the expedition. It failed because the Tzar had no fleet with which to invest Azof by sea, because the new army and its chiefs wanted experience, and because Jansen, the German engineer, ill-treated by Peter, passed over to the enemy. After two assaults, the siege was raised. This check appeared the more grave because the Tzar himself was with the army, because the first attempt to turn from the " amusements " of Preobrajenskoé to serious warfare had failed, and because this failure would furnish arms against innovations, against the *Germans* and the *heretics*, against the new tactics.

It might even compromise, in the eyes of the people, the work of regeneration (1695).

Although Peter had followed the example of Galitsyne, and entered Moscow in triumph, he felt he needed revenge. He sent for good officers from foreign countries. Artillerymen arrived from Holland and Austria, engineers from Prussia, and Admiral Lima from Venice. Peter hurried on the creation of a fleet with feverish impatience. He built of green wood twenty-two galleys, a hundred rafts, and seventeen hundred boats or barks. All the small ports of the Don were metamorphosed into dockyards; twenty-six thousand workmen were assembled there from all parts of the empire. It was like the camp of Boulogne. No misfortune—neither the desertion of the laborers, the burnings of the dockyards, nor even his own illness—could lessen his activity. Peter was able to write that, " following the advice God gave to Adam, he earned his bread by the sweat of his brow." At last the "marine caravan," the Russian armada, descended the Don. From the slopes of Azof he wrote to his sister Natalia : * " In obedience to thy counsels, I do not go to meet the shells and balls ; it is they who approach me, but tolerably courteously." Azof was blockaded by sea and land, and a breach was opened by the engineers. Preparations were being made for a general assault, when the place capitulated. The joy in Russia was great, and the *streltsi's* jealousy of the success of foreign tactics gave place to their enthusiasm as Christians for this victory over Islamism, which recalled those of Kazan and Astrakhan. The effect produced on Europe was considerable. At Warsaw the people shouted, " Long live the Tzar ! " The army entered Moscow under triumphal arches, on which were represented Hercules trampling a pacha and two Turks under foot, and Mars throwing to the earth a *mourza* and two Tatars. Admiral Lefort and Schein the generalissimo took part in the *cortége*, seated on magnificent sledges; whilst Peter, promoted to the rank of Captain, followed on foot. Jansen, destined to the gibbet, marched among the prisoners (1676).

Peter wished to profit by this great success to found the naval power of Russia. By the decision of the *douma* three thousand families were established at Azof, besides four hundred Kalmucks, and a garrison of Moscow *streltsi*. The Patriarch, the prelates, and the monasteries taxed themselves for the construction of one vessel to every eight thousand serfs. The nobles, the officials, and the merchants were seized with the fever of this holy war, and brought their contributions towards

* His mother died in 1694, his brother Ivan in 1696.

the infant navy. It was proposed to unite the Don and the Volga by means of a canal. A new appeal was made to the artisans and sailors of Europe. Fifty young nobles of the Court were sent to Venice, England, and the Low Countries, to learn seamanship and shipbuilding. But it was necessary that the Tzar himself should be able to judge of the science of his subjects; he must counteract Russian indolence and prejudice by the force of a great example; and Peter, after having begun his career in the navy at the rank of "skipper," and in the army at that of bombardier, was to become a carpenter of Saardam. He allowed himself, as a reward for his success at Azof, the much longed-for journey to the West.

In 1697 Admiral Lefort and Generals Golovine and Vosnitsyne prepared to depart for the countries of the West, under the title of "the great ambassadors of the Tzar." Their suite was composed of two hundred and seventy persons—young nobles, soldiers, interpreters, merchants, jesters, and buffoons. In the *cortége* was a young man who went by the name of Peter Mikhailof. This *incognito* would render the position of the Tzar easier, whether in his own personal studies or in delicate negotiations. On the journey to Riga, Peter allowed himself to be insulted by the governor, but laid up the recollection for future use. At Königsburg the Prussian Colonel Sternfeld delivered to "M. Peter Mikhailof" "a formal brevet of master of artillery." The great ambassadors and their travelling companion were cordially received by the Courts of Courland, Hanover, and Brandenburg. Sophia Charlotte of Hanover, afterwards Queen of Prussia, has left us some curious notes about the Tzar, then twenty-seven years of age. He astonished her by the vivacity of his mind, and the promptitude and point of his answers, not less than by the grossness of his manners, his bad habits at table, his wild timidity, like that of a badly brought-up child, his grimaces, and a frightful twitching which at times convulsed his whole face. Peter had then a beautiful brown skin, with great piercing eyes, but his features already bore traces of toil and debauchery. "He must have very good and very bad points," said the young Electress; and in this he represented contemporary Russia. "If he had received a better education," adds the princess, "he would have been an accomplished man." The suite of the Tzar were not less surprising than their master; the Muscovites danced with the Court ladies, and took the stiffening of their corsets for their bones. "The bones of these Germans are devilish hard!" said the Tzar.

Leaving the great embassy on the road, Peter travelled quickly, and reached Saardam. The very day of his arrival he took a lodging at a blacksmith's, procured himself a complete costume like those worn by Dutch workmen, and began to wield the axe. He bargained for a boat, bought it, and drank the traditional pint of beer with its owner. He visited cutleries, ropewalks, and other manufactories, and everywhere tried his hand at the work: in a paper manufactory he made some paper. However, in spite of the tradition, he only remained eight days at Saardam. At Amsterdam his eccentricities were no less astonishing. He neither took any rest himself, nor allowed others to do so; he exhausted all his *ciceroni*, always repeating, " I must see it." He inspected the most celebrated anatomical collections; engaged artists, workmen, officers, and engineers; and bought models of ships, and collections of naval laws and treaties. He entered familiarly the houses of private individuals, gained the good will of the Dutch by his *bonhomie*, penetrated into the recesses of the shops and stalls, and remained lost in admiration over a dentist.

But, amidst all these distractions, he never lost sight of his aim. "We labor," he wrote to the Patriarch Adrian, "in order thoroughly to master the art of the sea; so that, having once learnt it, we may return to Russia and conquer the enemies of Christ, and free by his grace the Christians who are oppressed. This is what I shall long for, to my last breath." He was vexed at making so little progress in shipbuilding, but in Holland everyone had to learn by personal experience. A naval captain told him that in England instruction was based on principles, and these he could learn in four months; so Peter crossed the sea, and spent three months in London and the neighboring towns. There he took into his service goldsmiths and gold-beaters, architects and bombardiers. He then returned to Holland, and, his ship being attacked by a violent tempest, he reassured those who trembled for his safety by the remark, " Did you ever hear of a Tzar of Russia who was drowned in the North Sea?" Though much occupied with his technical studies, he had not neglected policy; he had conversed with William III, but did not visit France in this tour, for "Louis XIV.," says St. Simon, "had procured the postponement of his visit;" the fact being that his alliance with the Emperor, and his wars with the Turks, were looked on with disfavor at Versailles. He went to Vienna to study the military art, and dissuaded Leopold from making peace with the Sultan. Peter wished to conquer Kertch in order to secure the Straits of Ienikale. He was preparing to go to Venice, when vexatious intelligence reached him from Moscow.

REVOLT AND DESTRUCTION OF THE STRELTSI.

The first reforms of Peter, his first attempts against the national prejudices and customs, had raised him up a crowd of enemies. Old Russia did not allow herself quietly to be set aside by the bold innovator. There was in the interior a sullen and resolute resistance, which sometimes gave birth to bloody scenes. The revolt of the *streltsi*, the insurrection of Astrakhan, the rebellion of the Cossacks, and later the trial of his son and first wife, are only episodes of the great struggle. Already the priests were teaching that Antichrist was born. Now it had been prophesied that Antichrist should be born of an adulteress, and Peter was the son of the *second* wife of Alexis, therefore his mother Natalia was the "false virgin," the adulterous woman of the prophecies. The increasingly heavy taxes that weighed on the people were another sign that the time had come. Others, disgusted by the taste shown by the Tzar for German clothes and foreign languages and adventurers, affirmed that he was not the son of Alexis, but of Lefort the Genevan, or that his father was a German surgeon. They were scandalized to see the Tzar, like another Gregory Otrépief, expose himself to blows in his military "amusements." The lower orders were indignant at the abolition of the long beards and national costume, and the *raskolniks* at the authorization of "the sacrilegious smell of tobacco." The journey to the West completed the general dissatisfaction. Had anyone ever before seen a Tzar of Moscow quit Holy Russia to wander in the kingdoms of foreigners? Who knew what adventures might befall him among the *niémtsi* and the *bousourmanes*? for the Russian people hardly knew how to distinguish between the Turks and the Germans, and were wholly ignorant of France and England. Under an unknown sky, at the extremity of the world, on the shores of the "ocean sea," what dangers might he not encounter? Then a singular legend was invented about the travels of the Tzar. It was said that he went to Stockholm disguised as a merchant, and that the queen had recognized him, and had tried in vain to capture him. According to another version, she had plunged him in a dungeon, and delivered him over to his enemies, who wished to put him into a cask lined with nails, and throw him into the sea. He had only been saved by a *streletz* who had taken his place. Some asserted that Peter was still kept there ; and in 1705 the *streltsi*, and *raskolniks* of Astrakhan still gave out that it was a false Tzar who had come back to Moscow—the true Tzar was a prisoner at *Stekoln*, attached to a stake.*

* A. Rambaud, 'La Russie Epique,' p. 303.

In the midst of this universal disturbance, caused by the absence of Peter, there were certain symptoms peculiarly disquieting. The Muscovite army grew more and more hostile to the new order of things. In 1694 Peter had discovered a fresh conspiracy, having for its object the deliverance of Sophia ; and at the very moment of his departure from Russia he had to put down a plot of *streltsi* and Cossacks, headed by Colonel Tsykler. Those of the *streltsi* who had been sent to form the garrison of Azof pined for their wives, their children, and the trades they had left in Moscow. When in the absence of the Tzar they were sent from Azof to the frontiers of Poland, they again began to murmur. "What a fate is ours ! It is the boyards who do all the mischief ; for three years they have kept us from our homes." Two hundred deserted and returned to Moscow ; but the *douma*, fearing their presence in the already troubled capital, expelled them by force. They brought back to their regiments a letter of Sophia. "You suffer," she wrote ; "later it will become worse. March on Moscow. What is it you wait for ? There is no news of the Tzar." It was repeated through the army that the Tzar had died in foreign lands, and that the boyards wished to put his son Alexis to death. It was necessary to march on Moscow and exterminate the nobles. The military sedition was complicated by the religious fanaticism of the *raskolniks* and the demagogic passions of the popular army. Four regiments revolted and deserted. Generals Schein and Gordon, with their regular troops, hastened after them, came up with them on the banks of the Iskra, and tried to persuade them to return to their duty. The *streltsi* replied by a petition setting forth all their grievances : " Many of them had died during the expedition to Azof, suggested by Lefort, a German, a heretic ; they had endured fatiguing marches over burning plains, their only food being bad meat ; their strength had been exhausted by severe tasks, and they had been banished to distant garrisons. Moscow was now a prey to all sorts of horrors. Foreigners had introduced the custom of shaving the beard and smoking tobacco. It was said that these *niémtsi* meant to seize the town. On this rumor, the *streltsi* had arrived, and also because Romodanovski wished to disperse and put them to the sword without anyone knowing why." A few cannon-shots were sufficient to scatter the rebels. A large number were arrested ; torture, the gibbet, and the dungeon awaited the captives.

When Peter hastened home from Vienna, he decided that his generals and his *douma* had been too lenient. He had old grievances against the *streltsi ;* they had been the army of Sophia, in opposition to the army of the Tzar ; he remembered the invasion of the Kremlin, the massacre of his mother's family, her terrors in Troïtsa, and the conspiracies which all but delayed his journey to the West. At the very time that he was travelling in Europe for the benefit of his people, these incorrigible mutineers had forced him to renounce his dearest projects, and had stopped him on the road to Venice. He resolved to take advantage of the opportunity by crushing his enemies *en masse*, and by making the Old Russia feel the weight of a terror that would recall the days of Ivan IV. The long beards had been the standard of revolt—they should fall. On the 26th of August he ordered all the gentlemen of his Court to shave themselves, and himself applied the razor to his great lords. The same day the Red Place was covered with gibbets. The Patriarch Adrian tried in vain to appease the anger of the Tzar by presenting to him the wonderworking image of the Mother of God "Why hast thou brought out the holy icon?" exclaimed the Tzar. "Retire and restore it to its place. Know that I venerate God and His Mother as much as thyself, but know also that it is my duty to protect the people and punish the rebels."

On the 30th of October there arrived at the Red Place the first instalment of 230 prisoners : they came in carts, with lighted torches in their hands, nearly all already broken by torture, and followed by their wives and children, who ran behind chanting a funeral wail. Their sentence was read, and they were slain, the Tzar ordering several officers to help the executioner. John George Korb, the Austrian agent, who as an eye-witness has left us an authentic account of the executions, heard that five rebel heads had been sent into the dust by blows from an axe wielded by the noblest hand in Russia." The terrible carpenter of Saardam worked and obliged his boyards to work at this horrible employment. Seven other days were employed in this way; a thousand victims were put to death. Some were broken on the wheel, and others died by various modes of torture. The removal of the corpses was forbidden : for five months Moscow had before its eyes the spectacle of the dead bodies hanging from the battlements of the Kremlin and the other ramparts; and for five months the *streltsi* suspended to the bars of Sophia's prison presented her the petition by which they had entreated her to reign. Two of her confidants were buried alive ; she herself, with Eudoxia Lapoukhine, Peter's wife, who had been repudiated for her obstinate attachment to the ancient customs, had their heads shaved and were confined in monasteries. After the revolt of the inhabitants of Astrakhan, who put their voïevode to death, the old militia was completely abolished, and the way left clear for the formation of new troops.

CONTEST WITH THE COSSACKS: REVOLT OF THE DON (1706);
MAZEPPA (1709).

The *streltsi* was not the only military force of ancient Russia whose existence and privileges had become incompatible with the organization of the modern State. The "armies" (*voïska*) of Cossacks—those republican and undisciplined warriors who had been formerly the rampart of Russia, and were her outposts against the barbarians—had to undergo a transformation. The empire had numerous grievances against them: the Cossacks of the Ukraine and those of the Don had given birth to the first and the second of the false Dmitris, and from the army of the Don had sprung the terrible Stenko Razine.

In 1706 the Cossacks of the Don revolted against the Tzarian government, because they were forbidden to give an asylum to the peasants who fled from their masters, or to those who took refuge from taxation in the camp. The ataman Boulavine, and his lieutenants Nekrassof, Frolof, and Dranyi, summoned them to arms. They murdered Prince George Dolgorouki, defeated the Russians on the Liskovata, took Tcherkask, threatened Azof, all the while protesting their fidelity to the Tzar, and accusing the voïevodes of having acted "without orders." They soon, however, suffered defeat at the hands of Vassili Dolgorouki, brother of the dead man. Boulavine was stabbed by his own soldiers, and Nekrassof fled with two thousand men to the Kuban. The rebel camp was laid waste, and Dolgorouki was able to write: "The chief mutineers and declared traitors have been hung; of the others, one out of every ten; and all these dead malefactors have been laid on rafts and abandoned to the river, to strike terror into the hearts of the Dontsi, and to cause them to repent."

Since Samoïlovitch had been removed, Mazeppa had been the hetman of the Little Russian Cossacks of the Ukraine. In his youth a page of John Casimir, King of Poland, that adventure had befallen him which the poem of Lord Byron and the pictures of Horace Vernet have rendered famous. Loosed from the back of the unbroken horse which had carried him into the solitudes of the Ukraine, he had entered the Cossack army, and, by betraying all chiefs and parties in turn, he had risen through all the grades of military service. He owed the office of hetman to Galitsyne and Sophia, but was one of the first to embrace the cause of Peter. His elevation gained him many enemies, but the Tzar, who admired his intelligence and believed in his fidelity, delivered up to him his accusers. He executed the monk

Salomon, who pretended to reveal Mazeppa's intrigues with the King of Poland and Sophia; Mikhaïlof in 1690, and the *diak* Souzlof in 1696, were likewise put to death.

All this time the Ukraine was being steadily undermined by factions. In the Cossack army there always existed a Russian party, a party who longed for Polish government, and a party who wished to do homage to the Turks. In 1693 Petrek, one of the chiefs, invaded the Ukraine with 40,000 Tatars, but was forced to retreat. Besides this, the views of the army and those of the sedentary populations of the Ukraine were always at variance. The hetman dreamed of becoming independent, the officers disliked being responsible to anyone, and the soldiers wished to live at the expense of the country, without either working or paying taxes, after the manner of the ancient nobles; but the farmers who had created the agricultural prosperity of the country, the citizens who could not work in security, in fact all the peaceful laboring population, determined to get rid of the turbulent military oligarchy, and hailed the Tzar of Moscow as a liberator.

Mazeppa represented the military element of the Ukraine, and was hated by the more peaceful classes. The Tzar overwhelmed him with proofs of confidence, but Mazeppa feared the strengthening of the Russian State. He remembered how one day in an orgie the Tzar had seized him by the beard and violently shaken him. The taxes imposed on the vassal State of Little Russia became daily heavier, and in the war with Charles XII. they increased still more. Everything was to be feared from the imperious humor and autocratic pretensions of Peter. The invasion of the Swedes, now imminent, would necessarily precipitate the crisis; and either Little Russia would gain her independence by the help of the foreigners, or their defeat on her soil would give a mortal blow to her prosperity and hopes for the future. Feeling the approach of the hour when he must obey the White Tzar, Mazeppa allowed himself to be drawn into communications with Stanislas Leszczinski, the King of Poland set up by the Swedish party. The witty Princess Dolskaïa had given him an alphabet in cipher. Up to that time Mazeppa had delivered to the Tzar all letters tampering with his fidelity, and, in return, the Tzar surrendered to him all his accusers. When he received the letters of the princess he smiled and said, " Wicked woman, she wants to detach me from the Tzar." He did not give up the letter, but burned it. When the hand of Menchikof's sister was refused to one of his cousins, when Menchikof himself began to give direct orders to the commanders of the *polks*, when the Swedish war and the march

of the Muscovite troops limited his power and augmented the
burdens of his territory, when the Tzar sent pressing injunctions
for the equipment of the army in European style, when he felt
around him the spirit of rebellion against Moscow, he wrote to
Leszczinski, saying that he did not think the Polish army sufficiently strong, but assuring him of his goodwill. His confidant, Orlik,
was in the secret of all his intrigues. Some of his subordinates who
had penetrated his designs made another attempt to denounce him
to the Tzar: among these were Paleï, celebrated in the songs of the
Ukraine; Kotchoubey, whose daughter Mazeppa had taken; and
Iskra. The information was very exact and revealed his secret conferences with the emissaries of the King and of Princess Dolskaïa
It failed, like former denunciations, through the blind confidence
of Peter: Paleï was sent to Siberia; Iskra and Kotchoubey were
tortured, forced to confess themselves false witnesses, delivered
up to the hetman, and beheaded. Mazeppa was conscious that
such extraordinary good fortune could not last, and the malcontents urged him to think of their common safety. At this moment
Charles XII. arrived in the neighborhood of Little Russia.
"The devil has brought him," cried Mazeppa; and he tried between the two powers to save the independence of his little
State, without delivering himself over completely either to
Charles XII. or Peter the Great. When the latter invited him
to join the army, he pretended that he was ill, and even received
extreme unction. But Menchikof and Charles were approaching—a choice must be made. Mazeppa left his bed, assembled
his most faithful Cossacks, and crossed the Desna to effect a
junction with the Swedish army. Then Peter the Great made a
proclamation denouncing the treason of Mazeppa, his alliance
with the heretics, his plot to restore the Ukraine to Poland, and
to fill the monasteries and temples of God with Uniates. He was
cursed in all the churches of Russia. Batourine, his capital, was
taken by Menchikof, sacked and destroyed; his accomplices, whom
he had abandoned, died on the wheel and the gibbet; he himself
fled, after the battle of Pultowa, to the Turkish territory, and perished miserably at Bender. A new hetman, Skoropadski, was
elected in his stead; the mass of the people and the Cossack army
pronounced loudly for the Tzar, and the Swedes had to cope with
the rising of the entire population of the Ukraine. In spite of
this, the independence of Little Russia was past. The privileges
of the Cossacks were over, and twelve hundred of them were
sent to work at the Canal of Ladoga. A Muscovite official was
joined to Skoropadski to govern "in concert with the advice of
the hetman." Muscovite subjects were allowed to hold lands in
the Ukraine by the same title as the Little Russians; Menchikof

and Chafirof were given large domains there by Skoropadski, whose daughter married another Muscovite, Tolstoï, created commandant of the *polk* of Niéjine. In 1722 Little Russia, whose affairs up to that time had been conducted by the department of Foreign Affairs, was governed by a special office founded at Moscow under the name of " Little Russian Affairs." This was clear proof that the Ukraine had ceased to be an autonomous State. When Skoropadski died, Peter did not nominate a successor, declaring that " the treasons of the preceding hetmans did not allow a decision to be made lightly in this grave matter of election, and that he needed time to find a man of assured fidelity."

From this time the institutions of the Ukraine were modified at the will of Peter the Great and his successors. The hetmannate was now abolished, now restored, till the last man who held the title, a courtier of Catherine II., abdicated in 1789. The affairs of the Ukraine were sometimes directed by the office of Little Russia, sometimes by the office of Foreign Affairs, till the time when, under Catherine II., it became an integral part of the empire. As to the Zaporogues, after their *sétcha* had been taken by Peter the Great, they emigrated to the Crimea, obtained their restoration to the Lower Dnieper from Anne, found the neighboring country already transformed, and, as their existence seemed incompatible with security and colonization, were finally expelled in 1775.

From the year 1709 we may say that there no longer existed in the empire a single military force that could oppose its privileges to the will of the Tzar.

www.ingramcontent.com/pod-product-compliance
Lightning Source LLC
Chambersburg PA
CBHW022044230426
43672CB00008B/1062